THE ASTOUNDING

WOLF-MAN

CREATED BY
ROBERT KIRKMAN & JASON HOWARD

image®

ROBERT KIRKMAN
writer

JASON HOWARD
penciler, inker, colorist

RUS WOOTON
letterer

past work and I was thrilled to have worked with Jason, but I figured I'd blown it with this guy and he'd never want to work with me again.

Months passed... and eventually, Jason sent me a pin-up of Science Dog that he'd done for fun. His son loves Science Dog and so I believe he drew it for him, but he colored it up and sent it to me so I could run it. As luck would have it... at that exact time, I'd been cooking up a new concept for a superhero.

I was trying to come up with something SIMPLE. When you're not doing Spider-Man or Batman you're at a huge disadvantage. The comic racks are littered with books with low-recognition value that sport titles and covers that tell you absolutely nothing about the book inside. As an example I'll pick on Warren Ellis and Ben Templesmith despite their series doing very well. A book like FELL often times features a dude standing looking cool on the cover. That along with the title doesn't tell you anything, no mention of the police angle, no mention of the crime themes, nothing about the super interesting setting in that book. It works despite all that, so it's not the best example but the comic racks are littered with comics that fail because their titles are vague and their covers often tell you nothing about the book.

So I wanted to avoid that at all costs and I was trying to think of a concept—that when you see the cover or even just the logo you know exactly what the book is about. What I came up with was "Wolf-Man" or "wolf dash man." The dash makes

you immediately think "superhero" and if you see a werewolf on the cover in a superheroish costume— you would immediately know from looking at that book exactly what it is about "a werewolf superhero." So that was the rough concept, I was in the middle of developing it further when Jason sent along his glorious Science Dog pin-up.

I thought—Science Dog has fur, Jason drew him very well, Werewolves have fur—maybe this is my guy? And the rest, as they say, is history. Jason started doing designs immediately— copious amounts of designs—which you'll see later in our sketchbook section—and all that brilliance saw in that first Invincible pin-up did came shining through in all his design work and suggestions for the series—it really brought my initial concept to life and allowed us to flesh it out, together, into something that eventually led to the seven issues you now hold, collected, in your hands.

So Jason Howard... if it weren't for him The Astounding Wolf-Man wouldn't be much more than a rough idea sitting in a drawer somewhere. So thank him, blame him, whatever—but when you read the following issues, maybe for the first time ever, I hope you appreciate the work Jason's put into them as much as I do.

And if you're an aspiring artist out there... and you don't suck, send me a pin-up... you never know what could happen, if you don't suck.

—Robert Kirkman
Backwoods, KY
2008

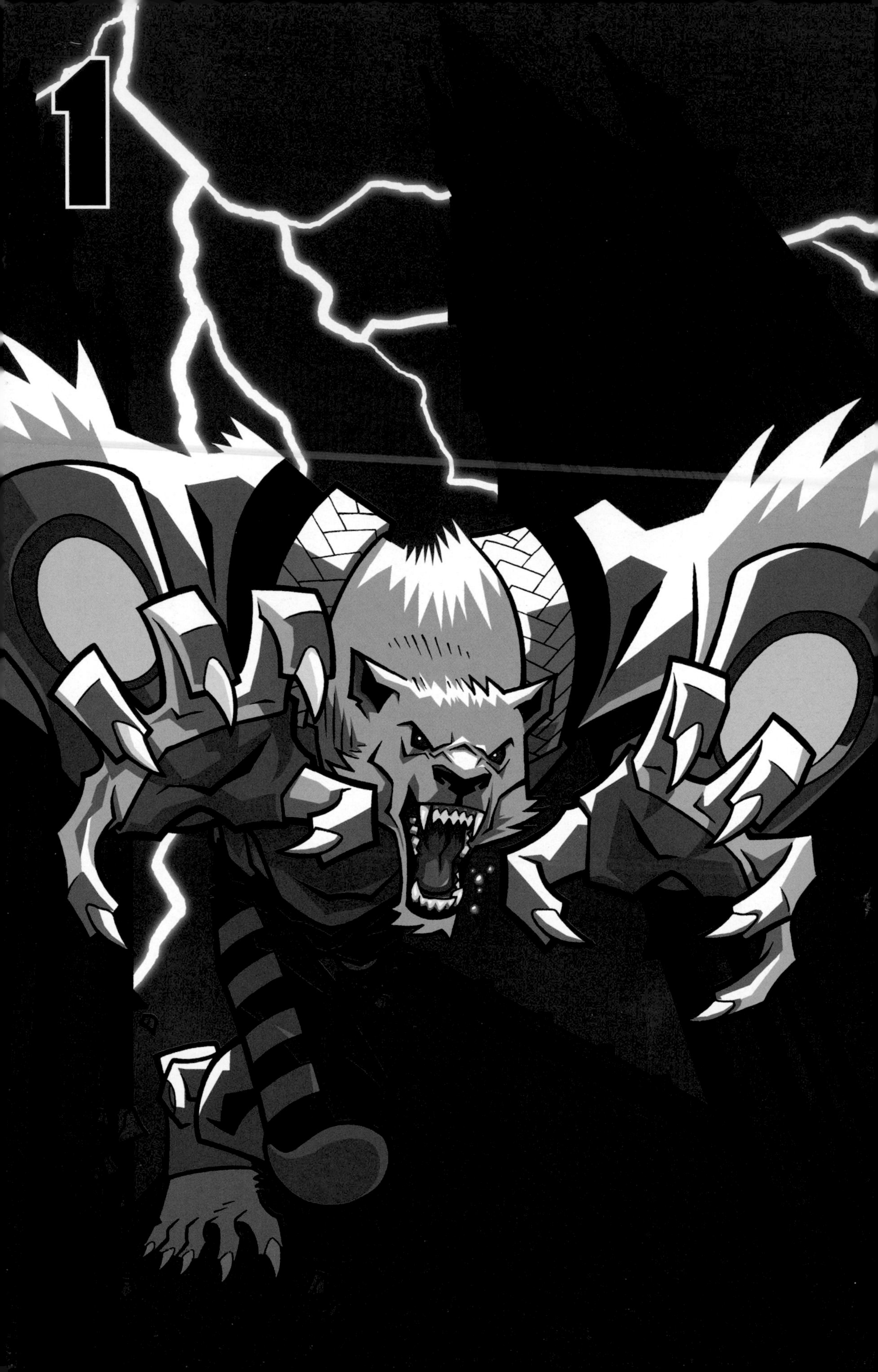
1

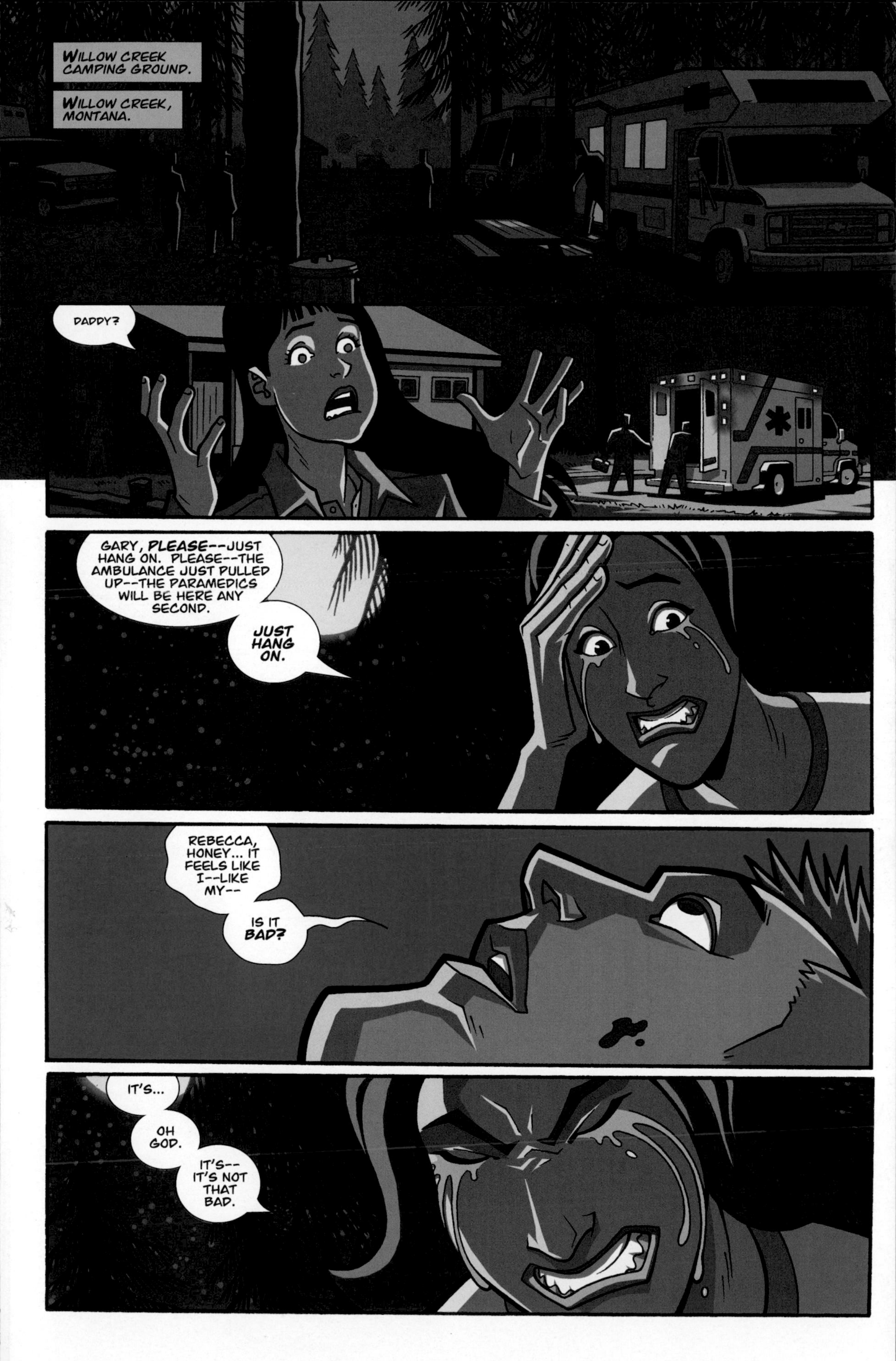
WILLOW CREEK CAMPING GROUND.
WILLOW CREEK, MONTANA.
DADDY?
GARY, PLEASE--JUST HANG ON. PLEASE--THE AMBULANCE JUST PULLED UP--THE PARAMEDICS WILL BE HERE ANY SECOND.
JUST HANG ON.
REBECCA, HONEY... IT FEELS LIKE I--LIKE MY--
IS IT BAD?
IT'S...
OH GOD.
IT'S-- IT'S NOT THAT BAD.

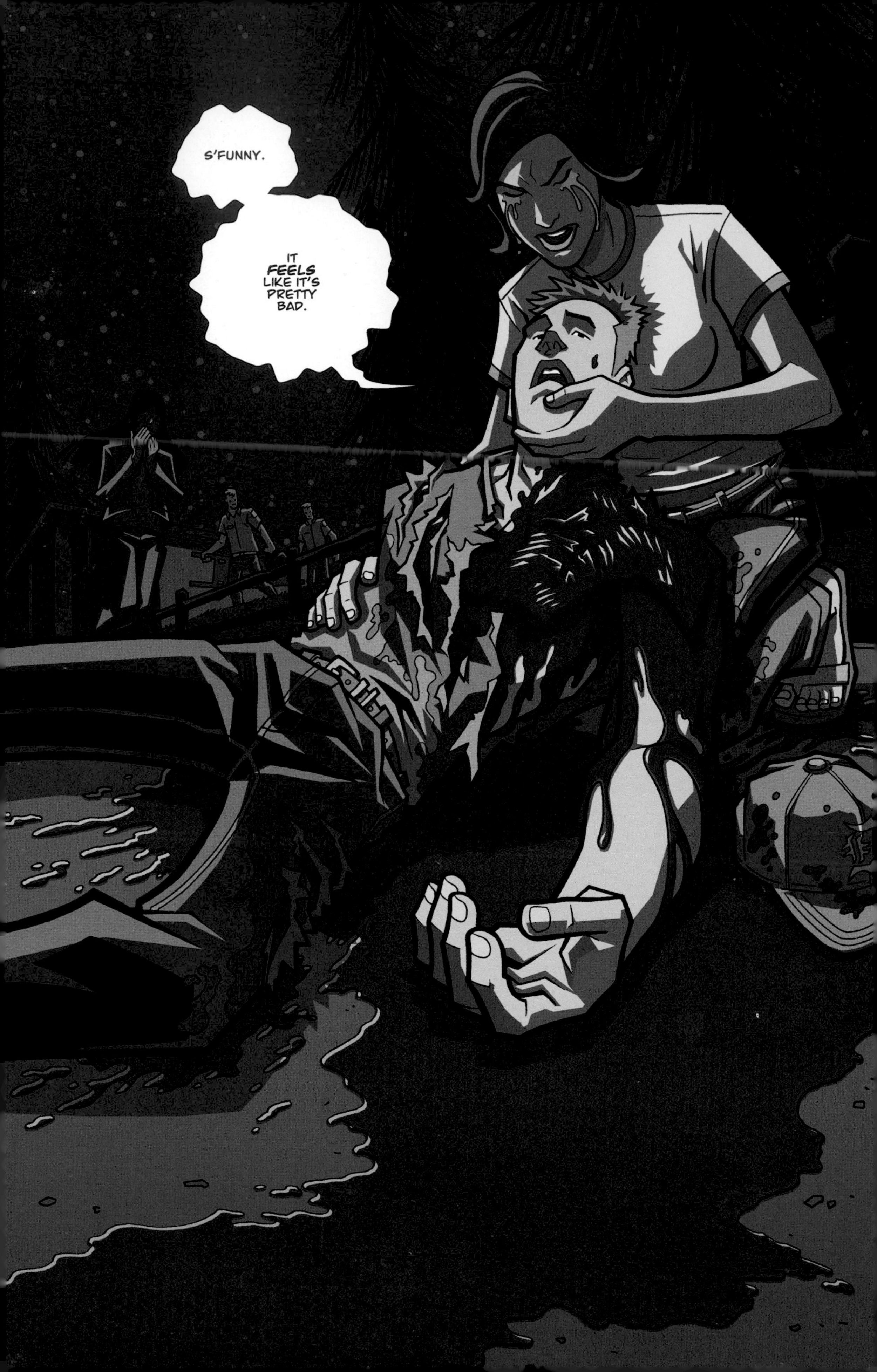
S'FUNNY.
IT FEELS LIKE IT'S PRETTY BAD.

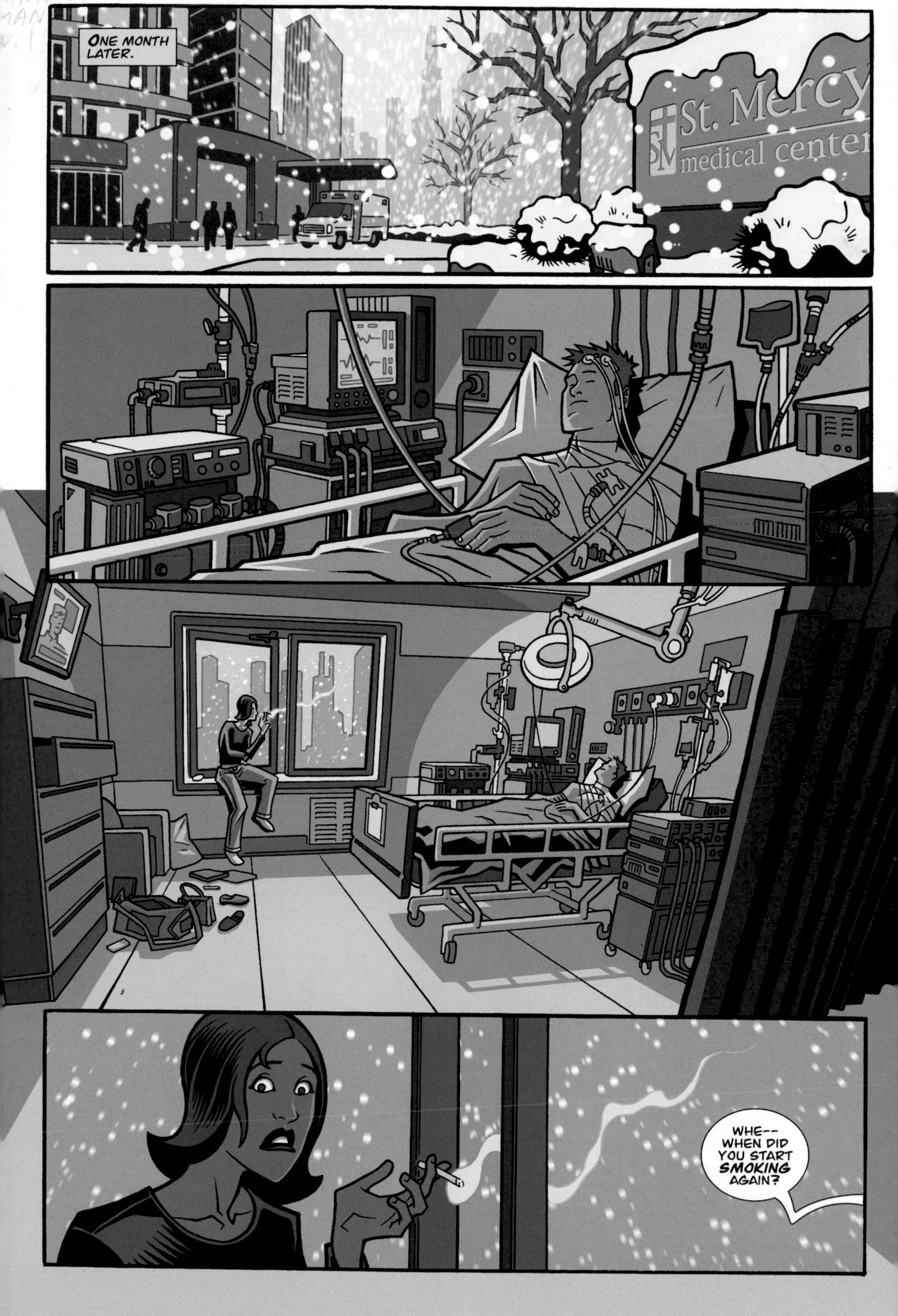
ONE MONTH LATER.
St. Mercy medical center
WHE-- WHEN DID YOU START SMOKING AGAIN?

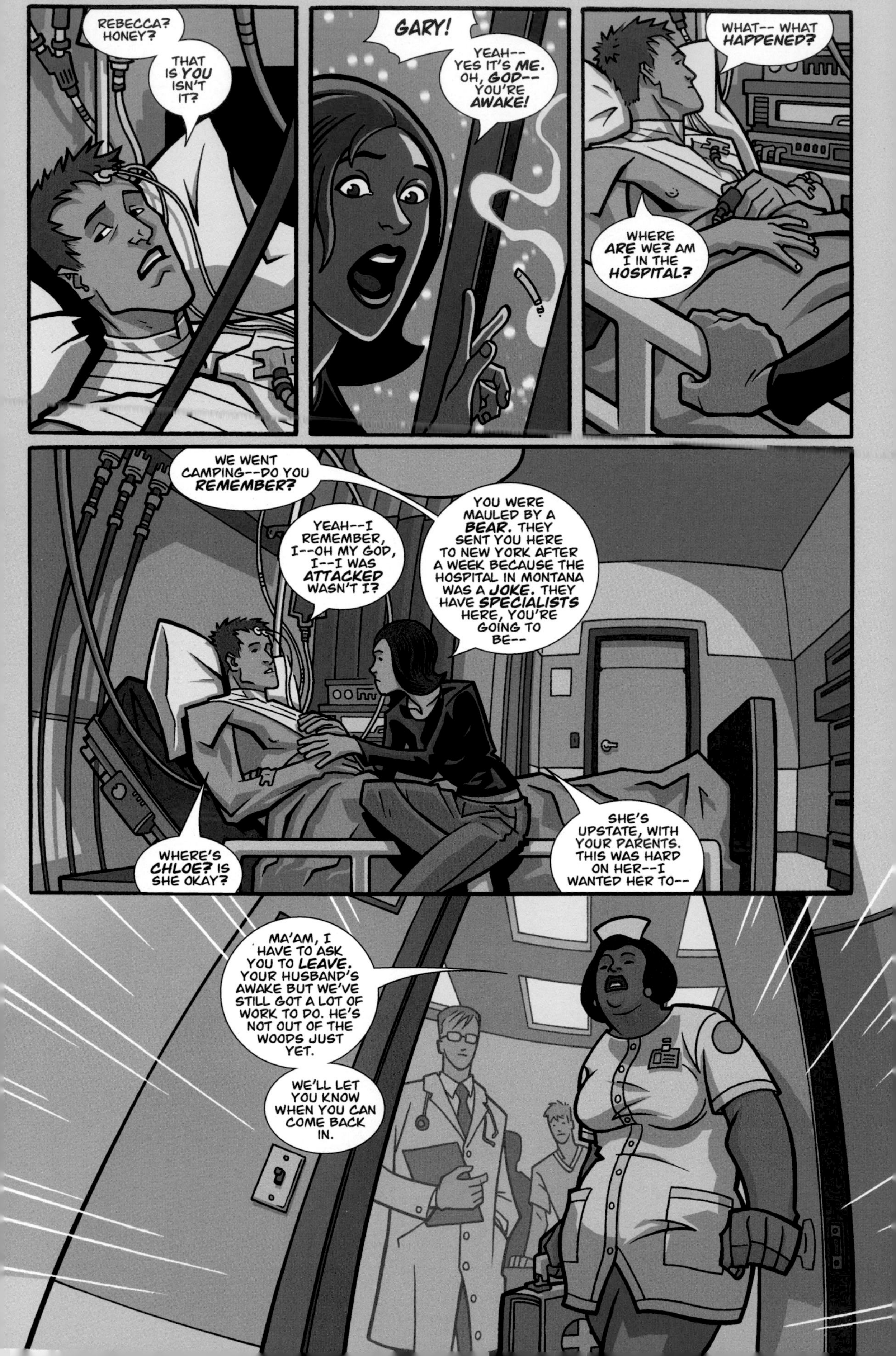
REBECCA? HONEY?
THAT IS YOU ISN'T IT?
GARY!
YEAH-- YES IT'S ME. OH, GOD-- YOU'RE AWAKE!
WHAT-- WHAT HAPPENED?
WHERE ARE WE? AM I IN THE HOSPITAL?
WE WENT CAMPING--DO YOU REMEMBER?
YEAH--I REMEMBER, I--OH MY GOD, I--I WAS ATTACKED WASN'T I?
YOU WERE MAULED BY A BEAR. THEY SENT YOU HERE TO NEW YORK AFTER A WEEK BECAUSE THE HOSPITAL IN MONTANA WAS A JOKE. THEY HAVE SPECIALISTS HERE, YOU'RE GOING TO BE--
WHERE'S CHLOE? IS SHE OKAY?
SHE'S UPSTATE, WITH YOUR PARENTS. THIS WAS HARD ON HER--I WANTED HER TO--
MA'AM, I HAVE TO ASK YOU TO LEAVE. YOUR HUSBAND'S AWAKE BUT WE'VE STILL GOT A LOT OF WORK TO DO. HE'S NOT OUT OF THE WOODS JUST YET.
WE'LL LET YOU KNOW WHEN YOU CAN COME BACK IN.

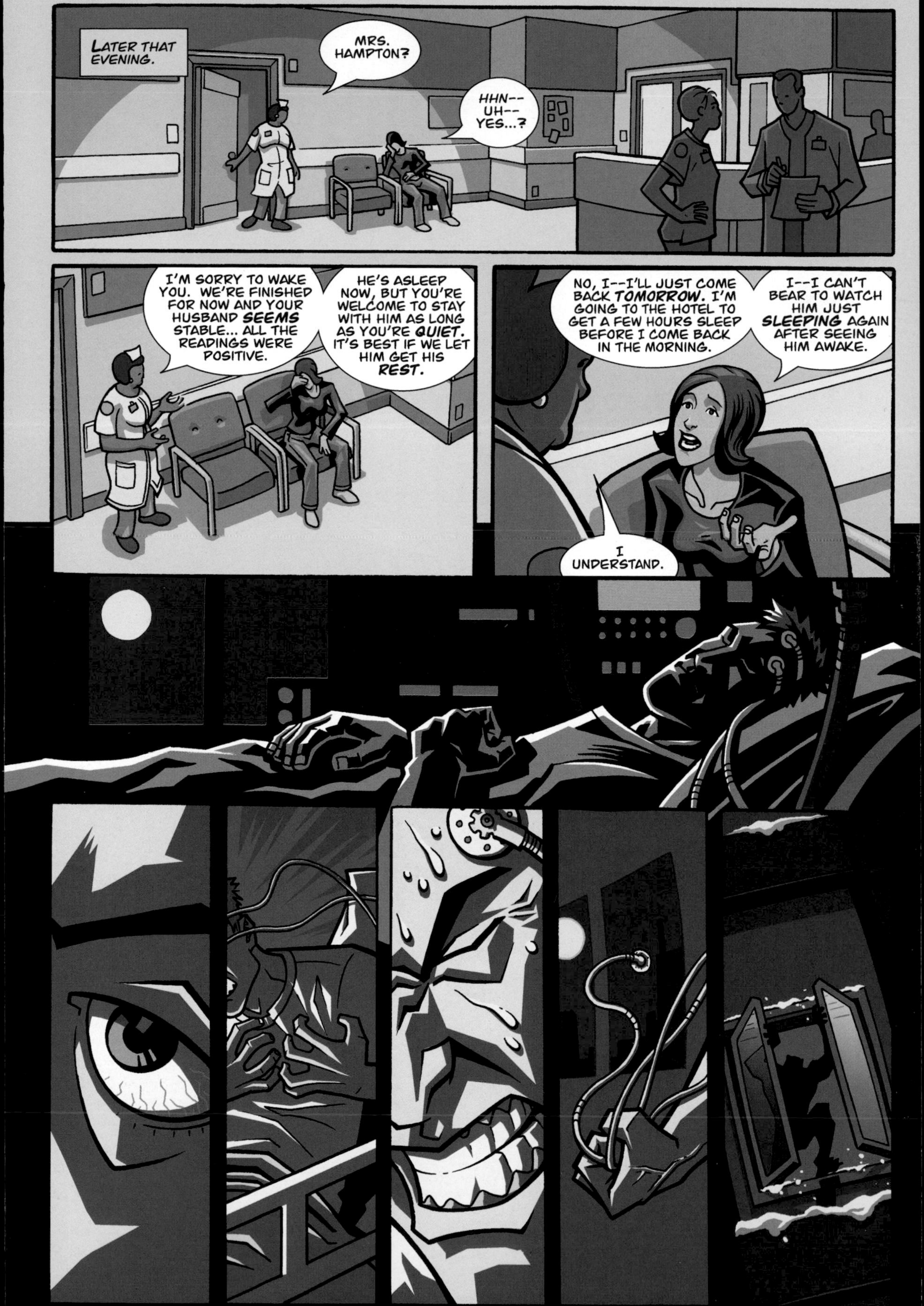

LATER THAT EVENING.
MRS. HAMPTON?
HHN-- UH-- YES...?
I'M SORRY TO WAKE YOU. WE'RE FINISHED FOR NOW AND YOUR HUSBAND SEEMS STABLE... ALL THE READINGS WERE POSITIVE.
HE'S ASLEEP NOW, BUT YOU'RE WELCOME TO STAY WITH HIM AS LONG AS YOU'RE QUIET. IT'S BEST IF WE LET HIM GET HIS REST.
NO, I--I'LL JUST COME BACK TOMORROW. I'M GOING TO THE HOTEL TO GET A FEW HOURS SLEEP BEFORE I COME BACK IN THE MORNING.
I--I CAN'T BEAR TO WATCH HIM JUST SLEEPING AGAIN AFTER SEEING HIM AWAKE.
I UNDERSTAND.

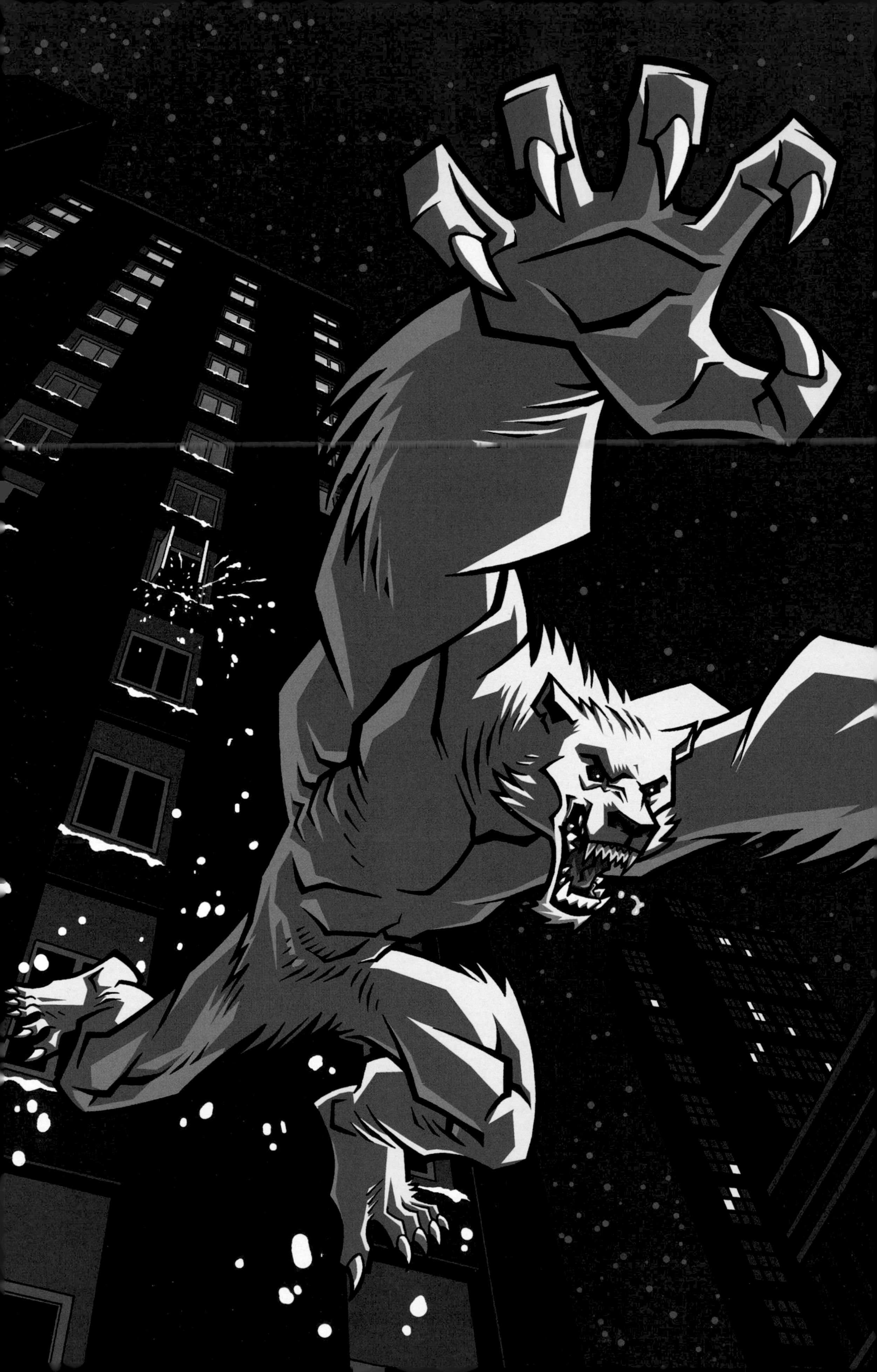

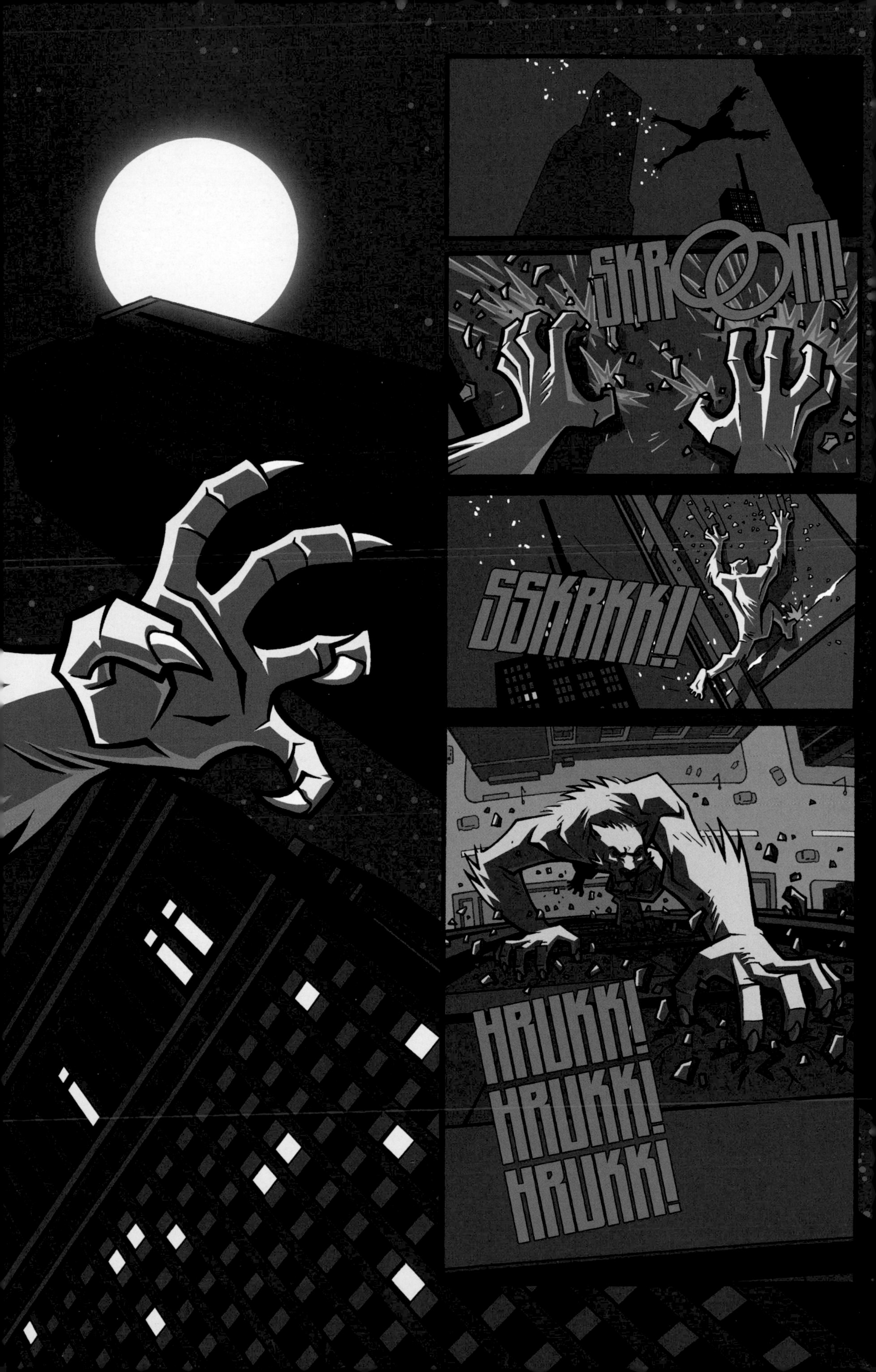
SKROOM!
SSKRKK!!
HRUKK!
HRUKK!
HRUKK!

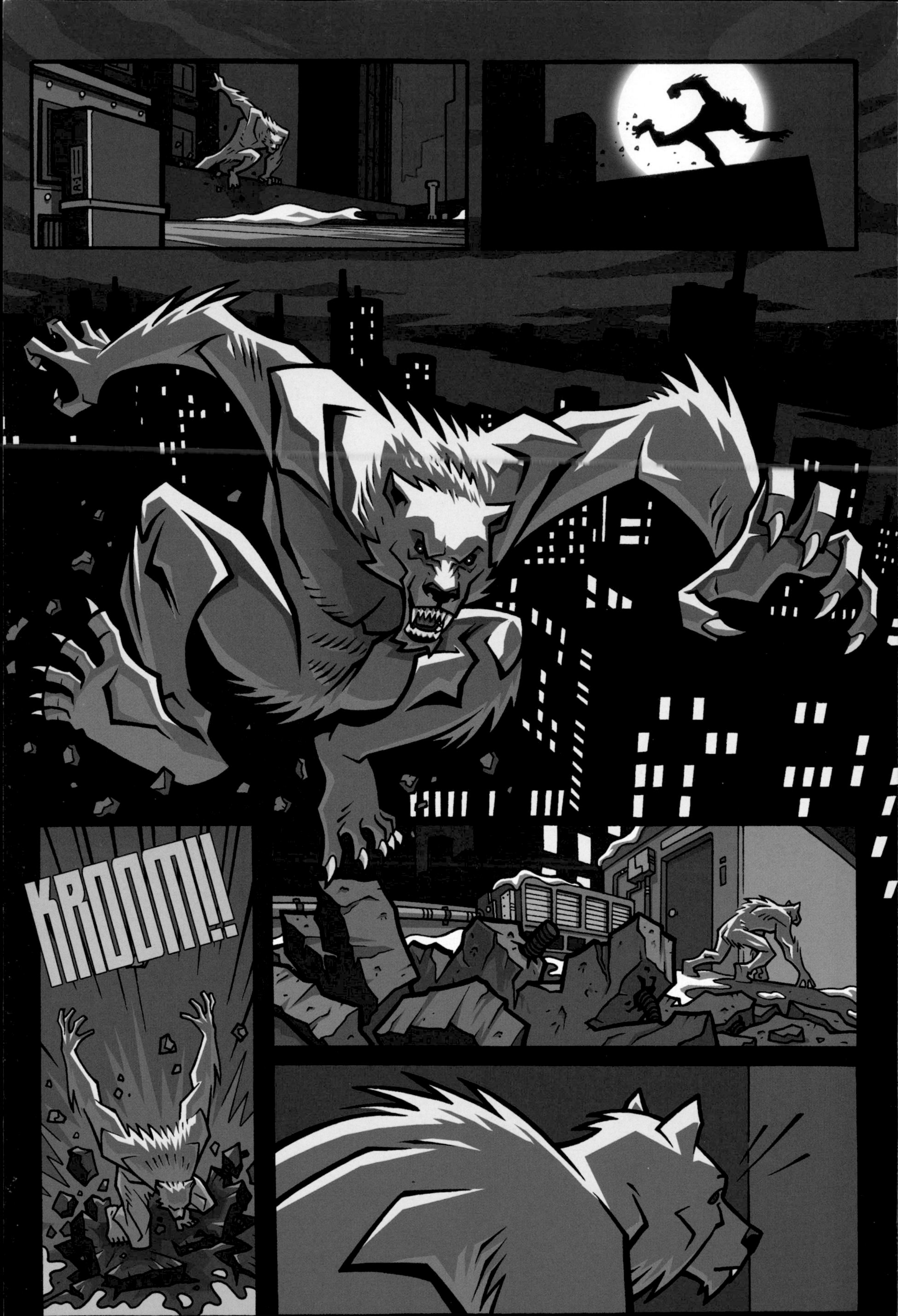

KROOM!!

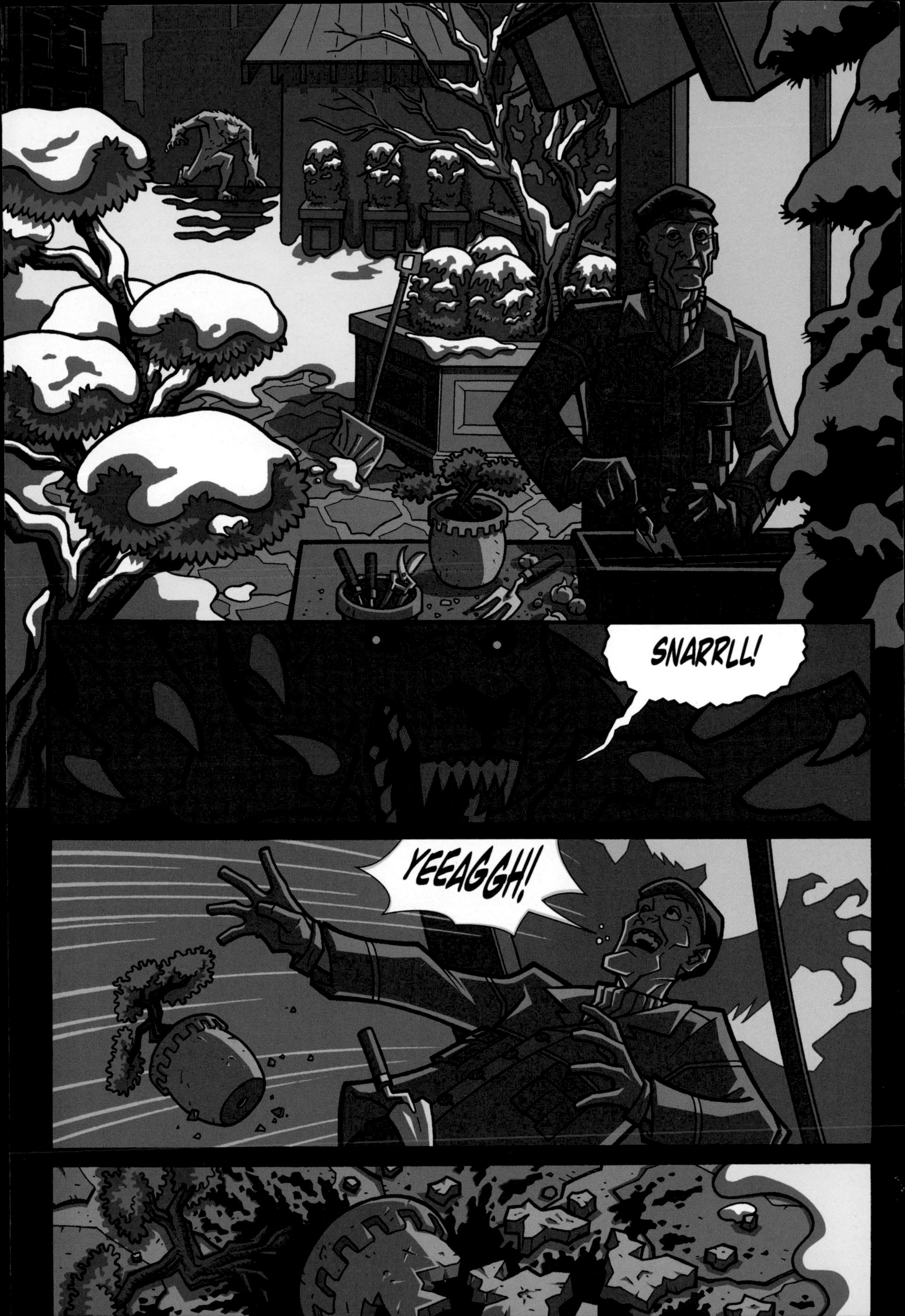
SNARRLL!
YEEAGGH!

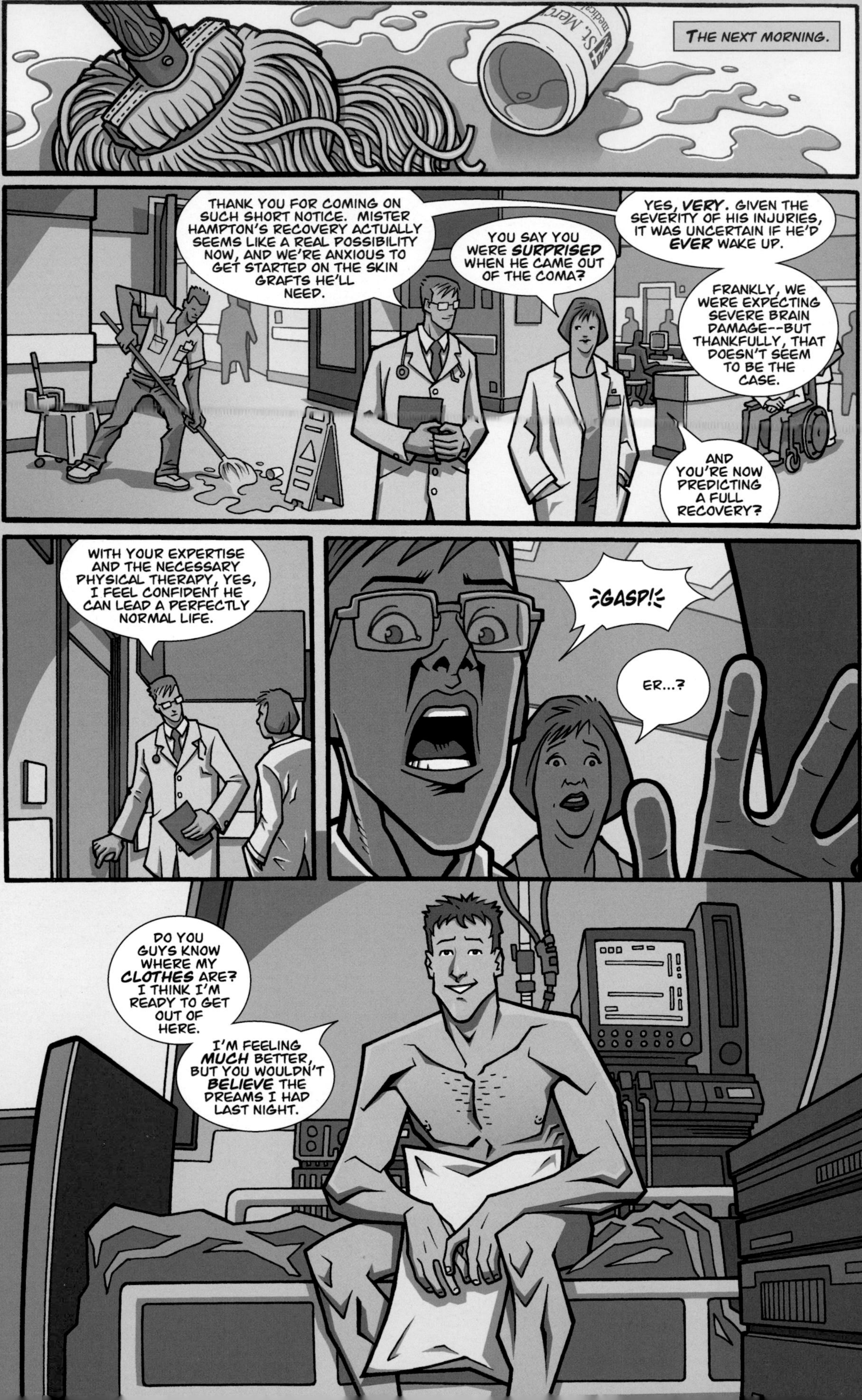
THE NEXT MORNING.
ST. MERCY MEDICAL
THANK YOU FOR COMING ON SUCH SHORT NOTICE. MISTER HAMPTON'S RECOVERY ACTUALLY SEEMS LIKE A REAL POSSIBILITY NOW, AND WE'RE ANXIOUS TO GET STARTED ON THE SKIN GRAFTS HE'LL NEED.
YOU SAY YOU WERE SURPRISED WHEN HE CAME OUT OF THE COMA?
YES, VERY. GIVEN THE SEVERITY OF HIS INJURIES, IT WAS UNCERTAIN IF HE'D EVER WAKE UP.
FRANKLY, WE WERE EXPECTING SEVERE BRAIN DAMAGE--BUT THANKFULLY, THAT DOESN'T SEEM TO BE THE CASE.
AND YOU'RE NOW PREDICTING A FULL RECOVERY?
WITH YOUR EXPERTISE AND THE NECESSARY PHYSICAL THERAPY, YES, I FEEL CONFIDENT HE CAN LEAD A PERFECTLY NORMAL LIFE.
GASP!
ER...?
DO YOU GUYS KNOW WHERE MY CLOTHES ARE? I THINK I'M READY TO GET OUT OF HERE.
I'M FEELING MUCH BETTER, BUT YOU WOULDN'T BELIEVE THE DREAMS I HAD LAST NIGHT.

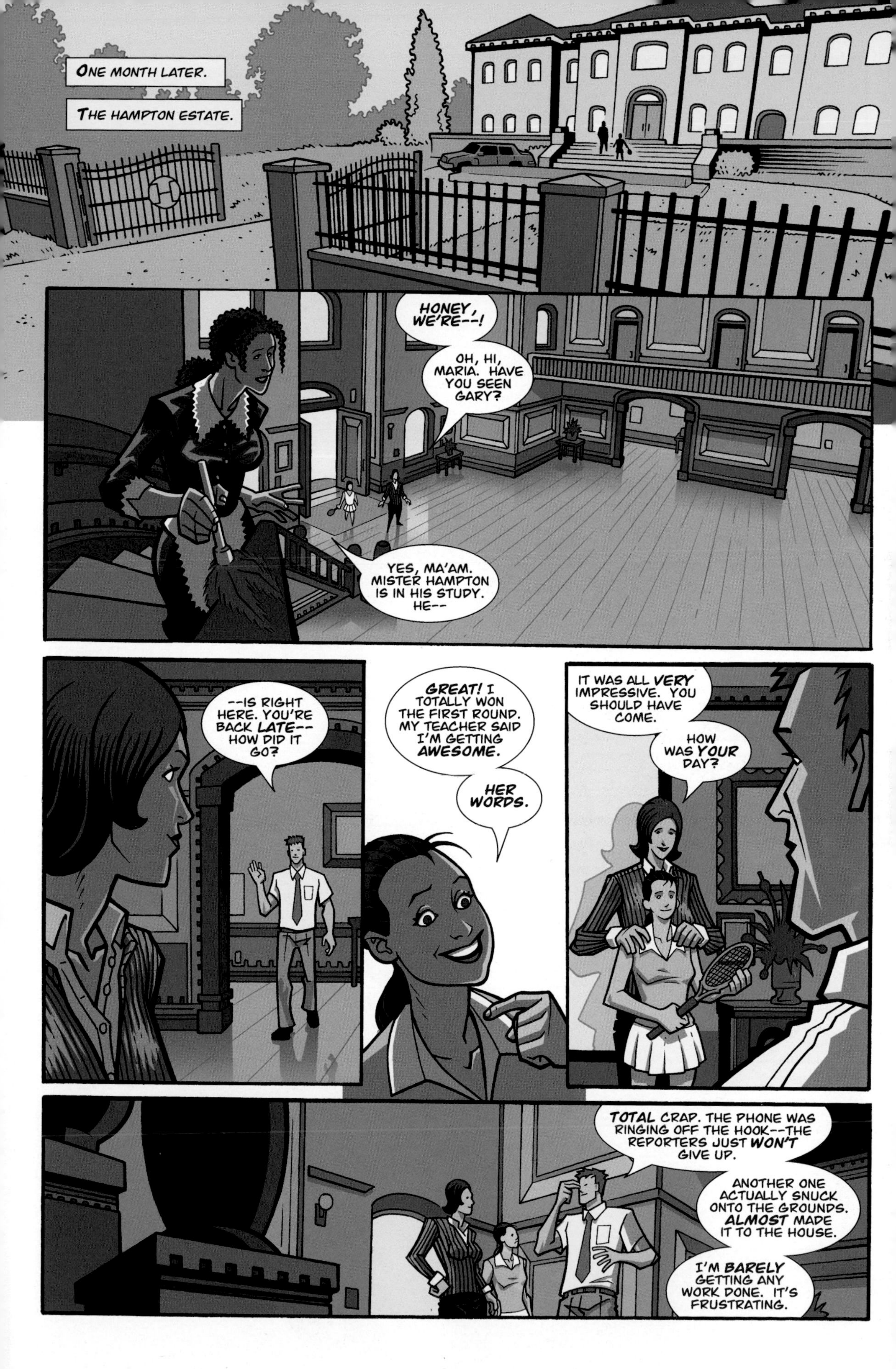
ONE MONTH LATER.
THE HAMPTON ESTATE.
HONEY, WE'RE--!
OH, HI, MARIA. HAVE YOU SEEN GARY?
YES, MA'AM. MISTER HAMPTON IS IN HIS STUDY. HE--
--IS RIGHT HERE. YOU'RE BACK LATE-- HOW DID IT GO?
GREAT! I TOTALLY WON THE FIRST ROUND. MY TEACHER SAID I'M GETTING AWESOME.
HER WORDS.
IT WAS ALL VERY IMPRESSIVE. YOU SHOULD HAVE COME.
HOW WAS YOUR DAY?
TOTAL CRAP. THE PHONE WAS RINGING OFF THE HOOK--THE REPORTERS JUST WON'T GIVE UP.
ANOTHER ONE ACTUALLY SNUCK ONTO THE GROUNDS. ALMOST MADE IT TO THE HOUSE.
I'M BARELY GETTING ANY WORK DONE. IT'S FRUSTRATING.

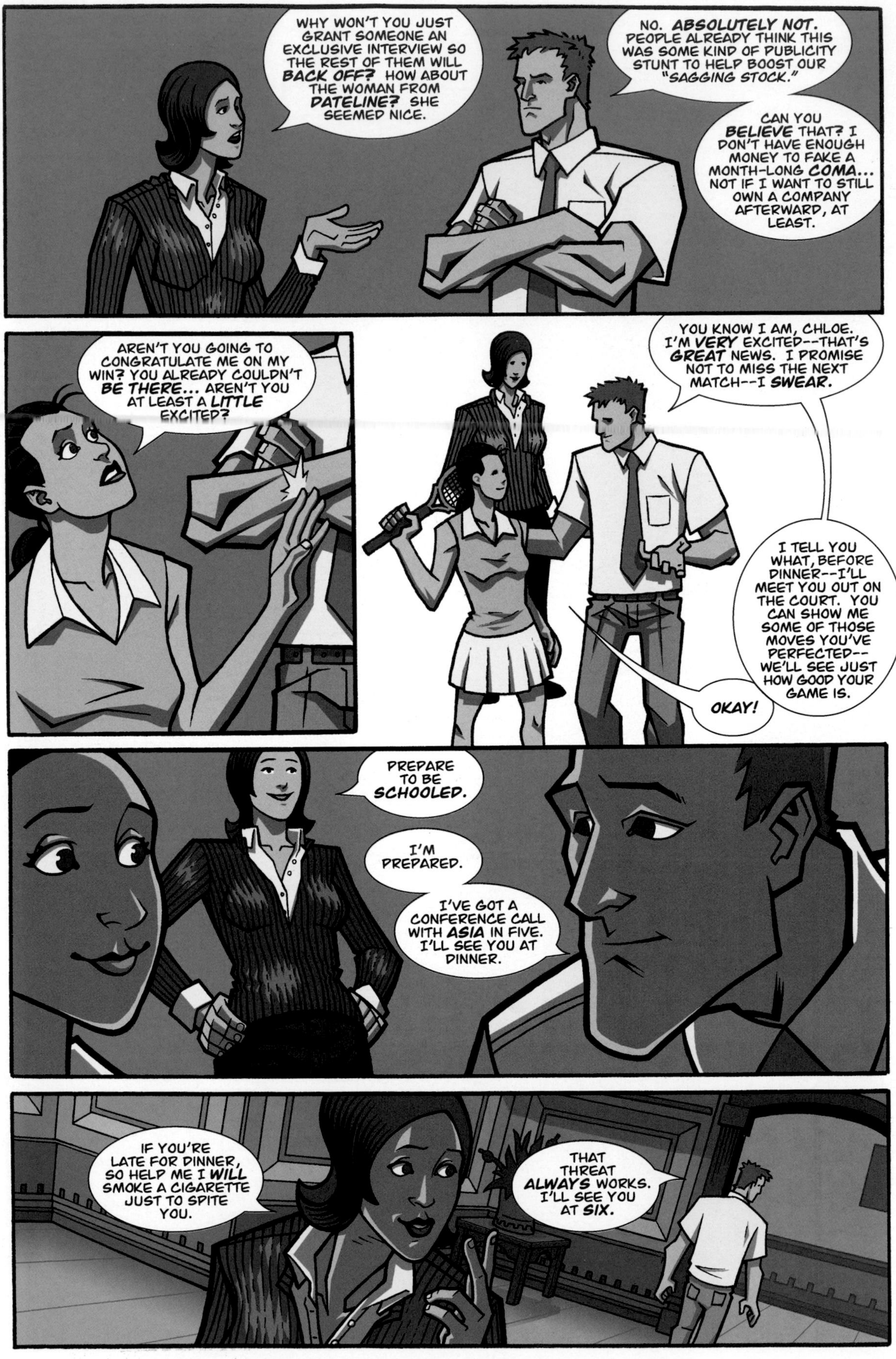
WHY WON'T YOU JUST GRANT SOMEONE AN EXCLUSIVE INTERVIEW SO THE REST OF THEM WILL BACK OFF? HOW ABOUT THE WOMAN FROM DATELINE? SHE SEEMED NICE.
NO. ABSOLUTELY NOT. PEOPLE ALREADY THINK THIS WAS SOME KIND OF PUBLICITY STUNT TO HELP BOOST OUR "SAGGING STOCK."
CAN YOU BELIEVE THAT? I DON'T HAVE ENOUGH MONEY TO FAKE A MONTH-LONG COMA... NOT IF I WANT TO STILL OWN A COMPANY AFTERWARD, AT LEAST.
AREN'T YOU GOING TO CONGRATULATE ME ON MY WIN? YOU ALREADY COULDN'T BE THERE... AREN'T YOU AT LEAST A LITTLE EXCITED?
YOU KNOW I AM, CHLOE. I'M VERY EXCITED--THAT'S GREAT NEWS. I PROMISE NOT TO MISS THE NEXT MATCH--I SWEAR.
I TELL YOU WHAT, BEFORE DINNER--I'LL MEET YOU OUT ON THE COURT. YOU CAN SHOW ME SOME OF THOSE MOVES YOU'VE PERFECTED--WE'LL SEE JUST HOW GOOD YOUR GAME IS.
OKAY!
PREPARE TO BE SCHOOLED.
I'M PREPARED.
I'VE GOT A CONFERENCE CALL WITH ASIA IN FIVE. I'LL SEE YOU AT DINNER.
IF YOU'RE LATE FOR DINNER, SO HELP ME I WILL SMOKE A CIGARETTE JUST TO SPITE YOU.
THAT THREAT ALWAYS WORKS. I'LL SEE YOU AT SIX.

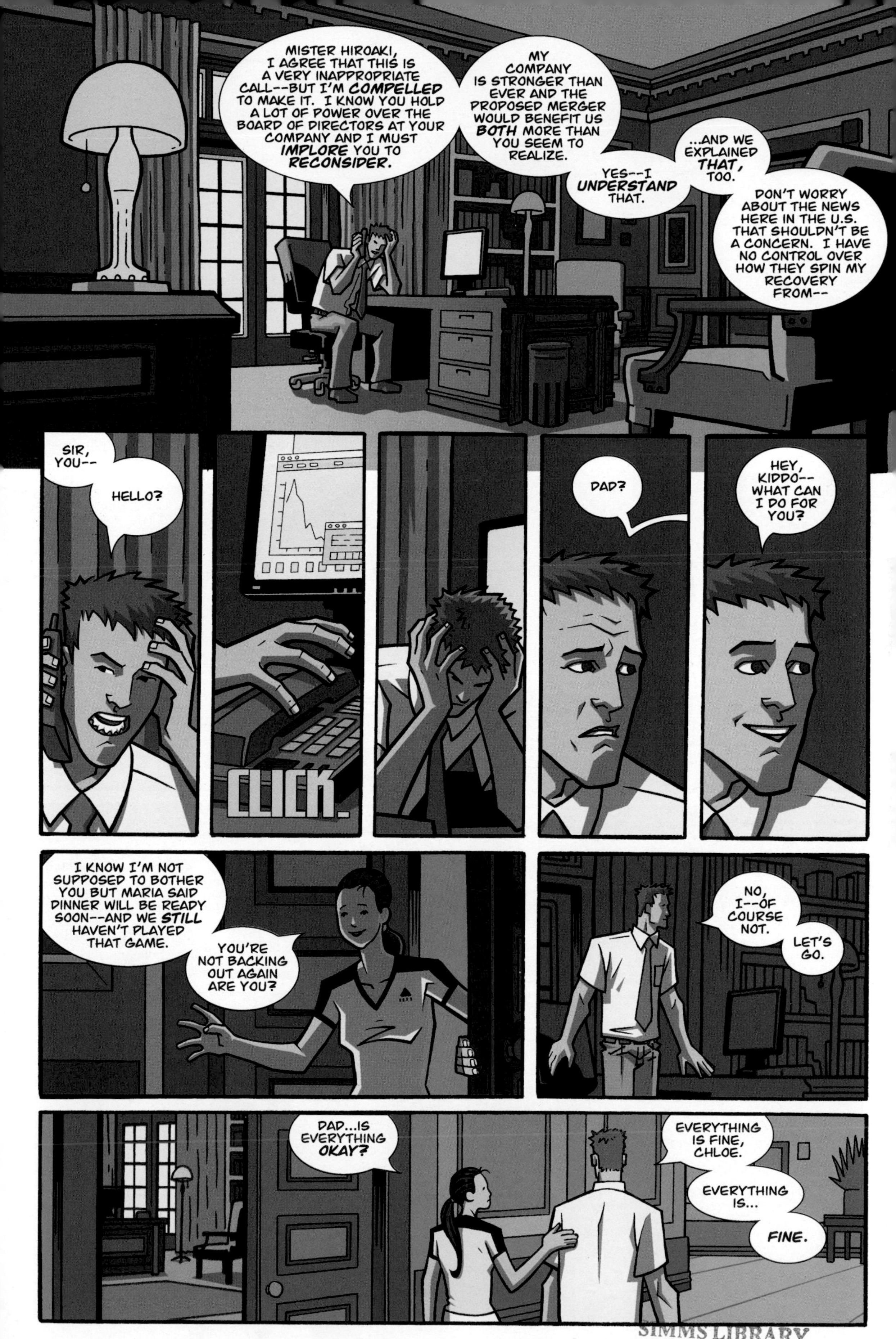
MISTER HIROAKI, I AGREE THAT THIS IS A VERY INAPPROPRIATE CALL--BUT I'M COMPELLED TO MAKE IT. I KNOW YOU HOLD A LOT OF POWER OVER THE BOARD OF DIRECTORS AT YOUR COMPANY AND I MUST IMPLORE YOU TO RECONSIDER.
MY COMPANY IS STRONGER THAN EVER AND THE PROPOSED MERGER WOULD BENEFIT US BOTH MORE THAN YOU SEEM TO REALIZE.
YES--I UNDERSTAND THAT.
...AND WE EXPLAINED THAT, TOO.
DON'T WORRY ABOUT THE NEWS HERE IN THE U.S. THAT SHOULDN'T BE A CONCERN. I HAVE NO CONTROL OVER HOW THEY SPIN MY RECOVERY FROM--
SIR, YOU--
HELLO?
CLICK.
DAD?
HEY, KIDDO--WHAT CAN I DO FOR YOU?
I KNOW I'M NOT SUPPOSED TO BOTHER YOU BUT MARIA SAID DINNER WILL BE READY SOON--AND WE STILL HAVEN'T PLAYED THAT GAME.
YOU'RE NOT BACKING OUT AGAIN ARE YOU?
NO, I--OF COURSE NOT.
LET'S GO.
DAD...IS EVERYTHING OKAY?
EVERYTHING IS FINE, CHLOE.
EVERYTHING IS...
FINE.

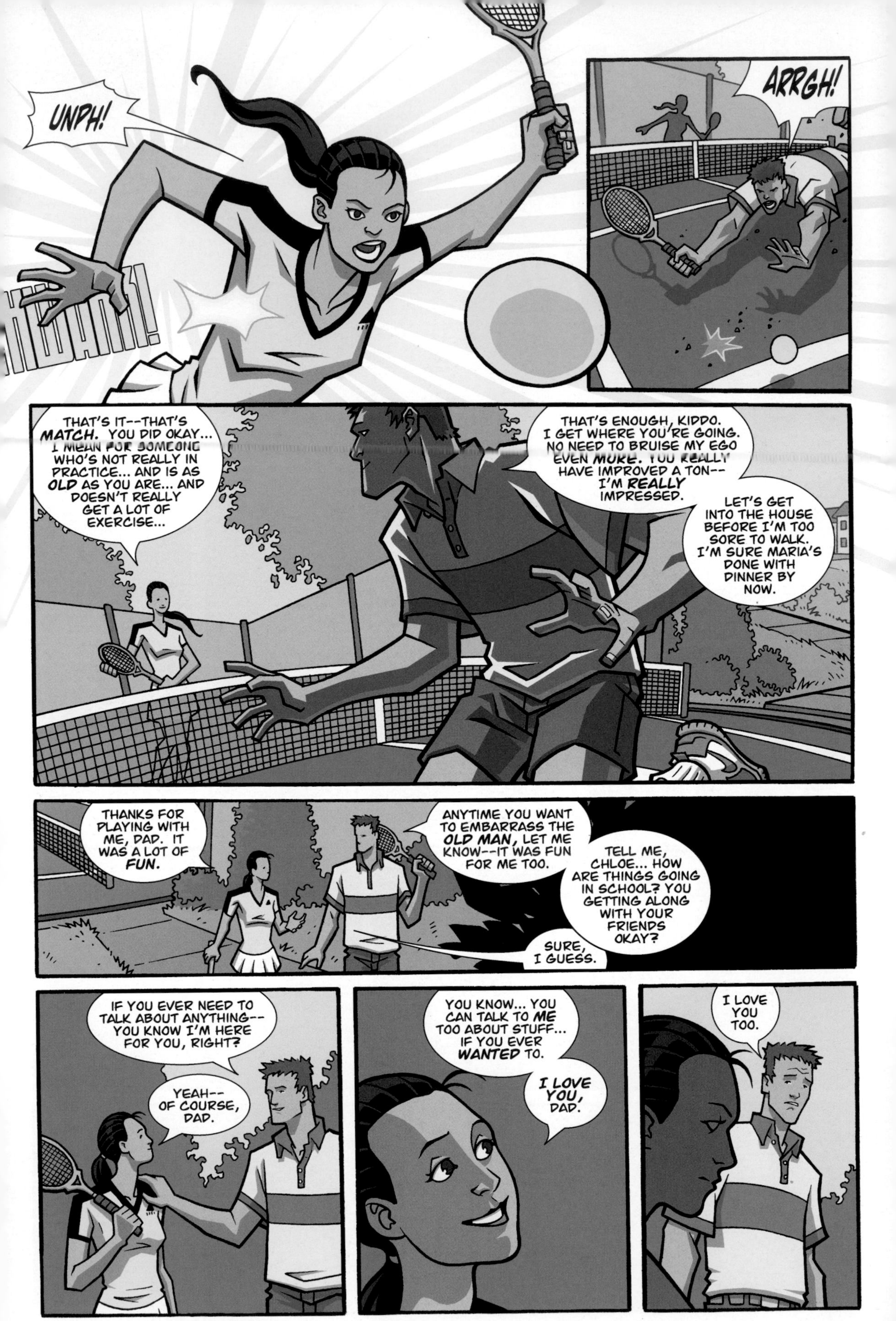
UNPH!
HWANN!
ARRGH!
THAT'S IT--THAT'S MATCH. YOU DID OKAY... I MEAN FOR SOMEONE WHO'S NOT REALLY IN PRACTICE... AND IS AS OLD AS YOU ARE... AND DOESN'T REALLY GET A LOT OF EXERCISE...
THAT'S ENOUGH, KIDDO. I GET WHERE YOU'RE GOING. NO NEED TO BRUISE MY EGO EVEN MORE. YOU REALLY HAVE IMPROVED A TON-- I'M REALLY IMPRESSED.
LET'S GET INTO THE HOUSE BEFORE I'M TOO SORE TO WALK. I'M SURE MARIA'S DONE WITH DINNER BY NOW.
THANKS FOR PLAYING WITH ME, DAD. IT WAS A LOT OF FUN.
ANYTIME YOU WANT TO EMBARRASS THE OLD MAN, LET ME KNOW--IT WAS FUN FOR ME TOO.
TELL ME, CHLOE... HOW ARE THINGS GOING IN SCHOOL? YOU GETTING ALONG WITH YOUR FRIENDS OKAY?
SURE, I GUESS.
IF YOU EVER NEED TO TALK ABOUT ANYTHING-- YOU KNOW I'M HERE FOR YOU, RIGHT?
YEAH-- OF COURSE, DAD.
YOU KNOW... YOU CAN TALK TO ME TOO ABOUT STUFF... IF YOU EVER WANTED TO.
I LOVE YOU, DAD.
I LOVE YOU TOO.

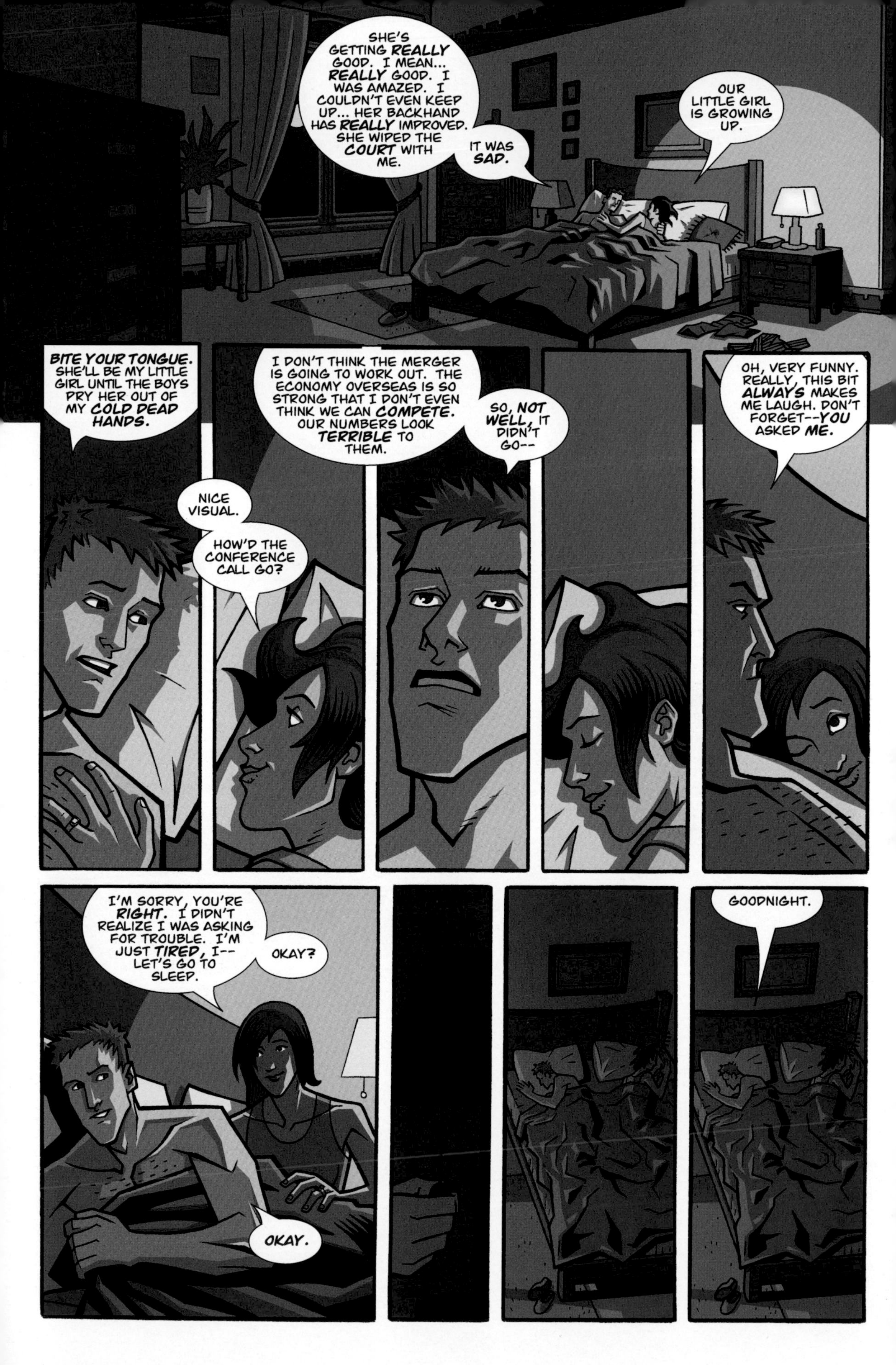
SHE'S GETTING REALLY GOOD. I MEAN... REALLY GOOD. I WAS AMAZED. I COULDN'T EVEN KEEP UP... HER BACKHAND HAS REALLY IMPROVED. SHE WIPED THE COURT WITH ME.
IT WAS SAD.
OUR LITTLE GIRL IS GROWING UP.
BITE YOUR TONGUE. SHE'LL BE MY LITTLE GIRL UNTIL THE BOYS PRY HER OUT OF MY COLD DEAD HANDS.
NICE VISUAL.
HOW'D THE CONFERENCE CALL GO?
I DON'T THINK THE MERGER IS GOING TO WORK OUT. THE ECONOMY OVERSEAS IS SO STRONG THAT I DON'T EVEN THINK WE CAN COMPETE. OUR NUMBERS LOOK TERRIBLE TO THEM.
SO, NOT WELL, IT DIDN'T GO--
OH, VERY FUNNY. REALLY, THIS BIT ALWAYS MAKES ME LAUGH. DON'T FORGET--YOU ASKED ME.
I'M SORRY, YOU'RE RIGHT. I DIDN'T REALIZE I WAS ASKING FOR TROUBLE. I'M JUST TIRED, I-- LET'S GO TO SLEEP.
OKAY?
OKAY.
GOODNIGHT.

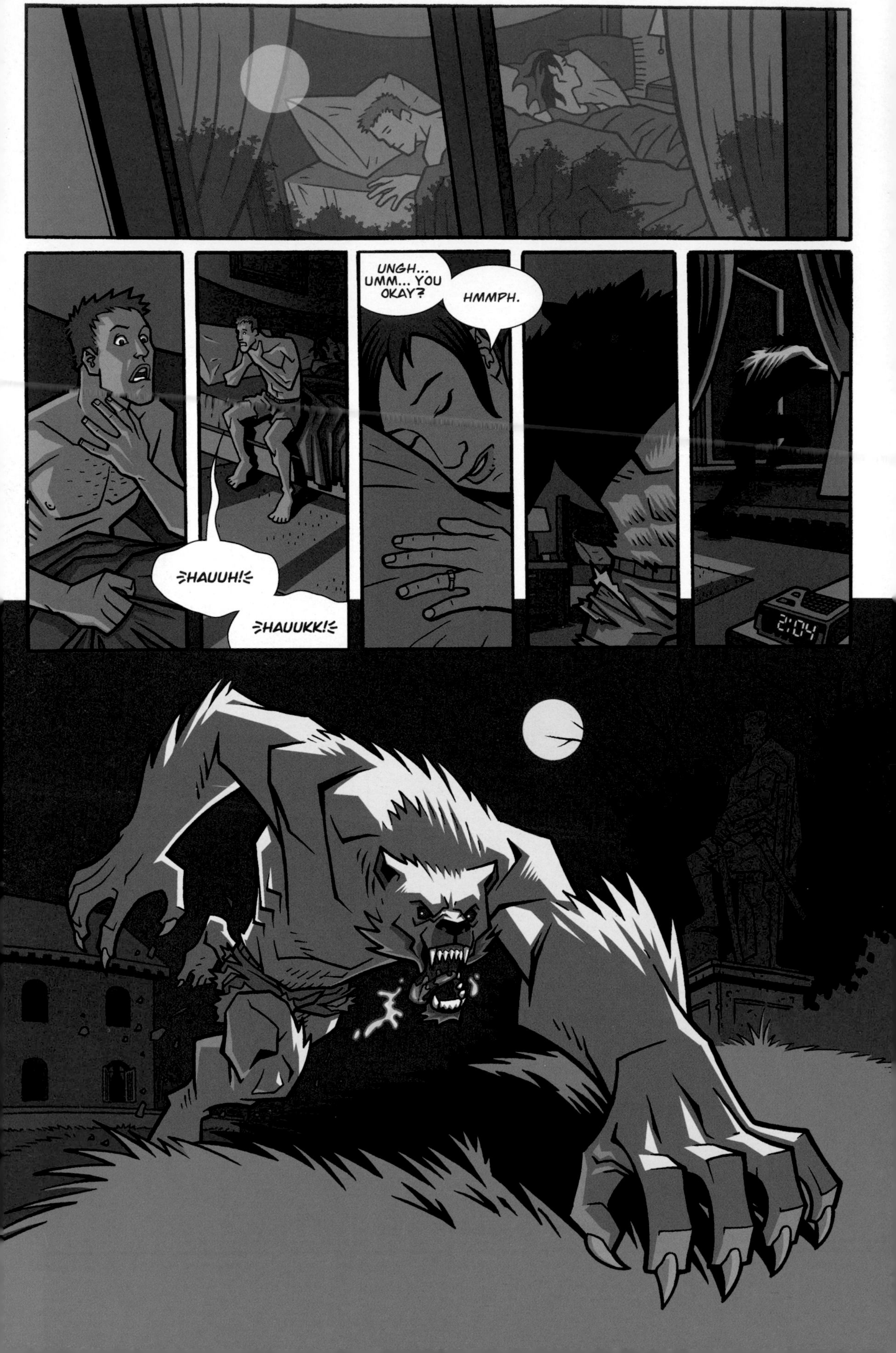
=HAUUH!=
=HAUUKK!=
UNGH... UMM... YOU OKAY?
HMMPH.
2:04

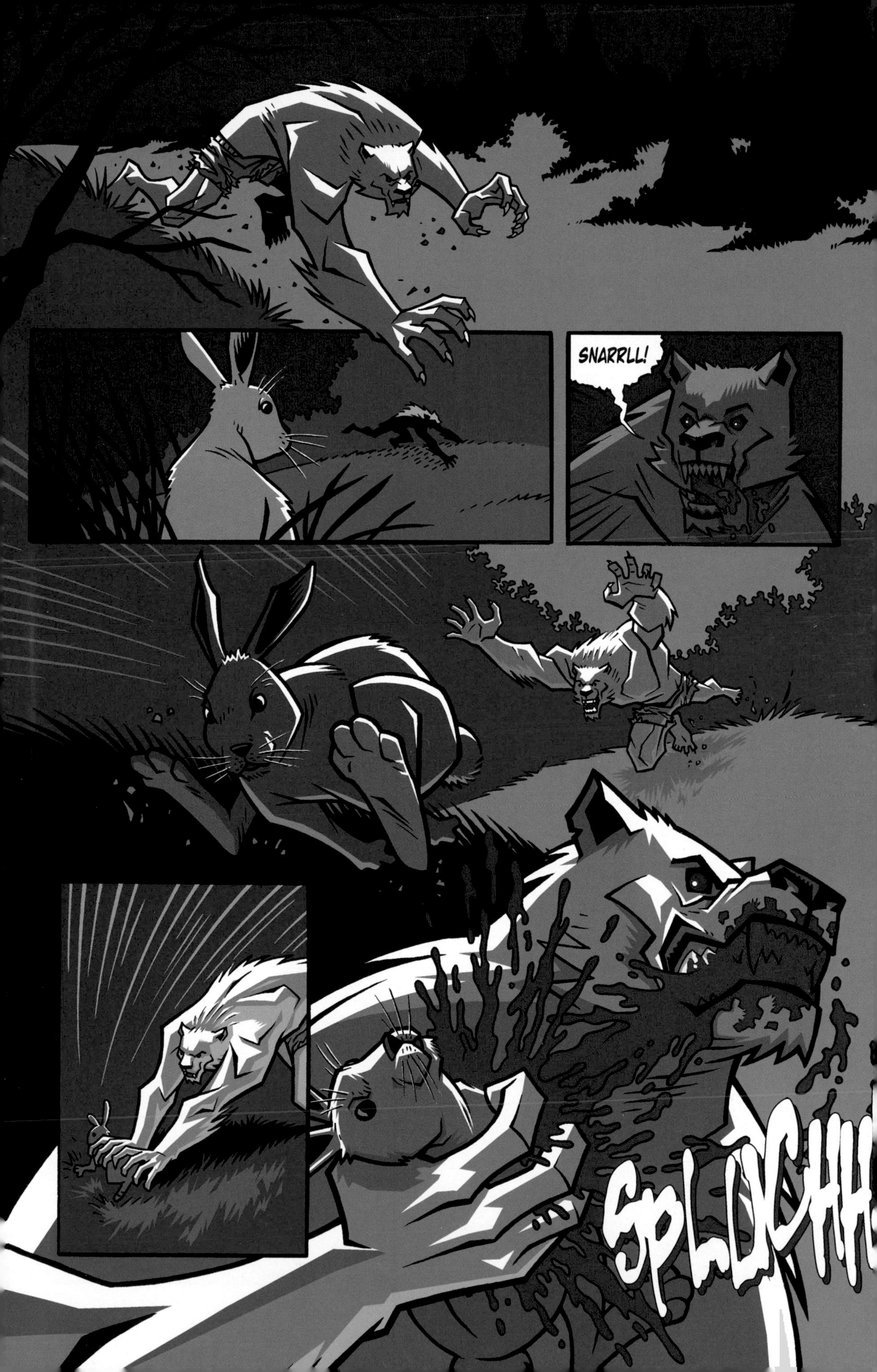
SNARRLL!
SPLOCHH!

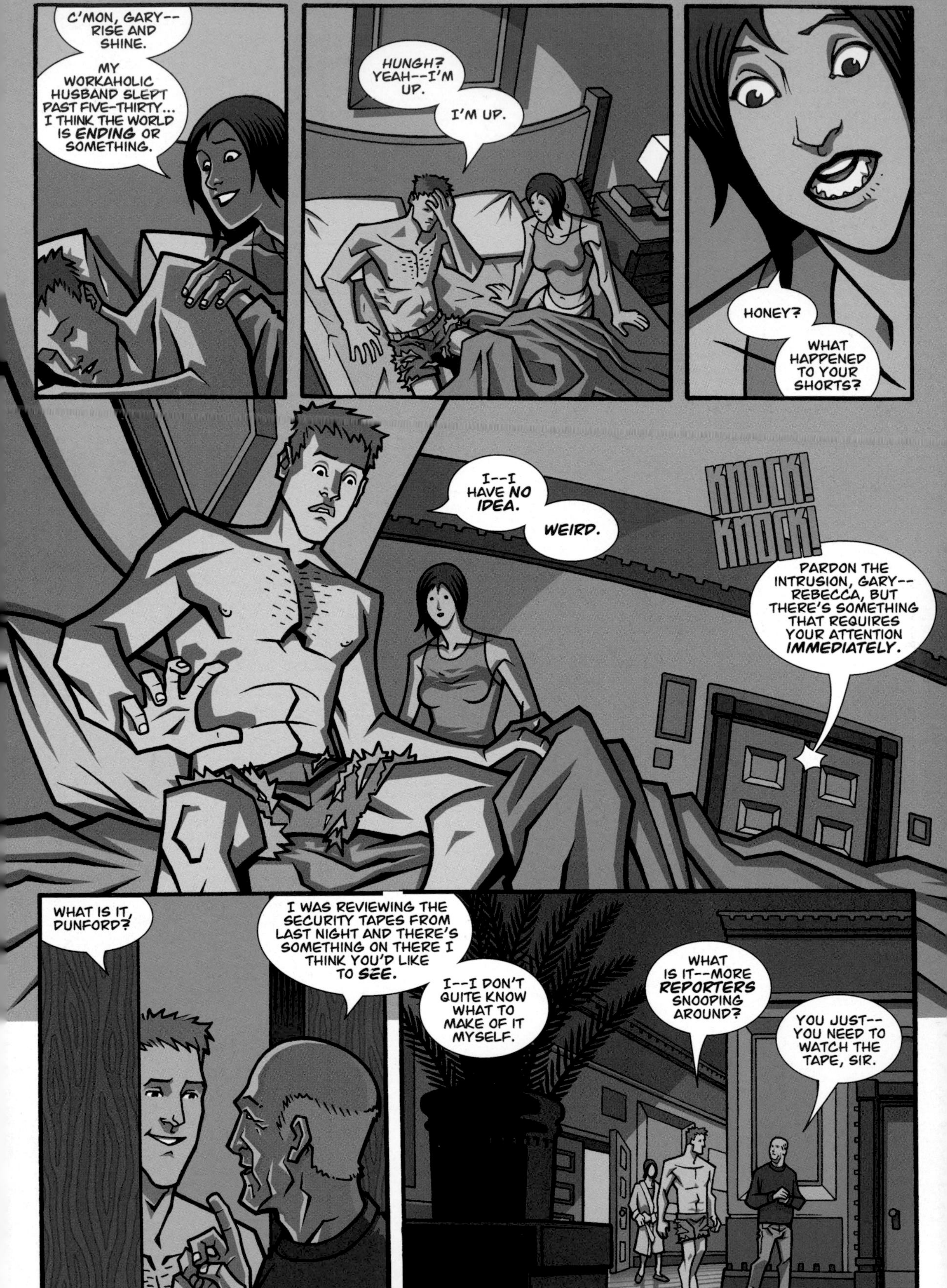
C'MON, GARY-- RISE AND SHINE.
MY WORKAHOLIC HUSBAND SLEPT PAST FIVE-THIRTY... I THINK THE WORLD IS ENDING OR SOMETHING.
HUNGH? YEAH--I'M UP.
I'M UP.
HONEY?
WHAT HAPPENED TO YOUR SHORTS?
I--I HAVE NO IDEA.
WEIRD.
KNOCK! KNOCK!
PARDON THE INTRUSION, GARY-- REBECCA, BUT THERE'S SOMETHING THAT REQUIRES YOUR ATTENTION IMMEDIATELY.
WHAT IS IT, DUNFORD?
I WAS REVIEWING THE SECURITY TAPES FROM LAST NIGHT AND THERE'S SOMETHING ON THERE I THINK YOU'D LIKE TO SEE.
I--I DON'T QUITE KNOW WHAT TO MAKE OF IT MYSELF.
WHAT IS IT--MORE REPORTERS SNOOPING AROUND?
YOU JUST-- YOU NEED TO WATCH THE TAPE, SIR.

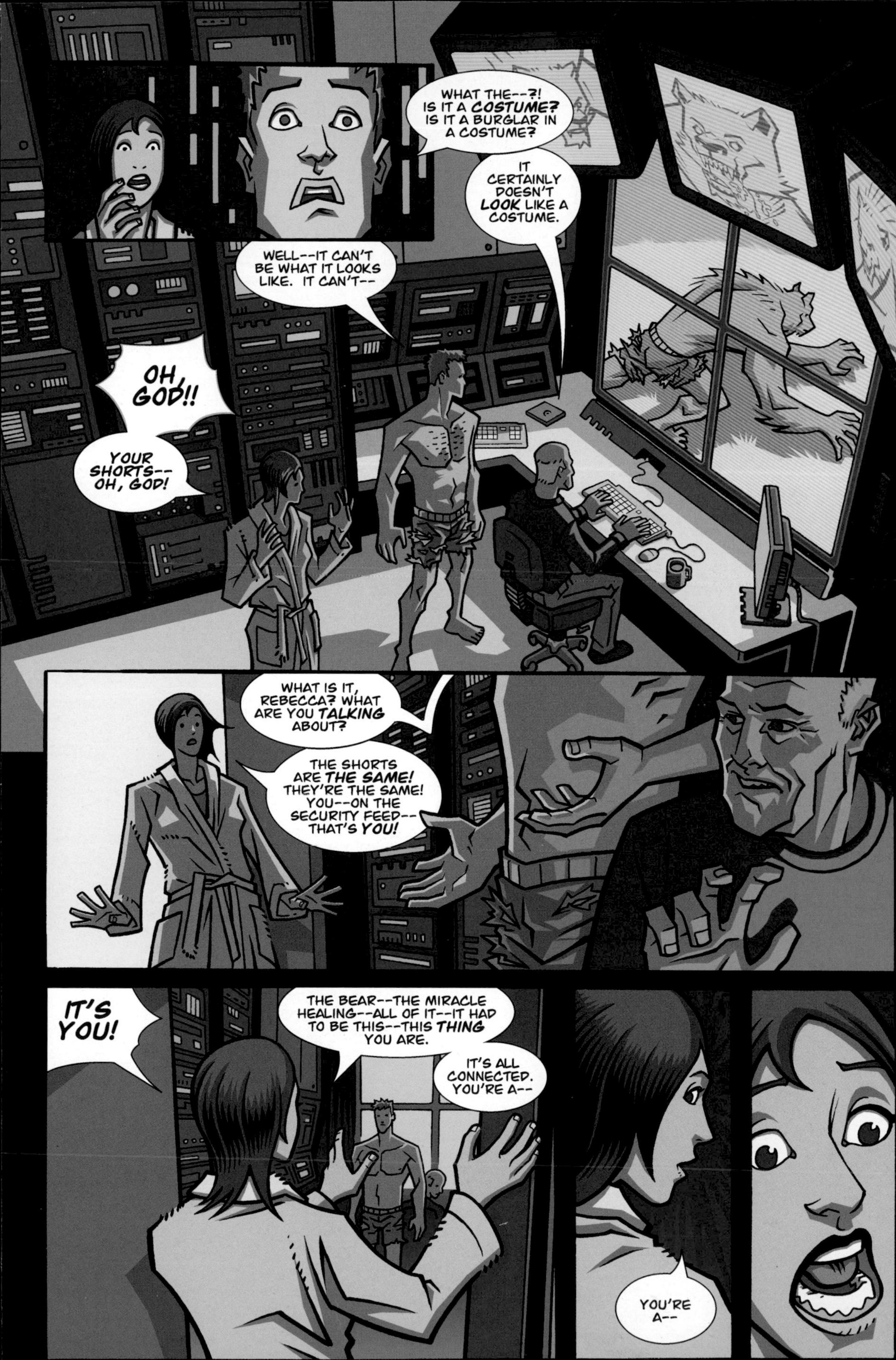
WHAT THE--?! IS IT A COSTUME? IS IT A BURGLAR IN A COSTUME?
IT CERTAINLY DOESN'T LOOK LIKE A COSTUME.
WELL--IT CAN'T BE WHAT IT LOOKS LIKE. IT CAN'T--
OH, GOD!!
YOUR SHORTS-- OH, GOD!
WHAT IS IT, REBECCA? WHAT ARE YOU TALKING ABOUT?
THE SHORTS ARE THE SAME! THEY'RE THE SAME! YOU--ON THE SECURITY FEED-- THAT'S YOU!
IT'S YOU!
THE BEAR--THE MIRACLE HEALING--ALL OF IT--IT HAD TO BE THIS--THIS THING YOU ARE.
IT'S ALL CONNECTED. YOU'RE A--
YOU'RE A--

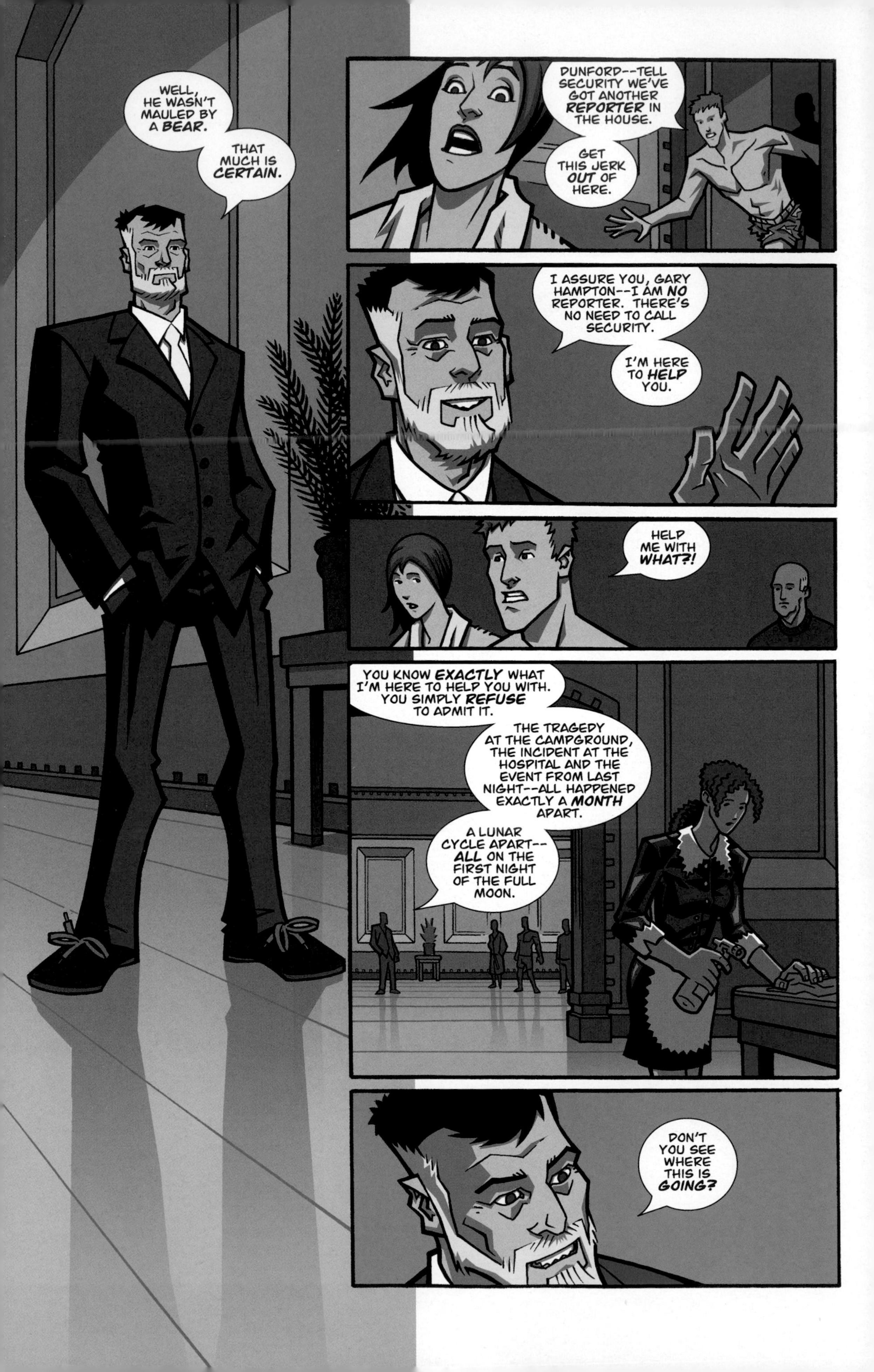
WELL, HE WASN'T MAULED BY A BEAR.
THAT MUCH IS CERTAIN.
DUNFORD--TELL SECURITY WE'VE GOT ANOTHER REPORTER IN THE HOUSE.
GET THIS JERK OUT OF HERE.
I ASSURE YOU, GARY HAMPTON--I AM NO REPORTER. THERE'S NO NEED TO CALL SECURITY.
I'M HERE TO HELP YOU.
HELP ME WITH WHAT?!
YOU KNOW EXACTLY WHAT I'M HERE TO HELP YOU WITH. YOU SIMPLY REFUSE TO ADMIT IT.
THE TRAGEDY AT THE CAMPGROUND, THE INCIDENT AT THE HOSPITAL AND THE EVENT FROM LAST NIGHT--ALL HAPPENED EXACTLY A MONTH APART.
A LUNAR CYCLE APART--ALL ON THE FIRST NIGHT OF THE FULL MOON.
DON'T YOU SEE WHERE THIS IS GOING?

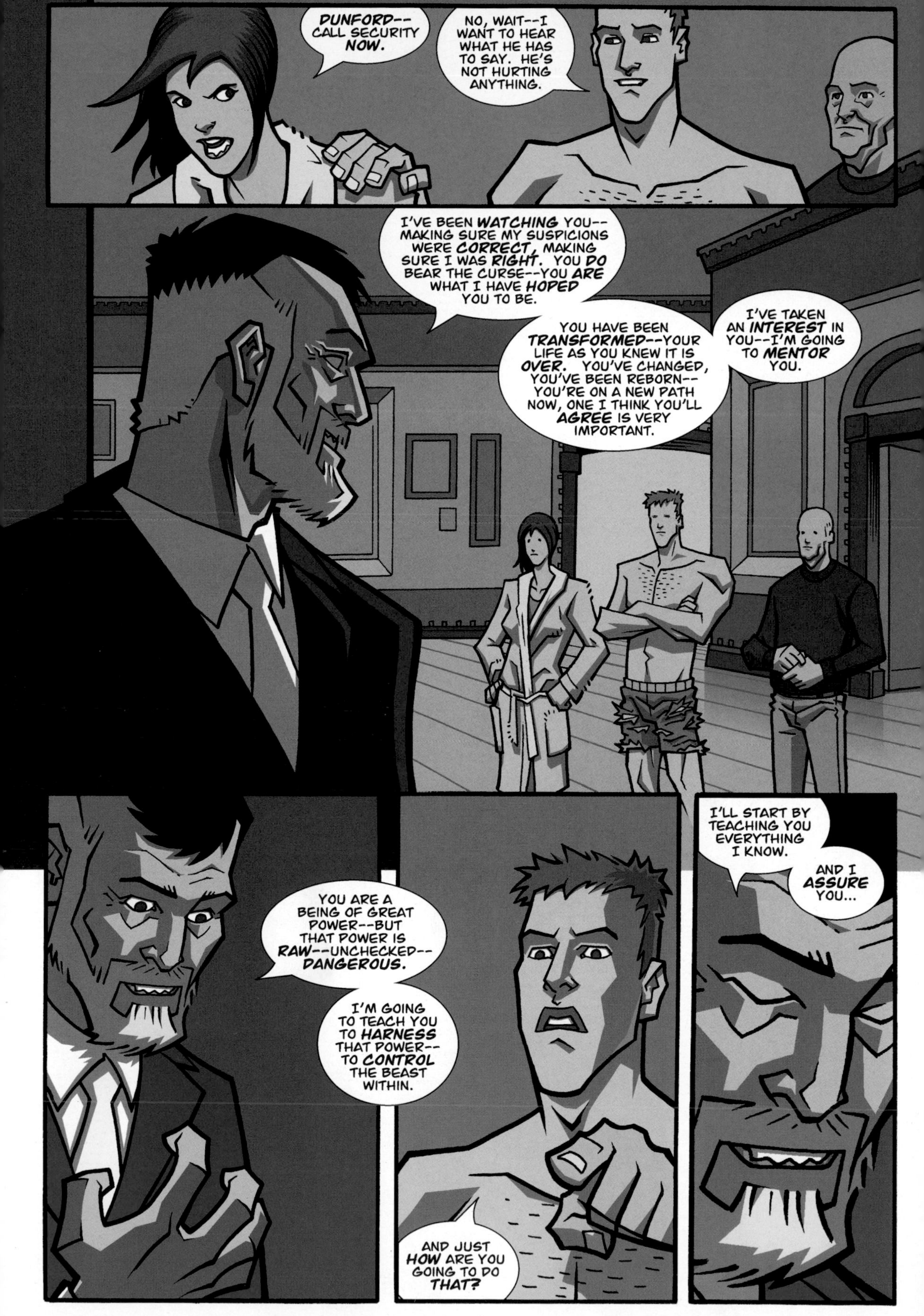
DUNFORD--
CALL SECURITY
NOW.
NO, WAIT--I WANT TO HEAR WHAT HE HAS TO SAY. HE'S NOT HURTING ANYTHING.
I'VE BEEN WATCHING YOU--MAKING SURE MY SUSPICIONS WERE CORRECT, MAKING SURE I WAS RIGHT. YOU DO BEAR THE CURSE--YOU ARE WHAT I HAVE HOPED YOU TO BE.
YOU HAVE BEEN TRANSFORMED--YOUR LIFE AS YOU KNEW IT IS OVER. YOU'VE CHANGED, YOU'VE BEEN REBORN--YOU'RE ON A NEW PATH NOW, ONE I THINK YOU'LL AGREE IS VERY IMPORTANT.
I'VE TAKEN AN INTEREST IN YOU--I'M GOING TO MENTOR YOU.
YOU ARE A BEING OF GREAT POWER--BUT THAT POWER IS RAW--UNCHECKED--DANGEROUS.
I'M GOING TO TEACH YOU TO HARNESS THAT POWER--TO CONTROL THE BEAST WITHIN.
AND JUST HOW ARE YOU GOING TO DO THAT?
I'LL START BY TEACHING YOU EVERYTHING I KNOW.
AND I ASSURE YOU...

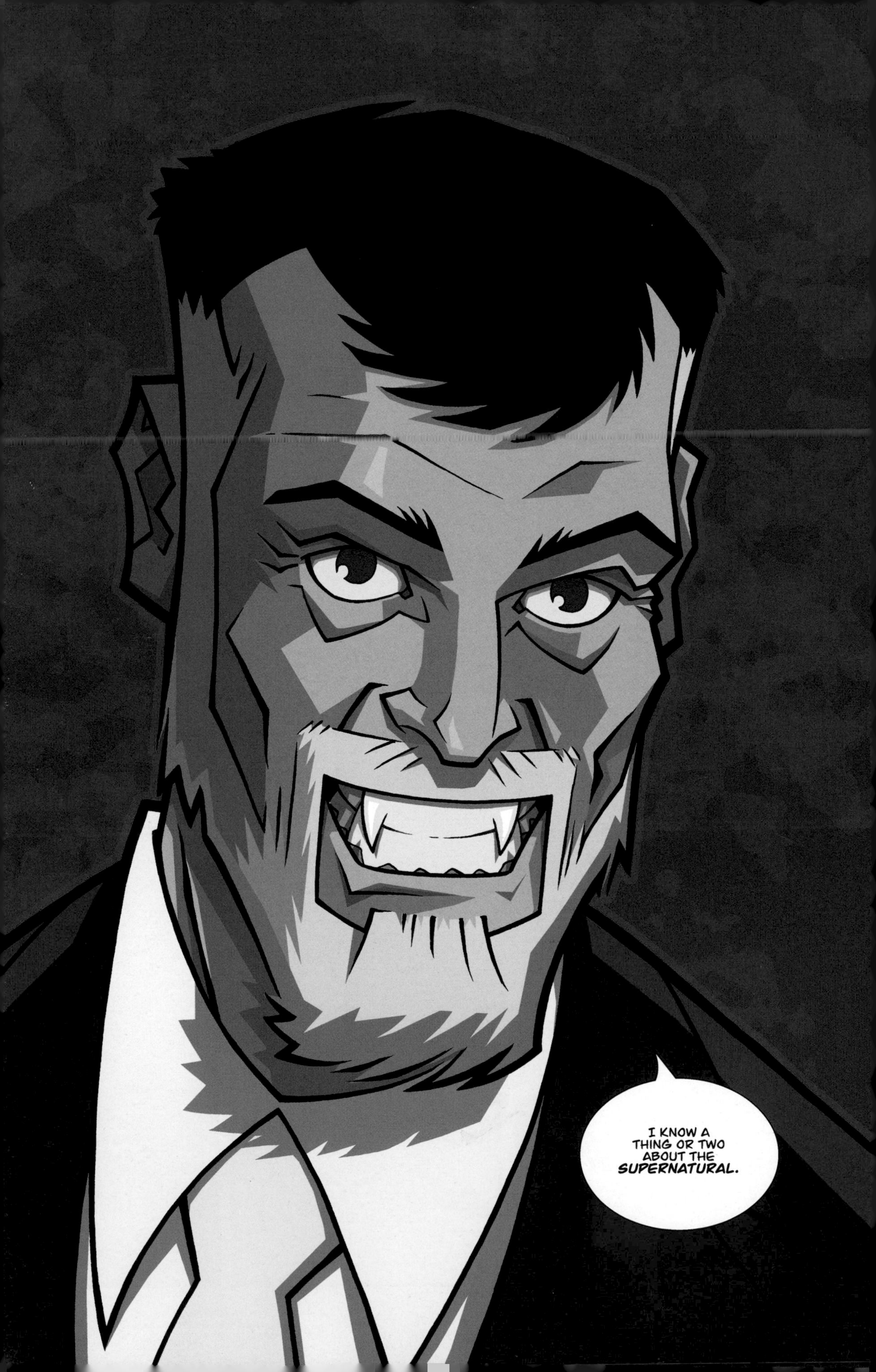
I KNOW A THING OR TWO ABOUT THE SUPERNATURAL.

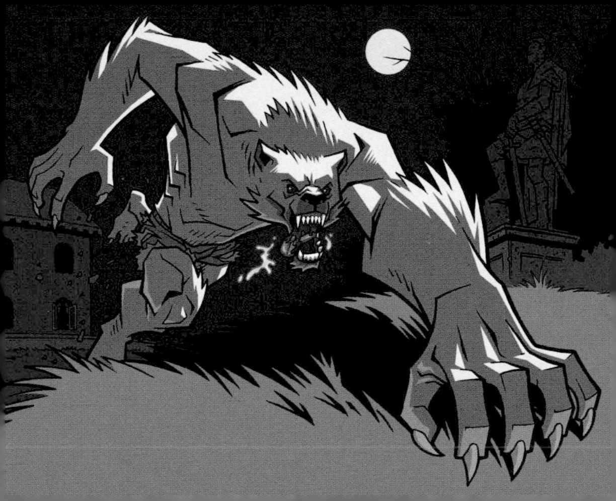

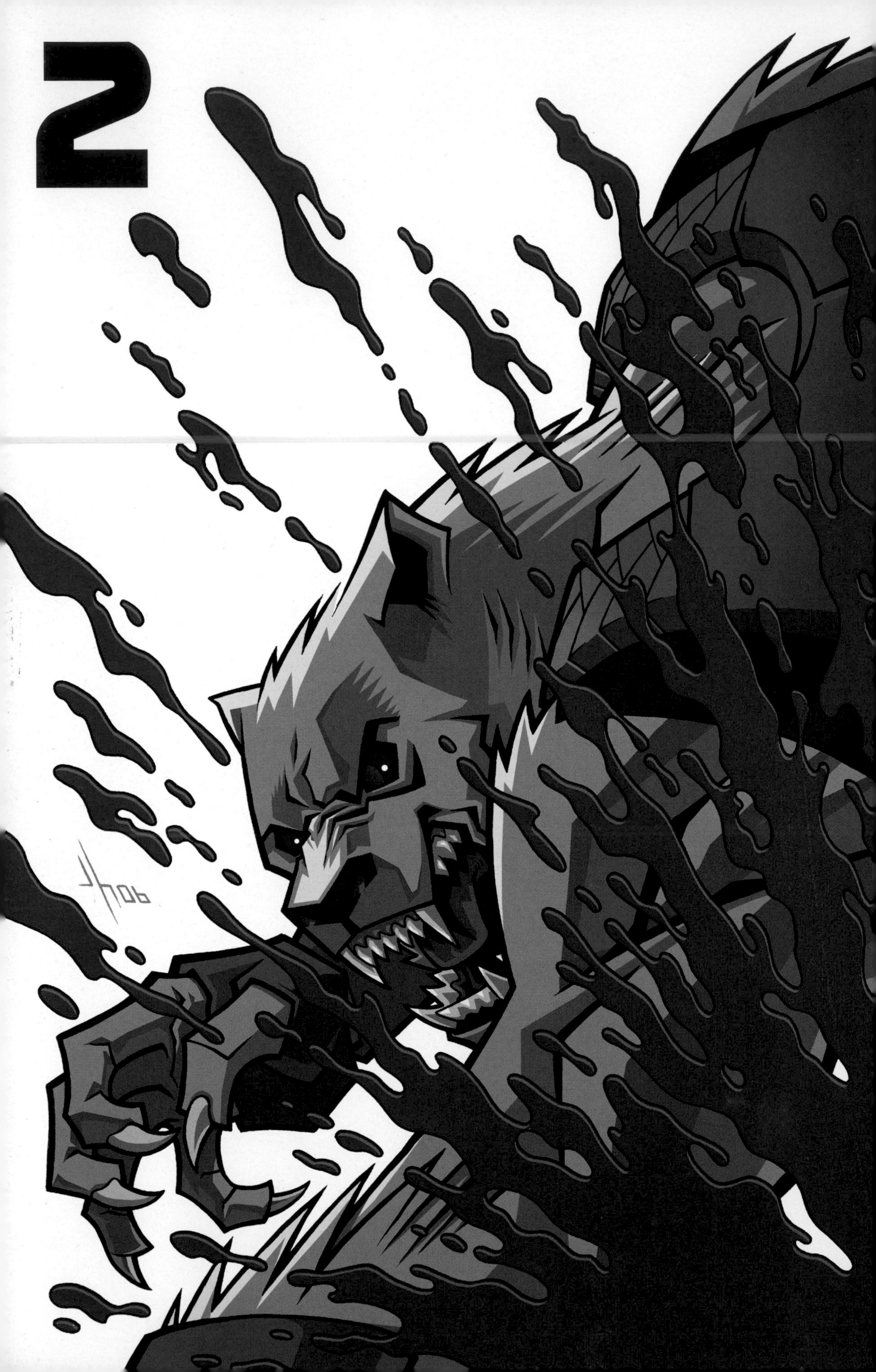
2

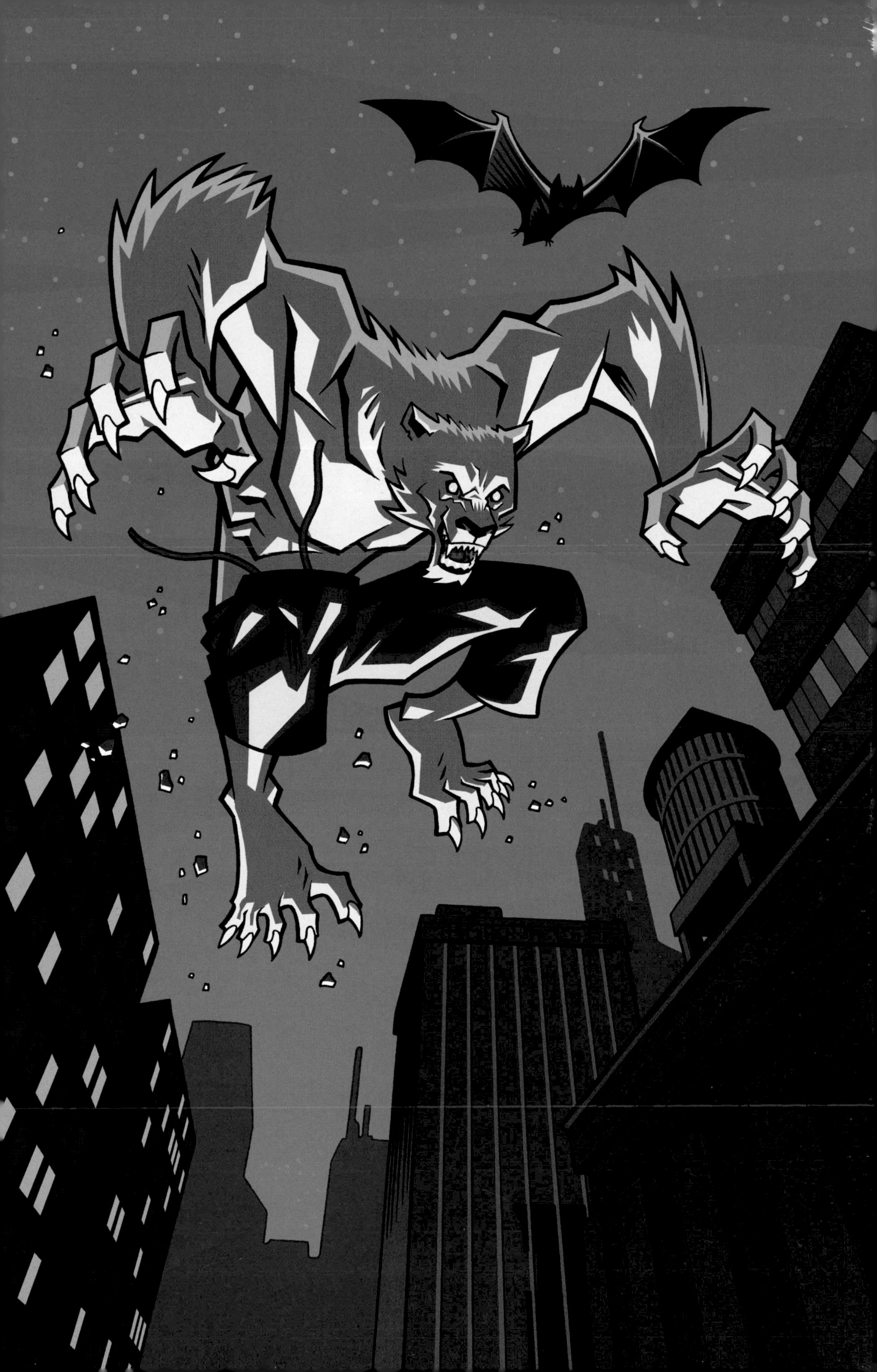

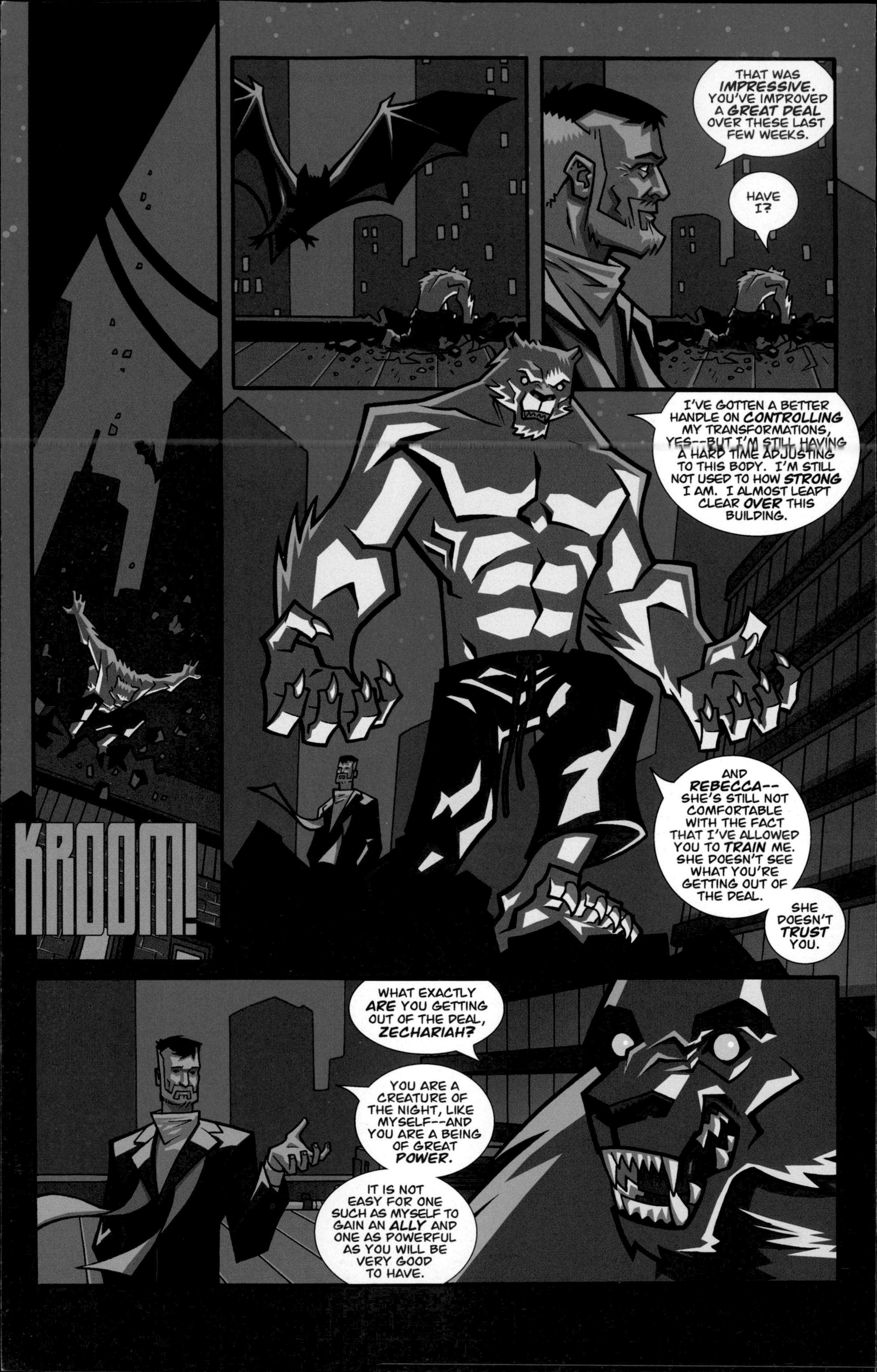
KROOM!
THAT WAS IMPRESSIVE. YOU'VE IMPROVED A GREAT DEAL OVER THESE LAST FEW WEEKS.
HAVE I?
I'VE GOTTEN A BETTER HANDLE ON CONTROLLING MY TRANSFORMATIONS, YES--BUT I'M STILL HAVING A HARD TIME ADJUSTING TO THIS BODY. I'M STILL NOT USED TO HOW STRONG I AM. I ALMOST LEAPT CLEAR OVER THIS BUILDING.
AND REBECCA-- SHE'S STILL NOT COMFORTABLE WITH THE FACT THAT I'VE ALLOWED YOU TO TRAIN ME. SHE DOESN'T SEE WHAT YOU'RE GETTING OUT OF THE DEAL.
SHE DOESN'T TRUST YOU.
WHAT EXACTLY ARE YOU GETTING OUT OF THE DEAL, ZECHARIAH?
YOU ARE A CREATURE OF THE NIGHT, LIKE MYSELF--AND YOU ARE A BEING OF GREAT POWER.
IT IS NOT EASY FOR ONE SUCH AS MYSELF TO GAIN AN ALLY AND ONE AS POWERFUL AS YOU WILL BE VERY GOOD TO HAVE.

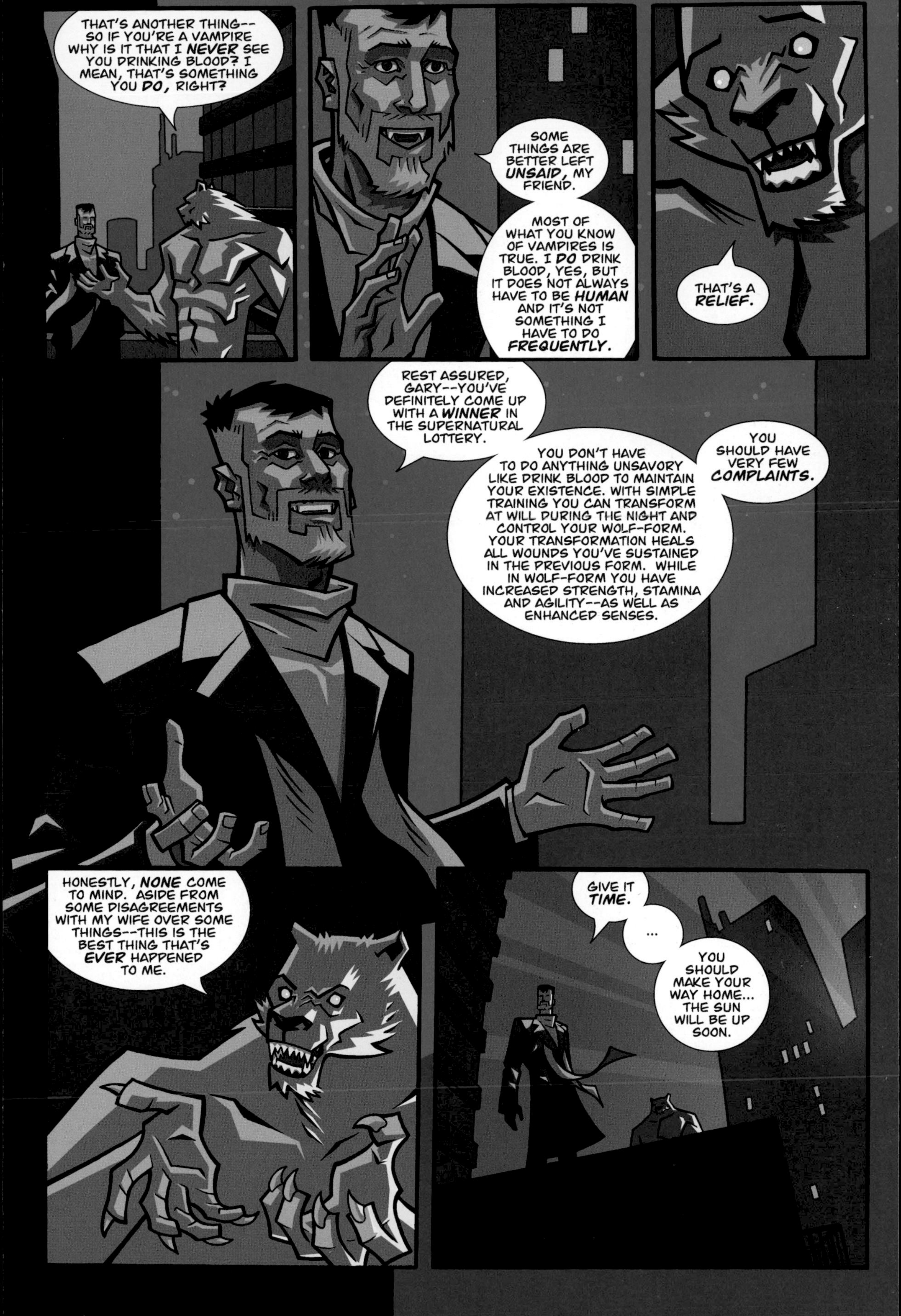
THAT'S ANOTHER THING-- SO IF YOU'RE A VAMPIRE WHY IS IT THAT I NEVER SEE YOU DRINKING BLOOD? I MEAN, THAT'S SOMETHING YOU DO, RIGHT?
SOME THINGS ARE BETTER LEFT UNSAID, MY FRIEND.
MOST OF WHAT YOU KNOW OF VAMPIRES IS TRUE. I DO DRINK BLOOD, YES, BUT IT DOES NOT ALWAYS HAVE TO BE HUMAN AND IT'S NOT SOMETHING I HAVE TO DO FREQUENTLY.
THAT'S A RELIEF.
REST ASSURED, GARY--YOU'VE DEFINITELY COME UP WITH A WINNER IN THE SUPERNATURAL LOTTERY.
YOU DON'T HAVE TO DO ANYTHING UNSAVORY LIKE DRINK BLOOD TO MAINTAIN YOUR EXISTENCE. WITH SIMPLE TRAINING YOU CAN TRANSFORM AT WILL DURING THE NIGHT AND CONTROL YOUR WOLF-FORM. YOUR TRANSFORMATION HEALS ALL WOUNDS YOU'VE SUSTAINED IN THE PREVIOUS FORM. WHILE IN WOLF-FORM YOU HAVE INCREASED STRENGTH, STAMINA AND AGILITY--AS WELL AS ENHANCED SENSES.
YOU SHOULD HAVE VERY FEW COMPLAINTS.
HONESTLY, NONE COME TO MIND. ASIDE FROM SOME DISAGREEMENTS WITH MY WIFE OVER SOME THINGS--THIS IS THE BEST THING THAT'S EVER HAPPENED TO ME.
GIVE IT TIME.
...
YOU SHOULD MAKE YOUR WAY HOME... THE SUN WILL BE UP SOON.

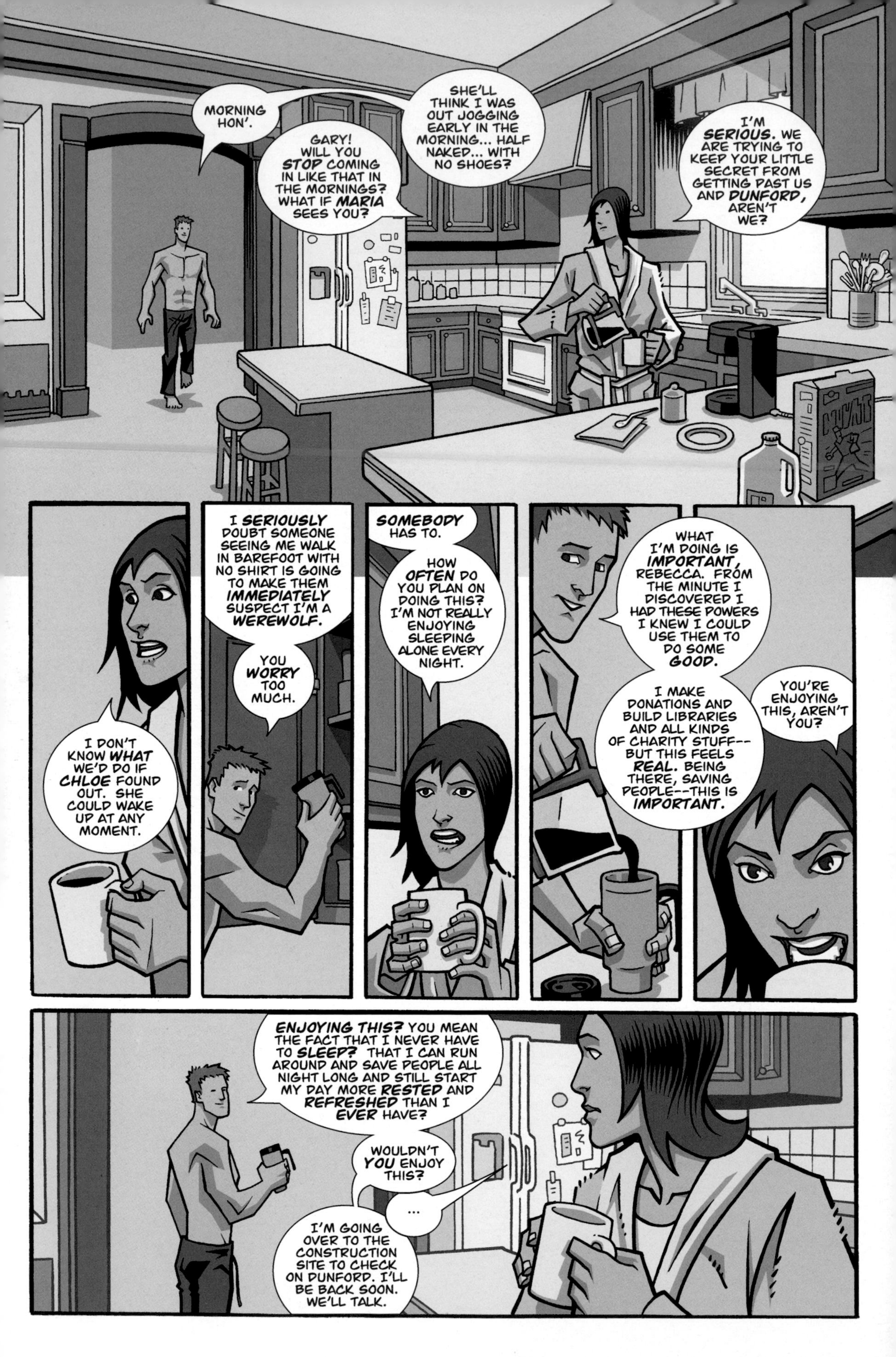
MORNING HON'.
GARY! WILL YOU STOP COMING IN LIKE THAT IN THE MORNINGS? WHAT IF MARIA SEES YOU?
SHE'LL THINK I WAS OUT JOGGING EARLY IN THE MORNING... HALF NAKED... WITH NO SHOES?
I'M SERIOUS. WE ARE TRYING TO KEEP YOUR LITTLE SECRET FROM GETTING PAST US AND DUNFORD, AREN'T WE?
I DON'T KNOW WHAT WE'D DO IF CHLOE FOUND OUT. SHE COULD WAKE UP AT ANY MOMENT.
I SERIOUSLY DOUBT SOMEONE SEEING ME WALK IN BAREFOOT WITH NO SHIRT IS GOING TO MAKE THEM IMMEDIATELY SUSPECT I'M A WEREWOLF.
YOU WORRY TOO MUCH.
SOMEBODY HAS TO.
HOW OFTEN DO YOU PLAN ON DOING THIS? I'M NOT REALLY ENJOYING SLEEPING ALONE EVERY NIGHT.
WHAT I'M DOING IS IMPORTANT, REBECCA. FROM THE MINUTE I DISCOVERED I HAD THESE POWERS I KNEW I COULD USE THEM TO DO SOME GOOD.
I MAKE DONATIONS AND BUILD LIBRARIES AND ALL KINDS OF CHARITY STUFF--BUT THIS FEELS REAL. BEING THERE, SAVING PEOPLE--THIS IS IMPORTANT.
YOU'RE ENJOYING THIS, AREN'T YOU?
ENJOYING THIS? YOU MEAN THE FACT THAT I NEVER HAVE TO SLEEP? THAT I CAN RUN AROUND AND SAVE PEOPLE ALL NIGHT LONG AND STILL START MY DAY MORE RESTED AND REFRESHED THAN I EVER HAVE?
WOULDN'T YOU ENJOY THIS?
...
I'M GOING OVER TO THE CONSTRUCTION SITE TO CHECK ON DUNFORD. I'LL BE BACK SOON. WE'LL TALK.

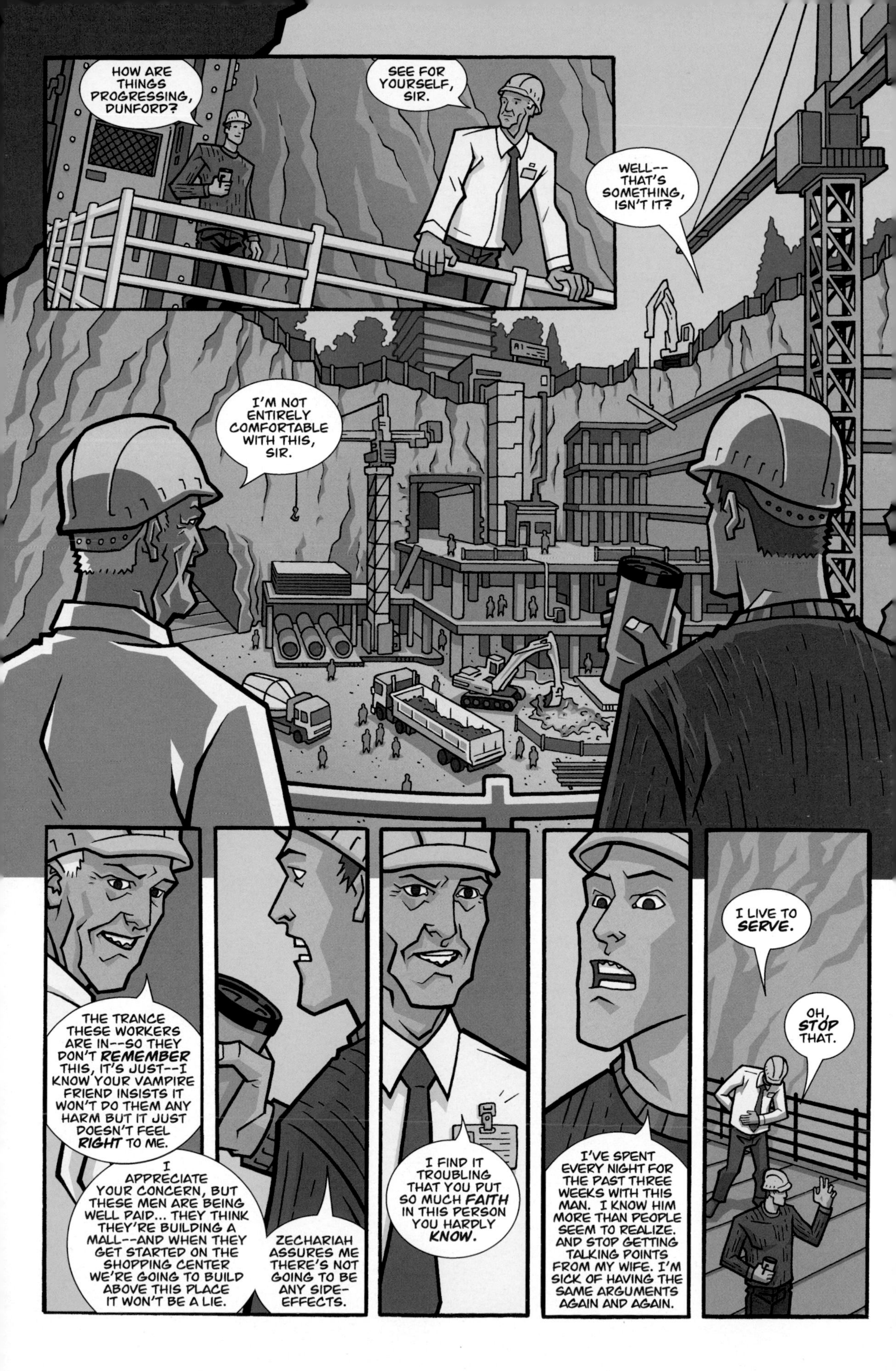
HOW ARE THINGS PROGRESSING, DUNFORD?
SEE FOR YOURSELF, SIR.
WELL-- THAT'S SOMETHING, ISN'T IT?
I'M NOT ENTIRELY COMFORTABLE WITH THIS, SIR.
THE TRANCE THESE WORKERS ARE IN--SO THEY DON'T REMEMBER THIS, IT'S JUST--I KNOW YOUR VAMPIRE FRIEND INSISTS IT WON'T DO THEM ANY HARM BUT IT JUST DOESN'T FEEL RIGHT TO ME.
I APPRECIATE YOUR CONCERN, BUT THESE MEN ARE BEING WELL PAID... THEY THINK THEY'RE BUILDING A MALL--AND WHEN THEY GET STARTED ON THE SHOPPING CENTER WE'RE GOING TO BUILD ABOVE THIS PLACE IT WON'T BE A LIE.
ZECHARIAH ASSURES ME THERE'S NOT GOING TO BE ANY SIDE-EFFECTS.
I FIND IT TROUBLING THAT YOU PUT SO MUCH FAITH IN THIS PERSON YOU HARDLY KNOW.
I'VE SPENT EVERY NIGHT FOR THE PAST THREE WEEKS WITH THIS MAN. I KNOW HIM MORE THAN PEOPLE SEEM TO REALIZE. AND STOP GETTING TALKING POINTS FROM MY WIFE. I'M SICK OF HAVING THE SAME ARGUMENTS AGAIN AND AGAIN.
I LIVE TO SERVE.
OH, STOP THAT.

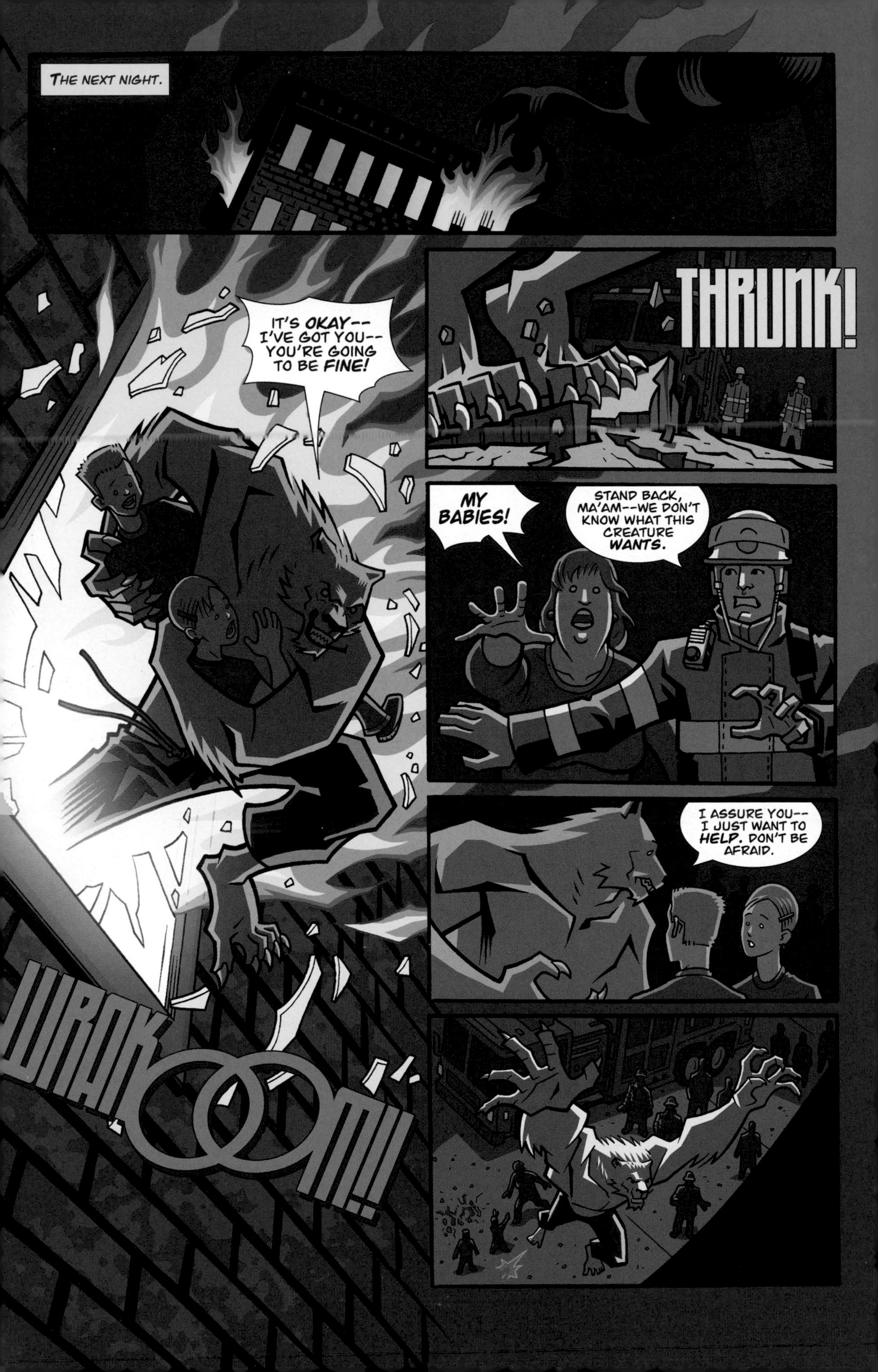
THE NEXT NIGHT.
IT'S OKAY-- I'VE GOT YOU-- YOU'RE GOING TO BE FINE!
WRAKOOOM!!
THRUNK!
MY BABIES!
STAND BACK, MA'AM--WE DON'T KNOW WHAT THIS CREATURE WANTS.
I ASSURE YOU-- I JUST WANT TO HELP. DON'T BE AFRAID.

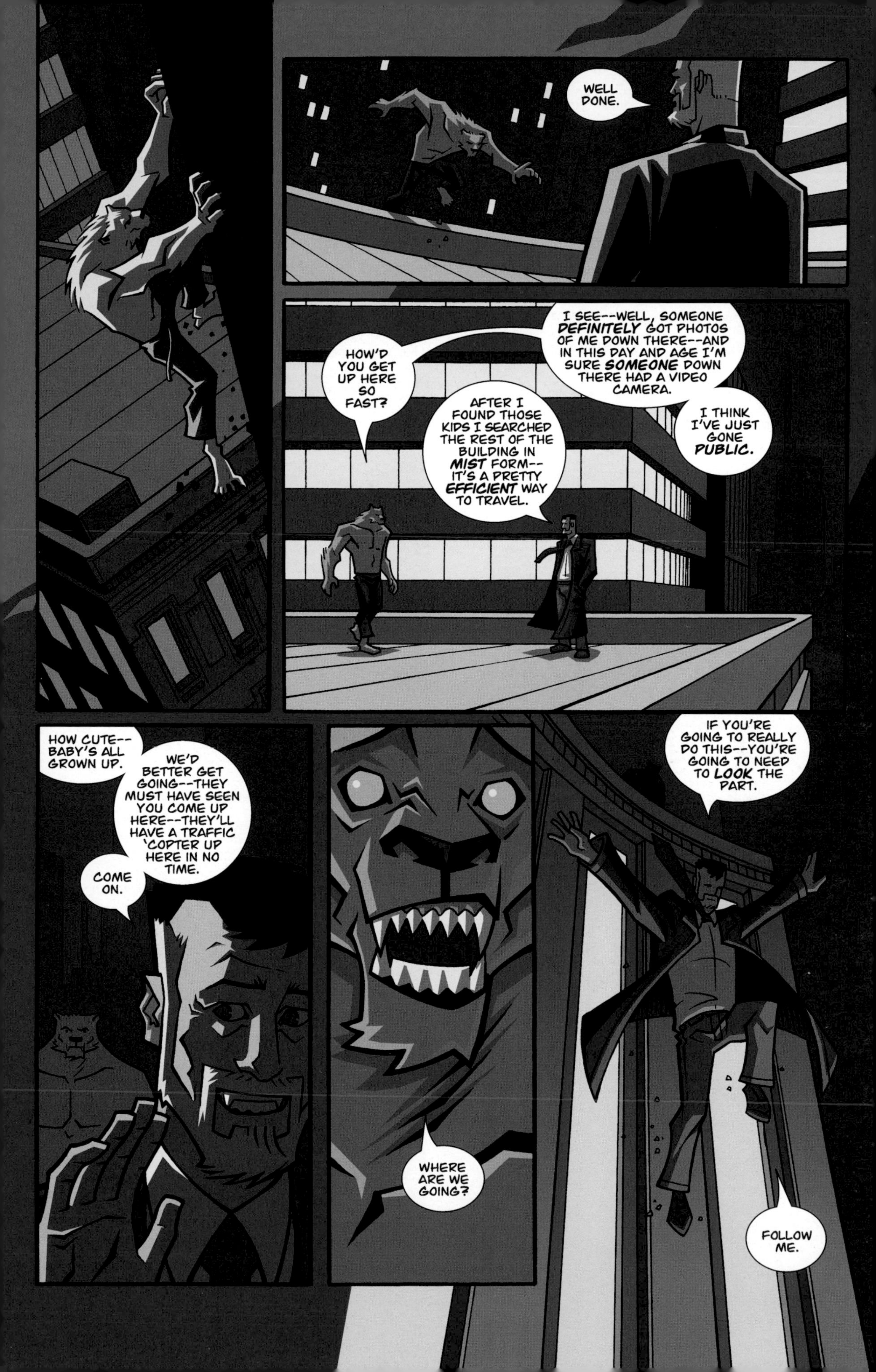
WELL DONE.
HOW'D YOU GET UP HERE SO FAST?
I SEE--WELL, SOMEONE DEFINITELY GOT PHOTOS OF ME DOWN THERE--AND IN THIS DAY AND AGE I'M SURE SOMEONE DOWN THERE HAD A VIDEO CAMERA.
I THINK I'VE JUST GONE PUBLIC.
AFTER I FOUND THOSE KIDS I SEARCHED THE REST OF THE BUILDING IN MIST FORM--IT'S A PRETTY EFFICIENT WAY TO TRAVEL.
HOW CUTE--BABY'S ALL GROWN UP.
WE'D BETTER GET GOING--THEY MUST HAVE SEEN YOU COME UP HERE--THEY'LL HAVE A TRAFFIC 'COPTER UP HERE IN NO TIME.
COME ON.
WHERE ARE WE GOING?
IF YOU'RE GOING TO REALLY DO THIS--YOU'RE GOING TO NEED TO LOOK THE PART.
FOLLOW ME.

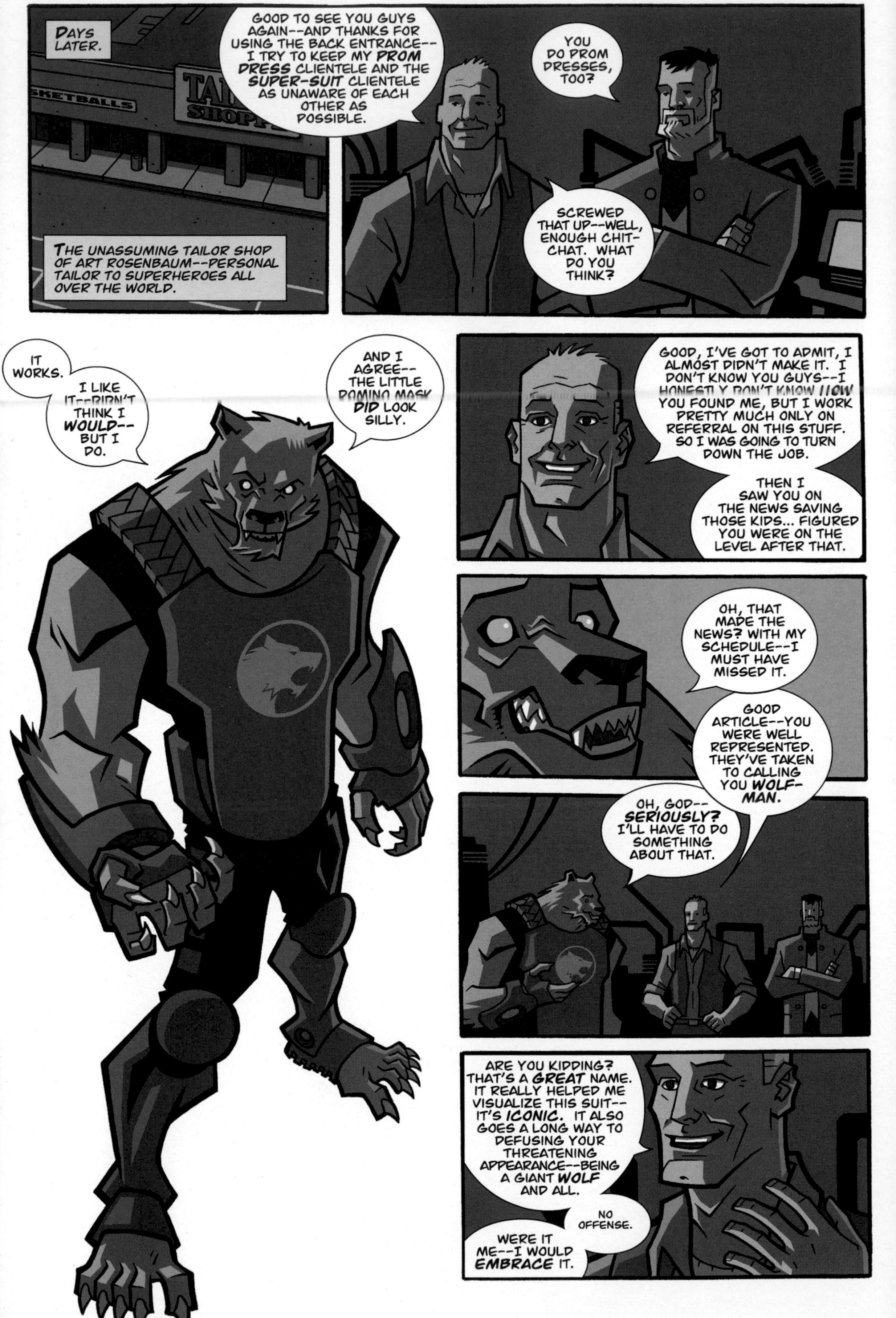
DAYS LATER.
TAILOR SHOPPE
SKETBALLS
THE UNASSUMING TAILOR SHOP OF ART ROSENBAUM--PERSONAL TAILOR TO SUPERHEROES ALL OVER THE WORLD.
GOOD TO SEE YOU GUYS AGAIN--AND THANKS FOR USING THE BACK ENTRANCE--I TRY TO KEEP MY PROM DRESS CLIENTELE AND THE SUPER-SUIT CLIENTELE AS UNAWARE OF EACH OTHER AS POSSIBLE.
YOU DO PROM DRESSES, TOO?
SCREWED THAT UP--WELL, ENOUGH CHIT-CHAT. WHAT DO YOU THINK?
IT WORKS.
I LIKE IT--DIDN'T THINK I WOULD--BUT I DO.
AND I AGREE--THE LITTLE DOMINO MASK DID LOOK SILLY.
GOOD, I'VE GOT TO ADMIT, I ALMOST DIDN'T MAKE IT. I DON'T KNOW YOU GUYS--I HONESTLY DON'T KNOW HOW YOU FOUND ME, BUT I WORK PRETTY MUCH ONLY ON REFERRAL ON THIS STUFF. SO I WAS GOING TO TURN DOWN THE JOB.
THEN I SAW YOU ON THE NEWS SAVING THOSE KIDS... FIGURED YOU WERE ON THE LEVEL AFTER THAT.
OH, THAT MADE THE NEWS? WITH MY SCHEDULE--I MUST HAVE MISSED IT.
GOOD ARTICLE--YOU WERE WELL REPRESENTED. THEY'VE TAKEN TO CALLING YOU WOLF-MAN.
OH, GOD--SERIOUSLY? I'LL HAVE TO DO SOMETHING ABOUT THAT.
ARE YOU KIDDING? THAT'S A GREAT NAME. IT REALLY HELPED ME VISUALIZE THIS SUIT--IT'S ICONIC. IT ALSO GOES A LONG WAY TO DEFUSING YOUR THREATENING APPEARANCE--BEING A GIANT WOLF AND ALL.
NO OFFENSE.
WERE IT ME--I WOULD EMBRACE IT.

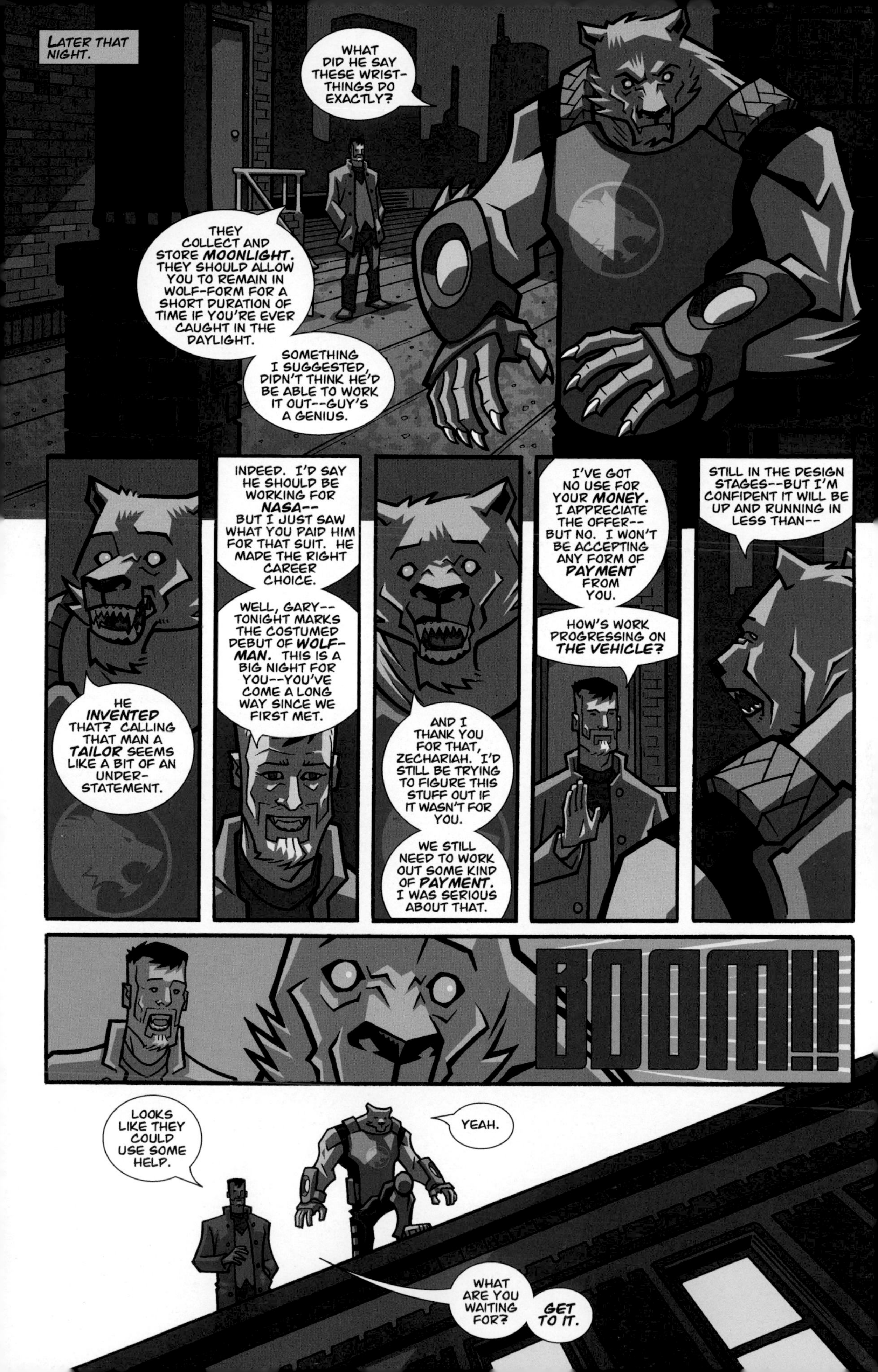
LATER THAT NIGHT.
WHAT DID HE SAY THESE WRIST-THINGS DO EXACTLY?
THEY COLLECT AND STORE MOONLIGHT. THEY SHOULD ALLOW YOU TO REMAIN IN WOLF-FORM FOR A SHORT DURATION OF TIME IF YOU'RE EVER CAUGHT IN THE DAYLIGHT.
SOMETHING I SUGGESTED, DIDN'T THINK HE'D BE ABLE TO WORK IT OUT--GUY'S A GENIUS.
HE INVENTED THAT? CALLING THAT MAN A TAILOR SEEMS LIKE A BIT OF AN UNDER-STATEMENT.
INDEED. I'D SAY HE SHOULD BE WORKING FOR NASA--
BUT I JUST SAW WHAT YOU PAID HIM FOR THAT SUIT. HE MADE THE RIGHT CAREER CHOICE.
WELL, GARY--TONIGHT MARKS THE COSTUMED DEBUT OF WOLF-MAN. THIS IS A BIG NIGHT FOR YOU--YOU'VE COME A LONG WAY SINCE WE FIRST MET.
AND I THANK YOU FOR THAT, ZECHARIAH. I'D STILL BE TRYING TO FIGURE THIS STUFF OUT IF IT WASN'T FOR YOU.
WE STILL NEED TO WORK OUT SOME KIND OF PAYMENT. I WAS SERIOUS ABOUT THAT.
I'VE GOT NO USE FOR YOUR MONEY. I APPRECIATE THE OFFER--BUT NO. I WON'T BE ACCEPTING ANY FORM OF PAYMENT FROM YOU.
HOW'S WORK PROGRESSING ON THE VEHICLE?
STILL IN THE DESIGN STAGES--BUT I'M CONFIDENT IT WILL BE UP AND RUNNING IN LESS THAN--
BOOM!!
LOOKS LIKE THEY COULD USE SOME HELP.
YEAH.
WHAT ARE YOU WAITING FOR?
GET TO IT.

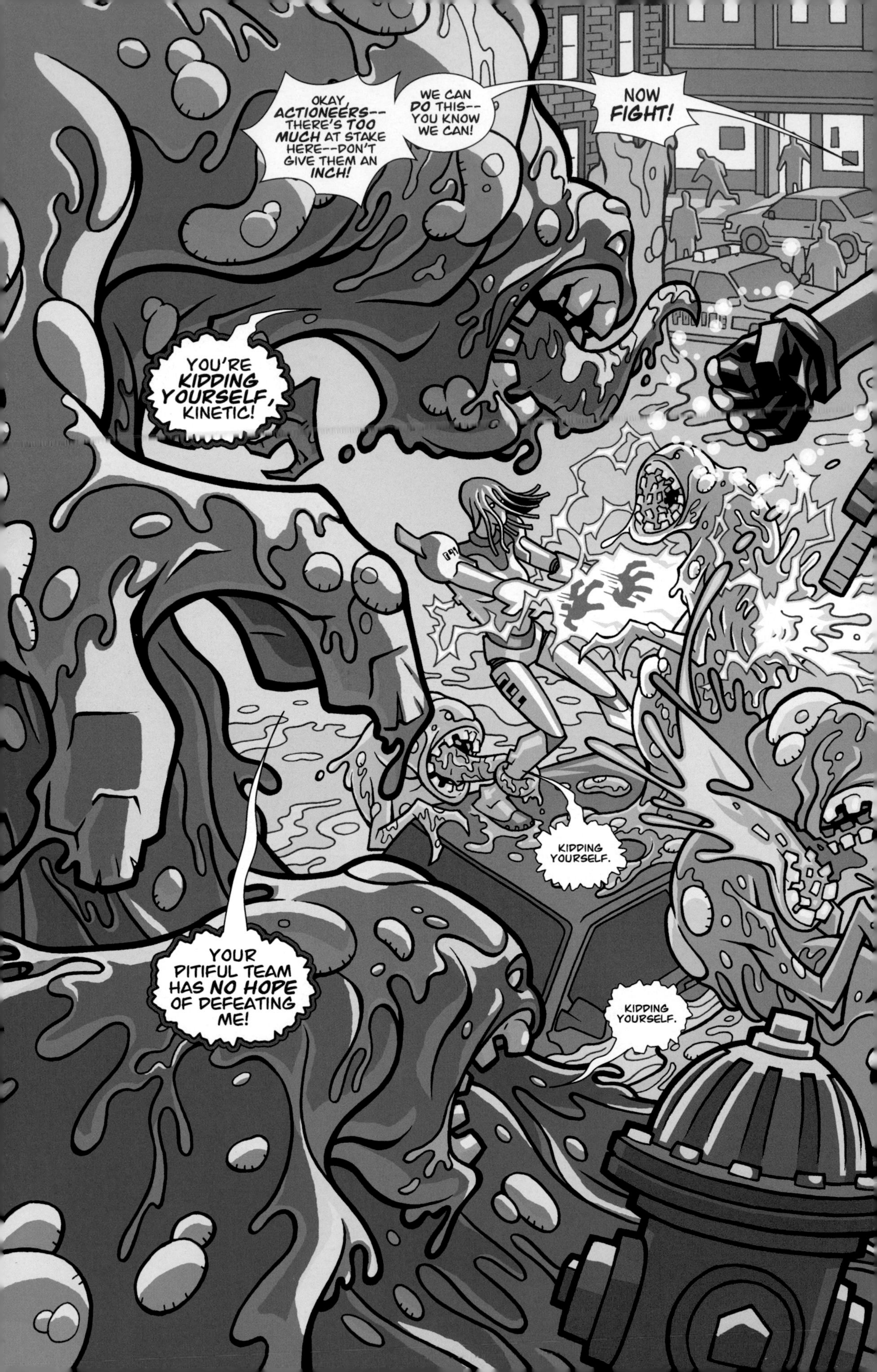
OKAY, ACTIONEERS-- THERE'S TOO MUCH AT STAKE HERE--DON'T GIVE THEM AN INCH!
WE CAN DO THIS-- YOU KNOW WE CAN!
NOW FIGHT!
YOU'RE KIDDING YOURSELF, KINETIC!
YOUR PITIFUL TEAM HAS NO HOPE OF DEFEATING ME!
KIDDING YOURSELF.
KIDDING YOURSELF.

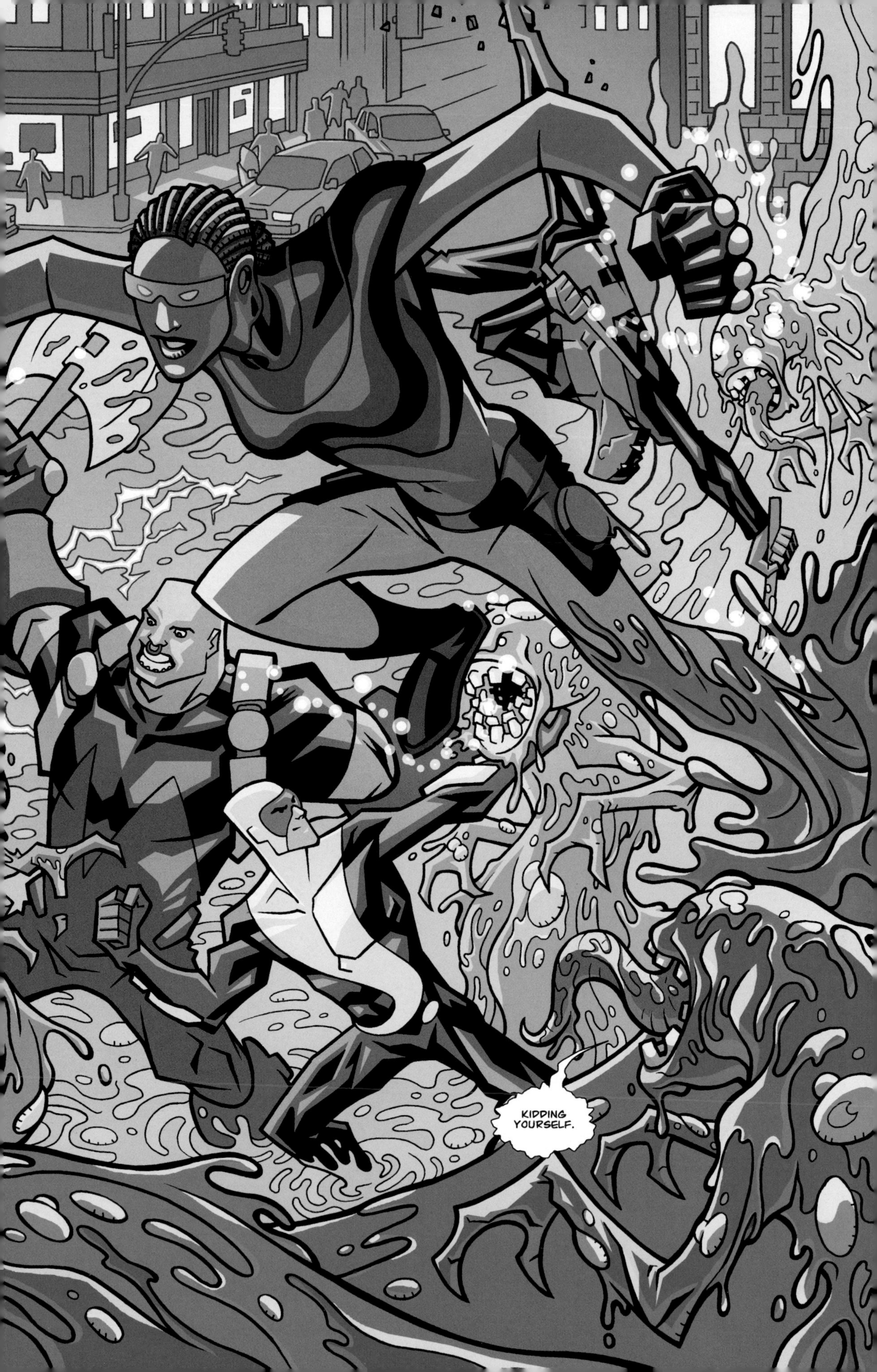
KIDDING YOURSELF.

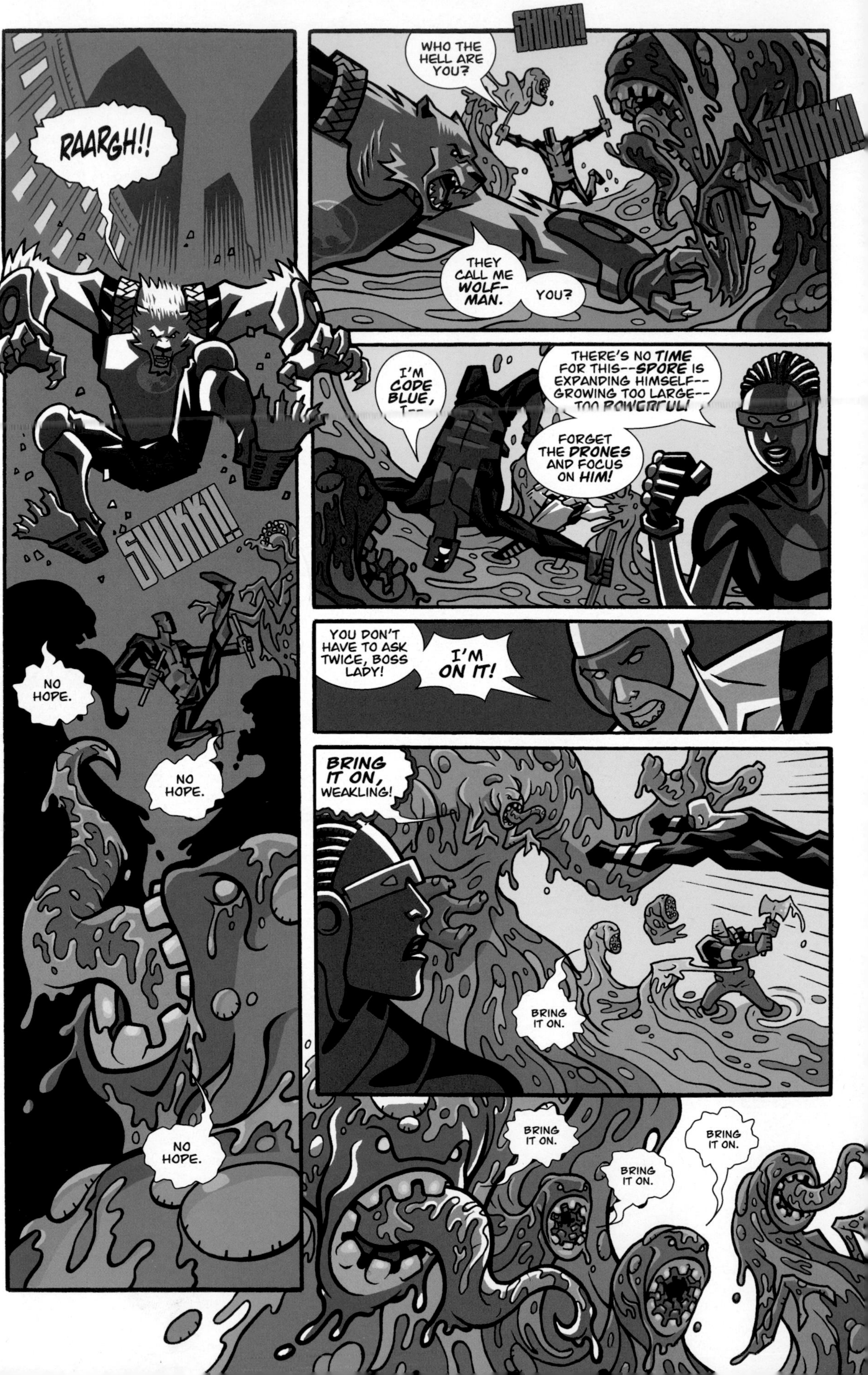
RAARGH!!
SHUKK!!
WHO THE HELL ARE YOU?
SHUKK!!
THEY CALL ME WOLF-MAN.
YOU?
I'M CODE BLUE, I--
THERE'S NO TIME FOR THIS--SPORE IS EXPANDING HIMSELF--GROWING TOO LARGE--TOO POWERFUL!
FORGET THE DRONES AND FOCUS ON HIM!
YOU DON'T HAVE TO ASK TWICE, BOSS LADY!
I'M ON IT!
SHUKK!!
NO HOPE.
NO HOPE.
BRING IT ON, WEAKLING!
BRING IT ON.
NO HOPE.
BRING IT ON.
BRING IT ON.
BRING IT ON.

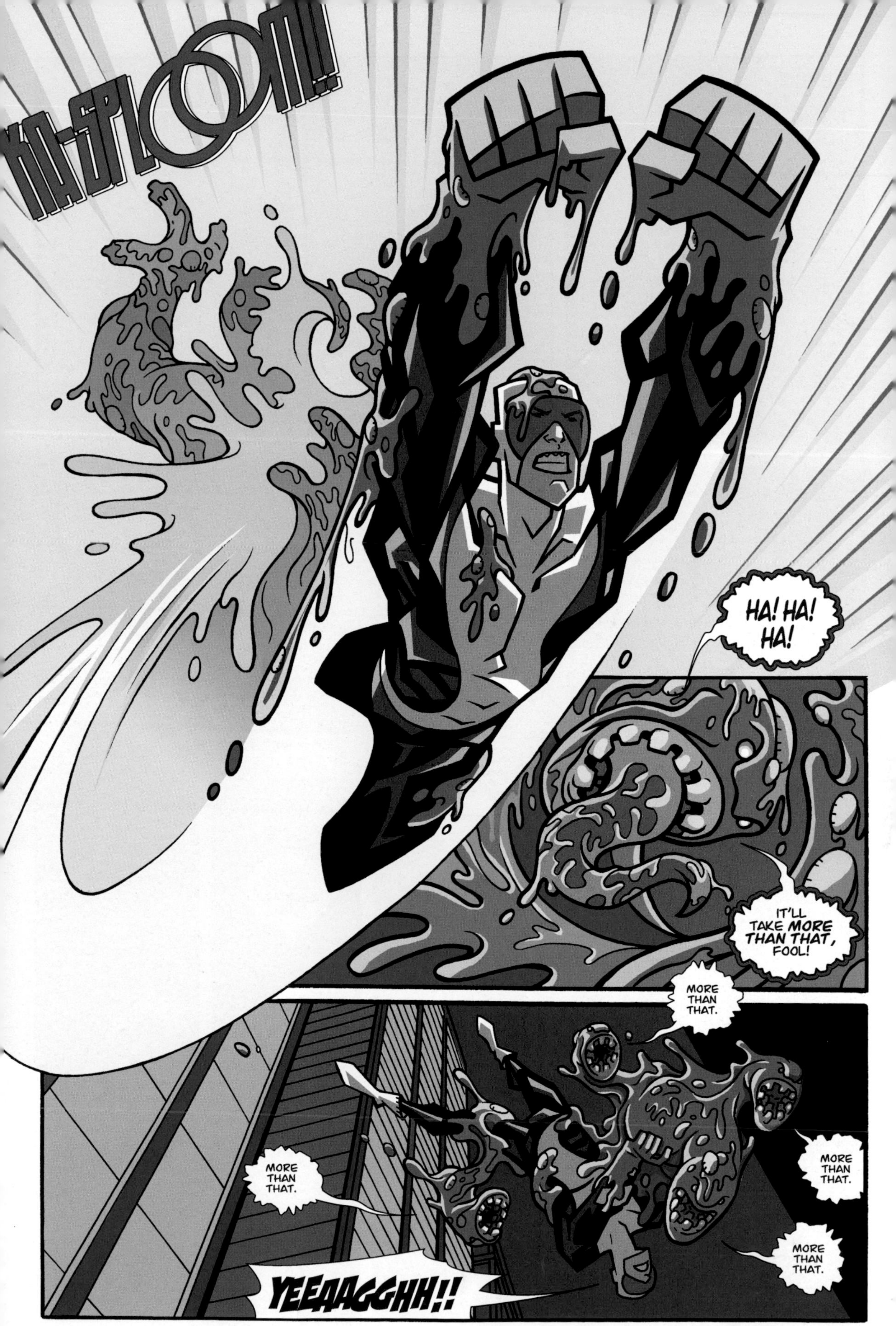
KA-SPLOOM!!
HA! HA! HA!
IT'LL TAKE MORE THAN THAT, FOOL!
MORE THAN THAT.
MORE THAN THAT.
MORE THAN THAT.
MORE THAN THAT.
YEEAAGGHH!!

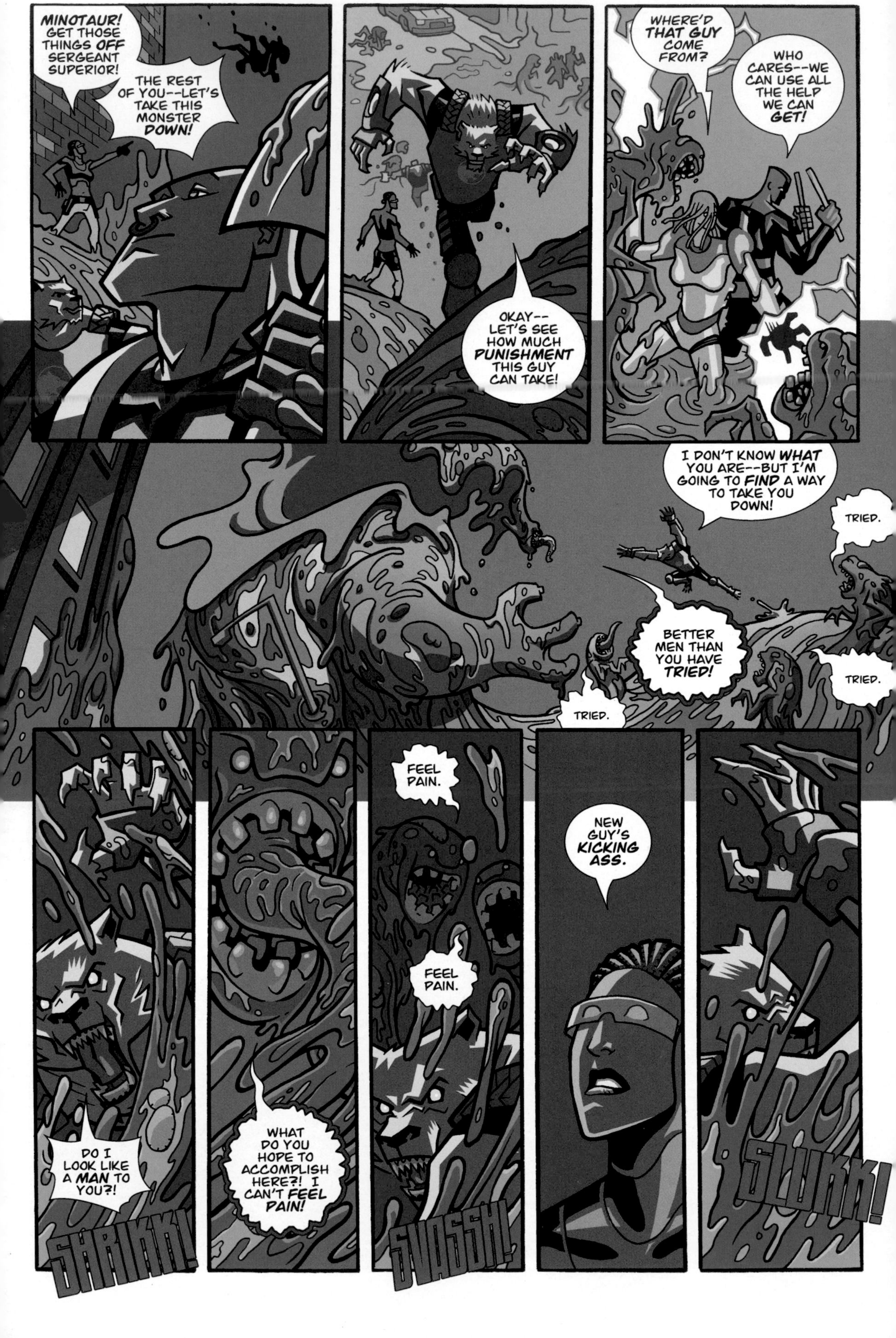
MINOTAUR! GET THOSE THINGS OFF SERGEANT SUPERIOR!
THE REST OF YOU--LET'S TAKE THIS MONSTER DOWN!
OKAY--LET'S SEE HOW MUCH PUNISHMENT THIS GUY CAN TAKE!
WHERE'D THAT GUY COME FROM?
WHO CARES--WE CAN USE ALL THE HELP WE CAN GET!
I DON'T KNOW WHAT YOU ARE--BUT I'M GOING TO FIND A WAY TO TAKE YOU DOWN!
TRIED.
BETTER MEN THAN YOU HAVE TRIED!
TRIED.
TRIED.
DO I LOOK LIKE A MAN TO YOU?!
SHRIKK!
WHAT DO YOU HOPE TO ACCOMPLISH HERE?! I CAN'T FEEL PAIN!
FEEL PAIN.
FEEL PAIN.
SVASSH!
NEW GUY'S KICKING ASS.
SLUKK!

THIS DOES **NOTHING!**

I STILL LIVE! I **LIVE!**

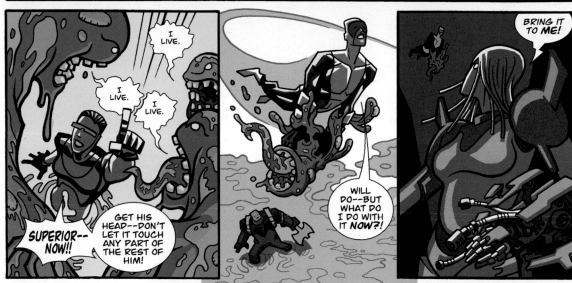

I LIVE.

I LIVE.

I LIVE.

SUPERIOR-- NOW!!

GET HIS HEAD--DON'T LET IT TOUCH ANY PART OF THE REST OF HIM!

WILL DO--BUT WHAT DO I DO WITH IT **NOW?!**

BRING IT TO ME!

WHAT'S LEFT OF THIS GUY ISN'T PUTTING UP A FIGHT ANYMORE-- IT'S DYING.

IT'S WORKING-- KEEP THE HEAD CONTAINED!

VWRRKK!

SHUKK!

SPLAKK

WE'VE GOT IT!

NICE WORK, MECHA-MAID.

HE'S NOT GOING ANYWHERE NOW.

WE DID IT--

IT'S OVER.

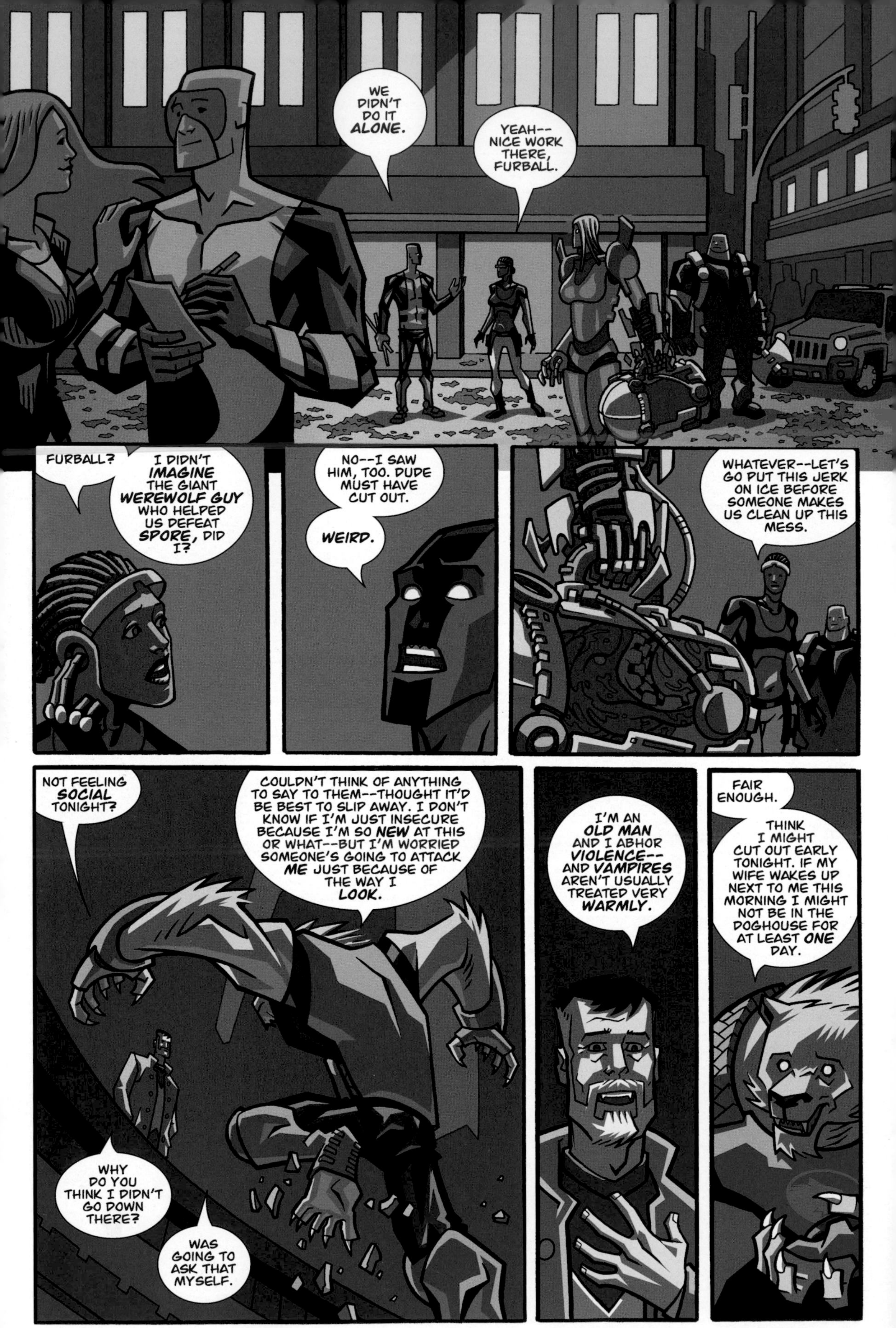
WE DIDN'T DO IT ALONE.
YEAH-- NICE WORK THERE, FURBALL.
FURBALL?
I DIDN'T IMAGINE THE GIANT WEREWOLF GUY WHO HELPED US DEFEAT SPORE, DID I?
NO--I SAW HIM, TOO. DUDE MUST HAVE CUT OUT.
WEIRD.
WHATEVER--LET'S GO PUT THIS JERK ON ICE BEFORE SOMEONE MAKES US CLEAN UP THIS MESS.
NOT FEELING SOCIAL TONIGHT?
COULDN'T THINK OF ANYTHING TO SAY TO THEM--THOUGHT IT'D BE BEST TO SLIP AWAY. I DON'T KNOW IF I'M JUST INSECURE BECAUSE I'M SO NEW AT THIS OR WHAT--BUT I'M WORRIED SOMEONE'S GOING TO ATTACK ME JUST BECAUSE OF THE WAY I LOOK.
WHY DO YOU THINK I DIDN'T GO DOWN THERE?
WAS GOING TO ASK THAT MYSELF.
I'M AN OLD MAN AND I ABHOR VIOLENCE-- AND VAMPIRES AREN'T USUALLY TREATED VERY WARMLY.
FAIR ENOUGH.
THINK I MIGHT CUT OUT EARLY TONIGHT. IF MY WIFE WAKES UP NEXT TO ME THIS MORNING I MIGHT NOT BE IN THE DOGHOUSE FOR AT LEAST ONE DAY.

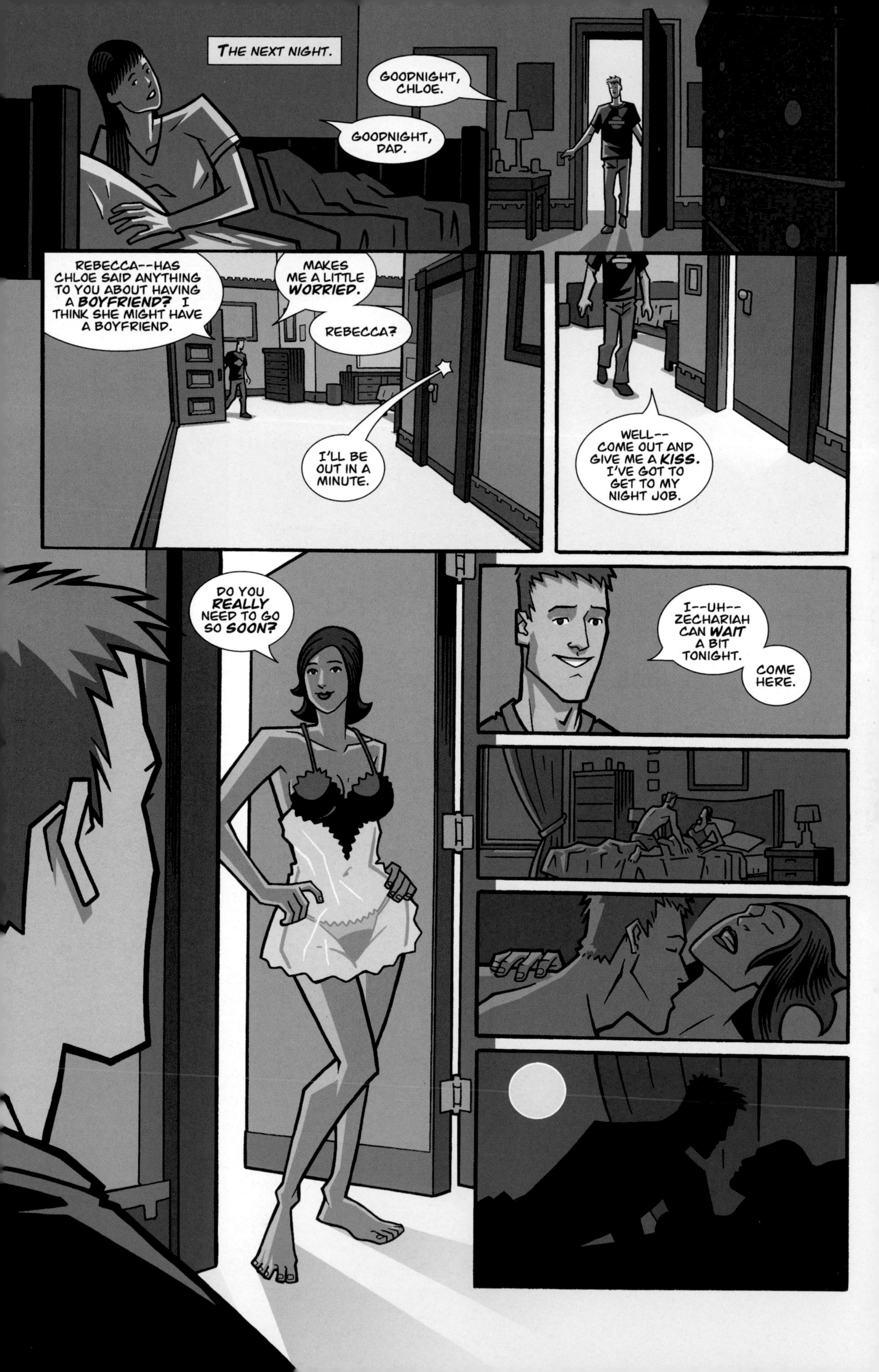
THE NEXT NIGHT.
GOODNIGHT, CHLOE.
GOODNIGHT, DAD.
REBECCA--HAS CHLOE SAID ANYTHING TO YOU ABOUT HAVING A BOYFRIEND? I THINK SHE MIGHT HAVE A BOYFRIEND.
MAKES ME A LITTLE WORRIED.
REBECCA?
I'LL BE OUT IN A MINUTE.
WELL-- COME OUT AND GIVE ME A KISS. I'VE GOT TO GET TO MY NIGHT JOB.
DO YOU REALLY NEED TO GO SO SOON?
I--UH-- ZECHARIAH CAN WAIT A BIT TONIGHT.
COME HERE.

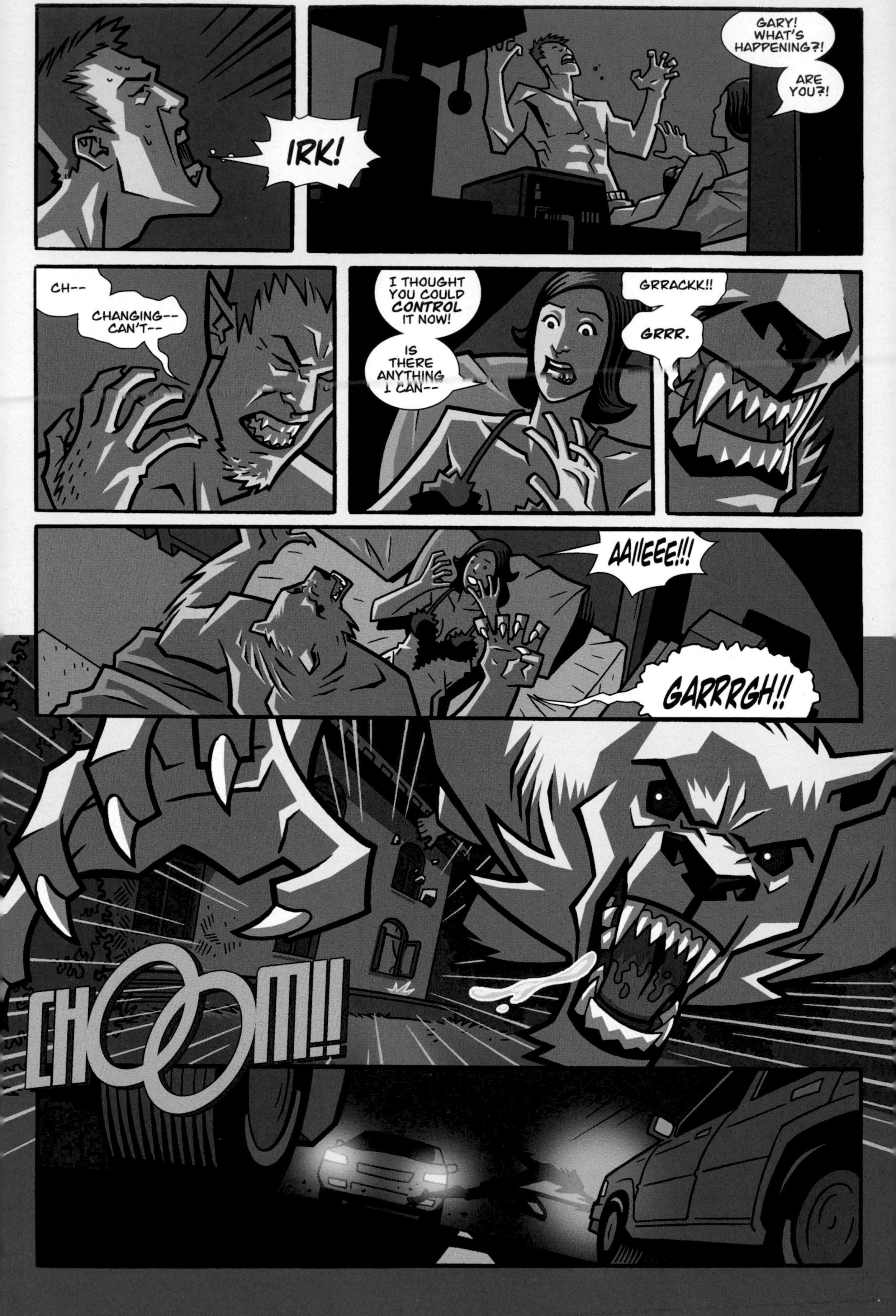
IRK!
GARY! WHAT'S HAPPENING?!
ARE YOU?!
CH--
CHANGING-- CAN'T--
I THOUGHT YOU COULD CONTROL IT NOW!
IS THERE ANYTHING I CAN--
GRRACKK!!
GRRR.
AAIIEEE!!!
GARRRGH!!
CHOOM!!

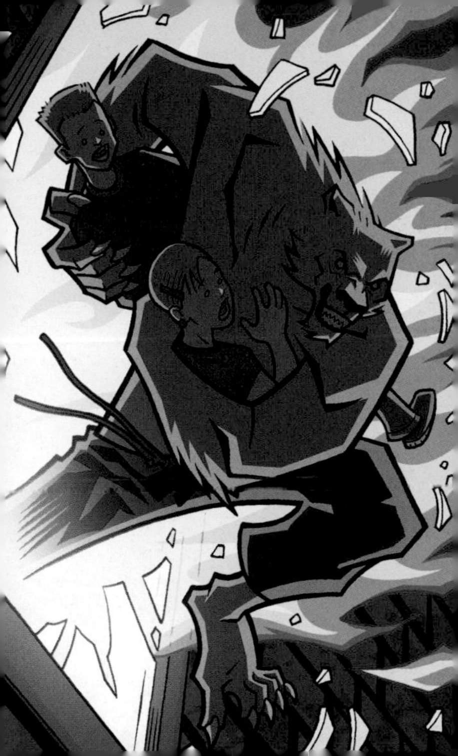

3

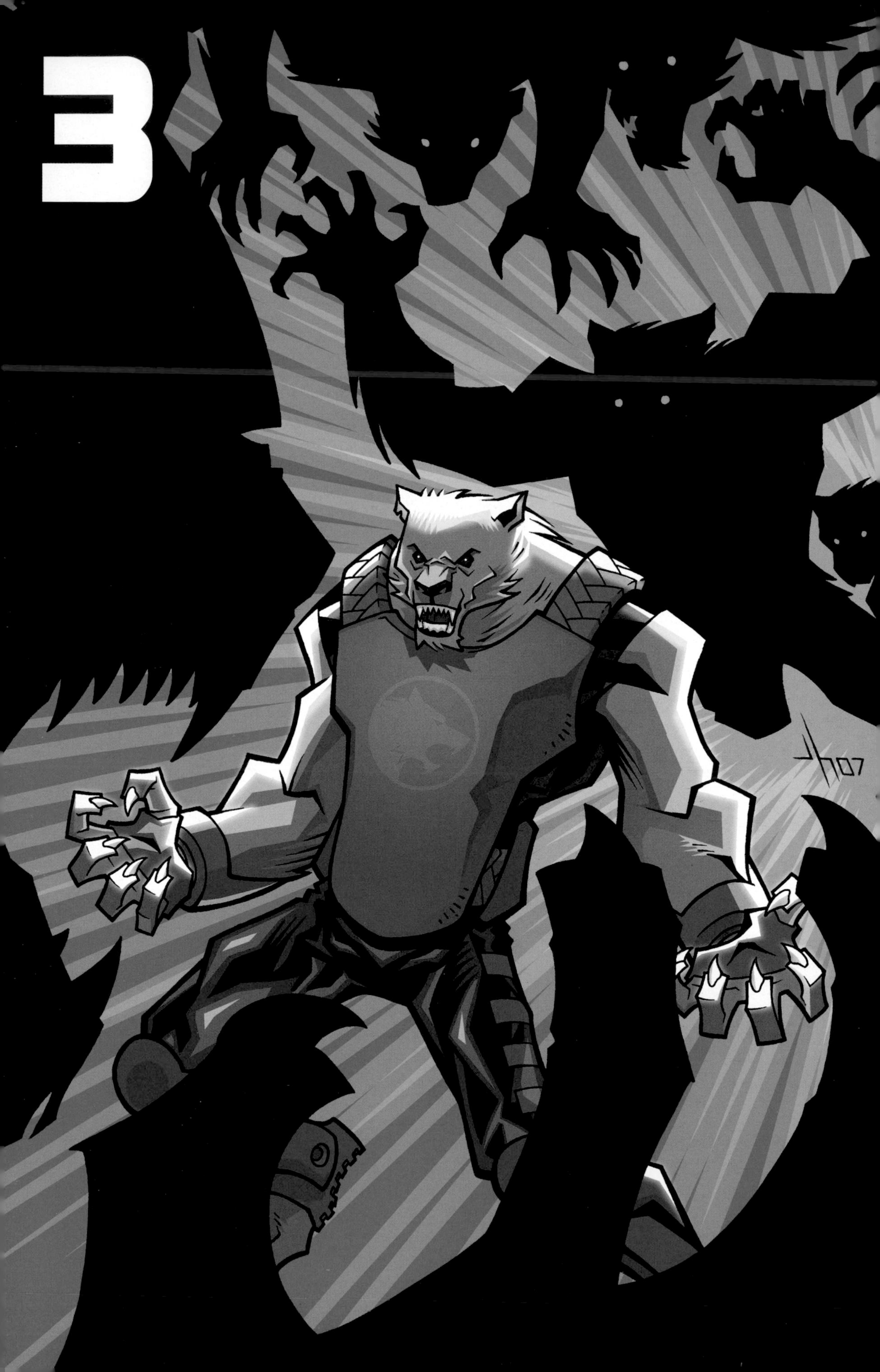

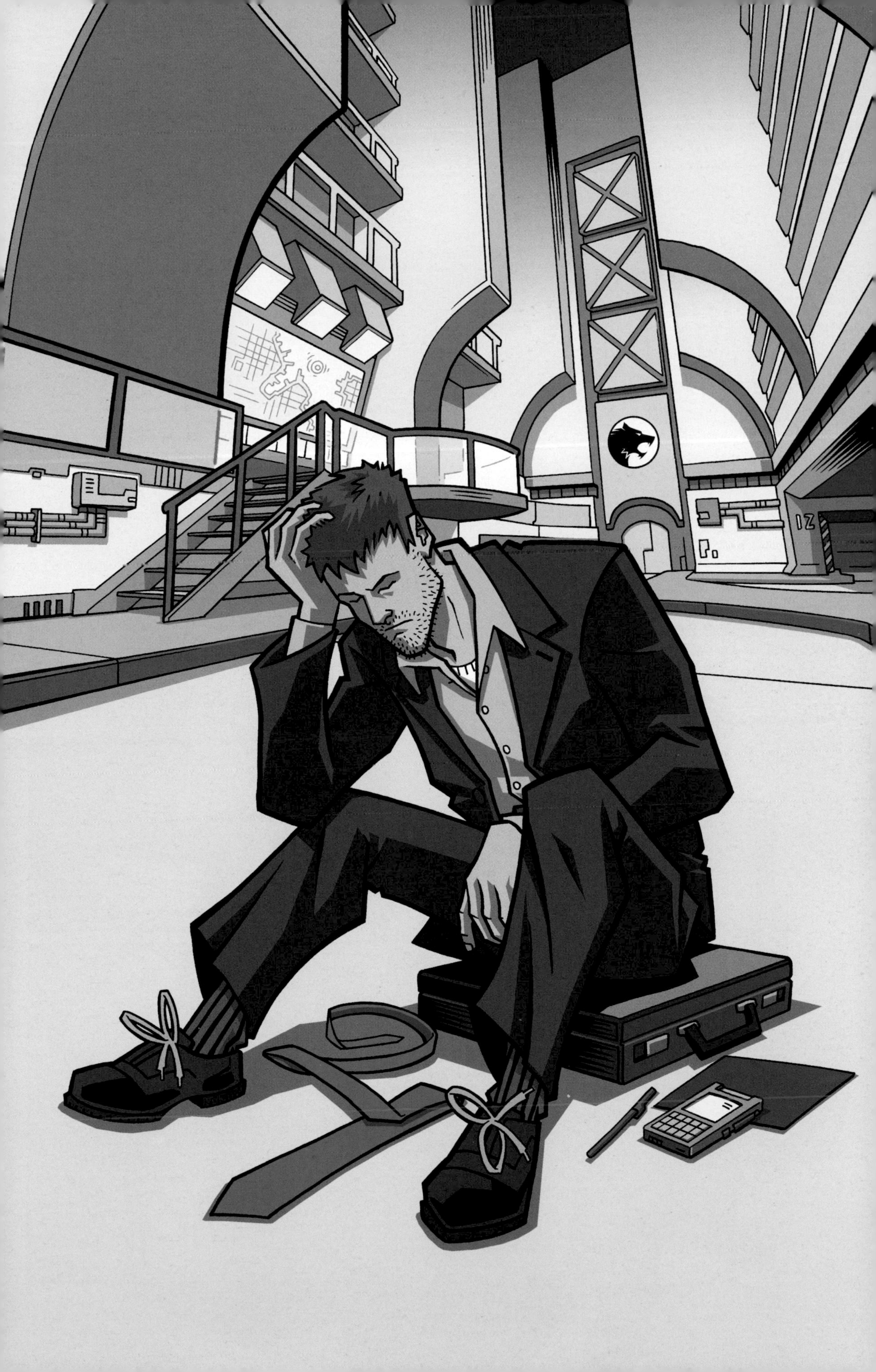

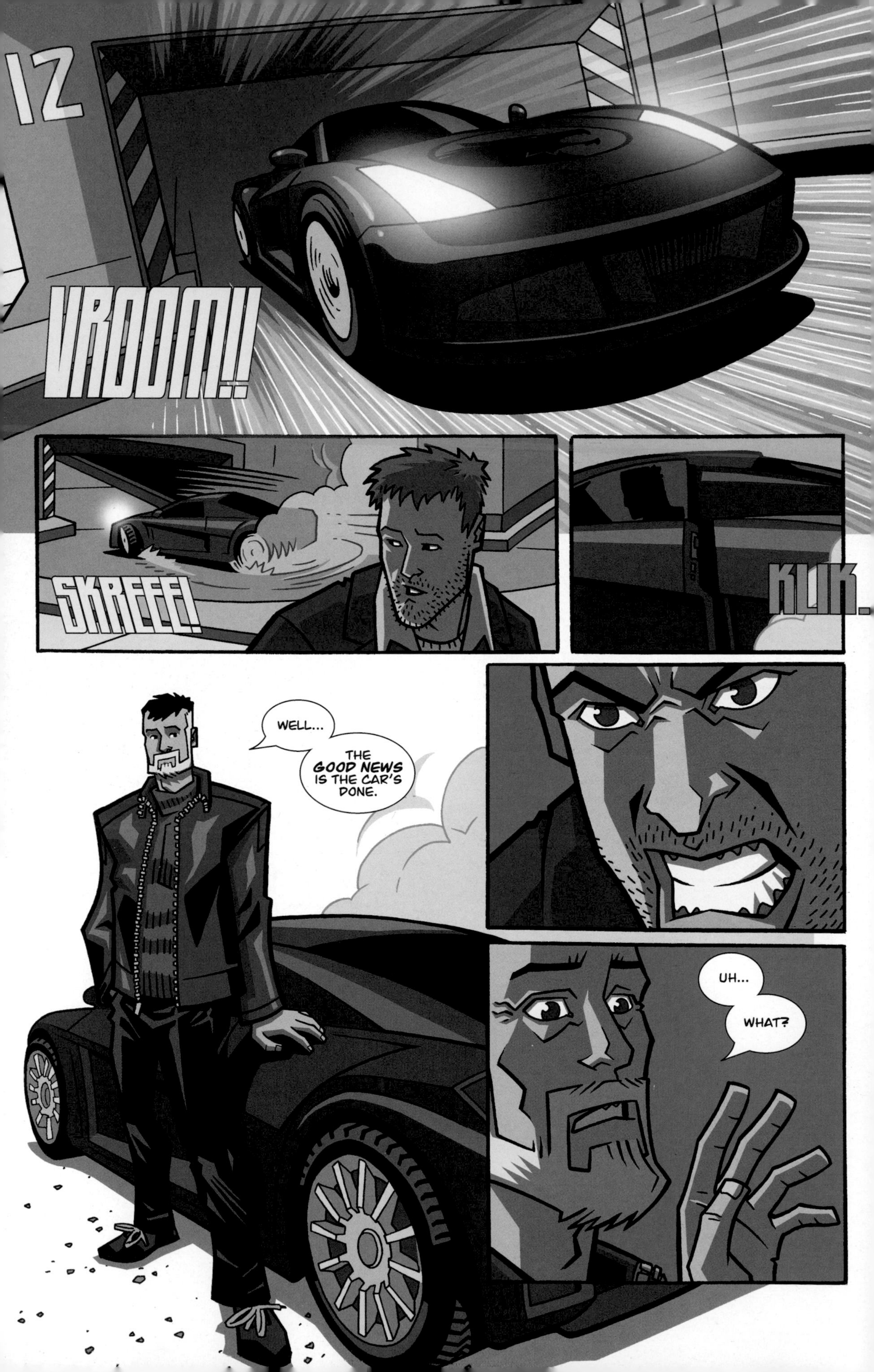
12
VROOM!!
SKREEE!
KLIK.
WELL...
THE GOOD NEWS IS THE CAR'S DONE.
UH...
WHAT?

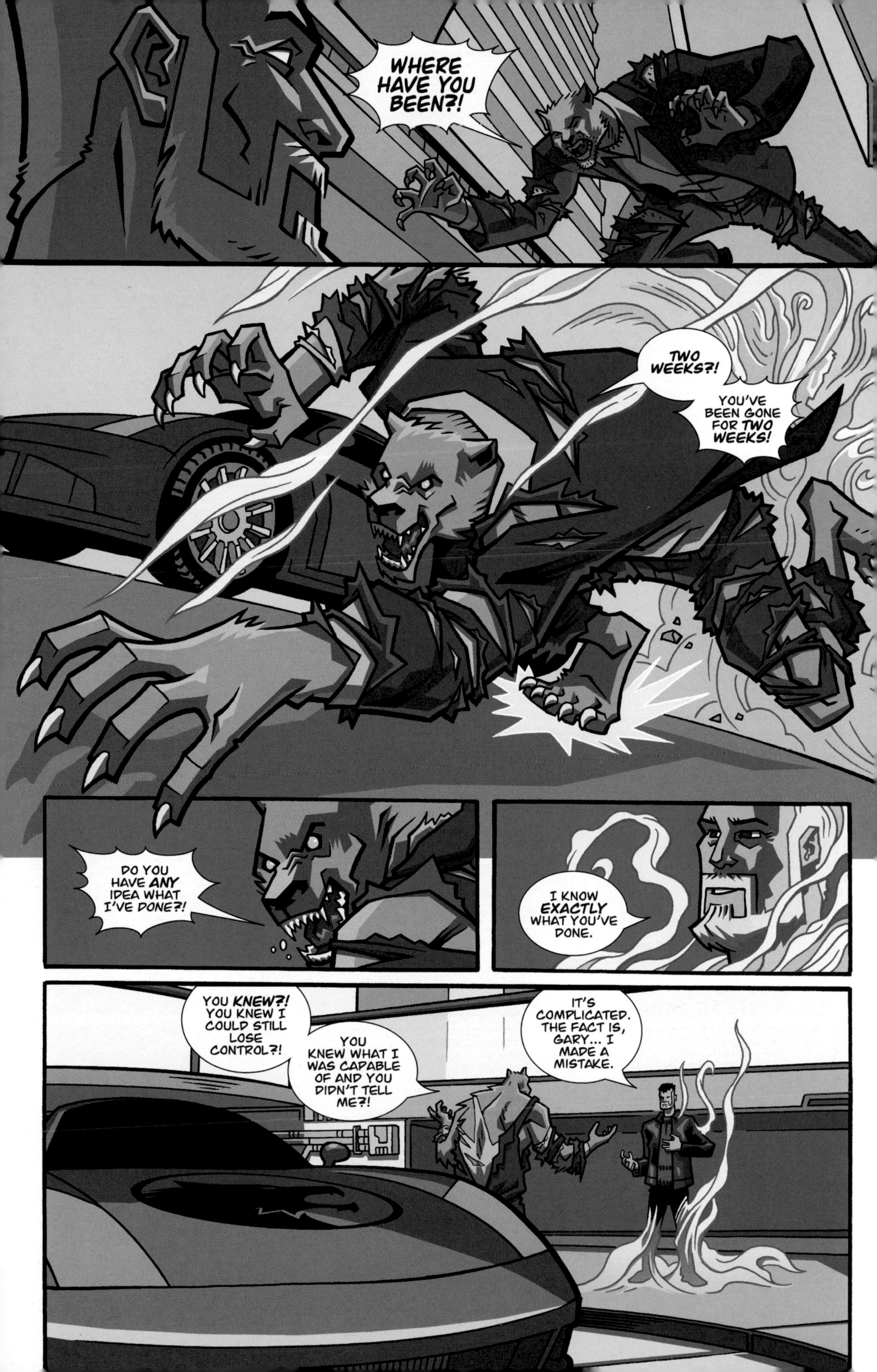
WHERE HAVE YOU BEEN?!
TWO WEEKS?!
YOU'VE BEEN GONE FOR TWO WEEKS!
DO YOU HAVE ANY IDEA WHAT I'VE DONE?!
I KNOW EXACTLY WHAT YOU'VE DONE.
YOU KNEW?! YOU KNEW I COULD STILL LOSE CONTROL?!
YOU KNEW WHAT I WAS CAPABLE OF AND YOU DIDN'T TELL ME?!
IT'S COMPLICATED. THE FACT IS, GARY... I MADE A MISTAKE.

IT WASN'T SUPPOSED TO BE LIKE THIS. I WANTED YOU TO EXPERIENCE IT--THE RAGE, THE FREEDOM, THE FEELING OF BEING OUT OF CONTROL.

I WANTED YOU TO **RESPECT** IT.

IF I JUST **TOLD** YOU ABOUT IT-- I DON'T THINK YOU WOULD HAVE TAKEN IT SERIOUSLY. THE POWER YOU HAVE-- HOW DANGEROUS IT IS... YOU NEEDED TO EXPERIENCE IT FIRST HAND.

I THOUGHT YOU'D STAY ON YOUR PROPERTY--RUN THROUGH THE WOODS, HUNT... I DIDN'T THINK YOU'D HURT ANYBODY. YOU RETAIN A BIT OF YOURSELF EVEN IN THAT STATE--YOU NEVER WOULD HAVE HURT REBECCA OR CHLOE. I **KNEW** THEY WERE SAFE.

YOU HAD NEVER KILLED **BEFORE**...

I'M NOT SO SURE THAT'S TRUE...

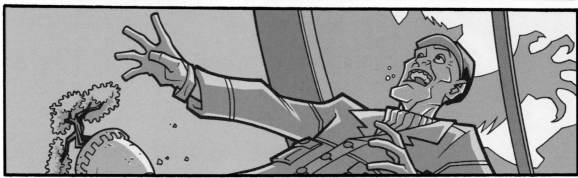

AT FIRST IT JUST SEEMED LIKE A DREAM. I WOKE UP IN THE HOSPITAL WITH A HAZY RECOLLECTION OF THE NIGHT BEFORE. RUNNING ACROSS ROOFTOPS, LEAPING, FALLING.

...

I ENCOUNTERED A MAN, TENDING A ROOFTOP GARDEN.

I HAD TRIED TO CONVINCE MYSELF IT WASN'T. AFTER WHAT I DID TO SERGEANT SUPERIOR... I KNEW I WAS JUST FOOLING MYSELF.

ONCE I STARTED TRAINING WITH YOU-- AND AFTER THAT NIGHT AT MY HOUSE, RIGHT BEFORE YOU CAME, I STARTED TO REALIZE... THOSE THINGS... THEY PROBABLY HAPPENED. THAT DREAM WAS PROBABLY REAL.

YOU CAN CONTROL YOUR TRANSFORMATIONS... YOU CAN BE WOLF-MAN AT NIGHT, EVERYTHING I TAUGHT YOU STILL APPLIES.

BUT ONCE A MONTH, ON THE FIRST NIGHT OF THE FULL MOON, YOU WILL LOSE ALL CONTROL AND REVERT BACK TO THE BEAST--THE CURSE WILL TAKE HOLD OF YOU AND THERE IS NOTHING YOU CAN DO TO STOP THIS.

I KNOW IT PROVIDES LITTLE COMFORT BUT YOU ARE NOT RESPONSIBLE FOR WHATEVER YOU DO IN THIS STATE. YOU ARE OUT OF CONTROL--YOU ARE YOU, BUT NOT... YOU'RE AN ANIMAL, A WILD BEAST.

SERGEANT SUPERIOR'S DEATH-- IF ANYTHING, THE BLAME FALLS ON ME. I SHOULD HAVE TOLD YOU--I SHOULD HAVE LOCKED YOU UP SOMEWHERE, CONTAINED YOU... BUT I DIDN'T.

I MADE A MISTAKE.

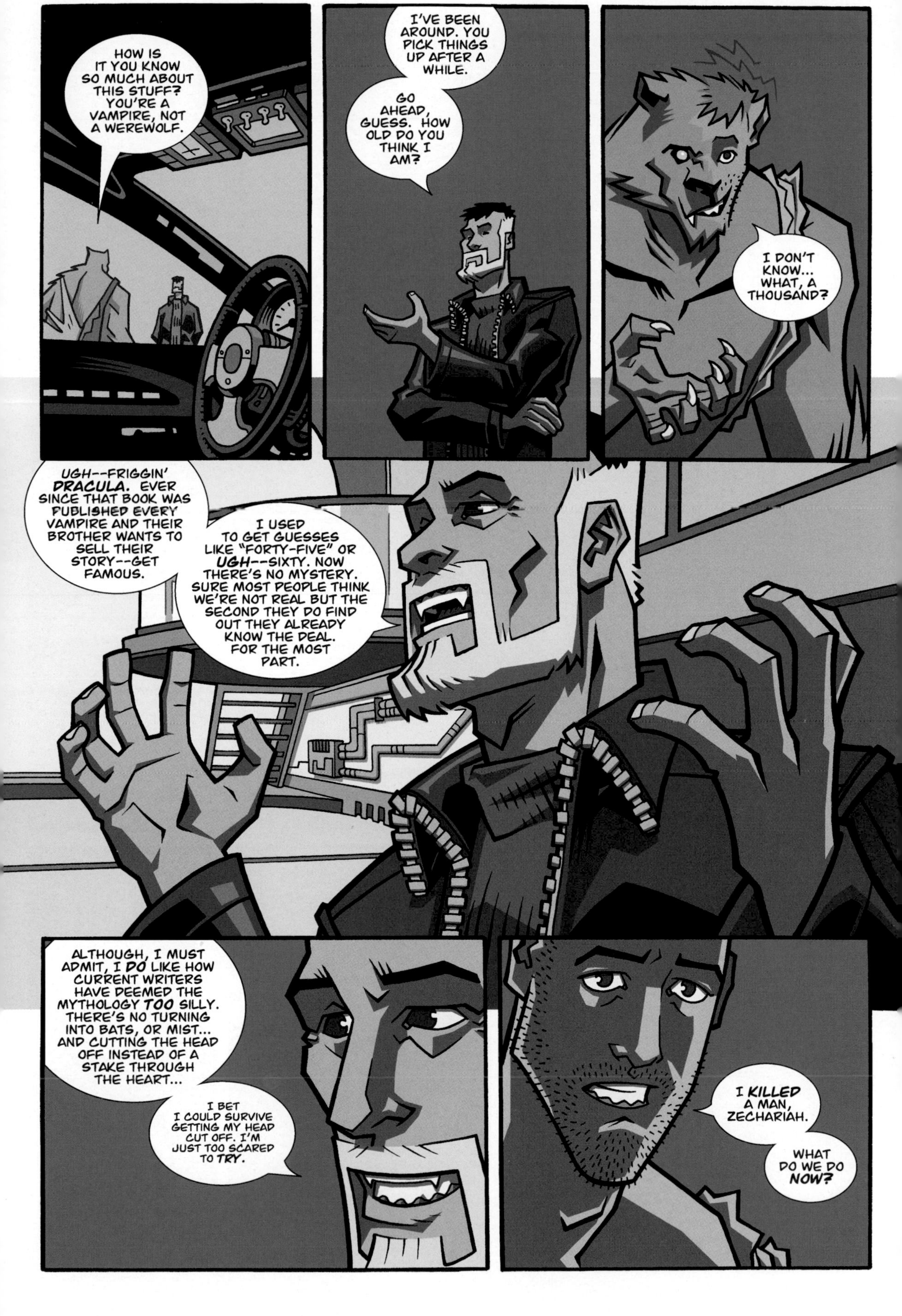
HOW IS IT YOU KNOW SO MUCH ABOUT THIS STUFF? YOU'RE A VAMPIRE, NOT A WEREWOLF.
I'VE BEEN AROUND. YOU PICK THINGS UP AFTER A WHILE.
GO AHEAD, GUESS. HOW OLD DO YOU THINK I AM?
I DON'T KNOW... WHAT, A THOUSAND?
UGH--FRIGGIN' DRACULA. EVER SINCE THAT BOOK WAS PUBLISHED EVERY VAMPIRE AND THEIR BROTHER WANTS TO SELL THEIR STORY--GET FAMOUS.
I USED TO GET GUESSES LIKE "FORTY-FIVE" OR UGH--SIXTY. NOW THERE'S NO MYSTERY. SURE MOST PEOPLE THINK WE'RE NOT REAL BUT THE SECOND THEY DO FIND OUT THEY ALREADY KNOW THE DEAL. FOR THE MOST PART.
ALTHOUGH, I MUST ADMIT, I DO LIKE HOW CURRENT WRITERS HAVE DEEMED THE MYTHOLOGY TOO SILLY. THERE'S NO TURNING INTO BATS, OR MIST... AND CUTTING THE HEAD OFF INSTEAD OF A STAKE THROUGH THE HEART...
I BET I COULD SURVIVE GETTING MY HEAD CUT OFF. I'M JUST TOO SCARED TO TRY.
I KILLED A MAN, ZECHARIAH.
WHAT DO WE DO NOW?

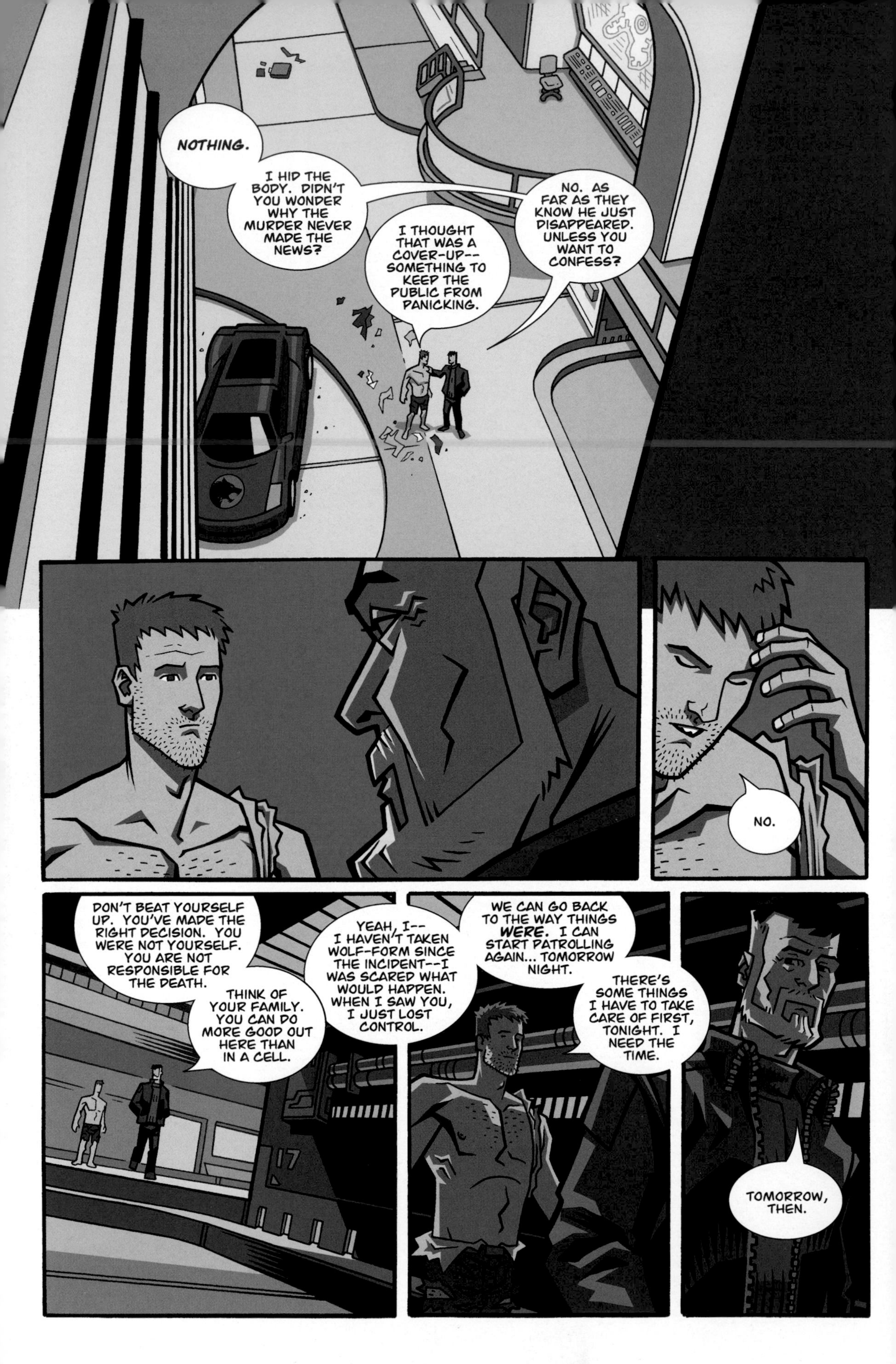
NOTHING.
I HID THE BODY. DIDN'T YOU WONDER WHY THE MURDER NEVER MADE THE NEWS?
I THOUGHT THAT WAS A COVER-UP-- SOMETHING TO KEEP THE PUBLIC FROM PANICKING.
NO. AS FAR AS THEY KNOW HE JUST DISAPPEARED. UNLESS YOU WANT TO CONFESS?
NO.
DON'T BEAT YOURSELF UP. YOU'VE MADE THE RIGHT DECISION. YOU WERE NOT YOURSELF. YOU ARE NOT RESPONSIBLE FOR THE DEATH.
THINK OF YOUR FAMILY. YOU CAN DO MORE GOOD OUT HERE THAN IN A CELL.
YEAH, I-- I HAVEN'T TAKEN WOLF-FORM SINCE THE INCIDENT--I WAS SCARED WHAT WOULD HAPPEN. WHEN I SAW YOU, I JUST LOST CONTROL.
WE CAN GO BACK TO THE WAY THINGS *WERE*. I CAN START PATROLLING AGAIN... TOMORROW NIGHT.
THERE'S SOME THINGS I HAVE TO TAKE CARE OF FIRST, TONIGHT. I NEED THE TIME.
TOMORROW, THEN.

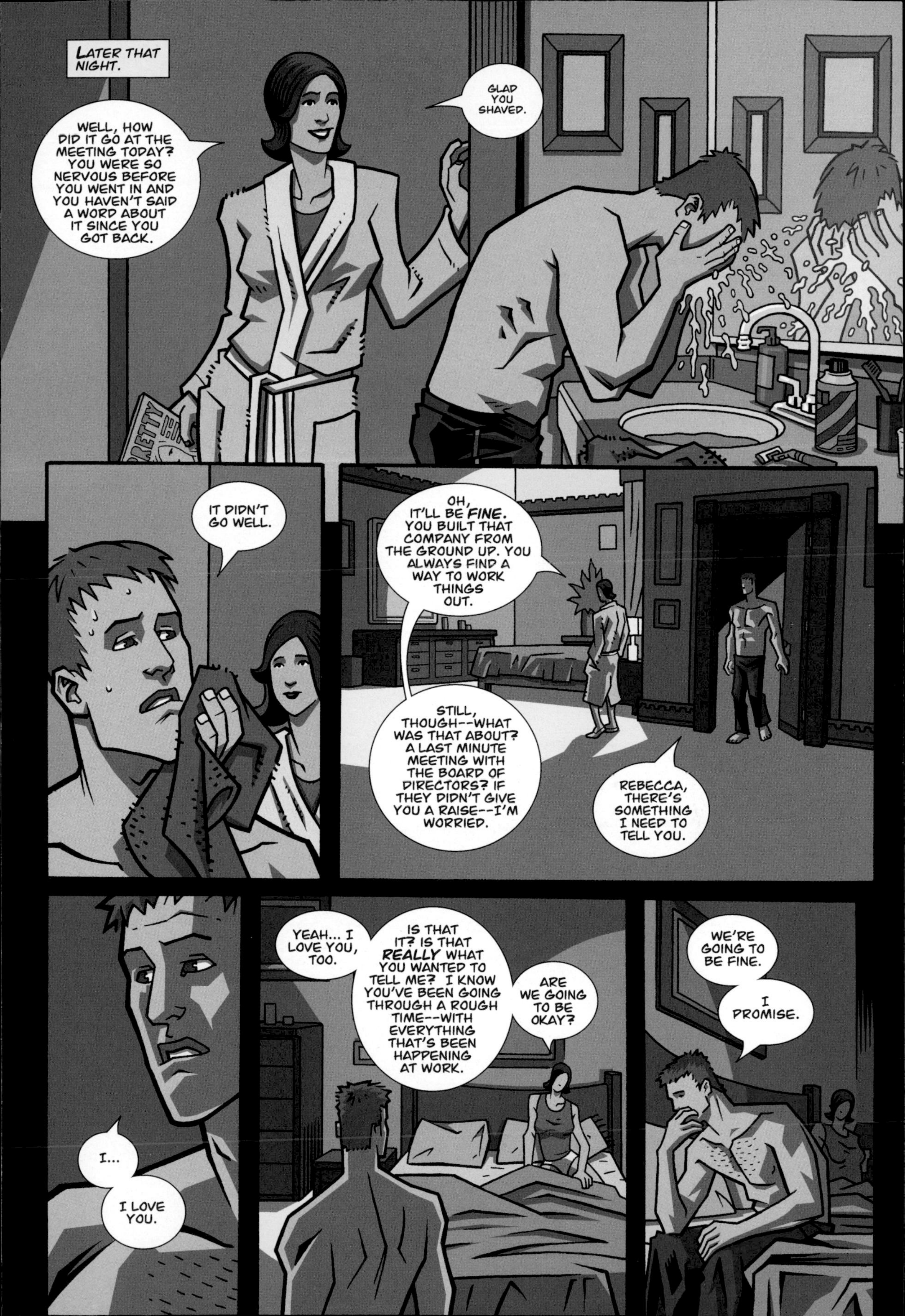
LATER THAT NIGHT.
WELL, HOW DID IT GO AT THE MEETING TODAY? YOU WERE SO NERVOUS BEFORE YOU WENT IN AND YOU HAVEN'T SAID A WORD ABOUT IT SINCE YOU GOT BACK.
GLAD YOU SHAVED.
PRETTY
IT DIDN'T GO WELL.
OH, IT'LL BE FINE. YOU BUILT THAT COMPANY FROM THE GROUND UP. YOU ALWAYS FIND A WAY TO WORK THINGS OUT.
STILL, THOUGH--WHAT WAS THAT ABOUT? A LAST MINUTE MEETING WITH THE BOARD OF DIRECTORS? IF THEY DIDN'T GIVE YOU A RAISE--I'M WORRIED.
REBECCA, THERE'S SOMETHING I NEED TO TELL YOU.
I...
I LOVE YOU.
YEAH... I LOVE YOU, TOO.
IS THAT IT? IS THAT REALLY WHAT YOU WANTED TO TELL ME? I KNOW YOU'VE BEEN GOING THROUGH A ROUGH TIME--WITH EVERYTHING THAT'S BEEN HAPPENING AT WORK.
ARE WE GOING TO BE OKAY?
WE'RE GOING TO BE FINE.
I PROMISE.

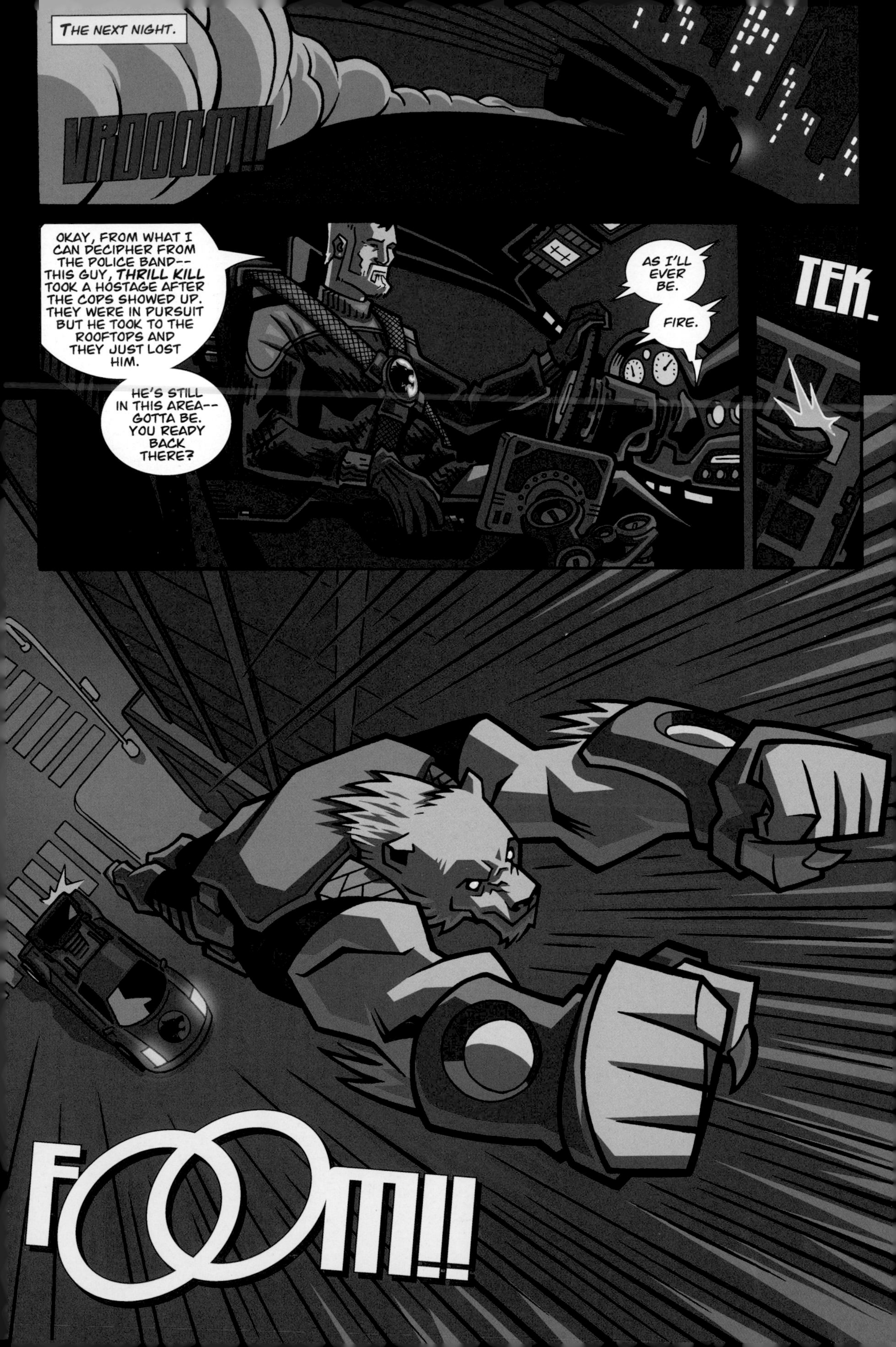
THE NEXT NIGHT.
VROOOM!!
OKAY, FROM WHAT I CAN DECIPHER FROM THE POLICE BAND-- THIS GUY, THRILL KILL TOOK A HOSTAGE AFTER THE COPS SHOWED UP. THEY WERE IN PURSUIT BUT HE TOOK TO THE ROOFTOPS AND THEY JUST LOST HIM.
HE'S STILL IN THIS AREA-- GOTTA BE. YOU READY BACK THERE?
AS I'LL EVER BE.
FIRE.
TEK.
FOOOM!!

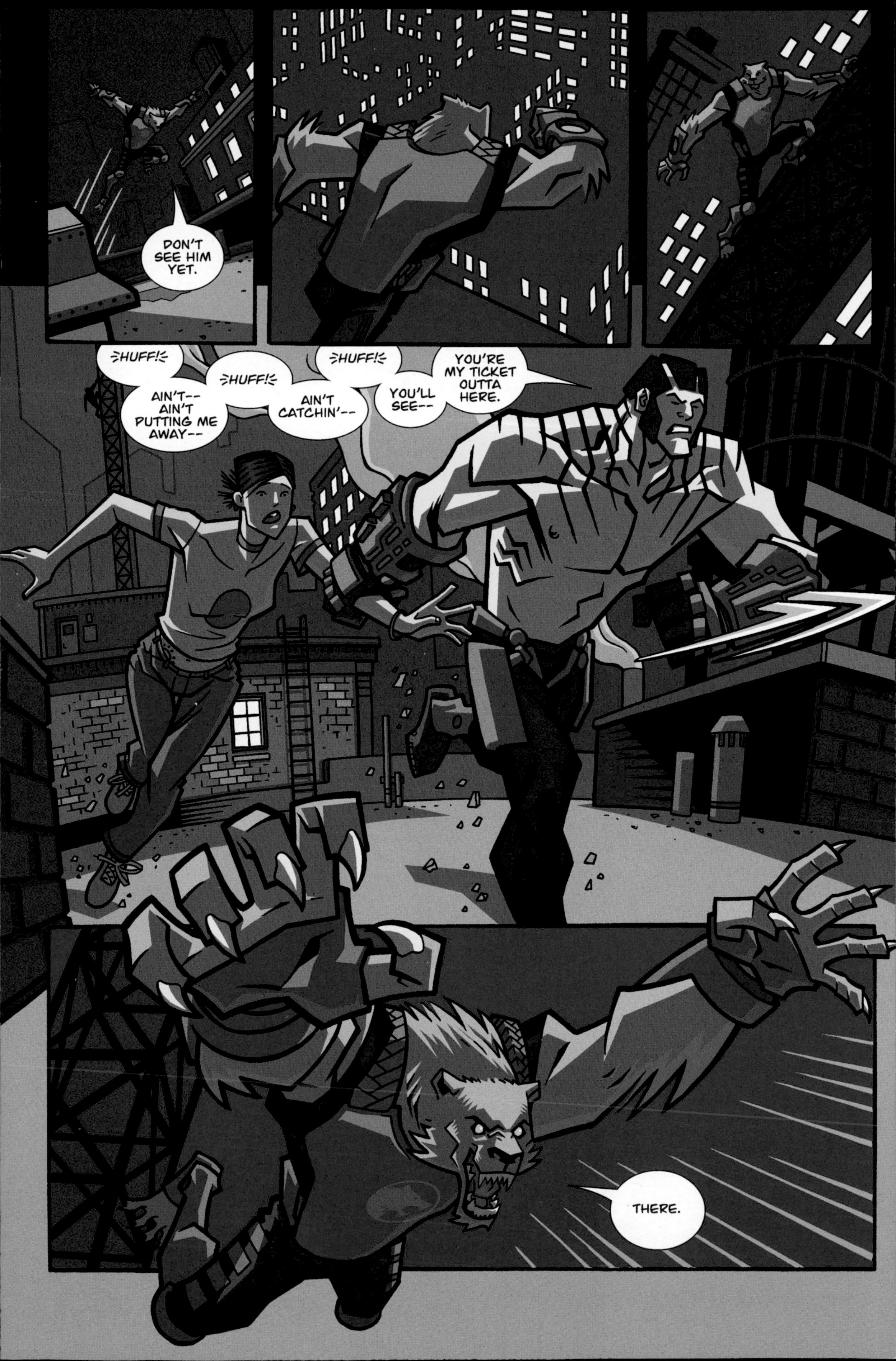
DON'T SEE HIM YET.
≥HUFF!≤
AIN'T-- AIN'T PUTTING ME AWAY--
≥HUFF!≤
AIN'T CATCHIN'--
≥HUFF!≤
YOU'LL SEE--
YOU'RE MY TICKET OUTTA HERE.
THERE.

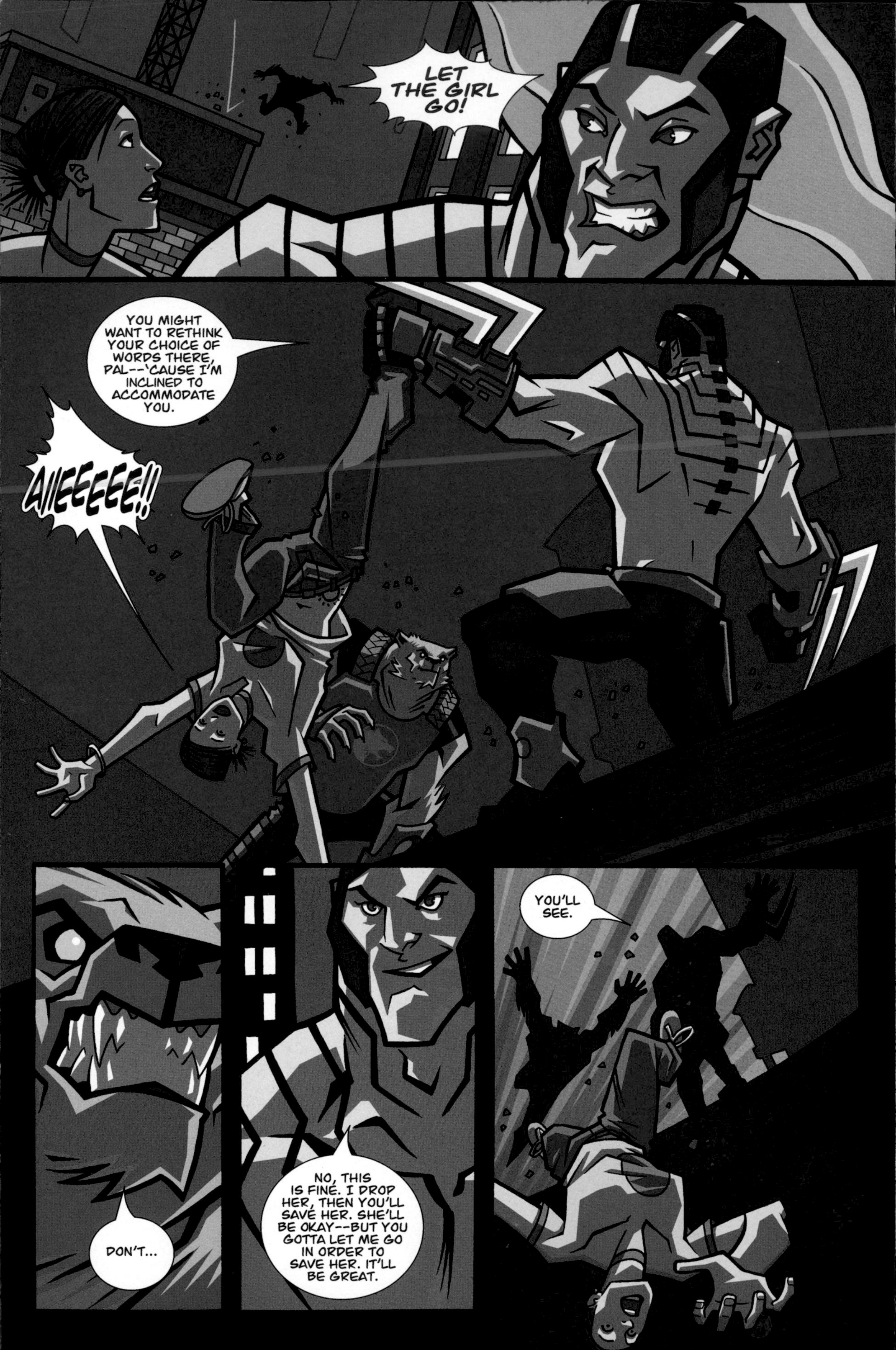
LET THE GIRL GO!
YOU MIGHT WANT TO RETHINK YOUR CHOICE OF WORDS THERE, PAL--'CAUSE I'M INCLINED TO ACCOMMODATE YOU.
AIIEEEEEE!!
DON'T...
NO, THIS IS FINE. I DROP HER, THEN YOU'LL SAVE HER. SHE'LL BE OKAY--BUT YOU GOTTA LET ME GO IN ORDER TO SAVE HER. IT'LL BE GREAT.
YOU'LL SEE.

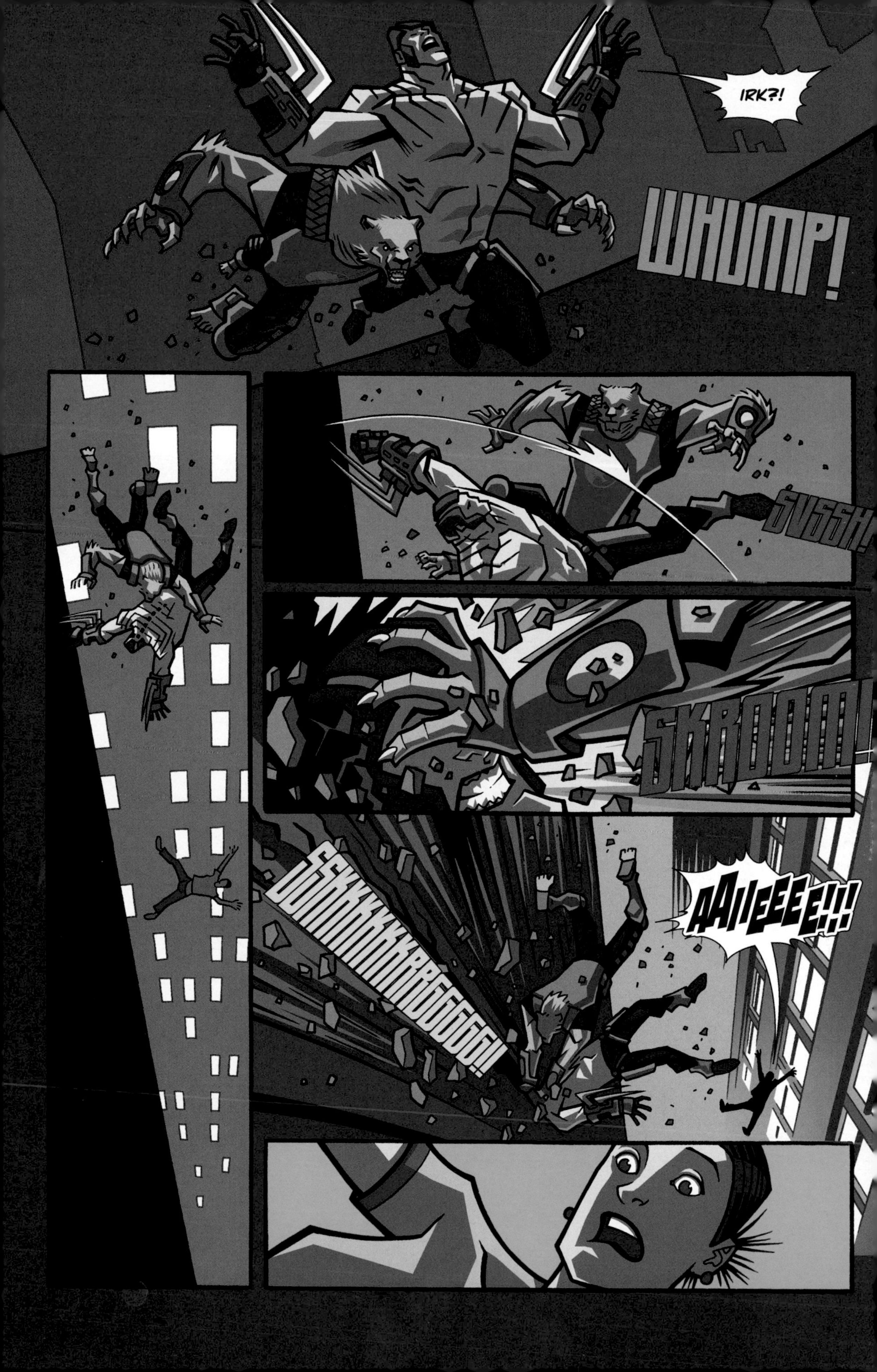
IRK?!
WHUMP!
SVSSH!
SKROOM!
SSKKKKKRRGGGG!!
AAIIEEEE!!!

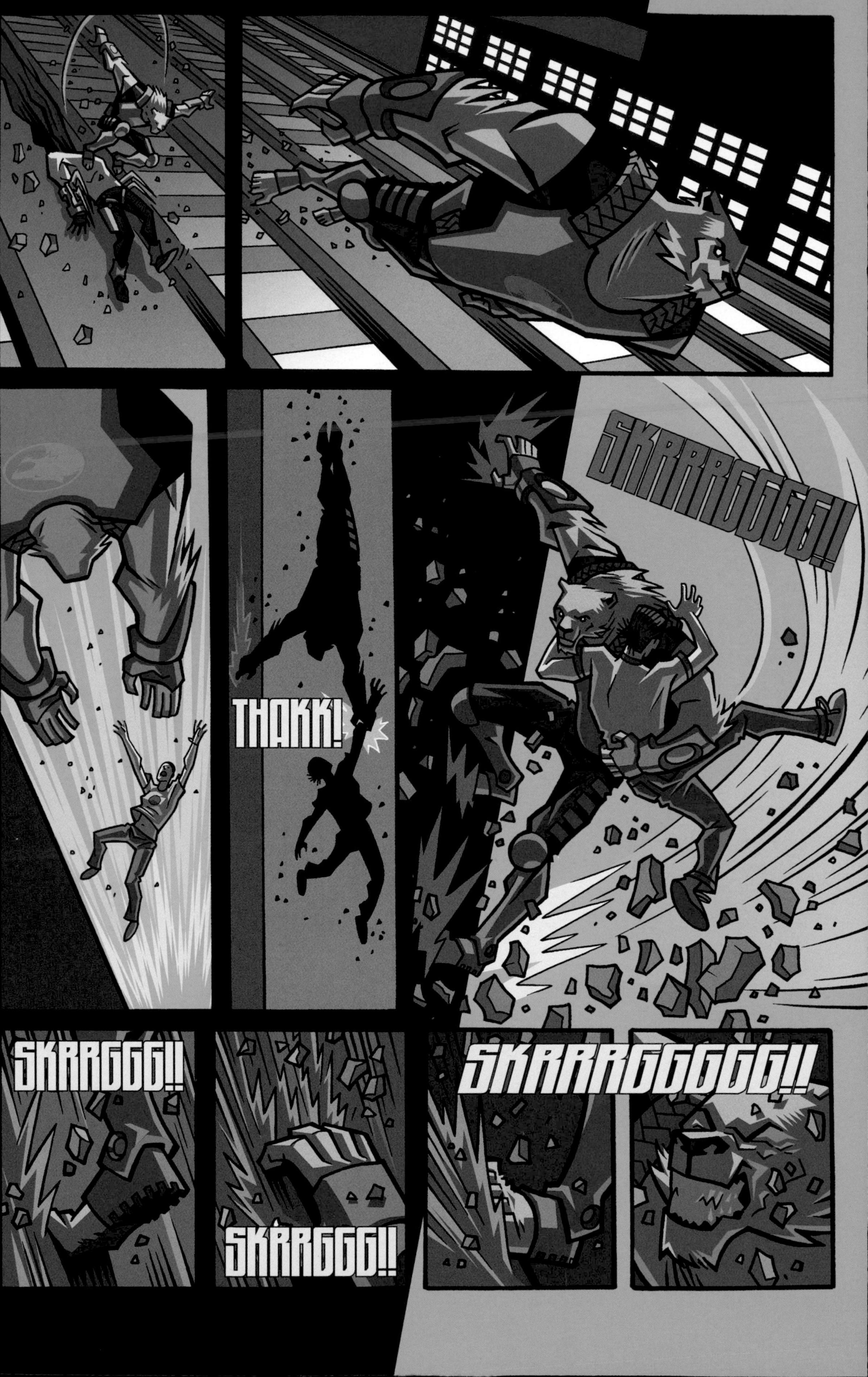
SKRRRGGG!!
THAKK!
SKRRGGG!!
SKRRGGG!!
SKRRRGGGGG!!

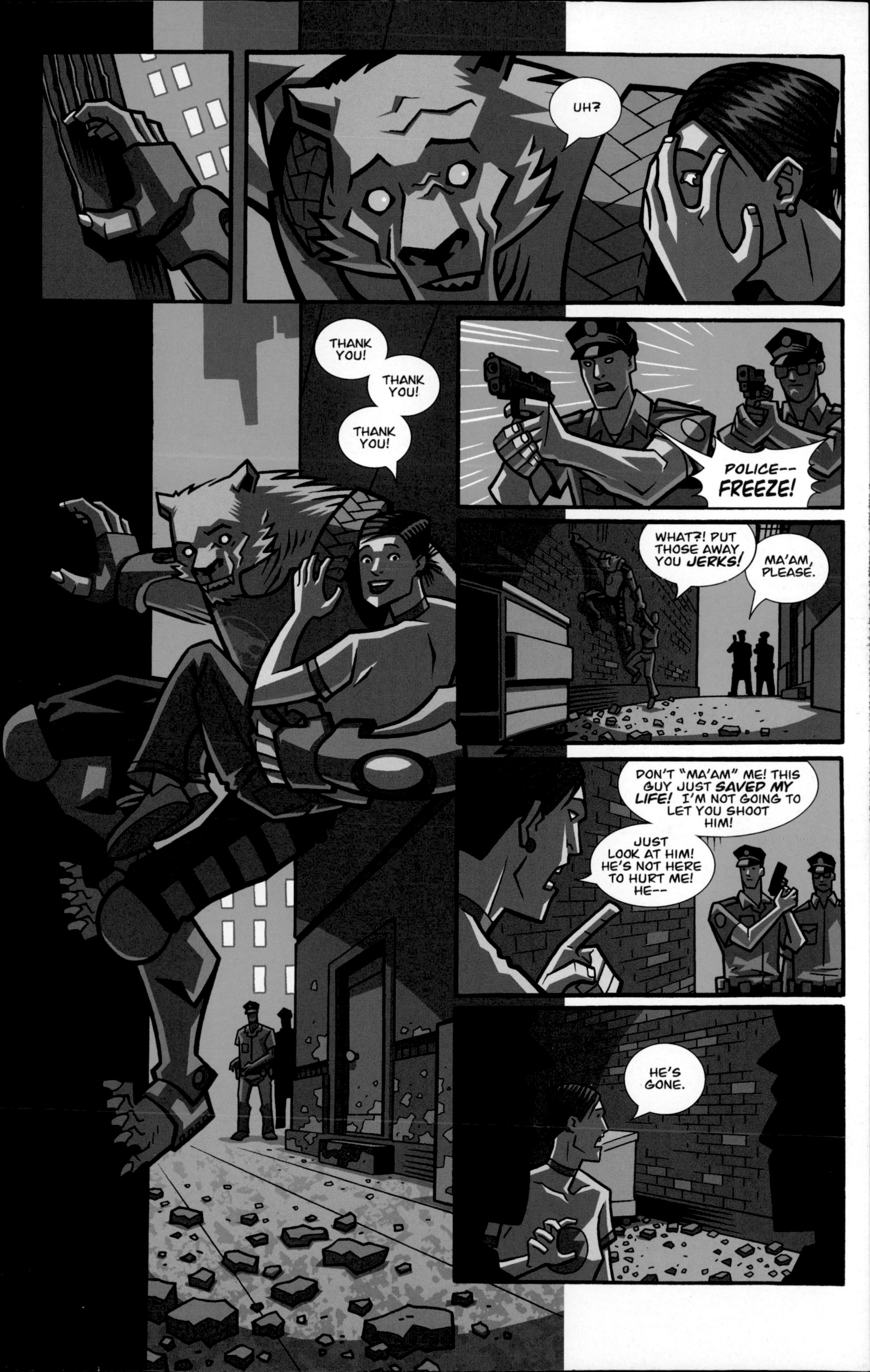
UH?
THANK YOU!
THANK YOU!
THANK YOU!
POLICE-- FREEZE!
WHAT?! PUT THOSE AWAY YOU JERKS!
MA'AM, PLEASE.
DON'T "MA'AM" ME! THIS GUY JUST SAVED MY LIFE! I'M NOT GOING TO LET YOU SHOOT HIM!
JUST LOOK AT HIM! HE'S NOT HERE TO HURT ME! HE--
HE'S GONE.

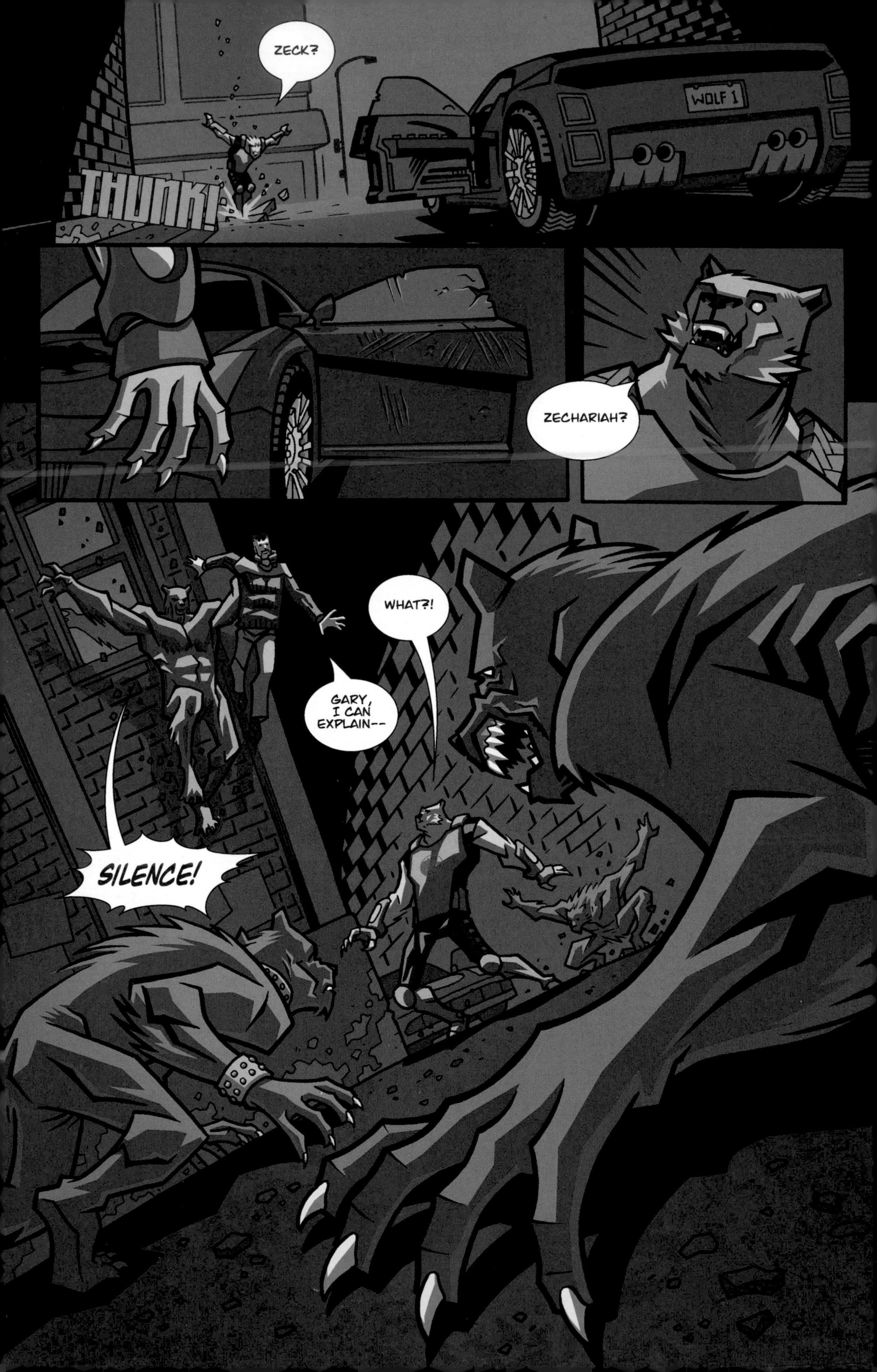
ZECK?
THUNK!
ZECHARIAH?
WHAT?!
GARY, I CAN EXPLAIN--
SILENCE!

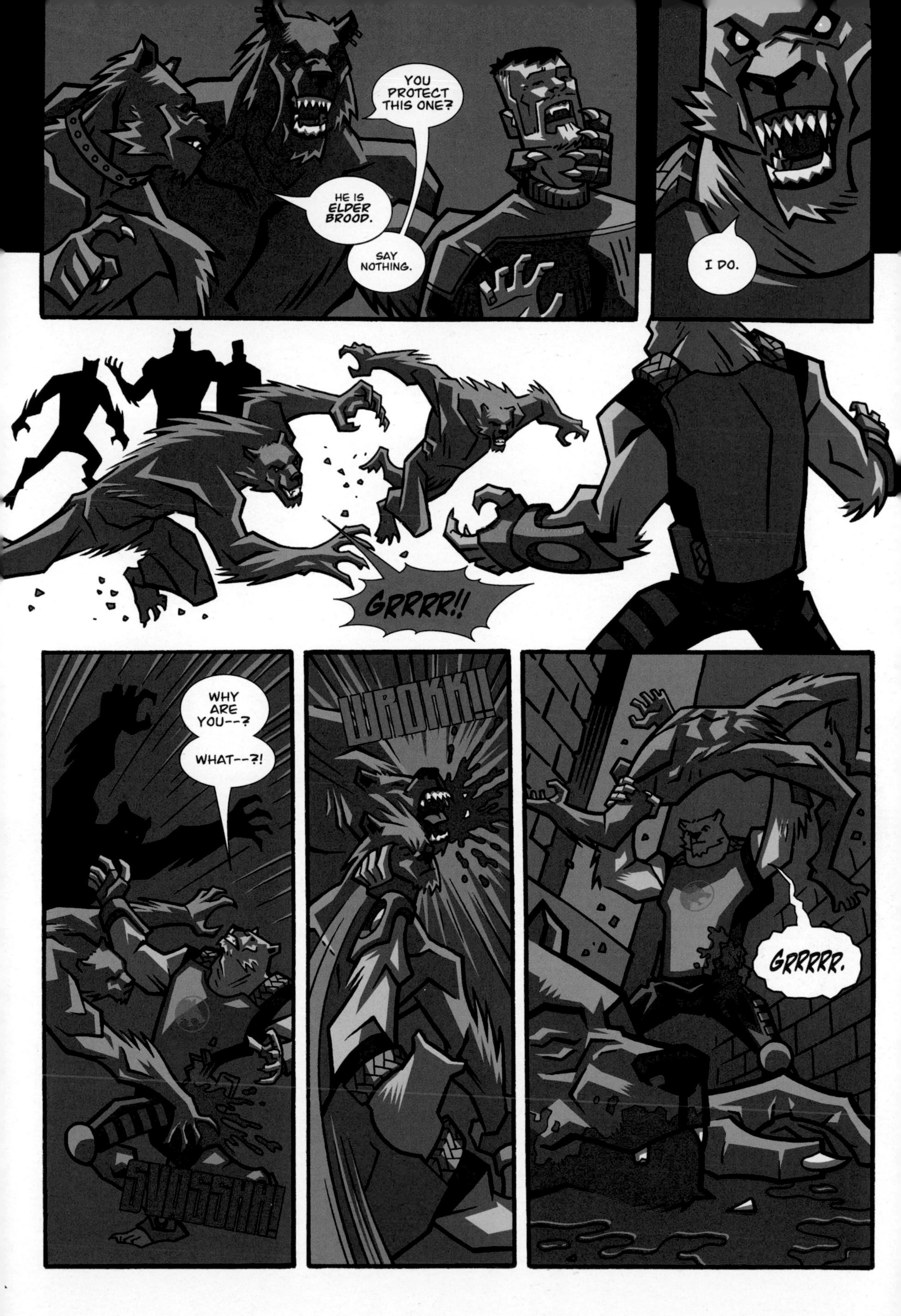
YOU PROTECT THIS ONE?
HE IS ELDER BROOD.
SAY NOTHING.
I DO.
GRRRR!!
WHY ARE YOU--?
WHAT--?!
SWISSHH!
WROKK!!
GRRRRR.

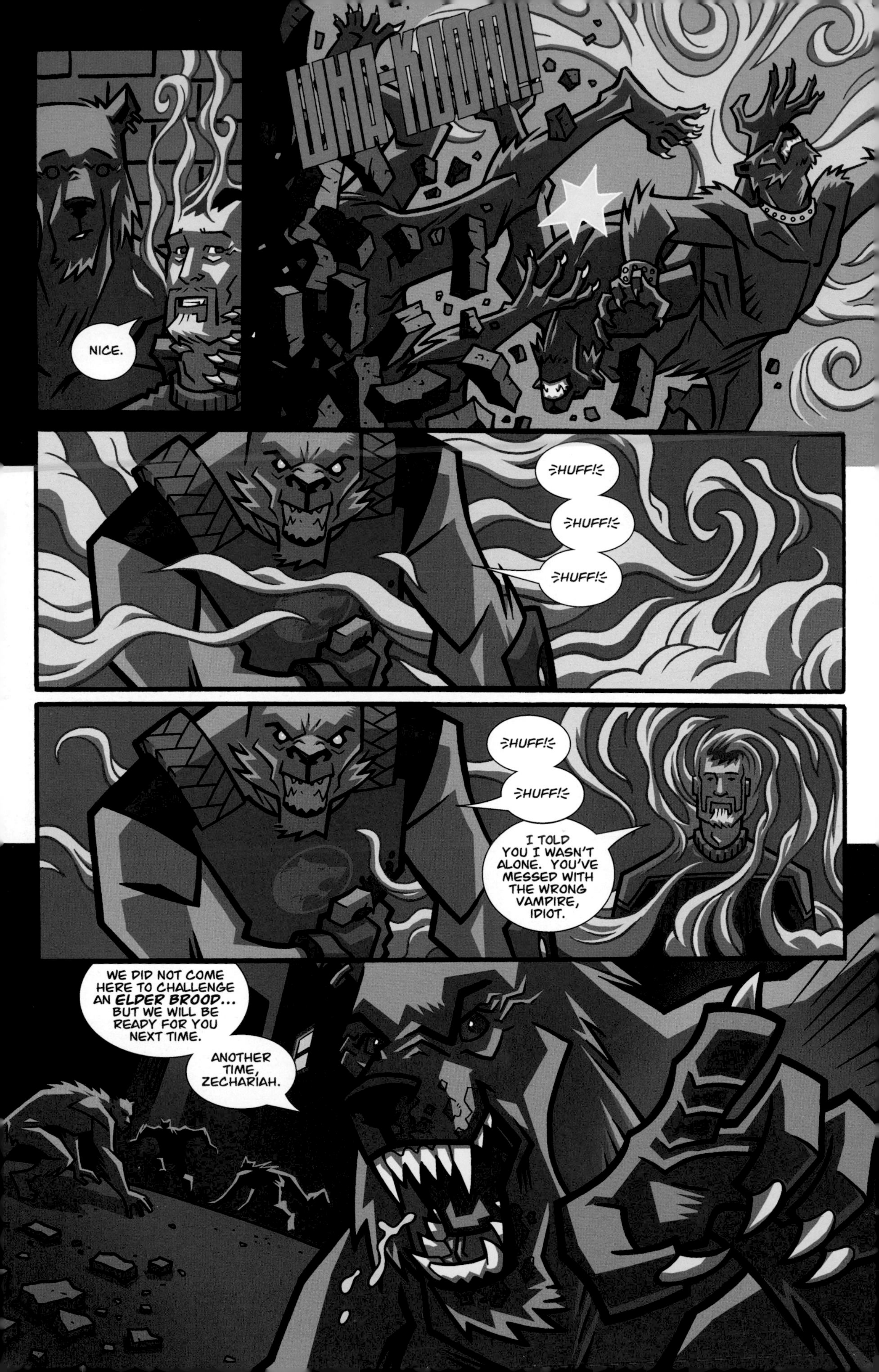
NICE.
WHA-KOOM!!
HUFF!
HUFF!
HUFF!
HUFF!
HUFF!
I TOLD YOU I WASN'T ALONE. YOU'VE MESSED WITH THE WRONG VAMPIRE, IDIOT.
WE DID NOT COME HERE TO CHALLENGE AN ELDER BROOD... BUT WE WILL BE READY FOR YOU NEXT TIME.
ANOTHER TIME, ZECHARIAH.

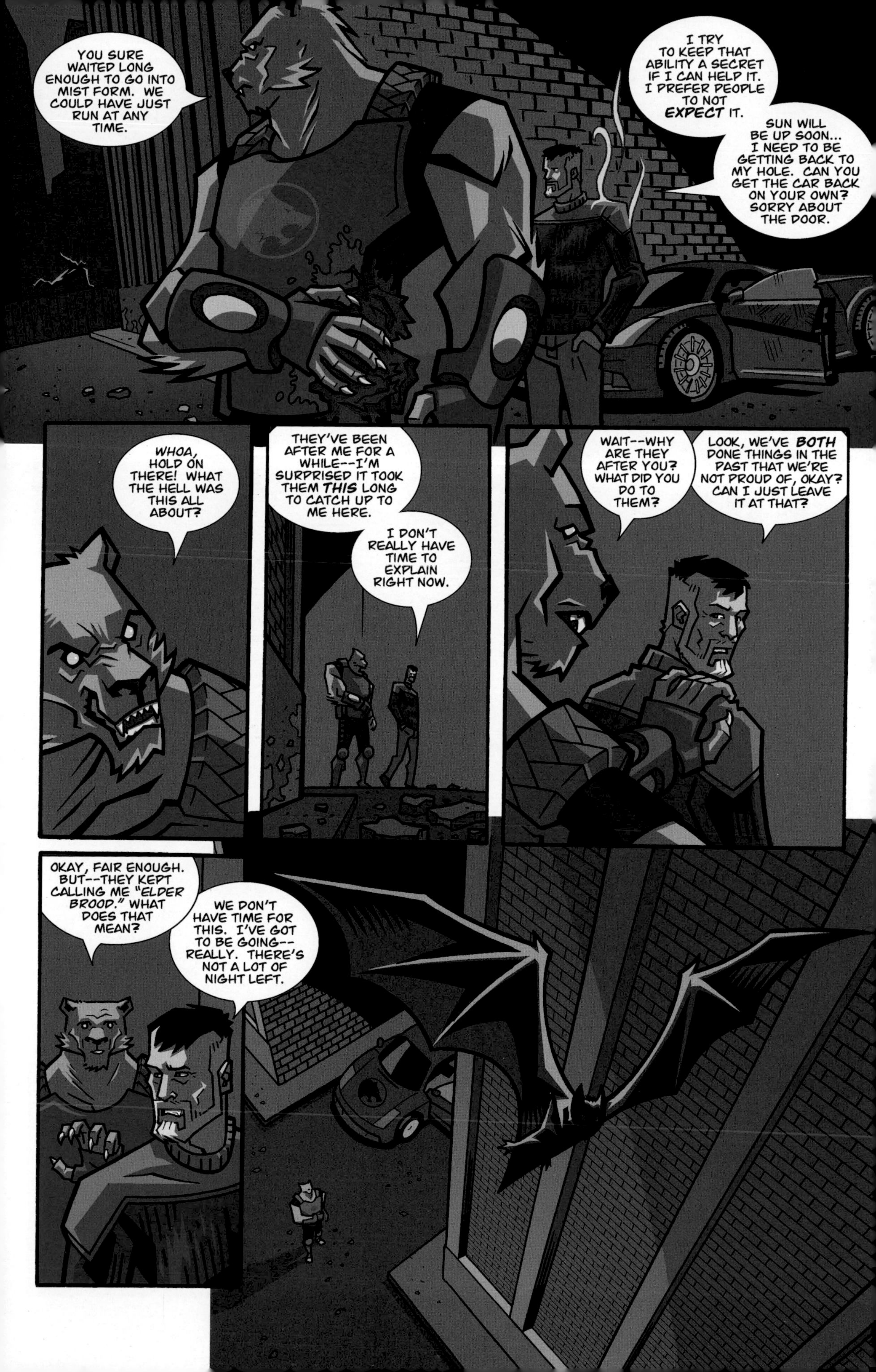
YOU SURE WAITED LONG ENOUGH TO GO INTO MIST FORM. WE COULD HAVE JUST RUN AT ANY TIME.
I TRY TO KEEP THAT ABILITY A SECRET IF I CAN HELP IT. I PREFER PEOPLE TO NOT EXPECT IT.
SUN WILL BE UP SOON... I NEED TO BE GETTING BACK TO MY HOLE. CAN YOU GET THE CAR BACK ON YOUR OWN? SORRY ABOUT THE DOOR.
WHOA, HOLD ON THERE! WHAT THE HELL WAS THIS ALL ABOUT?
THEY'VE BEEN AFTER ME FOR A WHILE--I'M SURPRISED IT TOOK THEM THIS LONG TO CATCH UP TO ME HERE.
I DON'T REALLY HAVE TIME TO EXPLAIN RIGHT NOW.
WAIT--WHY ARE THEY AFTER YOU? WHAT DID YOU DO TO THEM?
LOOK, WE'VE BOTH DONE THINGS IN THE PAST THAT WE'RE NOT PROUD OF, OKAY? CAN I JUST LEAVE IT AT THAT?
OKAY, FAIR ENOUGH. BUT--THEY KEPT CALLING ME "ELDER BROOD." WHAT DOES THAT MEAN?
WE DON'T HAVE TIME FOR THIS. I'VE GOT TO BE GOING--REALLY. THERE'S NOT A LOT OF NIGHT LEFT.

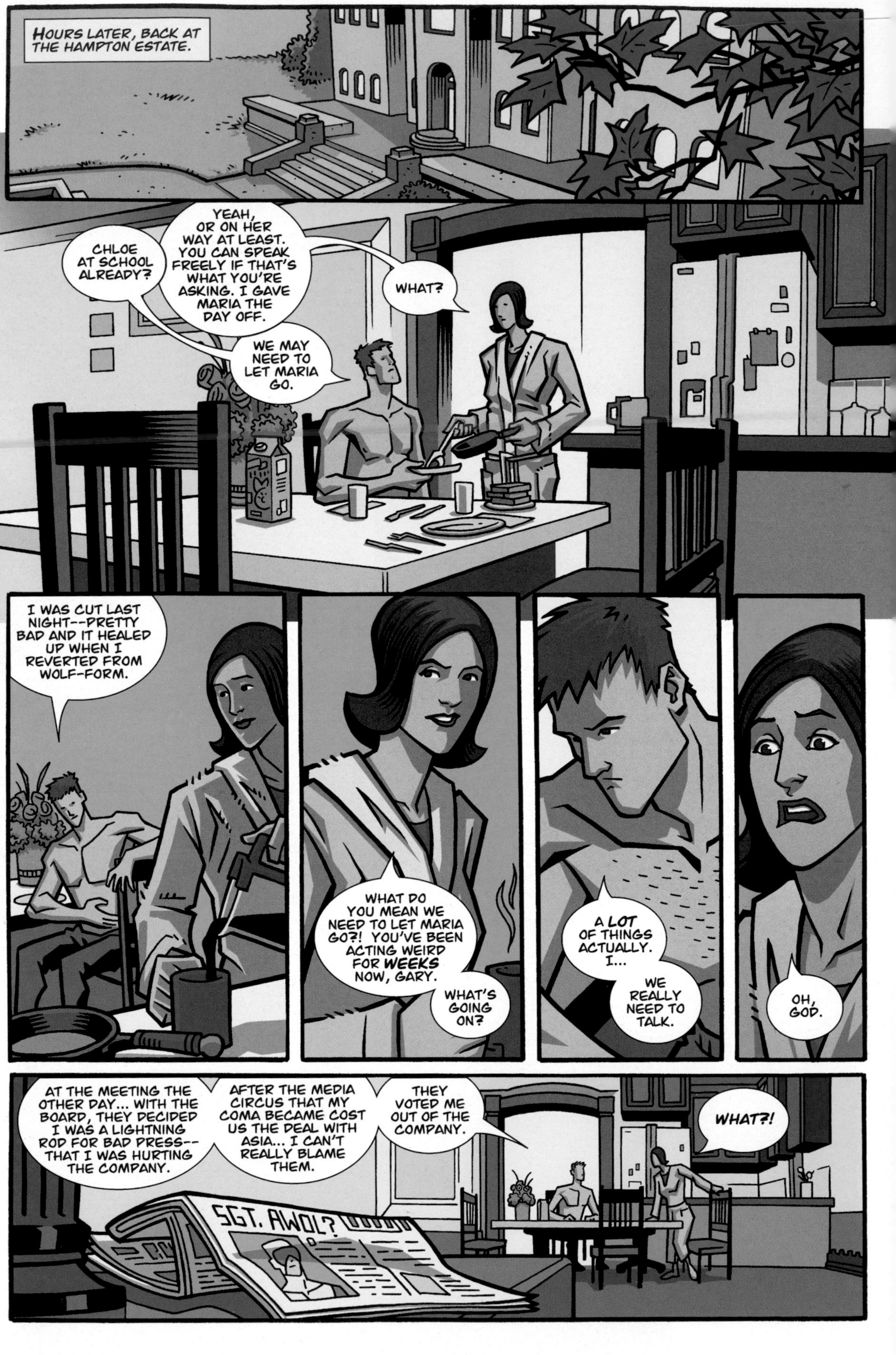

HOURS LATER, BACK AT THE HAMPTON ESTATE.
CHLOE AT SCHOOL ALREADY?
YEAH, OR ON HER WAY AT LEAST. YOU CAN SPEAK FREELY IF THAT'S WHAT YOU'RE ASKING. I GAVE MARIA THE DAY OFF.
WE MAY NEED TO LET MARIA GO.
WHAT?
I WAS CUT LAST NIGHT--PRETTY BAD AND IT HEALED UP WHEN I REVERTED FROM WOLF-FORM.
WHAT DO YOU MEAN WE NEED TO LET MARIA GO?! YOU'VE BEEN ACTING WEIRD FOR WEEKS NOW, GARY.
WHAT'S GOING ON?
A LOT OF THINGS ACTUALLY. I...
WE REALLY NEED TO TALK.
OH, GOD.
AT THE MEETING THE OTHER DAY... WITH THE BOARD, THEY DECIDED I WAS A LIGHTNING ROD FOR BAD PRESS--THAT I WAS HURTING THE COMPANY.
AFTER THE MEDIA CIRCUS THAT MY COMA BECAME COST US THE DEAL WITH ASIA... I CAN'T REALLY BLAME THEM.
THEY VOTED ME OUT OF THE COMPANY.
WHAT?!
SGT. AWOL?

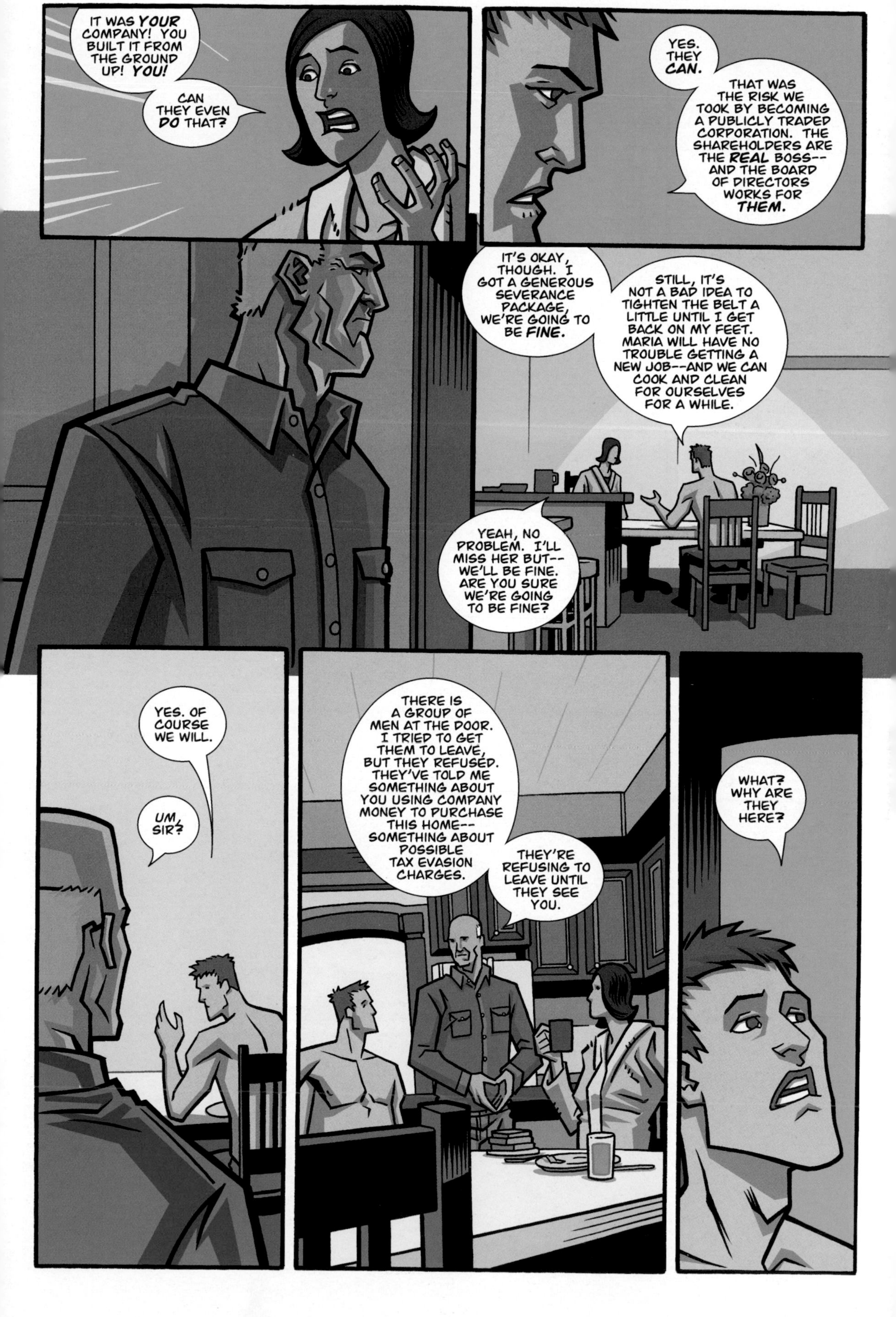
IT WAS YOUR COMPANY! YOU BUILT IT FROM THE GROUND UP! YOU!
CAN THEY EVEN DO THAT?
YES. THEY CAN.
THAT WAS THE RISK WE TOOK BY BECOMING A PUBLICLY TRADED CORPORATION. THE SHAREHOLDERS ARE THE REAL BOSS-- AND THE BOARD OF DIRECTORS WORKS FOR THEM.
IT'S OKAY, THOUGH. I GOT A GENEROUS SEVERANCE PACKAGE, WE'RE GOING TO BE FINE.
STILL, IT'S NOT A BAD IDEA TO TIGHTEN THE BELT A LITTLE UNTIL I GET BACK ON MY FEET. MARIA WILL HAVE NO TROUBLE GETTING A NEW JOB--AND WE CAN COOK AND CLEAN FOR OURSELVES FOR A WHILE.
YEAH, NO PROBLEM. I'LL MISS HER BUT-- WE'LL BE FINE. ARE YOU SURE WE'RE GOING TO BE FINE?
YES. OF COURSE WE WILL.
UM, SIR?
THERE IS A GROUP OF MEN AT THE DOOR. I TRIED TO GET THEM TO LEAVE, BUT THEY REFUSED. THEY'VE TOLD ME SOMETHING ABOUT YOU USING COMPANY MONEY TO PURCHASE THIS HOME-- SOMETHING ABOUT POSSIBLE TAX EVASION CHARGES.
THEY'RE REFUSING TO LEAVE UNTIL THEY SEE YOU.
WHAT? WHY ARE THEY HERE?

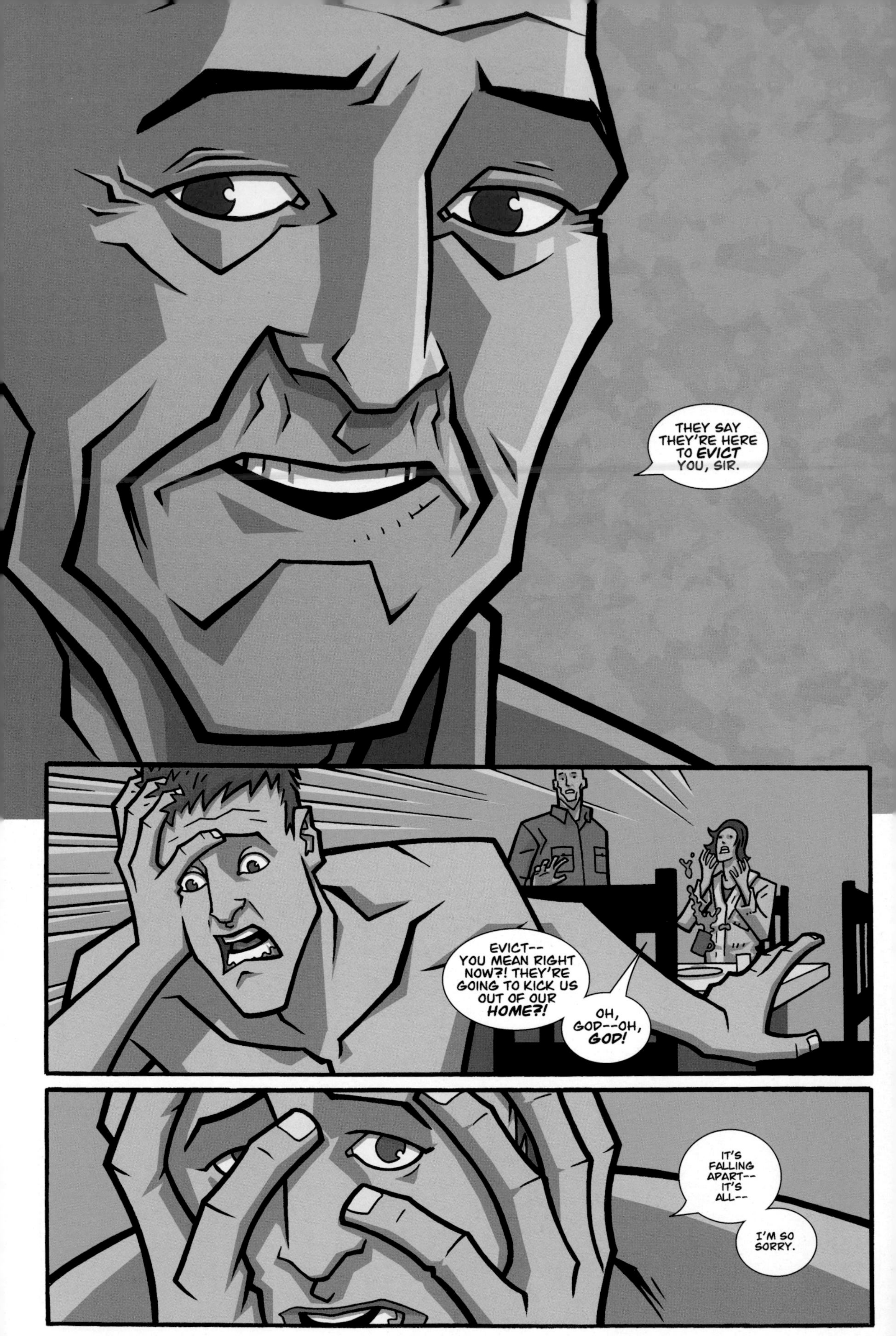
THEY SAY THEY'RE HERE TO EVICT YOU, SIR.
EVICT-- YOU MEAN RIGHT NOW?! THEY'RE GOING TO KICK US OUT OF OUR HOME?!
OH, GOD--OH, GOD!
IT'S FALLING APART-- IT'S ALL--
I'M SO SORRY.

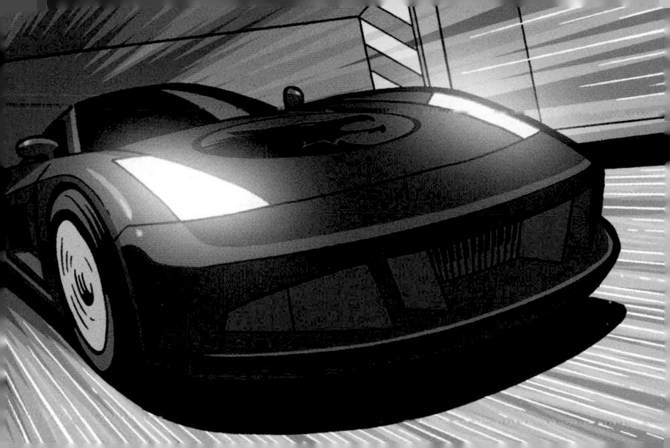

4

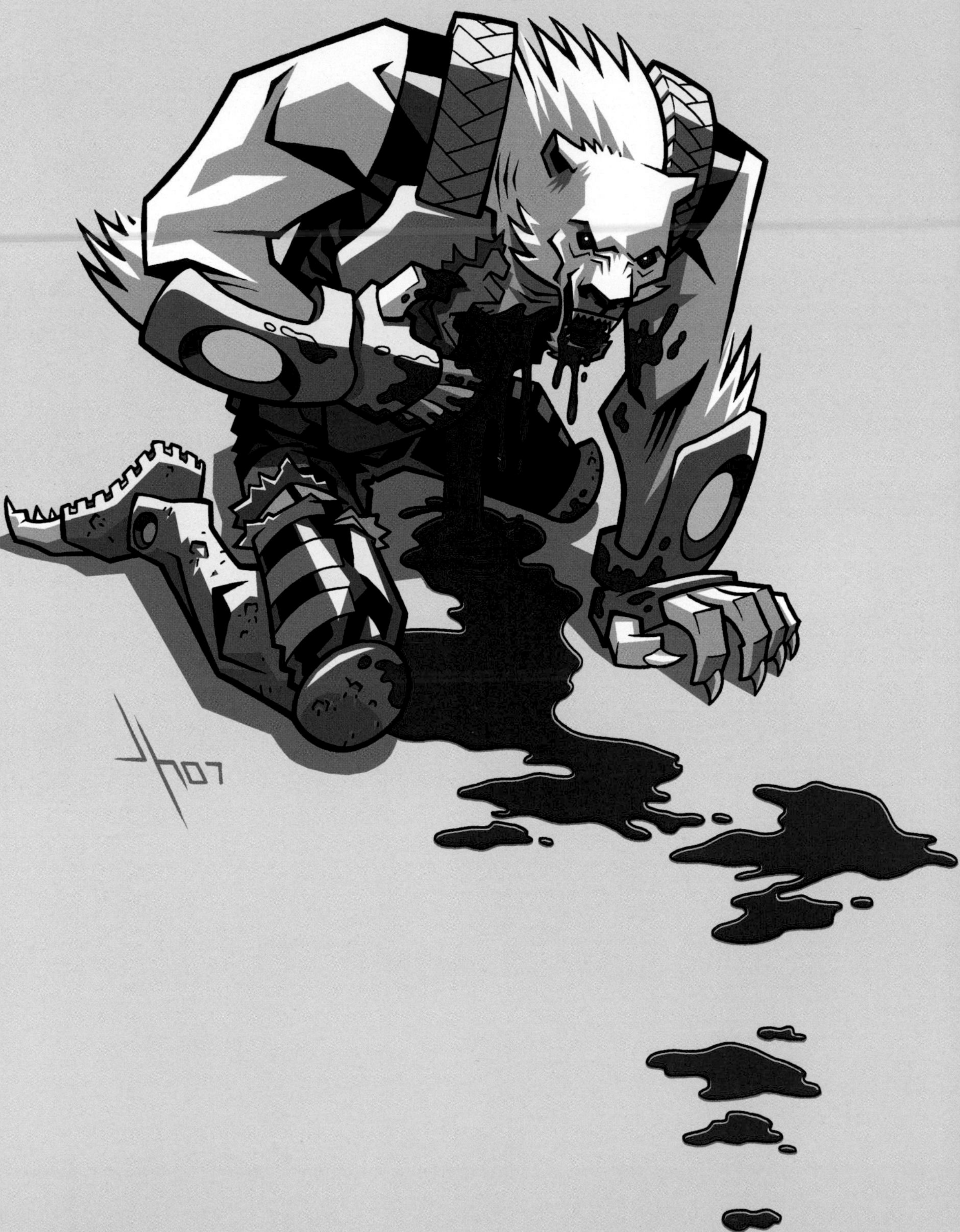

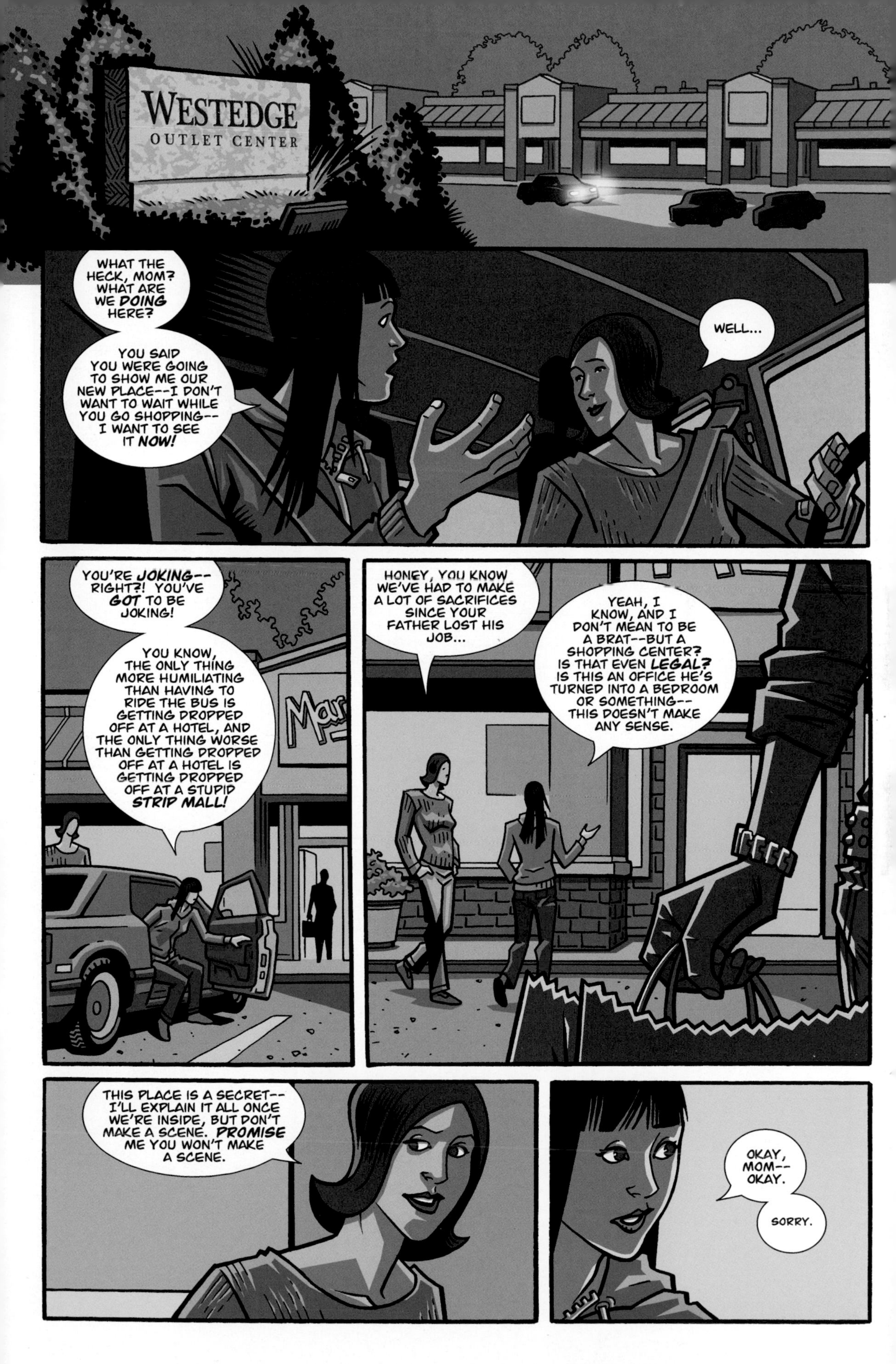
WESTEDGE OUTLET CENTER
WHAT THE HECK, MOM? WHAT ARE WE DOING HERE?
YOU SAID YOU WERE GOING TO SHOW ME OUR NEW PLACE--I DON'T WANT TO WAIT WHILE YOU GO SHOPPING--I WANT TO SEE IT NOW!
WELL...
YOU'RE JOKING--RIGHT?! YOU'VE GOT TO BE JOKING!
YOU KNOW, THE ONLY THING MORE HUMILIATING THAN HAVING TO RIDE THE BUS IS GETTING DROPPED OFF AT A HOTEL, AND THE ONLY THING WORSE THAN GETTING DROPPED OFF AT A HOTEL IS GETTING DROPPED OFF AT A STUPID STRIP MALL!
HONEY, YOU KNOW WE'VE HAD TO MAKE A LOT OF SACRIFICES SINCE YOUR FATHER LOST HIS JOB...
YEAH, I KNOW, AND I DON'T MEAN TO BE A BRAT--BUT A SHOPPING CENTER? IS THAT EVEN LEGAL? IS THIS AN OFFICE HE'S TURNED INTO A BEDROOM OR SOMETHING--THIS DOESN'T MAKE ANY SENSE.
THIS PLACE IS A SECRET--I'LL EXPLAIN IT ALL ONCE WE'RE INSIDE, BUT DON'T MAKE A SCENE. PROMISE ME YOU WON'T MAKE A SCENE.
OKAY, MOM--OKAY.
SORRY.

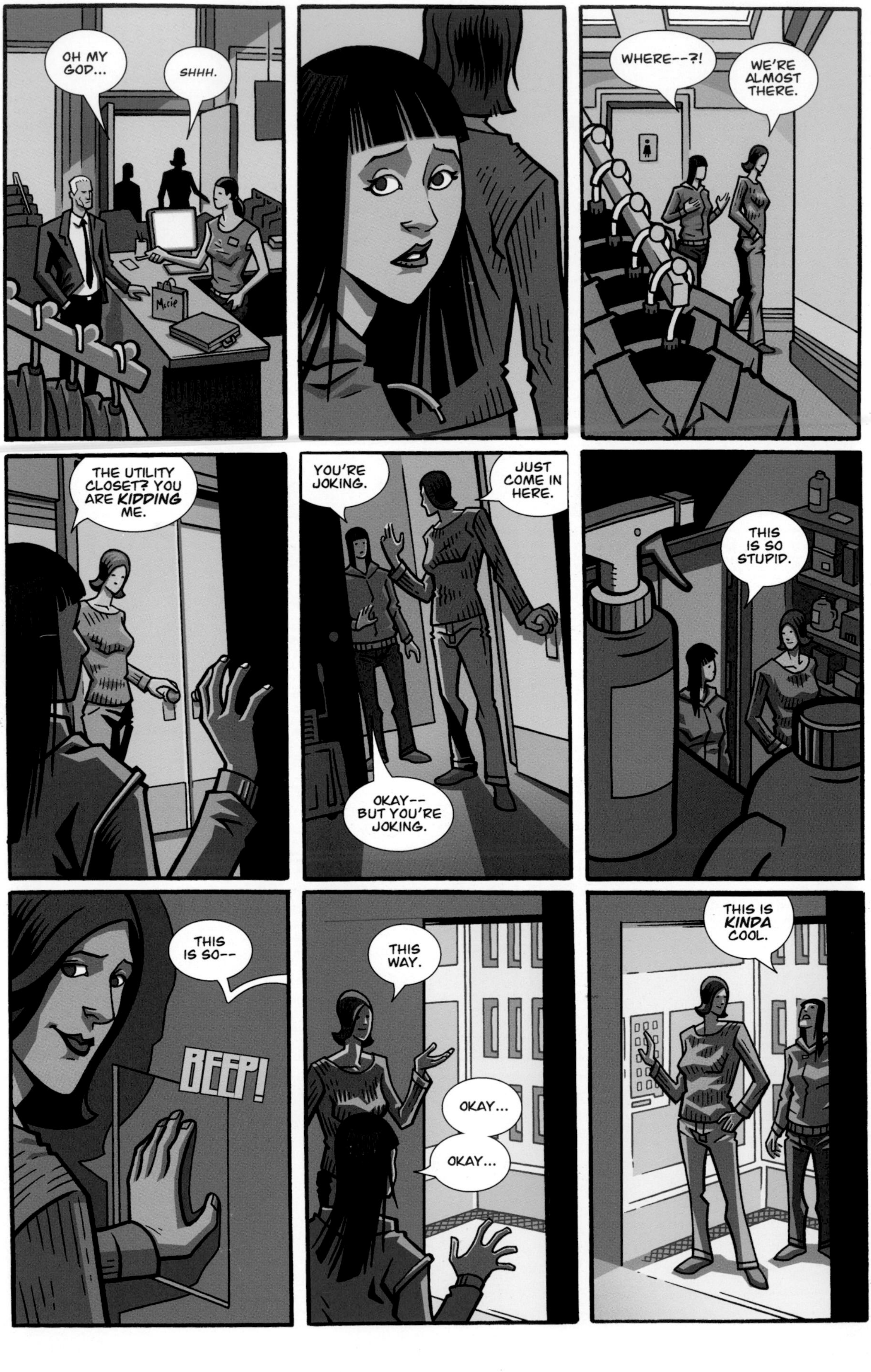
OH MY GOD...
SHHH.
Macie
WHERE--?!
WE'RE ALMOST THERE.
THE UTILITY CLOSET? YOU ARE KIDDING ME.
YOU'RE JOKING.
JUST COME IN HERE.
OKAY-- BUT YOU'RE JOKING.
THIS IS SO STUPID.
THIS IS SO--
BEEP!
THIS WAY.
OKAY...
OKAY...
THIS IS KINDA COOL.

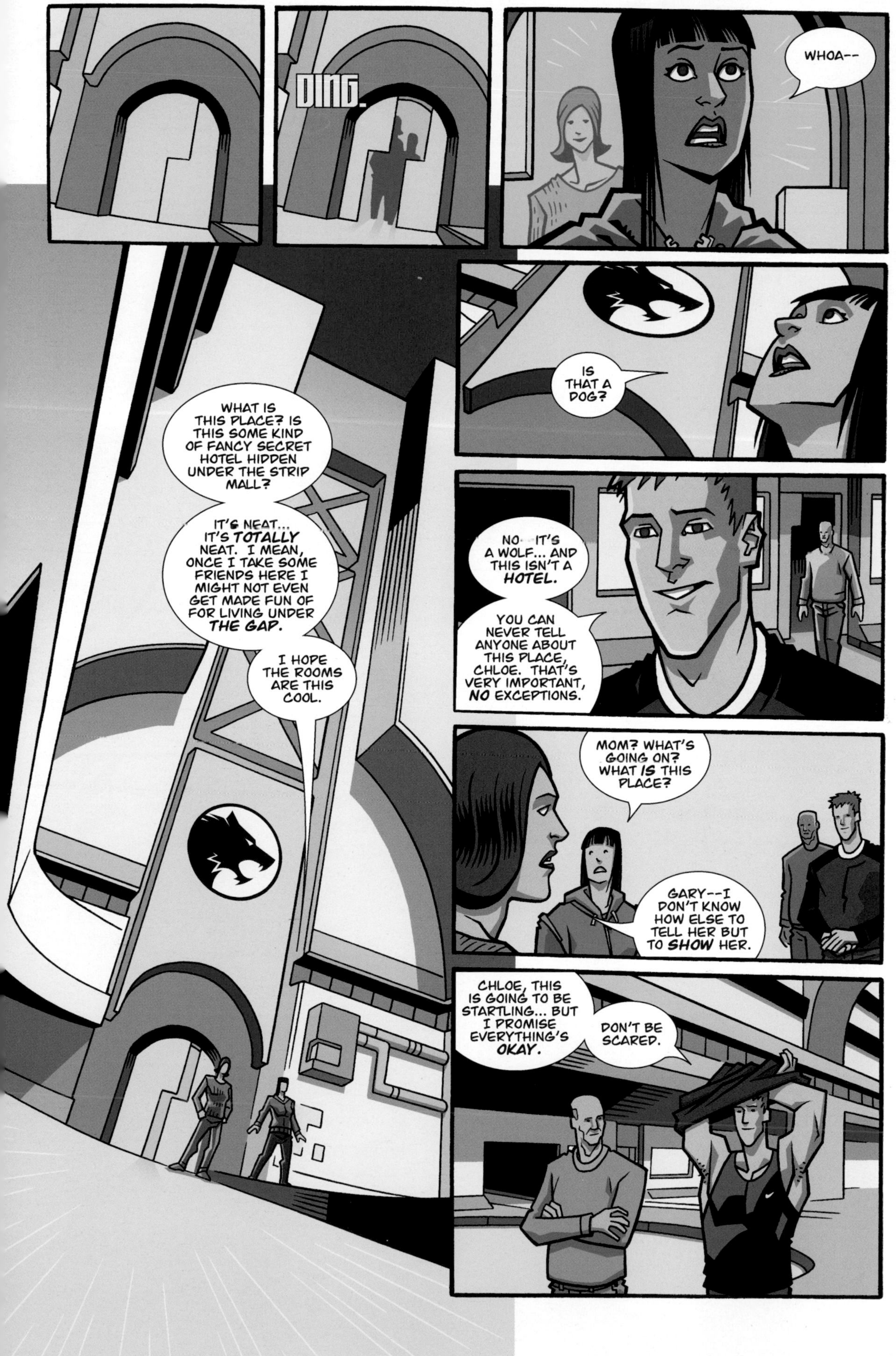
DING.
WHOA--
WHAT IS THIS PLACE? IS THIS SOME KIND OF FANCY SECRET HOTEL HIDDEN UNDER THE STRIP MALL?
IT'S NEAT... IT'S TOTALLY NEAT. I MEAN, ONCE I TAKE SOME FRIENDS HERE I MIGHT NOT EVEN GET MADE FUN OF FOR LIVING UNDER THE GAP.
I HOPE THE ROOMS ARE THIS COOL.
IS THAT A DOG?
NO. IT'S A WOLF... AND THIS ISN'T A HOTEL.
YOU CAN NEVER TELL ANYONE ABOUT THIS PLACE, CHLOE. THAT'S VERY IMPORTANT, NO EXCEPTIONS.
MOM? WHAT'S GOING ON? WHAT IS THIS PLACE?
GARY--I DON'T KNOW HOW ELSE TO TELL HER BUT TO SHOW HER.
CHLOE, THIS IS GOING TO BE STARTLING... BUT I PROMISE EVERYTHING'S OKAY.
DON'T BE SCARED.

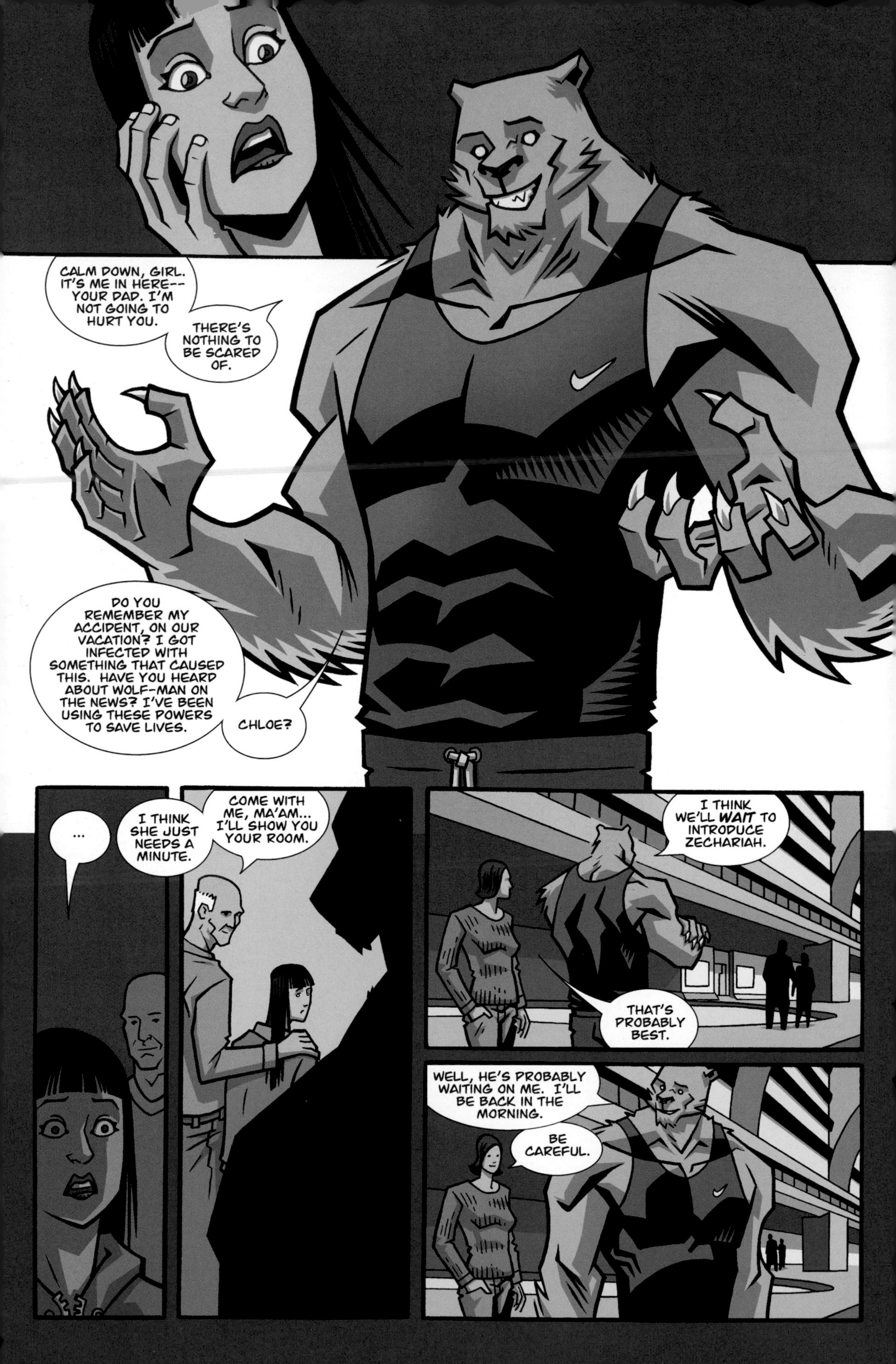
CALM DOWN, GIRL. IT'S ME IN HERE-- YOUR DAD. I'M NOT GOING TO HURT YOU.
THERE'S NOTHING TO BE SCARED OF.
DO YOU REMEMBER MY ACCIDENT, ON OUR VACATION? I GOT INFECTED WITH SOMETHING THAT CAUSED THIS. HAVE YOU HEARD ABOUT WOLF-MAN ON THE NEWS? I'VE BEEN USING THESE POWERS TO SAVE LIVES.
CHLOE?
...
I THINK SHE JUST NEEDS A MINUTE.
COME WITH ME, MA'AM... I'LL SHOW YOU YOUR ROOM.
I THINK WE'LL WAIT TO INTRODUCE ZECHARIAH.
THAT'S PROBABLY BEST.
WELL, HE'S PROBABLY WAITING ON ME. I'LL BE BACK IN THE MORNING.
BE CAREFUL.

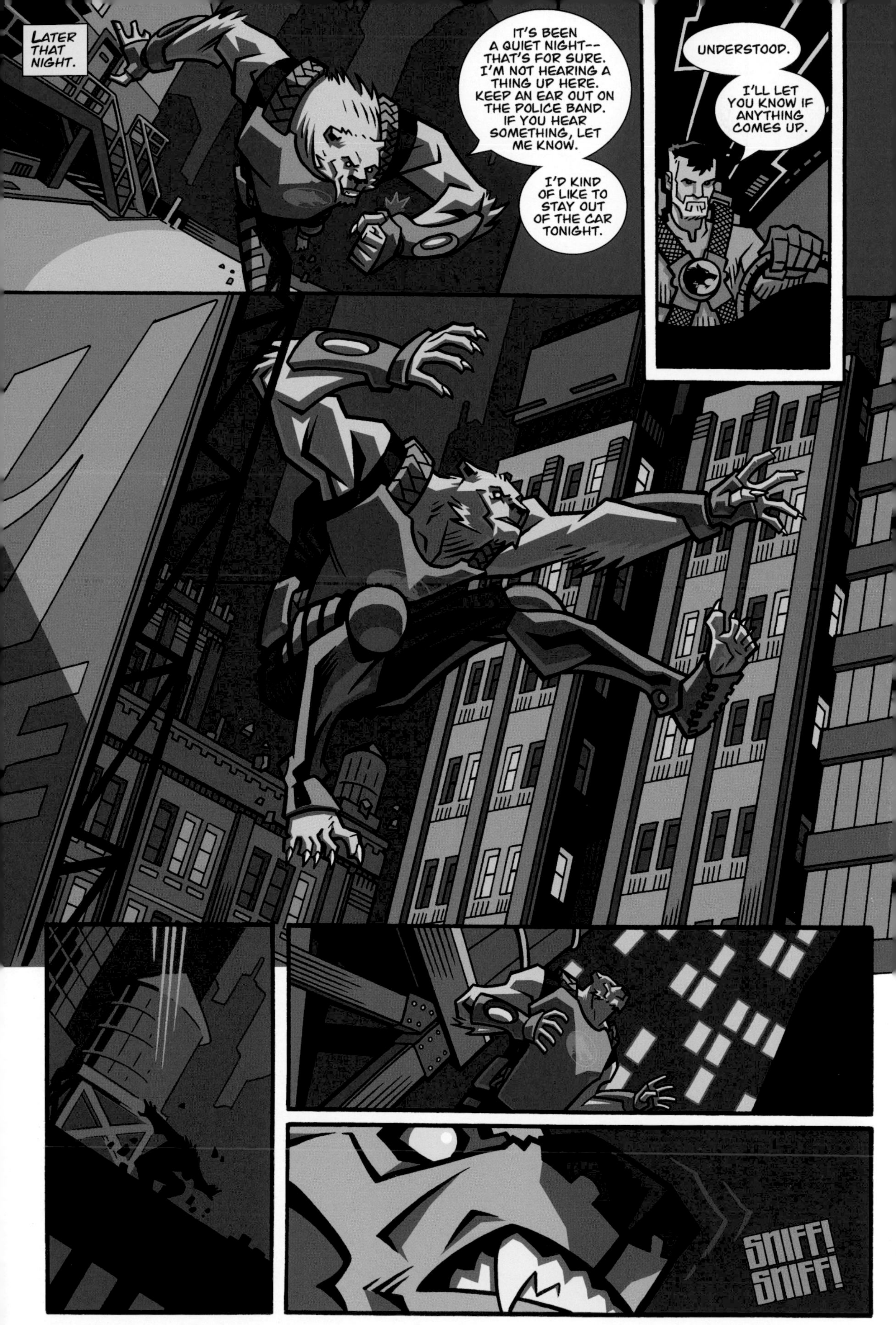
LATER THAT NIGHT.
IT'S BEEN A QUIET NIGHT--THAT'S FOR SURE. I'M NOT HEARING A THING UP HERE. KEEP AN EAR OUT ON THE POLICE BAND. IF YOU HEAR SOMETHING, LET ME KNOW.
I'D KIND OF LIKE TO STAY OUT OF THE CAR TONIGHT.
UNDERSTOOD.
I'LL LET YOU KNOW IF ANYTHING COMES UP.
SNIFF! SNIFF!

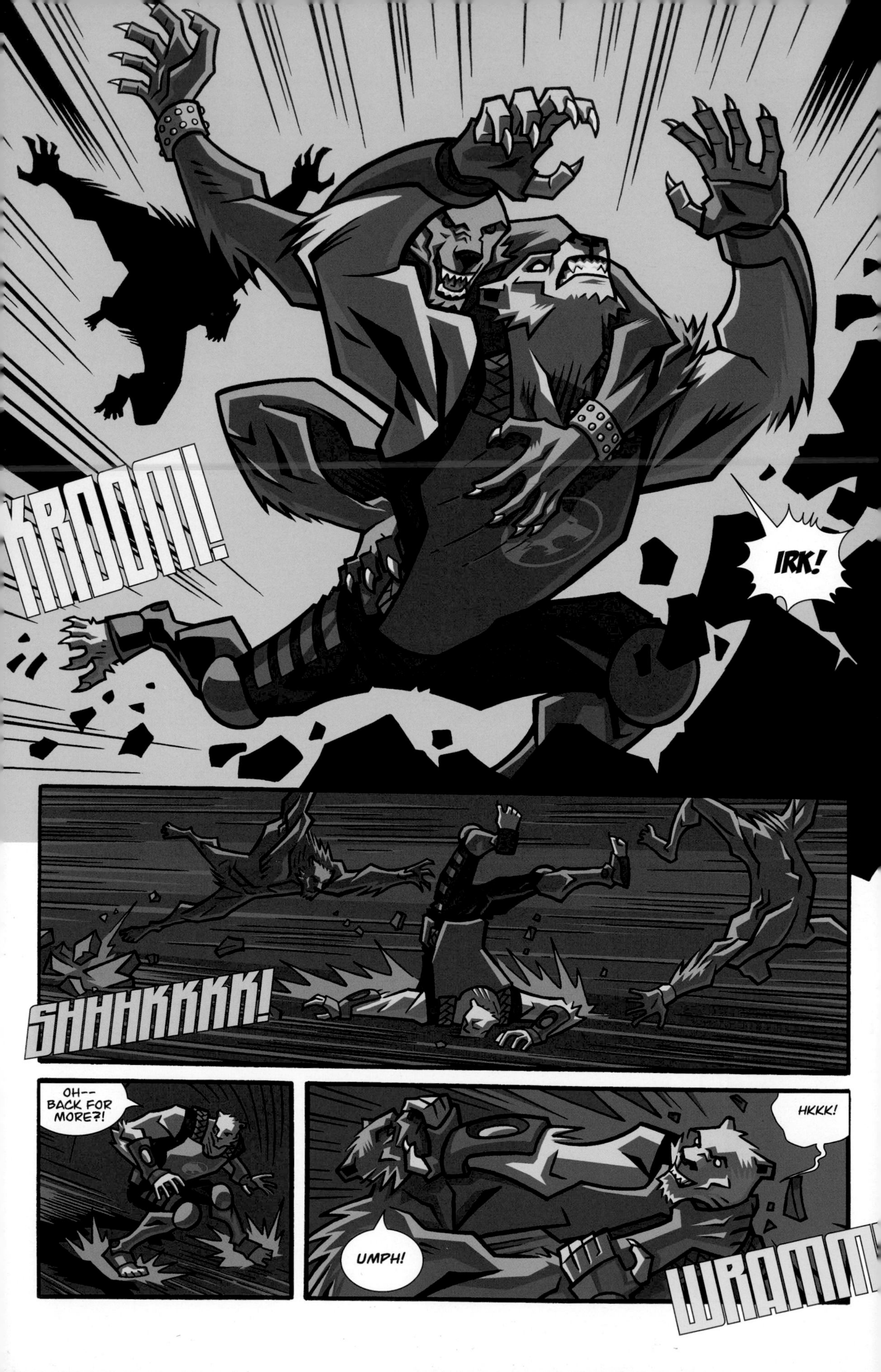
KROOM!
IRK!
SHHKKKK!
OH--
BACK FOR
MORE?!
HKKK!
UMPH!
WRAMM

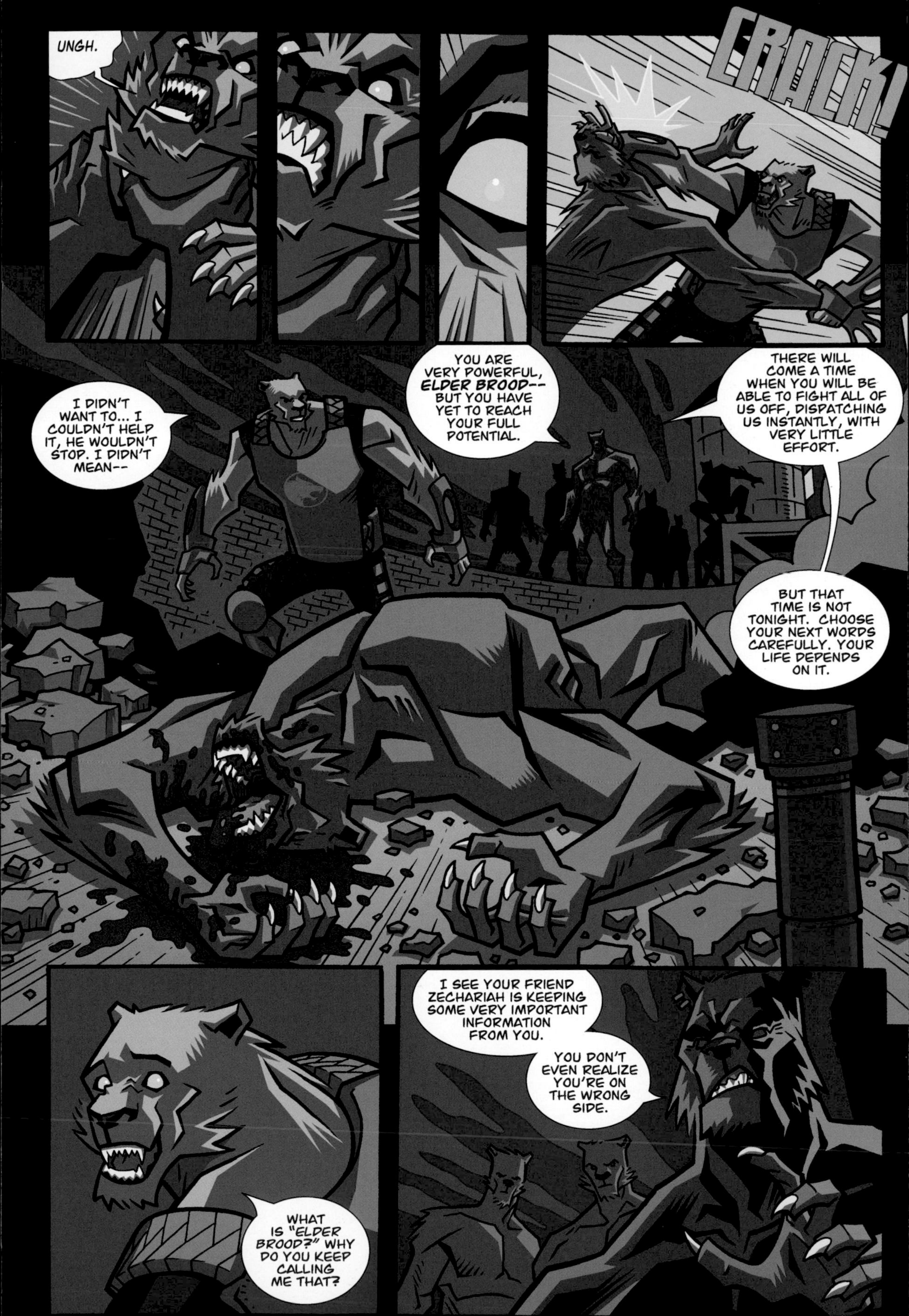
UNGH.
CRACK!
I DIDN'T WANT TO... I COULDN'T HELP IT, HE WOULDN'T STOP. I DIDN'T MEAN--
YOU ARE VERY POWERFUL, ELDER BROOD-- BUT YOU HAVE YET TO REACH YOUR FULL POTENTIAL.
THERE WILL COME A TIME WHEN YOU WILL BE ABLE TO FIGHT ALL OF US OFF, DISPATCHING US INSTANTLY, WITH VERY LITTLE EFFORT.
BUT THAT TIME IS NOT TONIGHT. CHOOSE YOUR NEXT WORDS CAREFULLY. YOUR LIFE DEPENDS ON IT.
WHAT IS "ELDER BROOD?" WHY DO YOU KEEP CALLING ME THAT?
I SEE YOUR FRIEND ZECHARIAH IS KEEPING SOME VERY IMPORTANT INFORMATION FROM YOU.
YOU DON'T EVEN REALIZE YOU'RE ON THE WRONG SIDE.

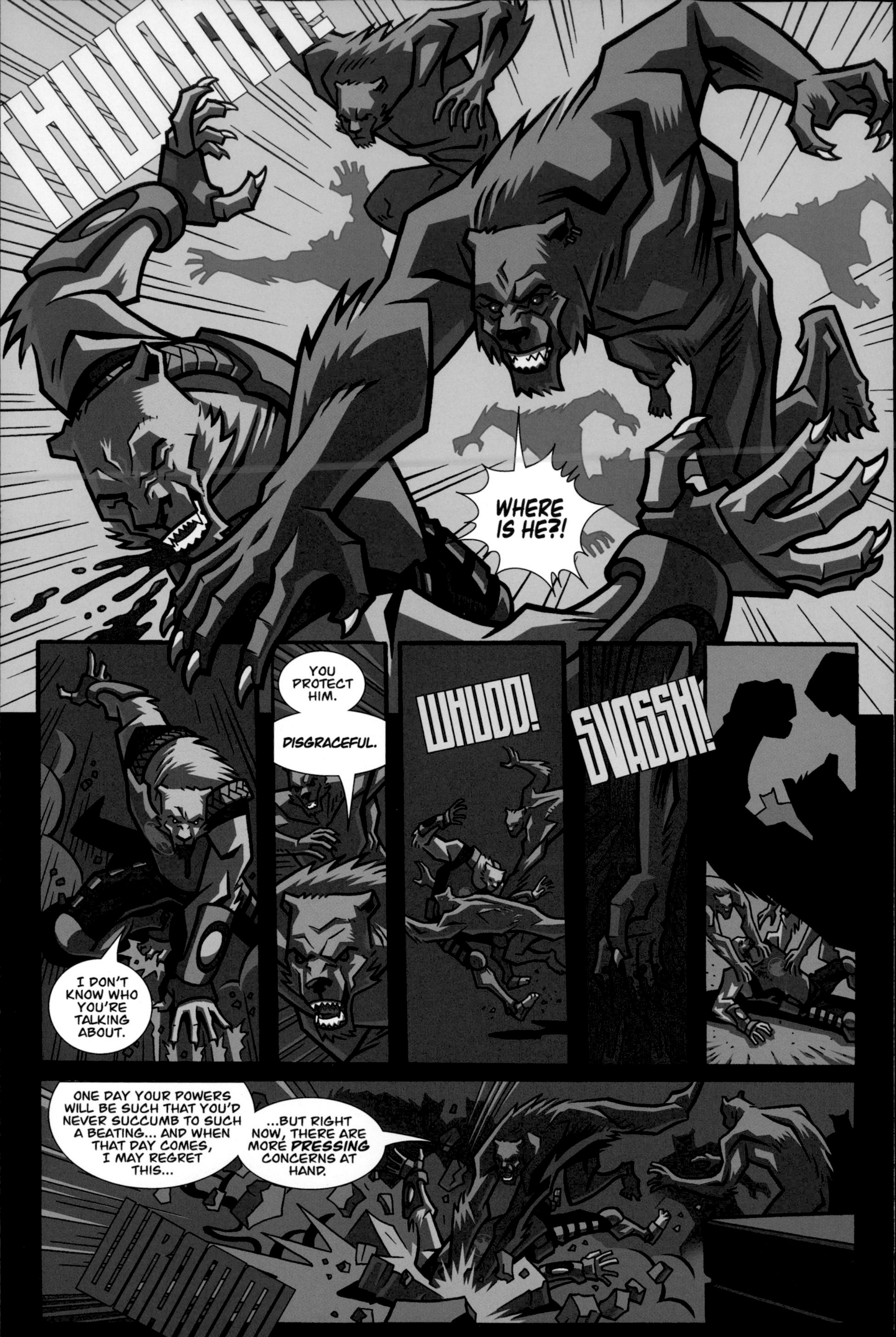
THHOOM!
WHERE IS HE?!
I DON'T KNOW WHO YOU'RE TALKING ABOUT.
YOU PROTECT HIM.
DISGRACEFUL.
WHUDD!
SWOSSH!
ONE DAY YOUR POWERS WILL BE SUCH THAT YOU'D NEVER SUCCUMB TO SUCH A BEATING... AND WHEN THAT DAY COMES, I MAY REGRET THIS...
...BUT RIGHT NOW, THERE ARE MORE PRESSING CONCERNS AT HAND.

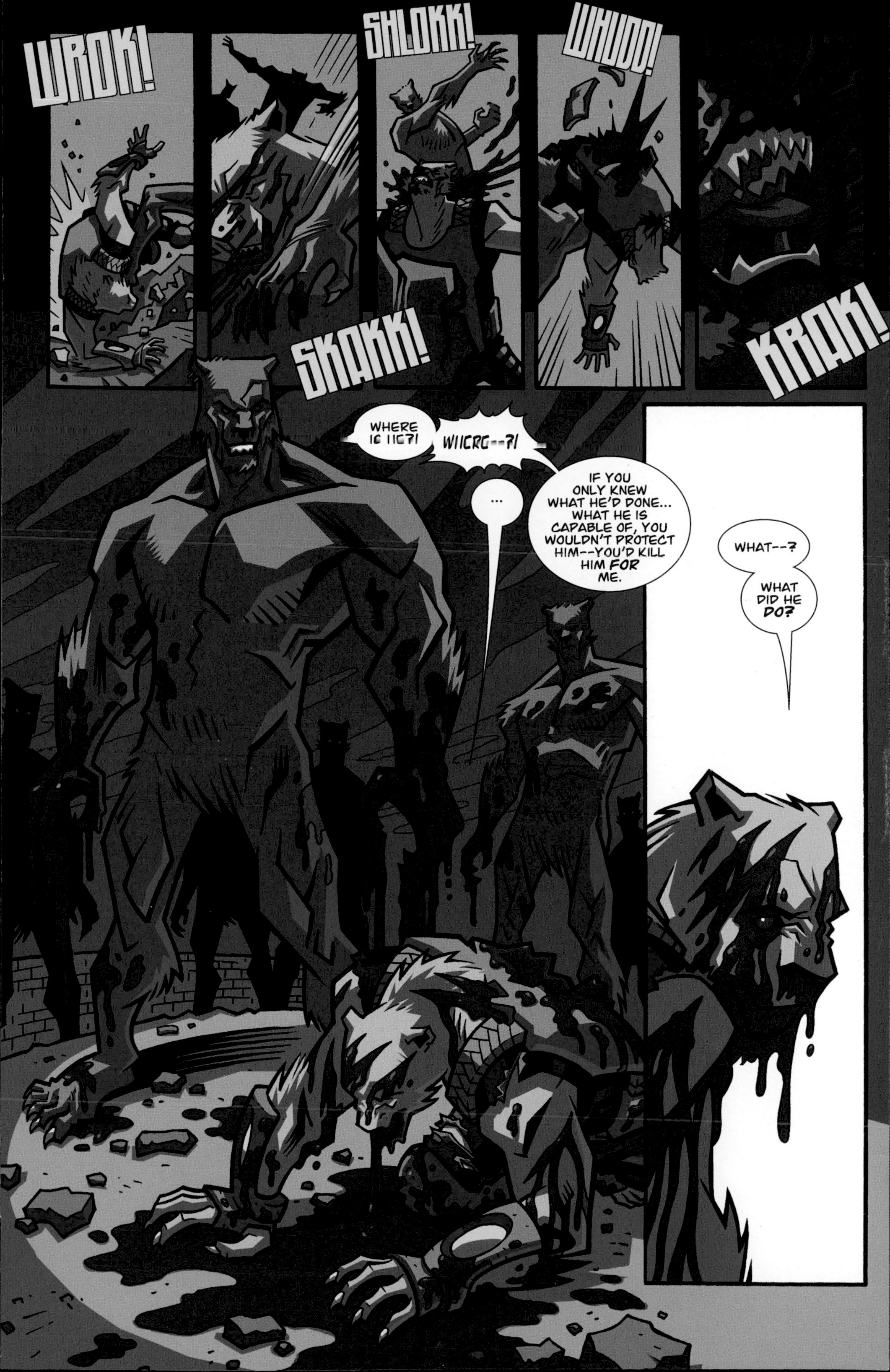
WROK!
SHLOKK!
WHUDD!
SKAKK!
KRAK!
WHERE IC IIC?!
WIICRC--?!
...
IF YOU ONLY KNEW WHAT HE'D DONE... WHAT HE IS CAPABLE OF, YOU WOULDN'T PROTECT HIM--YOU'D KILL HIM **FOR** ME.
WHAT--?
WHAT DID HE **DO?**

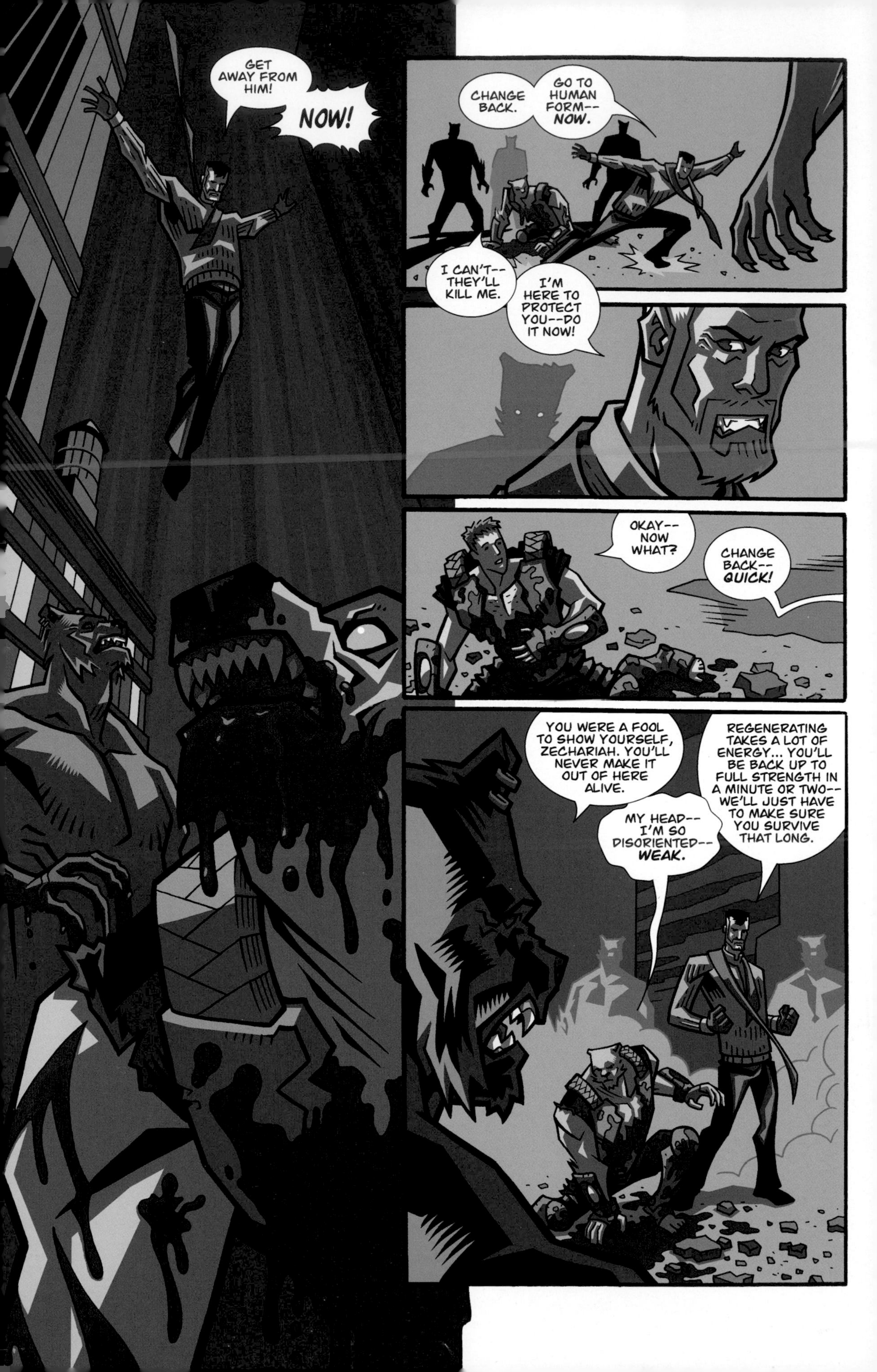
GET AWAY FROM HIM!
NOW!
CHANGE BACK.
GO TO HUMAN FORM--NOW.
I CAN'T--THEY'LL KILL ME.
I'M HERE TO PROTECT YOU--DO IT NOW!
OKAY--NOW WHAT?
CHANGE BACK--QUICK!
YOU WERE A FOOL TO SHOW YOURSELF, ZECHARIAH. YOU'LL NEVER MAKE IT OUT OF HERE ALIVE.
REGENERATING TAKES A LOT OF ENERGY... YOU'LL BE BACK UP TO FULL STRENGTH IN A MINUTE OR TWO--WE'LL JUST HAVE TO MAKE SURE YOU SURVIVE THAT LONG.
MY HEAD--I'M SO DISORIENTED--WEAK.

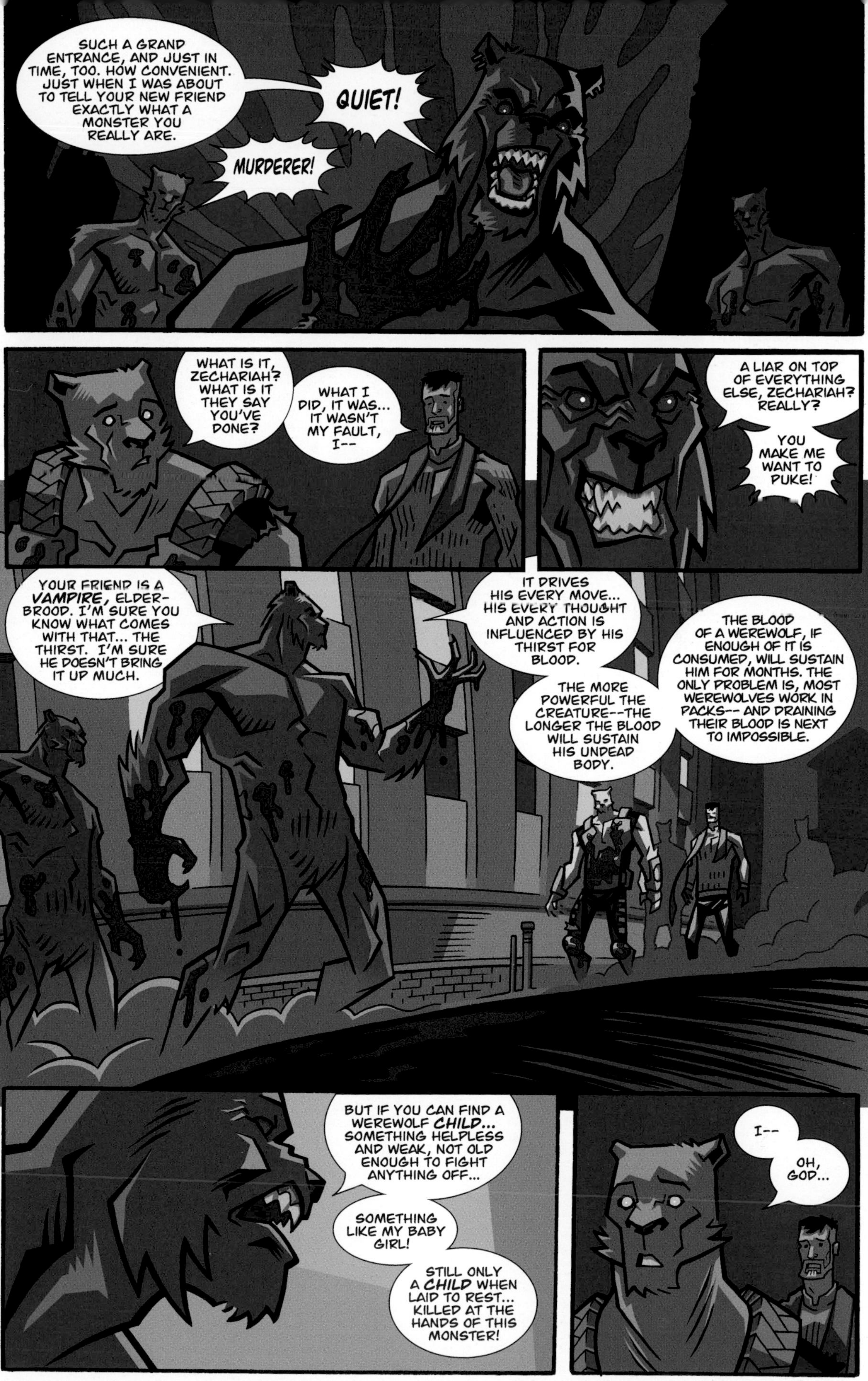
SUCH A GRAND ENTRANCE, AND JUST IN TIME, TOO. HOW CONVENIENT. JUST WHEN I WAS ABOUT TO TELL YOUR NEW FRIEND EXACTLY WHAT A MONSTER YOU REALLY ARE.
QUIET!
MURDERER!
WHAT IS IT, ZECHARIAH? WHAT IS IT THEY SAY YOU'VE DONE?
WHAT I DID, IT WAS... IT WASN'T MY FAULT, I--
A LIAR ON TOP OF EVERYTHING ELSE, ZECHARIAH? REALLY?
YOU MAKE ME WANT TO PUKE!
YOUR FRIEND IS A VAMPIRE, ELDER-BROOD. I'M SURE YOU KNOW WHAT COMES WITH THAT... THE THIRST. I'M SURE HE DOESN'T BRING IT UP MUCH.
IT DRIVES HIS EVERY MOVE... HIS EVERY THOUGHT AND ACTION IS INFLUENCED BY HIS THIRST FOR BLOOD.
THE MORE POWERFUL THE CREATURE--THE LONGER THE BLOOD WILL SUSTAIN HIS UNDEAD BODY.
THE BLOOD OF A WEREWOLF, IF ENOUGH OF IT IS CONSUMED, WILL SUSTAIN HIM FOR MONTHS. THE ONLY PROBLEM IS, MOST WEREWOLVES WORK IN PACKS-- AND DRAINING THEIR BLOOD IS NEXT TO IMPOSSIBLE.
BUT IF YOU CAN FIND A WEREWOLF CHILD... SOMETHING HELPLESS AND WEAK, NOT OLD ENOUGH TO FIGHT ANYTHING OFF...
SOMETHING LIKE MY BABY GIRL!
STILL ONLY A CHILD WHEN LAID TO REST... KILLED AT THE HANDS OF THIS MONSTER!
I--
OH, GOD...

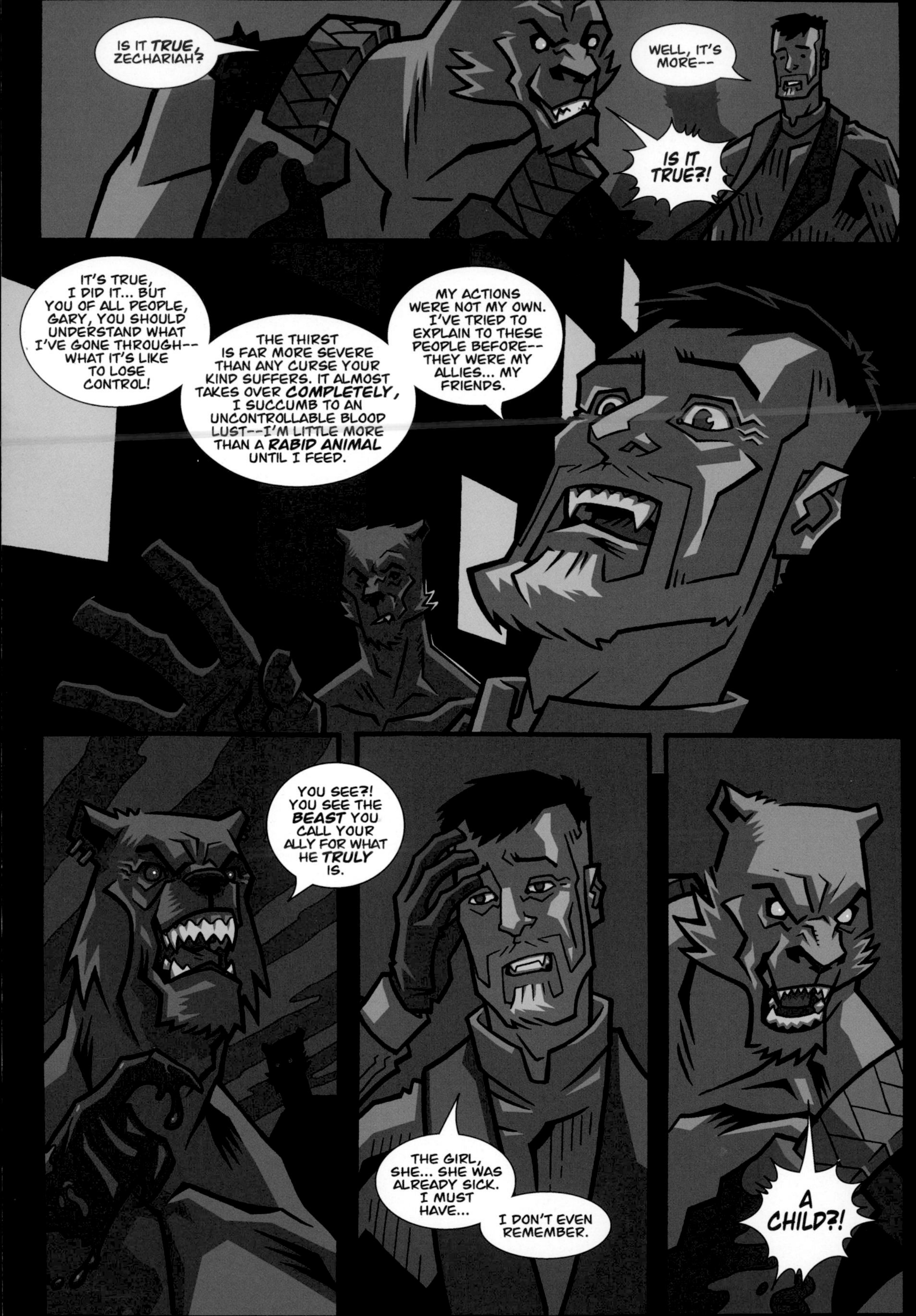
IS IT TRUE, ZECHARIAH?
WELL, IT'S MORE--
IS IT TRUE?!
IT'S TRUE, I DID IT... BUT YOU OF ALL PEOPLE, GARY, YOU SHOULD UNDERSTAND WHAT I'VE GONE THROUGH-- WHAT IT'S LIKE TO LOSE CONTROL!
THE THIRST IS FAR MORE SEVERE THAN ANY CURSE YOUR KIND SUFFERS. IT ALMOST TAKES OVER COMPLETELY, I SUCCUMB TO AN UNCONTROLLABLE BLOOD LUST--I'M LITTLE MORE THAN A RABID ANIMAL UNTIL I FEED.
MY ACTIONS WERE NOT MY OWN. I'VE TRIED TO EXPLAIN TO THESE PEOPLE BEFORE-- THEY WERE MY ALLIES... MY FRIENDS.
YOU SEE?! YOU SEE THE BEAST YOU CALL YOUR ALLY FOR WHAT HE TRULY IS.
THE GIRL, SHE... SHE WAS ALREADY SICK. I MUST HAVE...
I DON'T EVEN REMEMBER.
A CHILD?!

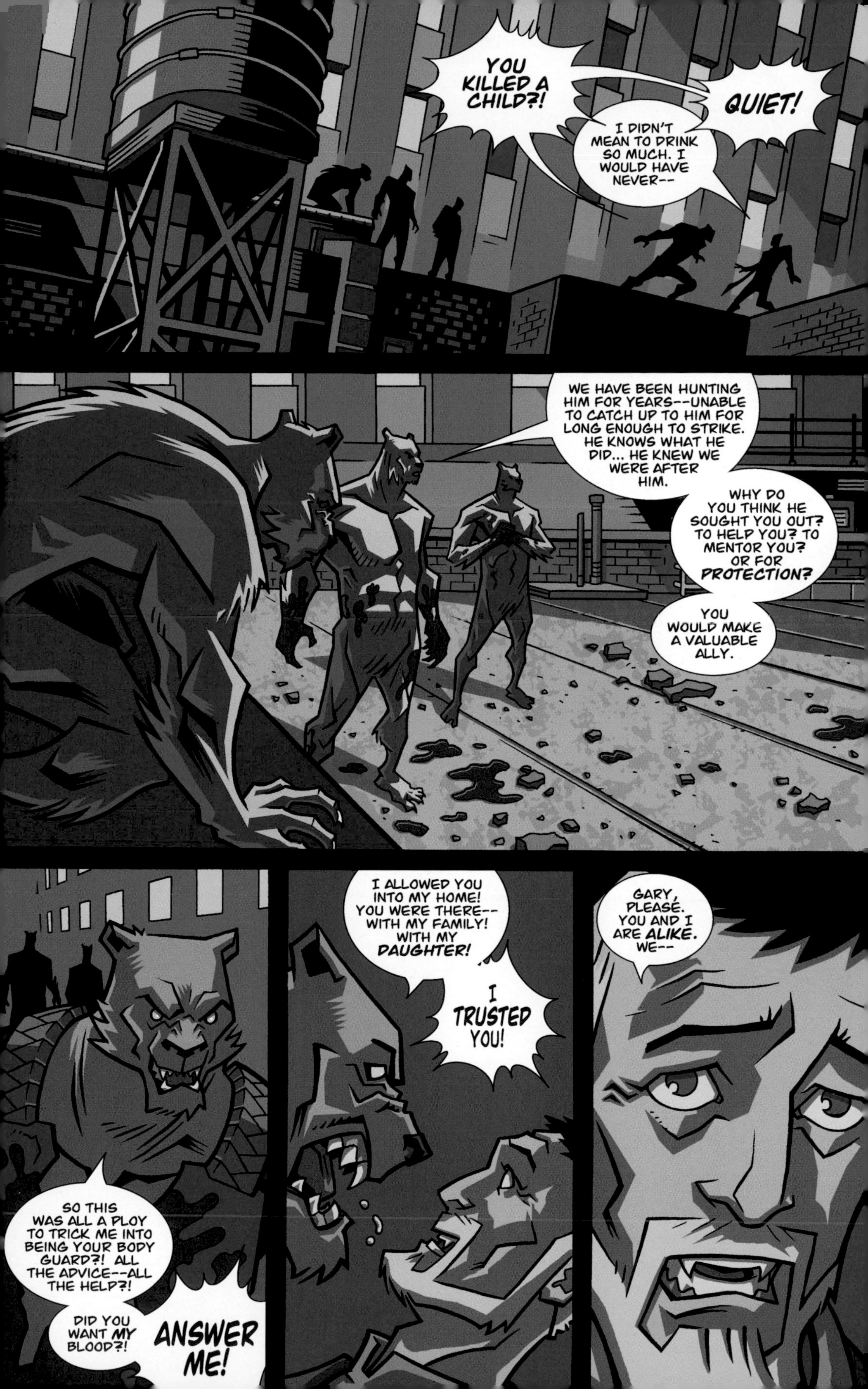
YOU KILLED A CHILD?!
I DIDN'T MEAN TO DRINK SO MUCH. I WOULD HAVE NEVER--
QUIET!
WE HAVE BEEN HUNTING HIM FOR YEARS--UNABLE TO CATCH UP TO HIM FOR LONG ENOUGH TO STRIKE. HE KNOWS WHAT HE DID... HE KNEW WE WERE AFTER HIM.
WHY DO YOU THINK HE SOUGHT YOU OUT? TO HELP YOU? TO MENTOR YOU? OR FOR PROTECTION?
YOU WOULD MAKE A VALUABLE ALLY.
SO THIS WAS ALL A PLOY TO TRICK ME INTO BEING YOUR BODY GUARD?! ALL THE ADVICE--ALL THE HELP?!
DID YOU WANT MY BLOOD?!
ANSWER ME!
I ALLOWED YOU INTO MY HOME! YOU WERE THERE--WITH MY FAMILY! WITH MY DAUGHTER!
I TRUSTED YOU!
GARY, PLEASE. YOU AND I ARE ALIKE. WE--

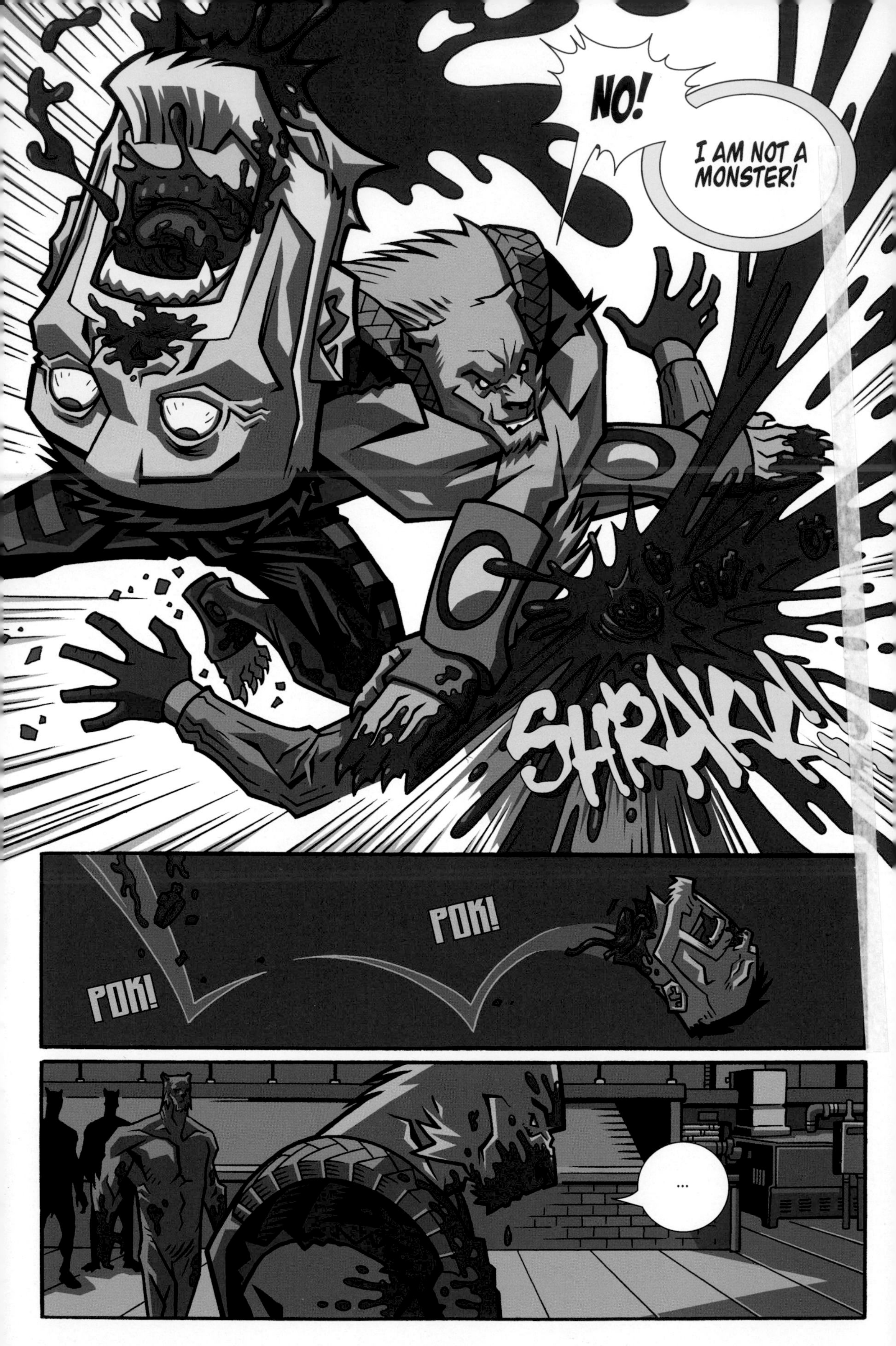
NO!
I AM NOT A MONSTER!
SHRAKK!
POK!
POK!
...

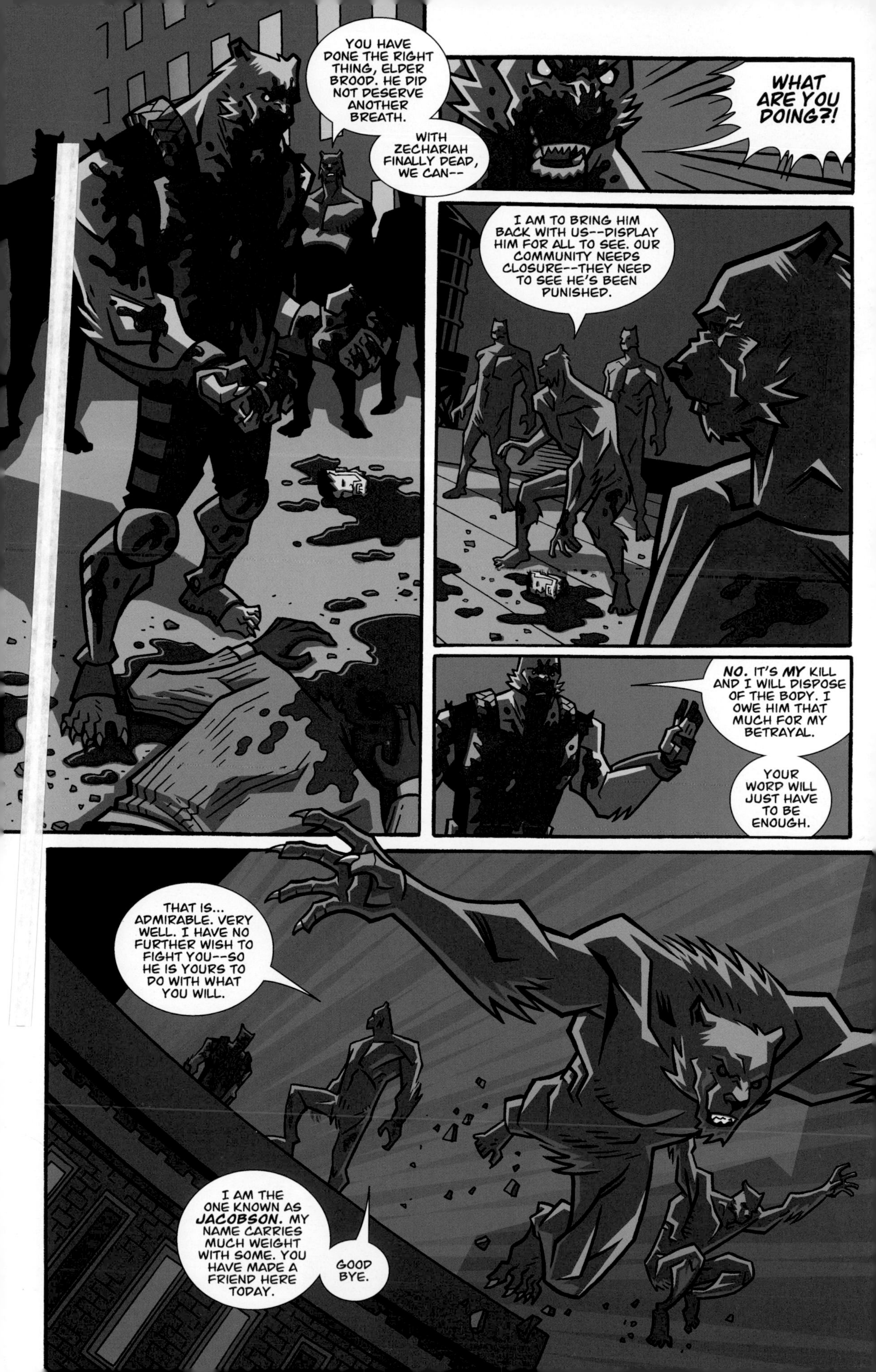
YOU HAVE DONE THE RIGHT THING, ELDER BROOD. HE DID NOT DESERVE ANOTHER BREATH.
WITH ZECHARIAH FINALLY DEAD, WE CAN--
WHAT ARE YOU DOING?!
I AM TO BRING HIM BACK WITH US--DISPLAY HIM FOR ALL TO SEE. OUR COMMUNITY NEEDS CLOSURE--THEY NEED TO SEE HE'S BEEN PUNISHED.
NO. IT'S MY KILL AND I WILL DISPOSE OF THE BODY. I OWE HIM THAT MUCH FOR MY BETRAYAL.
YOUR WORD WILL JUST HAVE TO BE ENOUGH.
THAT IS... ADMIRABLE. VERY WELL. I HAVE NO FURTHER WISH TO FIGHT YOU--SO HE IS YOURS TO DO WITH WHAT YOU WILL.
I AM THE ONE KNOWN AS JACOBSON. MY NAME CARRIES MUCH WEIGHT WITH SOME. YOU HAVE MADE A FRIEND HERE TODAY.
GOOD BYE.

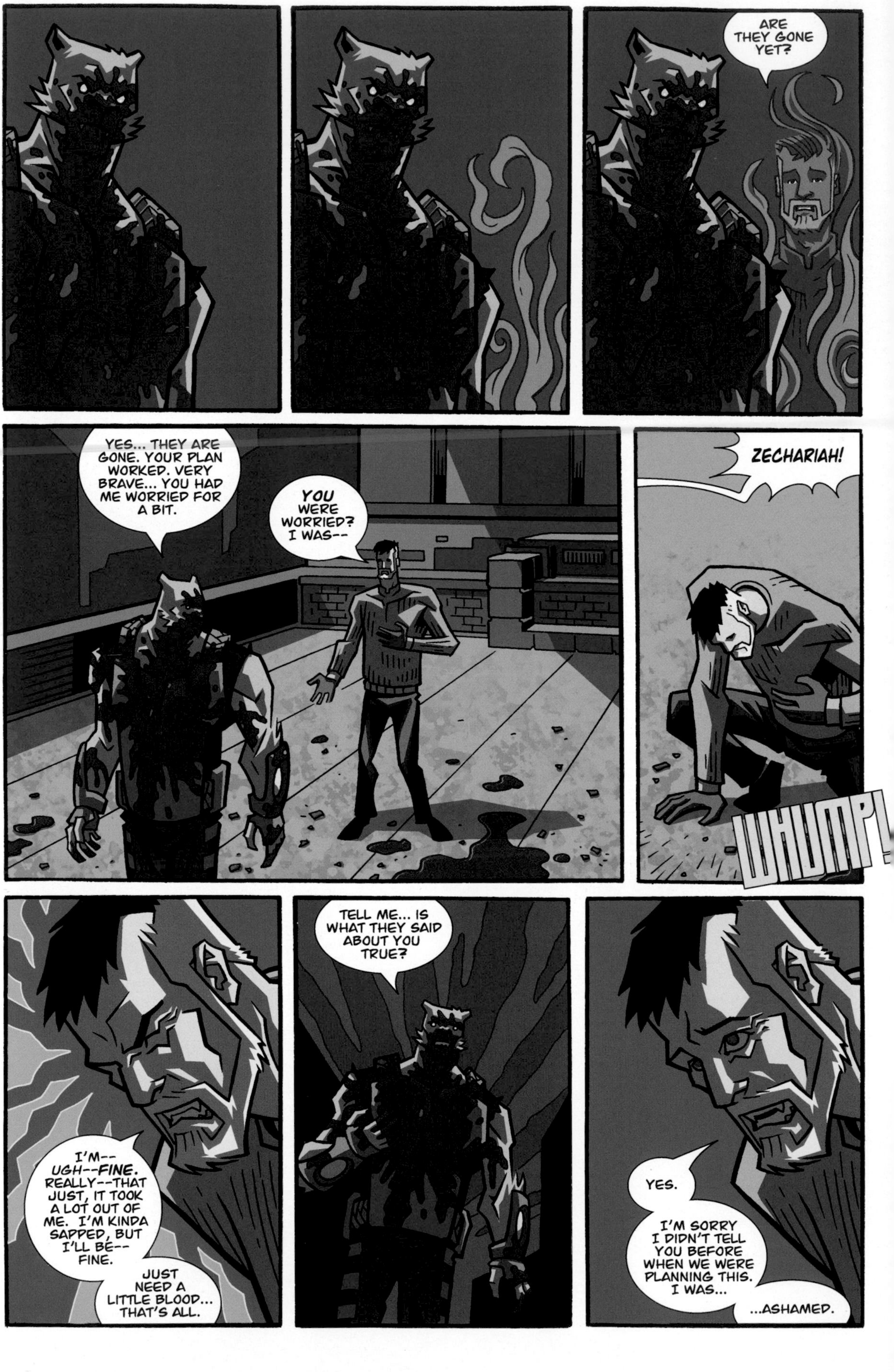
ARE THEY GONE YET?
YES... THEY ARE GONE. YOUR PLAN WORKED. VERY BRAVE... YOU HAD ME WORRIED FOR A BIT.
YOU WERE WORRIED? I WAS--
ZECHARIAH!
WHUMP!
I'M-- UGH--FINE. REALLY--THAT JUST, IT TOOK A LOT OUT OF ME. I'M KINDA SAPPED, BUT I'LL BE-- FINE.
JUST NEED A LITTLE BLOOD... THAT'S ALL.
TELL ME... IS WHAT THEY SAID ABOUT YOU TRUE?
YES.
I'M SORRY I DIDN'T TELL YOU BEFORE WHEN WE WERE PLANNING THIS. I WAS...
...ASHAMED.

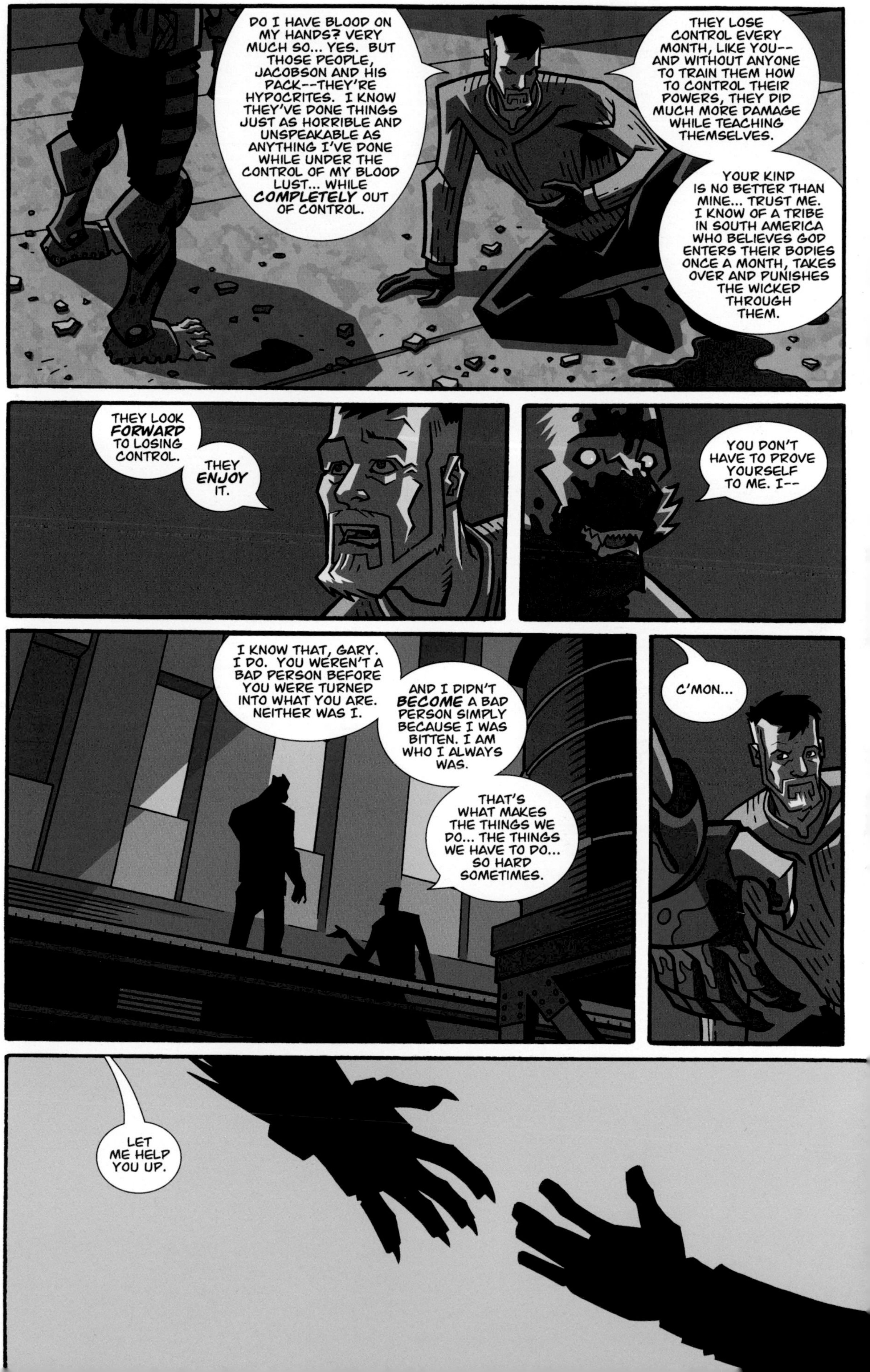
DO I HAVE BLOOD ON MY HANDS? VERY MUCH SO... YES. BUT THOSE PEOPLE, JACOBSON AND HIS PACK--THEY'RE HYPOCRITES. I KNOW THEY'VE DONE THINGS JUST AS HORRIBLE AND UNSPEAKABLE AS ANYTHING I'VE DONE WHILE UNDER THE CONTROL OF MY BLOOD LUST... WHILE COMPLETELY OUT OF CONTROL.
THEY LOSE CONTROL EVERY MONTH, LIKE YOU-- AND WITHOUT ANYONE TO TRAIN THEM HOW TO CONTROL THEIR POWERS, THEY DID MUCH MORE DAMAGE WHILE TEACHING THEMSELVES.
YOUR KIND IS NO BETTER THAN MINE... TRUST ME. I KNOW OF A TRIBE IN SOUTH AMERICA WHO BELIEVES GOD ENTERS THEIR BODIES ONCE A MONTH, TAKES OVER AND PUNISHES THE WICKED THROUGH THEM.
THEY LOOK FORWARD TO LOSING CONTROL.
THEY ENJOY IT.
YOU DON'T HAVE TO PROVE YOURSELF TO ME. I--
I KNOW THAT, GARY. I DO. YOU WEREN'T A BAD PERSON BEFORE YOU WERE TURNED INTO WHAT YOU ARE. NEITHER WAS I.
AND I DIDN'T BECOME A BAD PERSON SIMPLY BECAUSE I WAS BITTEN. I AM WHO I ALWAYS WAS.
THAT'S WHAT MAKES THE THINGS WE DO... THE THINGS WE HAVE TO DO... SO HARD SOMETIMES.
C'MON...
LET ME HELP YOU UP.

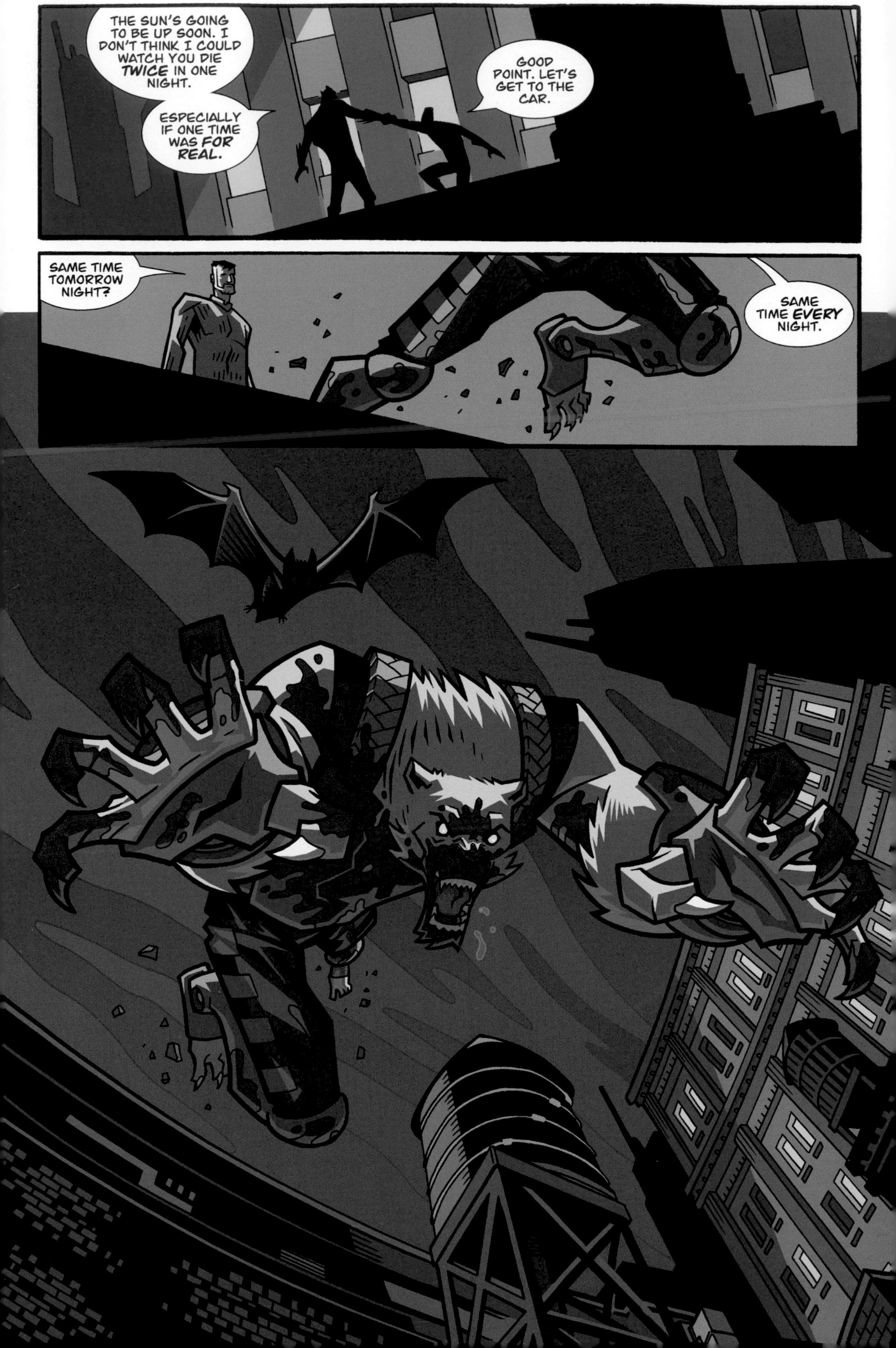
THE SUN'S GOING TO BE UP SOON. I DON'T THINK I COULD WATCH YOU DIE TWICE IN ONE NIGHT.
ESPECIALLY IF ONE TIME WAS FOR REAL.
GOOD POINT. LET'S GET TO THE CAR.
SAME TIME TOMORROW NIGHT?
SAME TIME EVERY NIGHT.

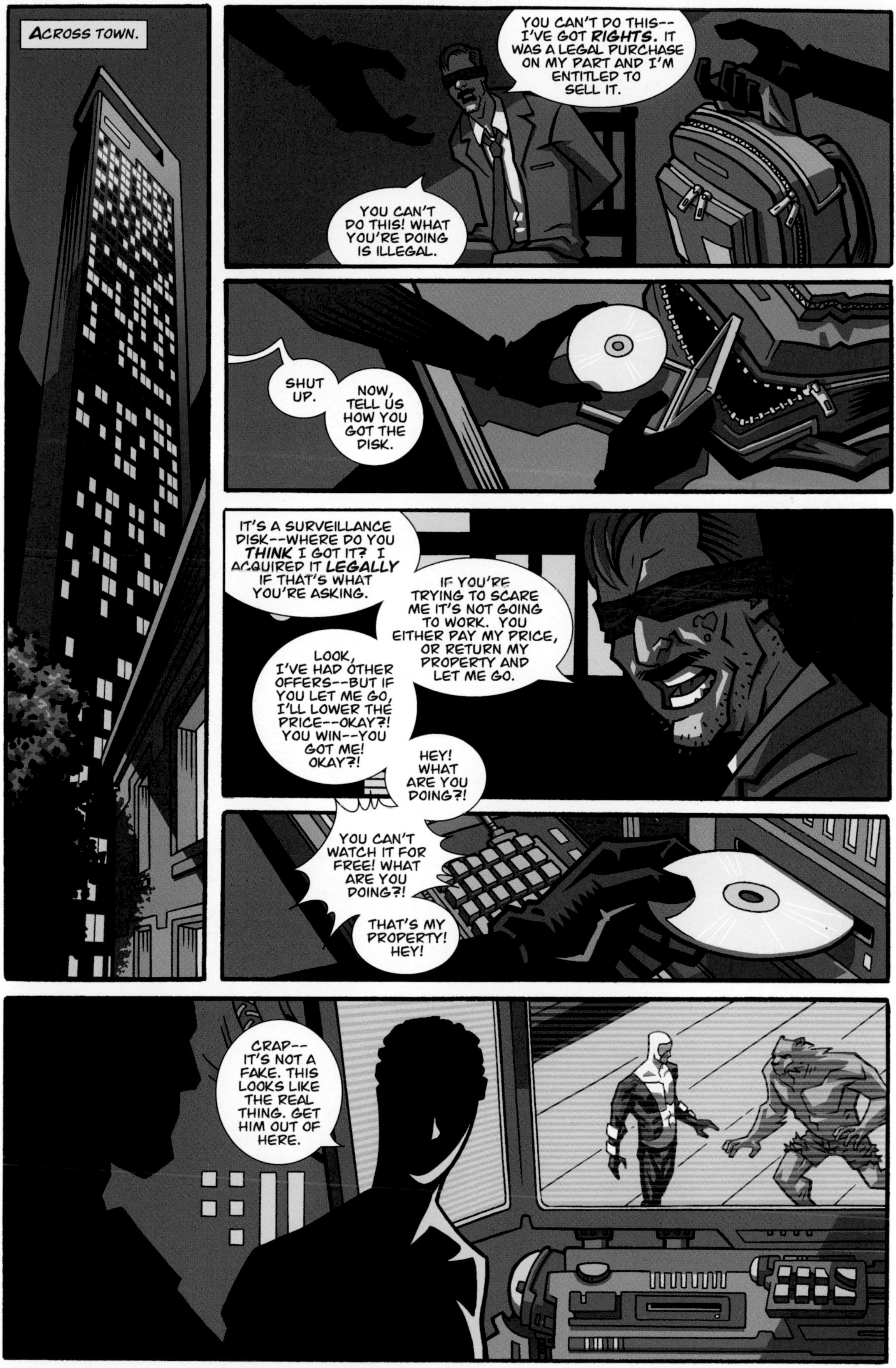

ACROSS TOWN.
YOU CAN'T DO THIS--I'VE GOT RIGHTS. IT WAS A LEGAL PURCHASE ON MY PART AND I'M ENTITLED TO SELL IT.
YOU CAN'T DO THIS! WHAT YOU'RE DOING IS ILLEGAL.
SHUT UP.
NOW, TELL US HOW YOU GOT THE DISK.
IT'S A SURVEILLANCE DISK--WHERE DO YOU THINK I GOT IT? I ACQUIRED IT LEGALLY IF THAT'S WHAT YOU'RE ASKING.
IF YOU'RE TRYING TO SCARE ME IT'S NOT GOING TO WORK. YOU EITHER PAY MY PRICE, OR RETURN MY PROPERTY AND LET ME GO.
LOOK, I'VE HAD OTHER OFFERS--BUT IF YOU LET ME GO, I'LL LOWER THE PRICE--OKAY?! YOU WIN--YOU GOT ME! OKAY?!
HEY! WHAT ARE YOU DOING?!
YOU CAN'T WATCH IT FOR FREE! WHAT ARE YOU DOING?!
THAT'S MY PROPERTY! HEY!
CRAP--IT'S NOT A FAKE. THIS LOOKS LIKE THE REAL THING. GET HIM OUT OF HERE.

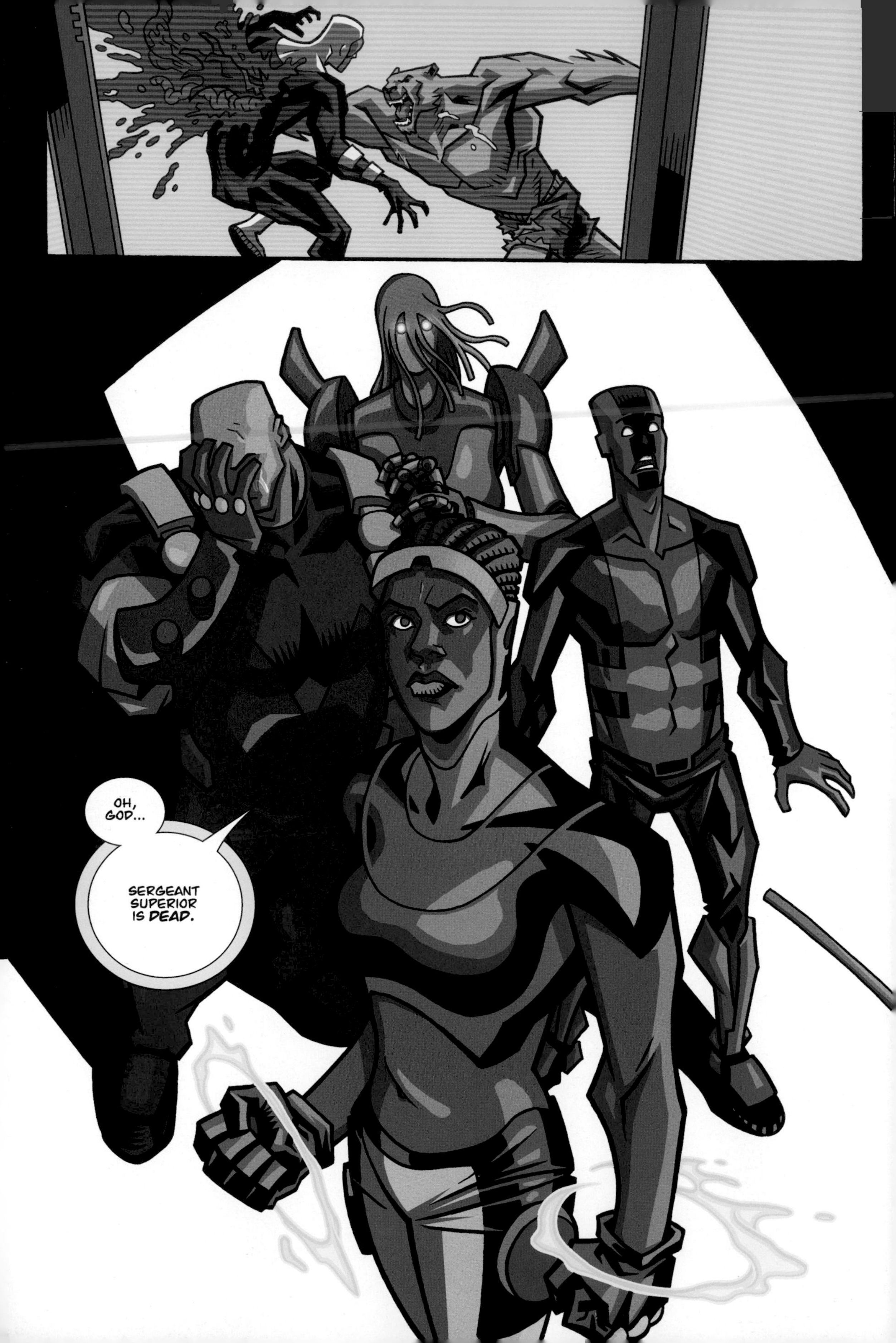
OH, GOD...
SERGEANT SUPERIOR IS DEAD.

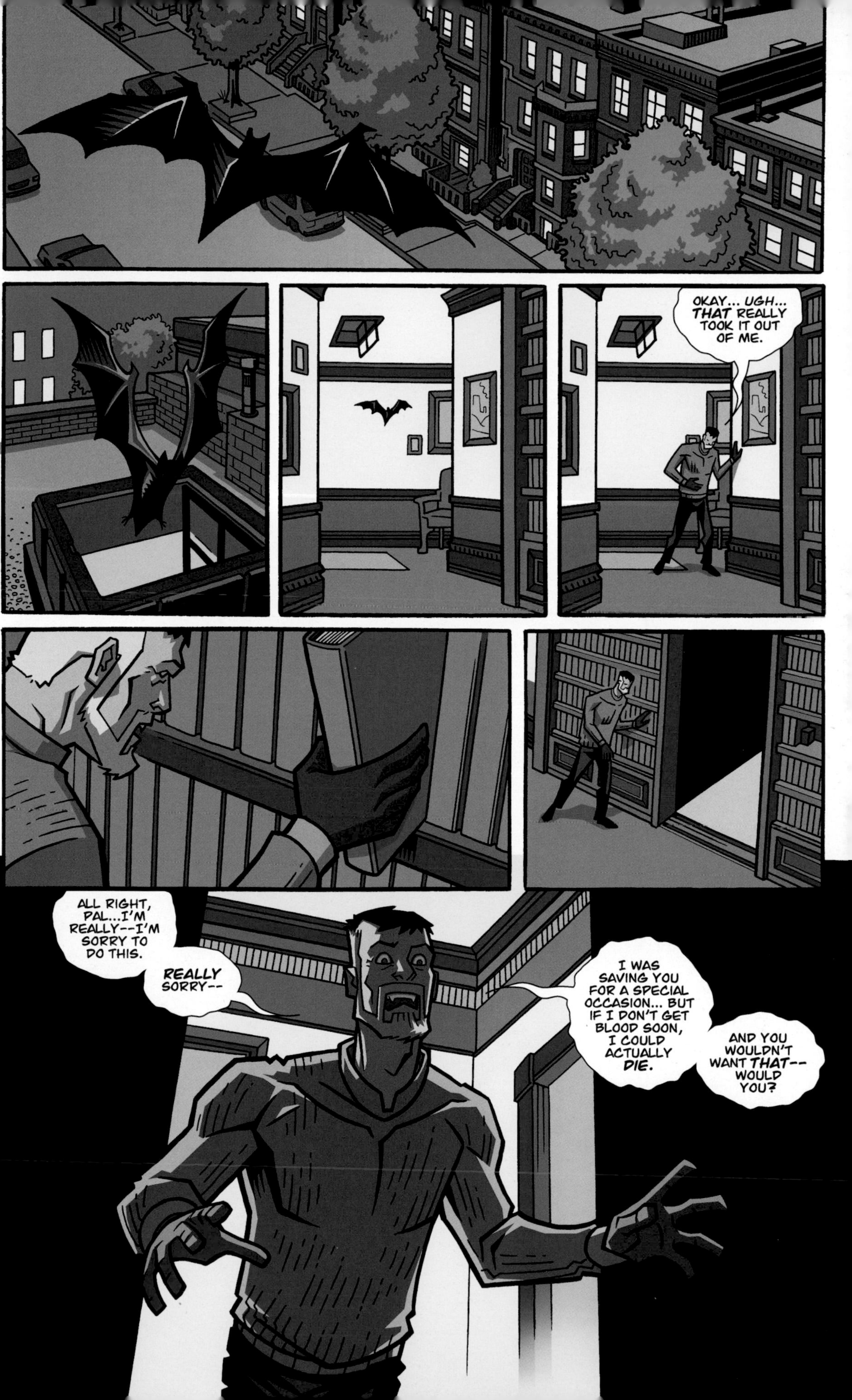
OKAY... UGH... THAT REALLY TOOK IT OUT OF ME.
ALL RIGHT, PAL...I'M REALLY--I'M SORRY TO DO THIS.
REALLY SORRY--
I WAS SAVING YOU FOR A SPECIAL OCCASION... BUT IF I DON'T GET BLOOD SOON, I COULD ACTUALLY DIE.
AND YOU WOULDN'T WANT THAT--WOULD YOU?

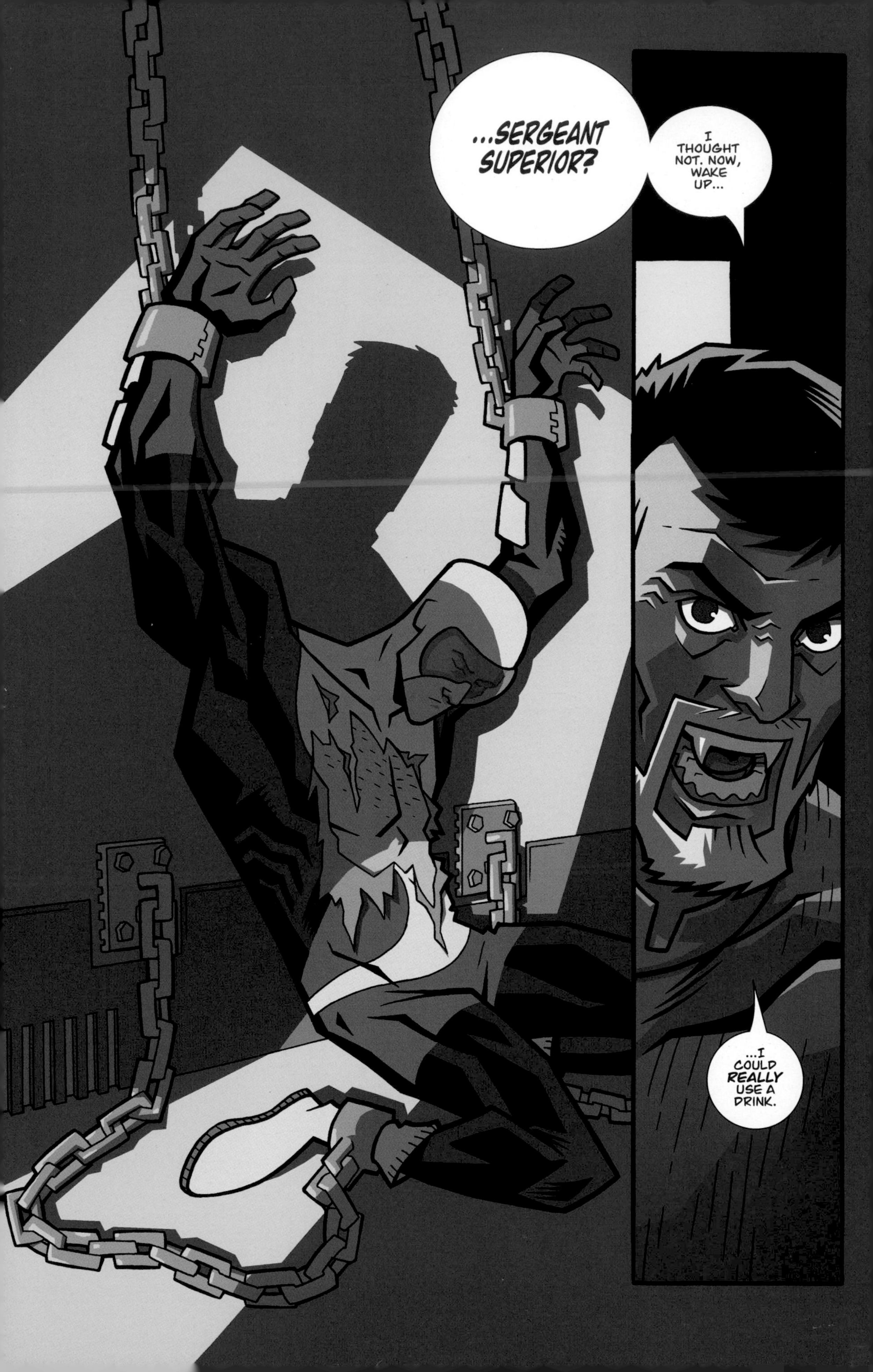
...SERGEANT SUPERIOR?
I THOUGHT NOT. NOW, WAKE UP...
...I COULD **REALLY** USE A DRINK.

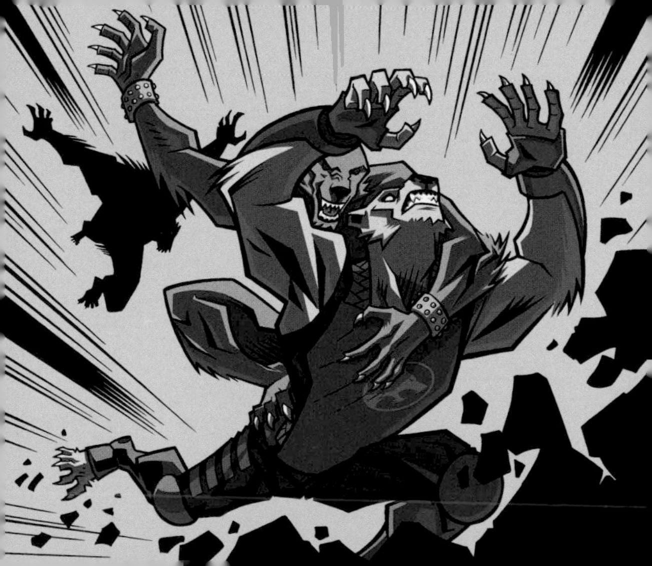

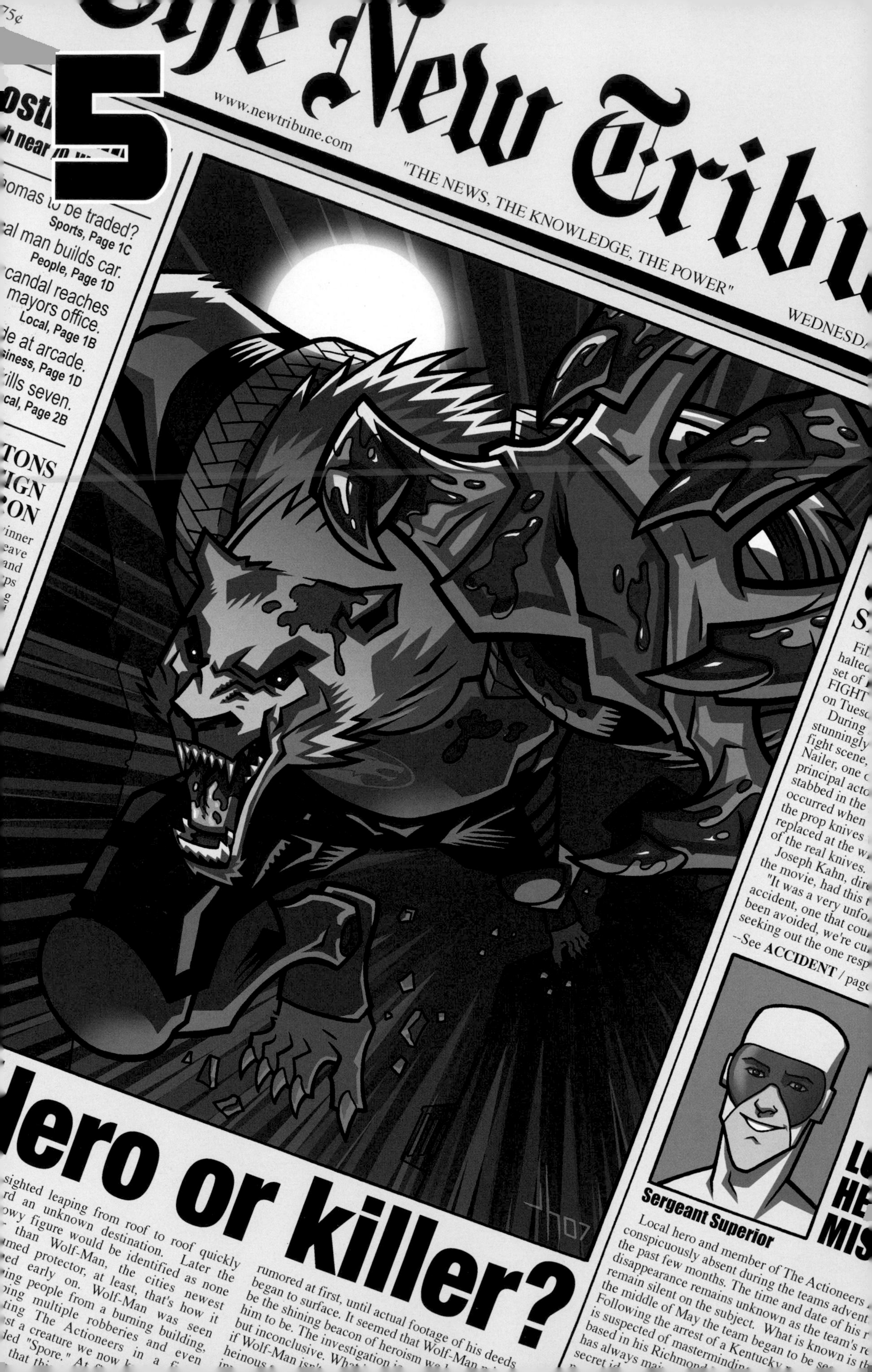
5
75¢
The New Tribu
www.newtribune.com
"THE NEWS, THE KNOWLEDGE, THE POWER"
WEDNESDA
omas to be traded?
Sports, Page 1C
al man builds car.
People, Page 1D
candal reaches
mayors office.
Local, Page 1B
de at arcade.
siness, Page 1D
ills seven.
cal, Page 2B
TONS
IGN
ON
Hero or killer?
sighted leaping from roof to roof quickly
rd an unknown destination. Later the
owy figure would be identified as none
than Wolf-Man, the cities newest
med protector, at least, that's how it
ed early on. Wolf-Man was seen
ing people from a burning building,
ping multiple robberies and even
ting The Actioneers in a
st a creature we now
led "Spore."
rumored at first, until actual footage of his deeds
began to surface. It seemed that Wolf-Man
be the shining beacon of heroism
him to be. The investigation
but inconclusive.
if Wolf-Man isn't
halted
set of
FIGHT
on Tuesd
During
stunningly
fight scene,
Nailer, one o
principal acto
stabbed in the
occurred when
the prop knives
replaced at the w
of the real knives.
Joseph Kahn, dire
the movie, had this
"It was a very unfo
accident, one that cou
been avoided, we're cu
seeking out the one resp
--See ACCIDENT / page
Sergeant Superior
Local hero and member of The Actioneers
conspicuously absent during the teams advent
the past few months. The time and date of his
disappearance remains unknown as the team's
remain silent on the subject. What is known is th
the middle of May the team began to be
Following the arrest of a Kentucky
is suspected of masterminding
based in his Richmond
has always
LO
HE
MIS

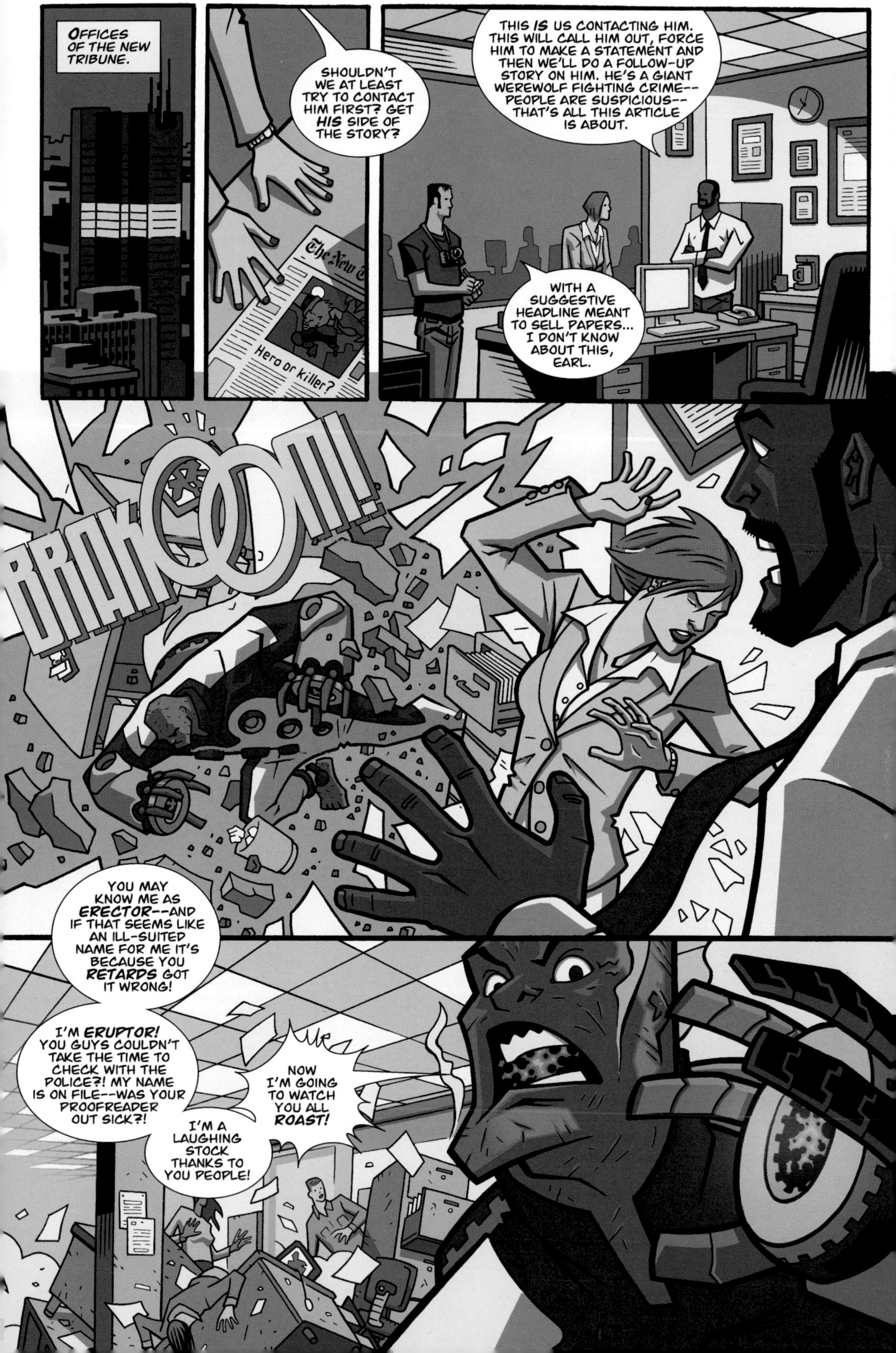
OFFICES OF THE NEW TRIBUNE.
SHOULDN'T WE AT LEAST TRY TO CONTACT HIM FIRST? GET HIS SIDE OF THE STORY?
The New
Hero or killer?
THIS IS US CONTACTING HIM. THIS WILL CALL HIM OUT, FORCE HIM TO MAKE A STATEMENT AND THEN WE'LL DO A FOLLOW-UP STORY ON HIM. HE'S A GIANT WEREWOLF FIGHTING CRIME--PEOPLE ARE SUSPICIOUS--THAT'S ALL THIS ARTICLE IS ABOUT.
WITH A SUGGESTIVE HEADLINE MEANT TO SELL PAPERS... I DON'T KNOW ABOUT THIS, EARL.
BROKOOOM!!
YOU MAY KNOW ME AS ERECTOR--AND IF THAT SEEMS LIKE AN ILL-SUITED NAME FOR ME IT'S BECAUSE YOU RETARDS GOT IT WRONG!
I'M ERUPTOR! YOU GUYS COULDN'T TAKE THE TIME TO CHECK WITH THE POLICE?! MY NAME IS ON FILE--WAS YOUR PROOFREADER OUT SICK?!
I'M A LAUGHING STOCK THANKS TO YOU PEOPLE!
NOW I'M GOING TO WATCH YOU ALL ROAST!

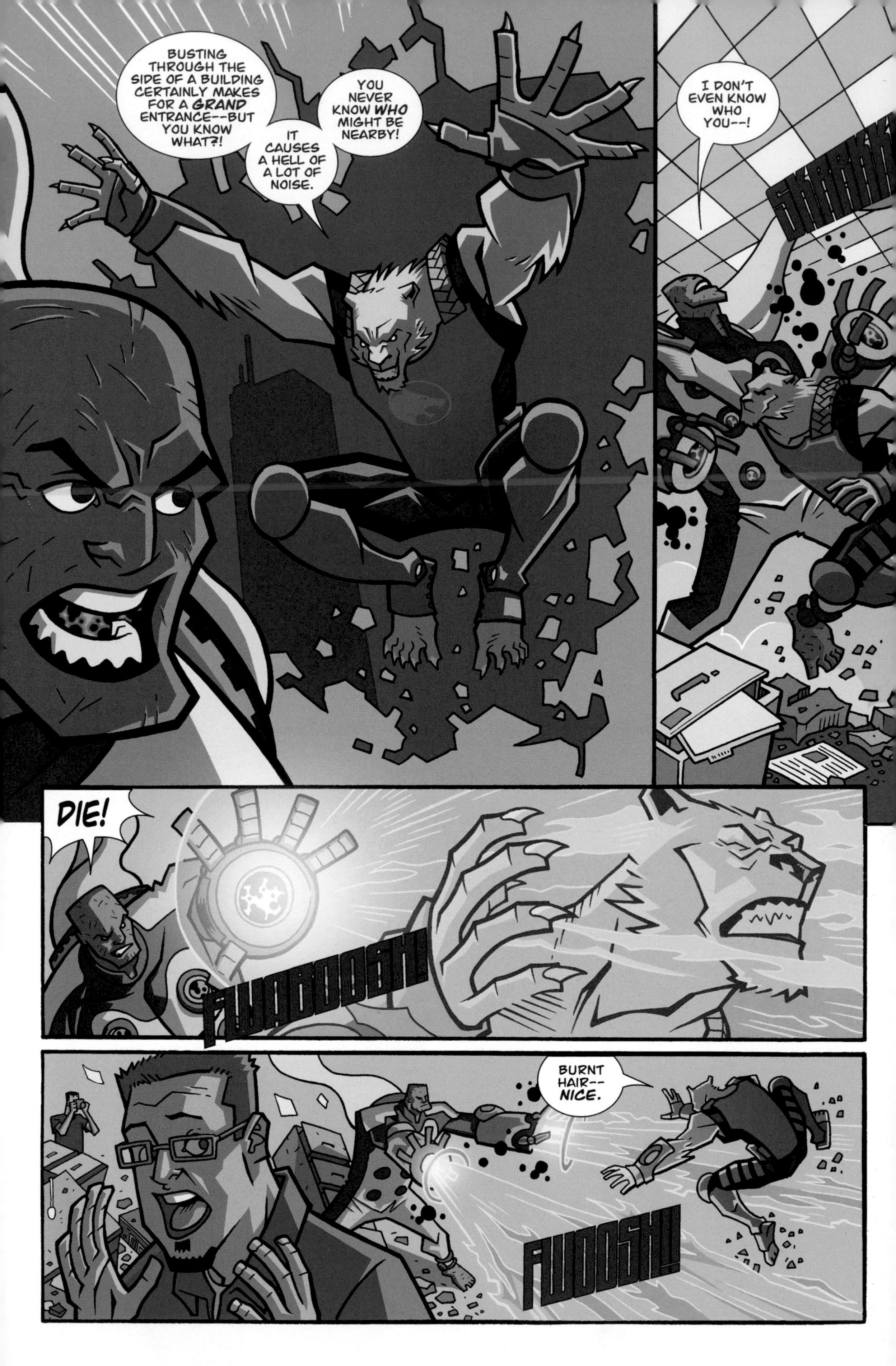
BUSTING THROUGH THE SIDE OF A BUILDING CERTAINLY MAKES FOR A GRAND ENTRANCE--BUT YOU KNOW WHAT?!
IT CAUSES A HELL OF A LOT OF NOISE.
YOU NEVER KNOW WHO MIGHT BE NEARBY!
I DON'T EVEN KNOW WHO YOU--!
DIE!
FWABOOSH!
BURNT HAIR-- NICE.
FWOOSH!

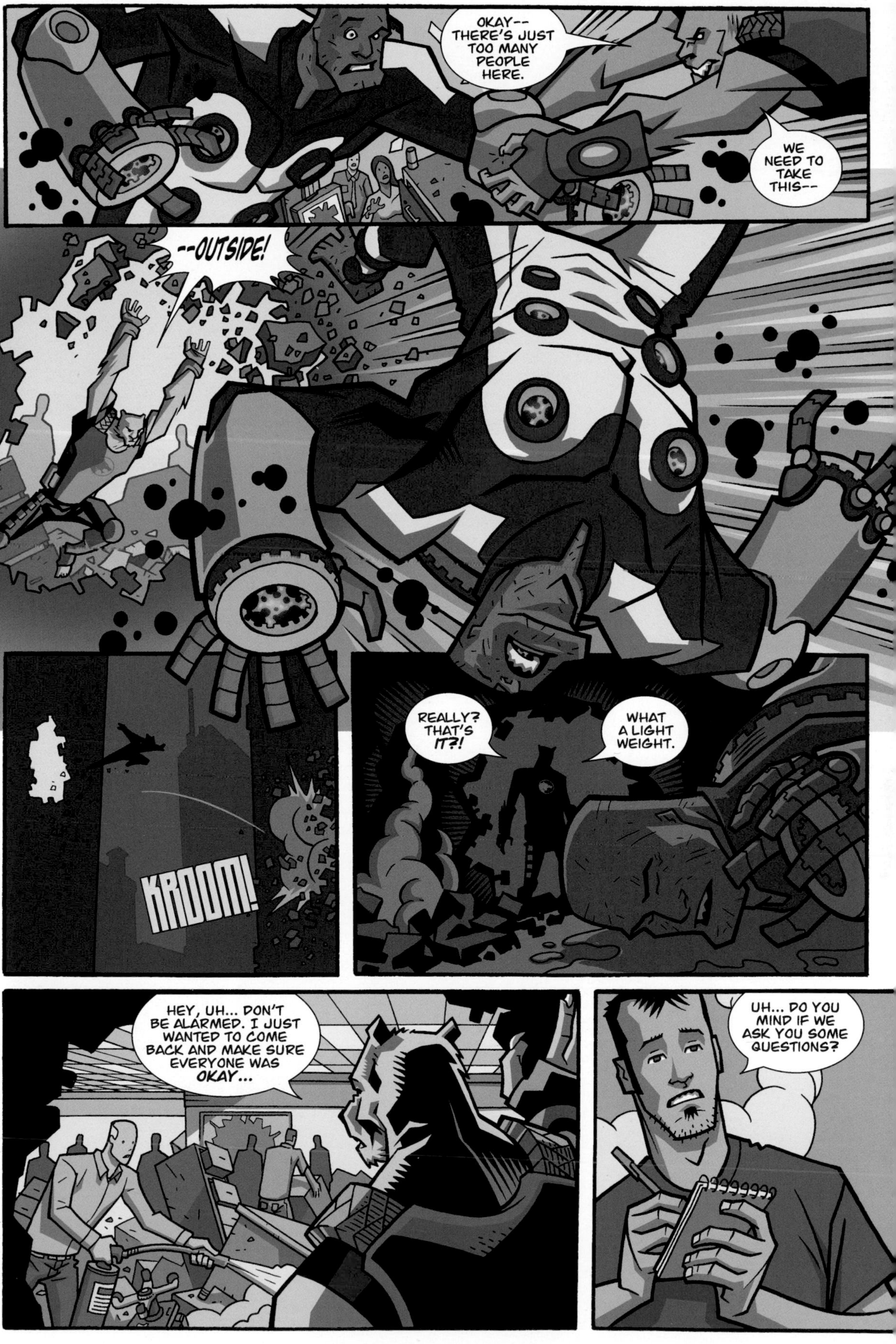

OKAY-- THERE'S JUST TOO MANY PEOPLE HERE.
WE NEED TO TAKE THIS--
--OUTSIDE!
KROOM!
REALLY? THAT'S IT?!
WHAT A LIGHT WEIGHT.
HEY, UH... DON'T BE ALARMED. I JUST WANTED TO COME BACK AND MAKE SURE EVERYONE WAS OKAY...
UH... DO YOU MIND IF WE ASK YOU SOME QUESTIONS?

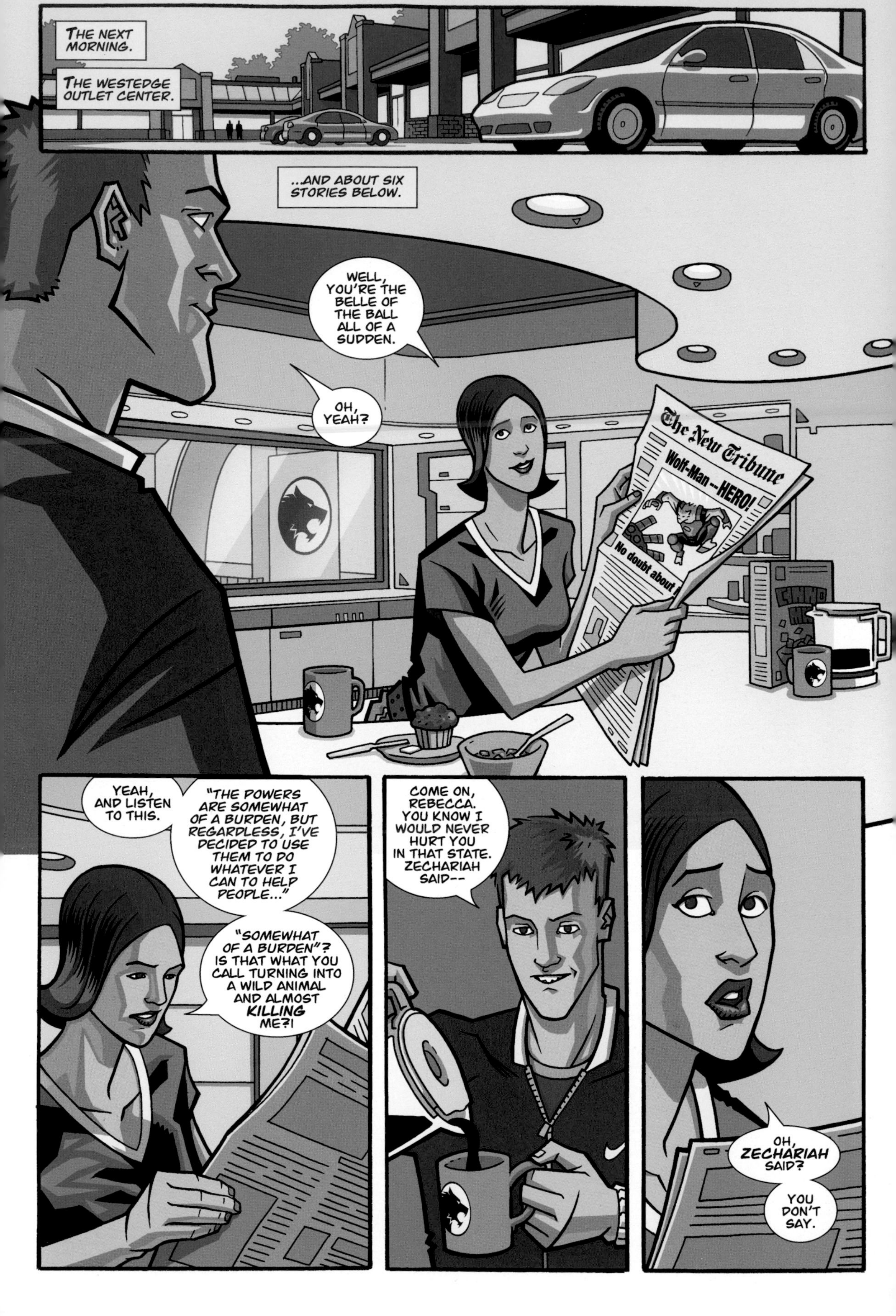
THE NEXT MORNING.
THE WESTEDGE OUTLET CENTER.
...AND ABOUT SIX STORIES BELOW.
WELL, YOU'RE THE BELLE OF THE BALL ALL OF A SUDDEN.
OH, YEAH?
The New Tribune
Wolf-Man --HERO!
No doubt about
YEAH, AND LISTEN TO THIS.
"THE POWERS ARE SOMEWHAT OF A BURDEN, BUT REGARDLESS, I'VE DECIDED TO USE THEM TO DO WHATEVER I CAN TO HELP PEOPLE..."
"SOMEWHAT OF A BURDEN"? IS THAT WHAT YOU CALL TURNING INTO A WILD ANIMAL AND ALMOST KILLING ME?!
COME ON, REBECCA. YOU KNOW I WOULD NEVER HURT YOU IN THAT STATE. ZECHARIAH SAID--
OH, ZECHARIAH SAID?
YOU DON'T SAY.

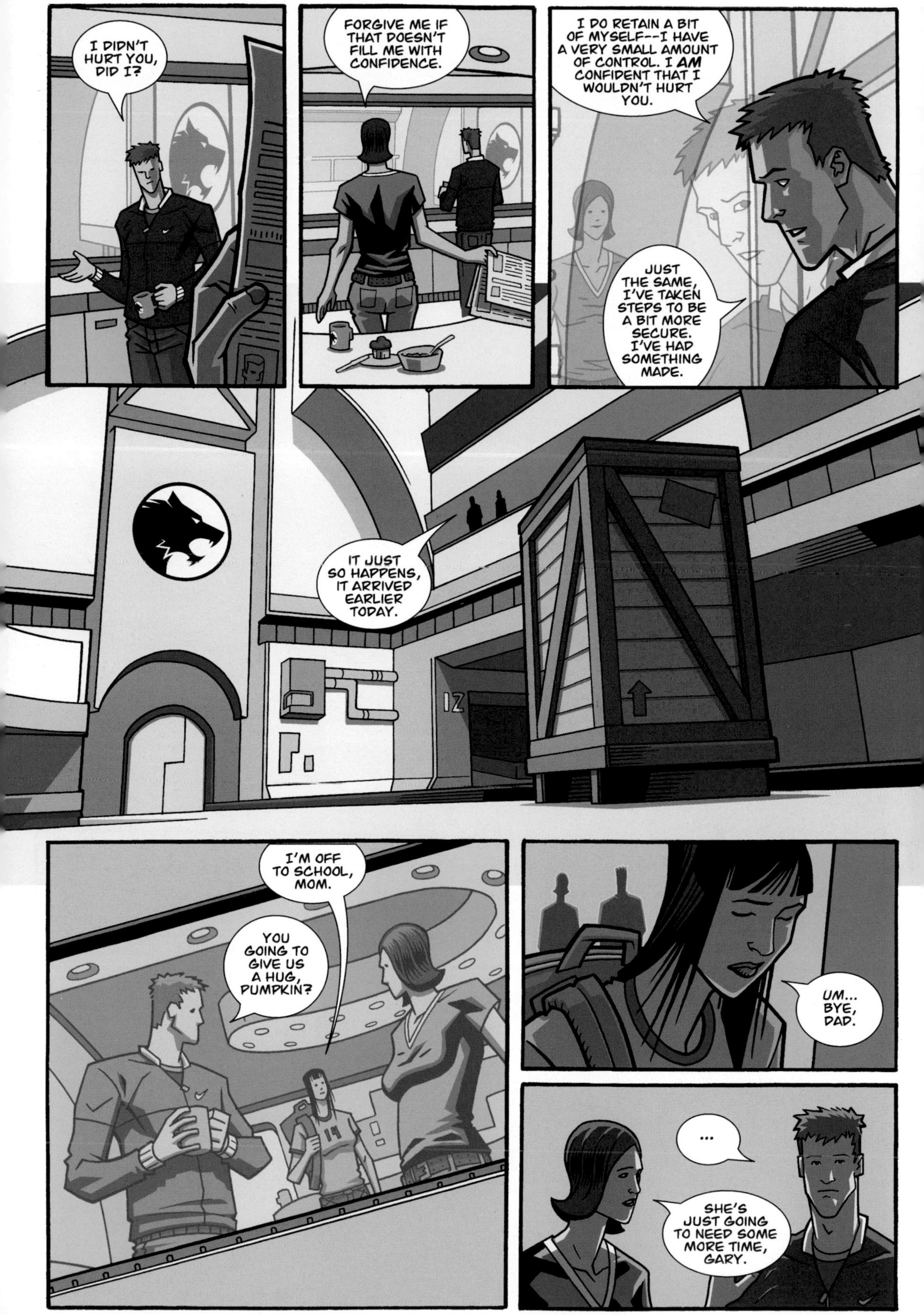
I DIDN'T HURT YOU, DID I?
FORGIVE ME IF THAT DOESN'T FILL ME WITH CONFIDENCE.
I DO RETAIN A BIT OF MYSELF--I HAVE A VERY SMALL AMOUNT OF CONTROL. I AM CONFIDENT THAT I WOULDN'T HURT YOU.
JUST THE SAME, I'VE TAKEN STEPS TO BE A BIT MORE SECURE. I'VE HAD SOMETHING MADE.
IT JUST SO HAPPENS, IT ARRIVED EARLIER TODAY.
12
I'M OFF TO SCHOOL, MOM.
YOU GOING TO GIVE US A HUG, PUMPKIN?
UM... BYE, DAD.
...
SHE'S JUST GOING TO NEED SOME MORE TIME, GARY.

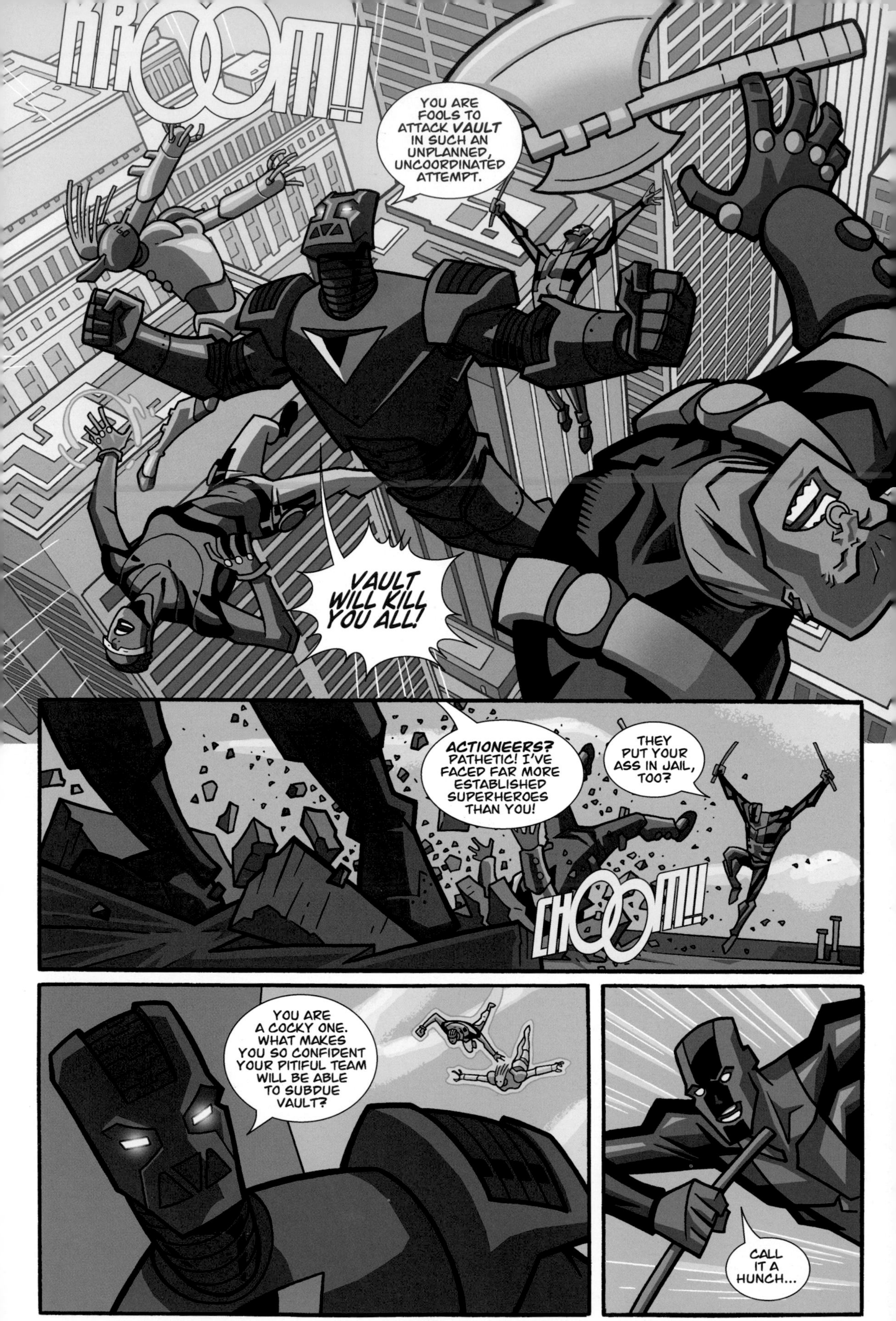
KROOM!!
YOU ARE FOOLS TO ATTACK VAULT IN SUCH AN UNPLANNED, UNCOORDINATED ATTEMPT.
VAULT WILL KILL YOU ALL!
ACTIONEERS? PATHETIC! I'VE FACED FAR MORE ESTABLISHED SUPERHEROES THAN YOU!
THEY PUT YOUR ASS IN JAIL, TOO?
CHOOM!!
YOU ARE A COCKY ONE. WHAT MAKES YOU SO CONFIDENT YOUR PITIFUL TEAM WILL BE ABLE TO SUBDUE VAULT?
CALL IT A HUNCH...

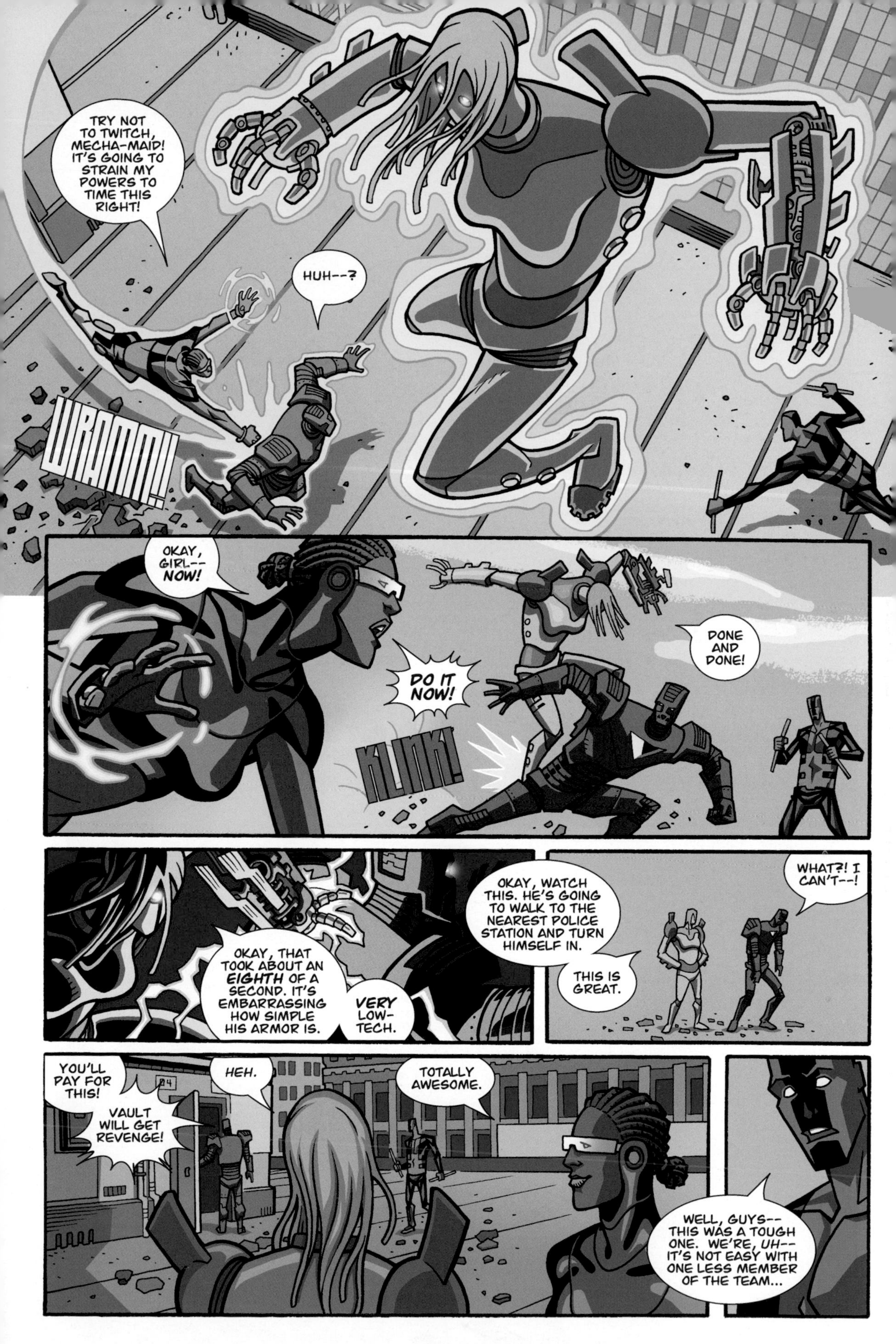

TRY NOT TO TWITCH, MECHA-MAID! IT'S GOING TO STRAIN MY POWERS TO TIME THIS RIGHT!
HUH--?
WRAMM!
OKAY, GIRL-- NOW!
DO IT NOW!
DONE AND DONE!
KLINK!
OKAY, THAT TOOK ABOUT AN EIGHTH OF A SECOND. IT'S EMBARRASSING HOW SIMPLE HIS ARMOR IS.
VERY LOW-TECH.
OKAY, WATCH THIS. HE'S GOING TO WALK TO THE NEAREST POLICE STATION AND TURN HIMSELF IN.
THIS IS GREAT.
WHAT?! I CAN'T--!
YOU'LL PAY FOR THIS!
VAULT WILL GET REVENGE!
HEH.
TOTALLY AWESOME.
WELL, GUYS-- THIS WAS A TOUGH ONE. WE'RE, UH-- IT'S NOT EASY WITH ONE LESS MEMBER OF THE TEAM...

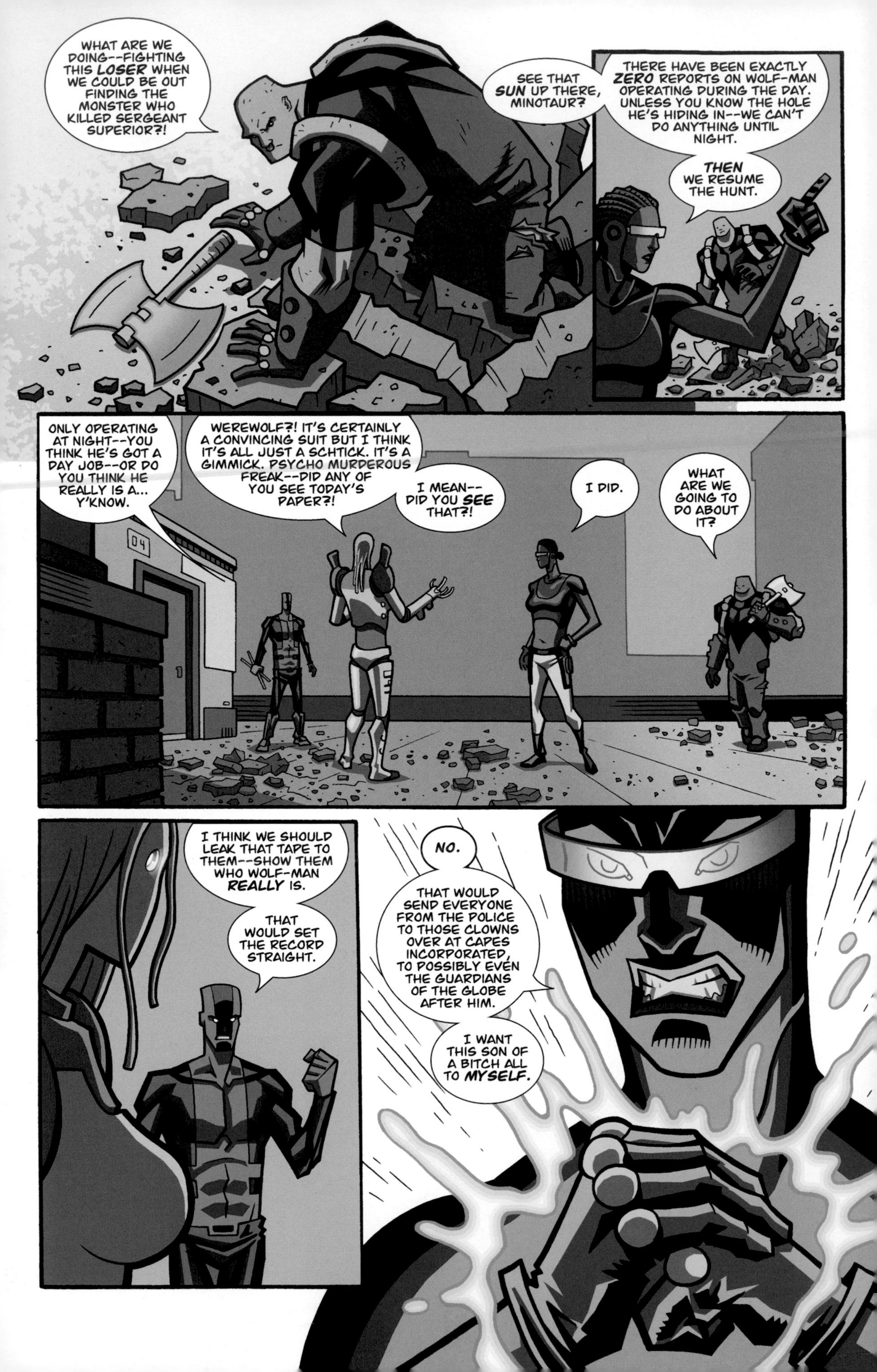
WHAT ARE WE DOING--FIGHTING THIS LOSER WHEN WE COULD BE OUT FINDING THE MONSTER WHO KILLED SERGEANT SUPERIOR?!
SEE THAT SUN UP THERE, MINOTAUR?
THERE HAVE BEEN EXACTLY ZERO REPORTS ON WOLF-MAN OPERATING DURING THE DAY. UNLESS YOU KNOW THE HOLE HE'S HIDING IN--WE CAN'T DO ANYTHING UNTIL NIGHT.
THEN WE RESUME THE HUNT.
ONLY OPERATING AT NIGHT--YOU THINK HE'S GOT A DAY JOB--OR DO YOU THINK HE REALLY IS A... Y'KNOW.
WEREWOLF?! IT'S CERTAINLY A CONVINCING SUIT BUT I THINK IT'S ALL JUST A SCHTICK. IT'S A GIMMICK. PSYCHO MURDEROUS FREAK--DID ANY OF YOU SEE TODAY'S PAPER?!
I MEAN-- DID YOU SEE THAT?!
I DID.
WHAT ARE WE GOING TO DO ABOUT IT?
04
I THINK WE SHOULD LEAK THAT TAPE TO THEM--SHOW THEM WHO WOLF-MAN REALLY IS.
THAT WOULD SET THE RECORD STRAIGHT.
NO.
THAT WOULD SEND EVERYONE FROM THE POLICE TO THOSE CLOWNS OVER AT CAPES INCORPORATED, TO POSSIBLY EVEN THE GUARDIANS OF THE GLOBE AFTER HIM.
I WANT THIS SON OF A BITCH ALL TO MYSELF.

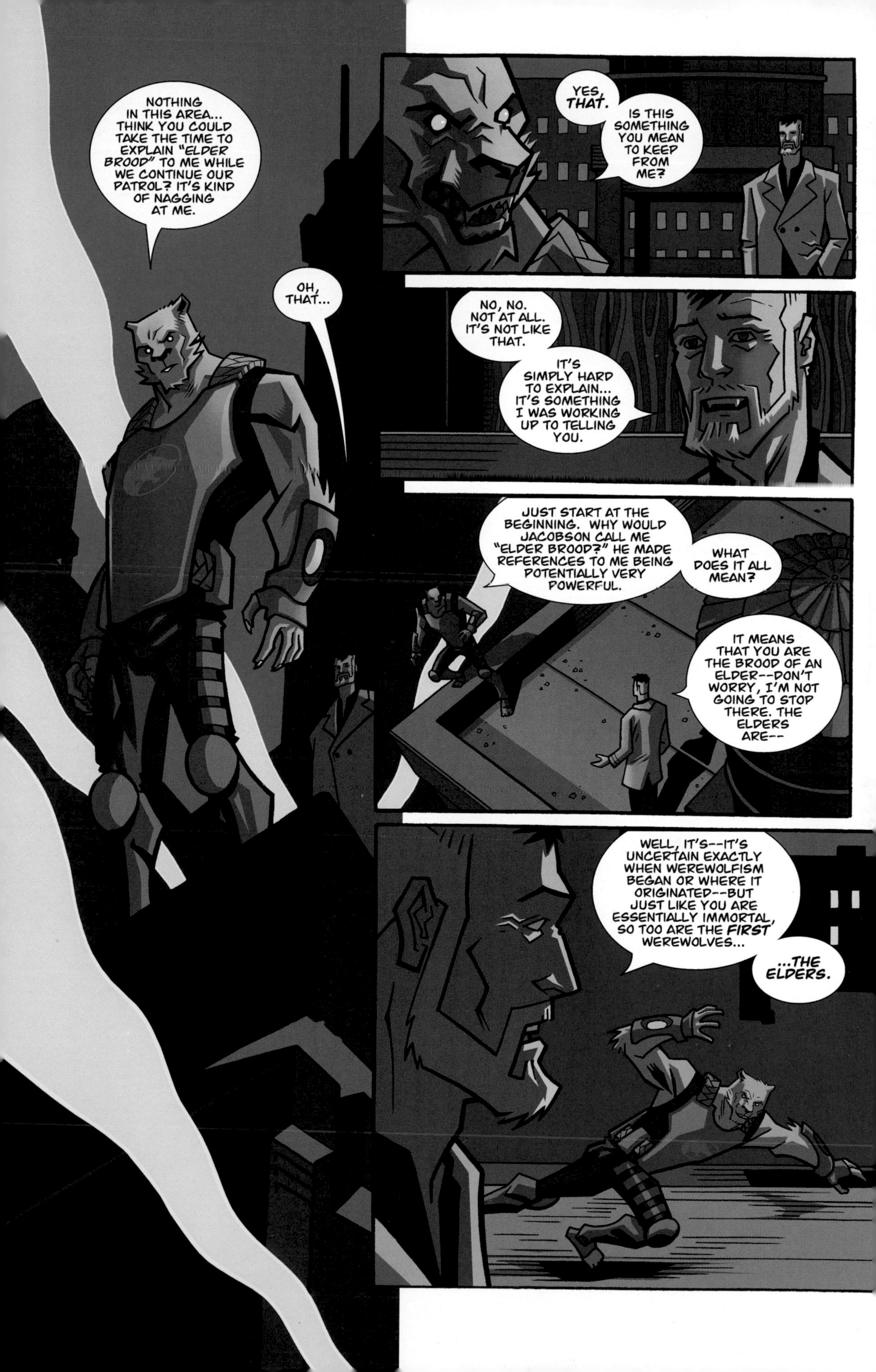
NOTHING IN THIS AREA... THINK YOU COULD TAKE THE TIME TO EXPLAIN "ELDER BROOD" TO ME WHILE WE CONTINUE OUR PATROL? IT'S KIND OF NAGGING AT ME.
OH, THAT...
YES, THAT.
IS THIS SOMETHING YOU MEAN TO KEEP FROM ME?
NO, NO. NOT AT ALL. IT'S NOT LIKE THAT.
IT'S SIMPLY HARD TO EXPLAIN... IT'S SOMETHING I WAS WORKING UP TO TELLING YOU.
JUST START AT THE BEGINNING. WHY WOULD JACOBSON CALL ME "ELDER BROOD?" HE MADE REFERENCES TO ME BEING POTENTIALLY VERY POWERFUL.
WHAT DOES IT ALL MEAN?
IT MEANS THAT YOU ARE THE BROOD OF AN ELDER--DON'T WORRY, I'M NOT GOING TO STOP THERE. THE ELDERS ARE--
WELL, IT'S--IT'S UNCERTAIN EXACTLY WHEN WEREWOLFISM BEGAN OR WHERE IT ORIGINATED--BUT JUST LIKE YOU ARE ESSENTIALLY IMMORTAL, SO TOO ARE THE FIRST WEREWOLVES...
...THE ELDERS.

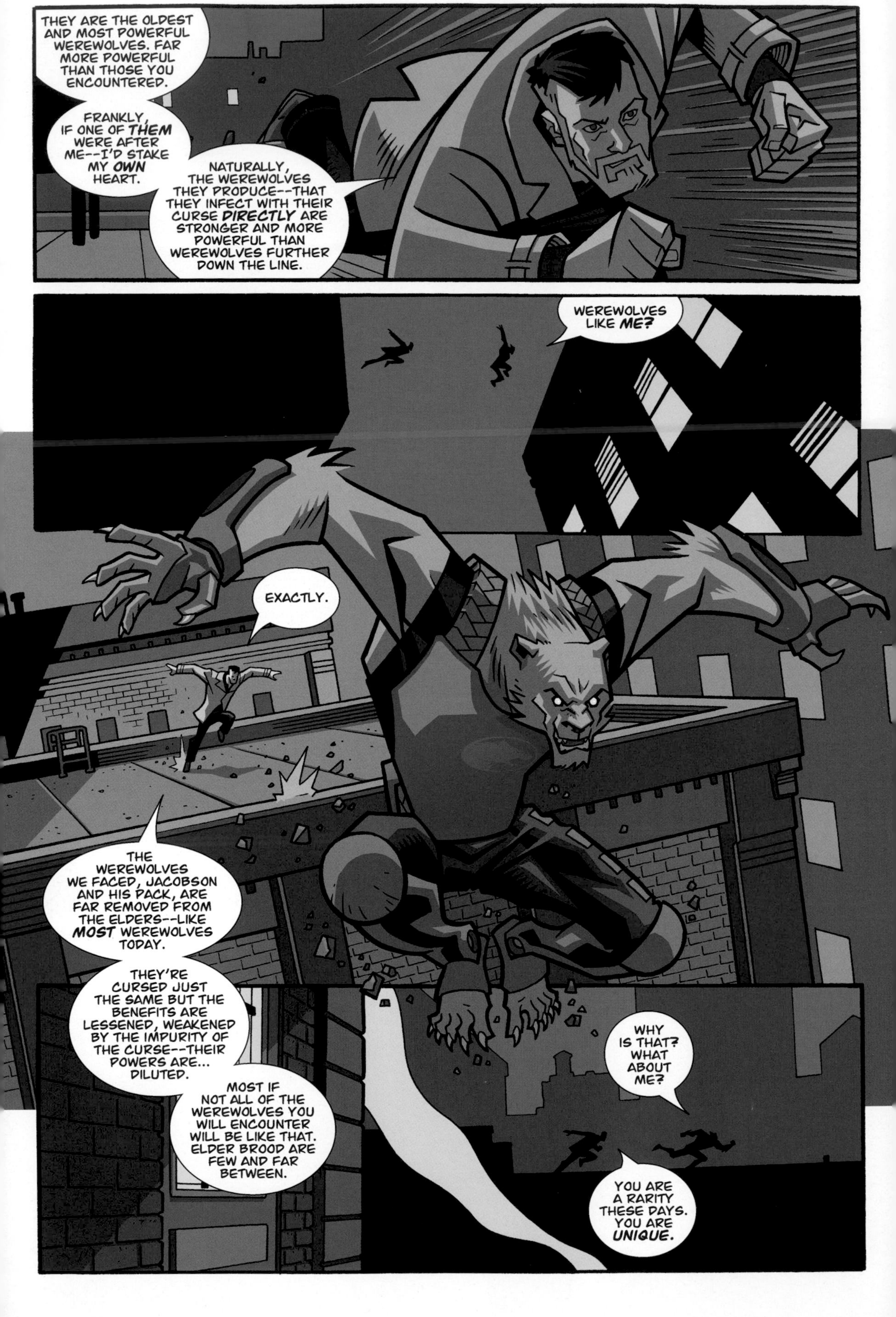
THEY ARE THE OLDEST AND MOST POWERFUL WEREWOLVES. FAR MORE POWERFUL THAN THOSE YOU ENCOUNTERED.
FRANKLY, IF ONE OF THEM WERE AFTER ME--I'D STAKE MY OWN HEART.
NATURALLY, THE WEREWOLVES THEY PRODUCE--THAT THEY INFECT WITH THEIR CURSE DIRECTLY ARE STRONGER AND MORE POWERFUL THAN WEREWOLVES FURTHER DOWN THE LINE.
WEREWOLVES LIKE ME?
EXACTLY.
THE WEREWOLVES WE FACED, JACOBSON AND HIS PACK, ARE FAR REMOVED FROM THE ELDERS--LIKE MOST WEREWOLVES TODAY.
THEY'RE CURSED JUST THE SAME BUT THE BENEFITS ARE LESSENED, WEAKENED BY THE IMPURITY OF THE CURSE--THEIR POWERS ARE... DILUTED.
MOST IF NOT ALL OF THE WEREWOLVES YOU WILL ENCOUNTER WILL BE LIKE THAT. ELDER BROOD ARE FEW AND FAR BETWEEN.
WHY IS THAT? WHAT ABOUT ME?
YOU ARE A RARITY THESE DAYS. YOU ARE UNIQUE.

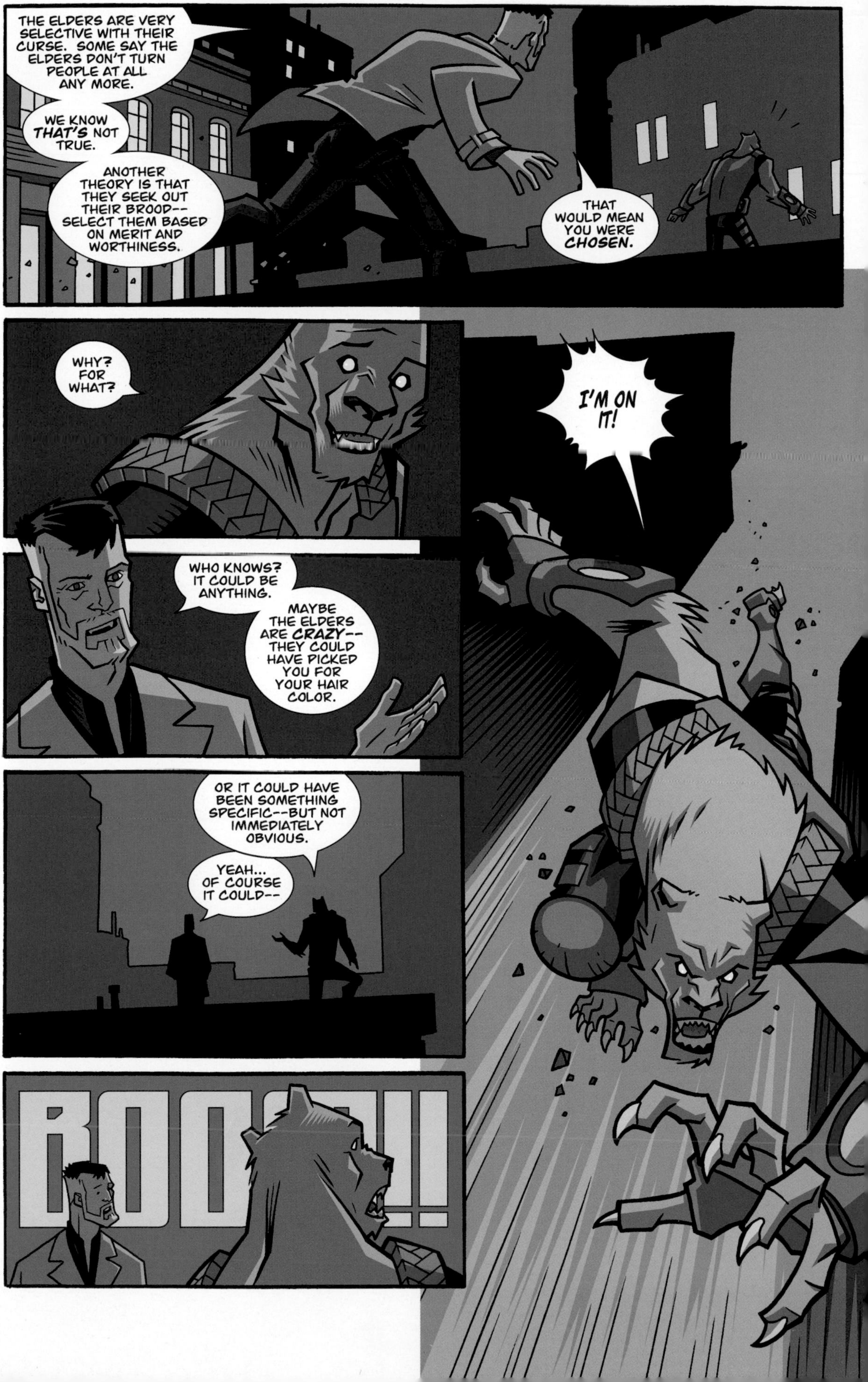
THE ELDERS ARE VERY SELECTIVE WITH THEIR CURSE. SOME SAY THE ELDERS DON'T TURN PEOPLE AT ALL ANY MORE.
WE KNOW THAT'S NOT TRUE.
ANOTHER THEORY IS THAT THEY SEEK OUT THEIR BROOD--SELECT THEM BASED ON MERIT AND WORTHINESS.
THAT WOULD MEAN YOU WERE CHOSEN.
WHY? FOR WHAT?
WHO KNOWS? IT COULD BE ANYTHING.
MAYBE THE ELDERS ARE CRAZY--THEY COULD HAVE PICKED YOU FOR YOUR HAIR COLOR.
OR IT COULD HAVE BEEN SOMETHING SPECIFIC--BUT NOT IMMEDIATELY OBVIOUS.
YEAH... OF COURSE IT COULD--
I'M ON IT!

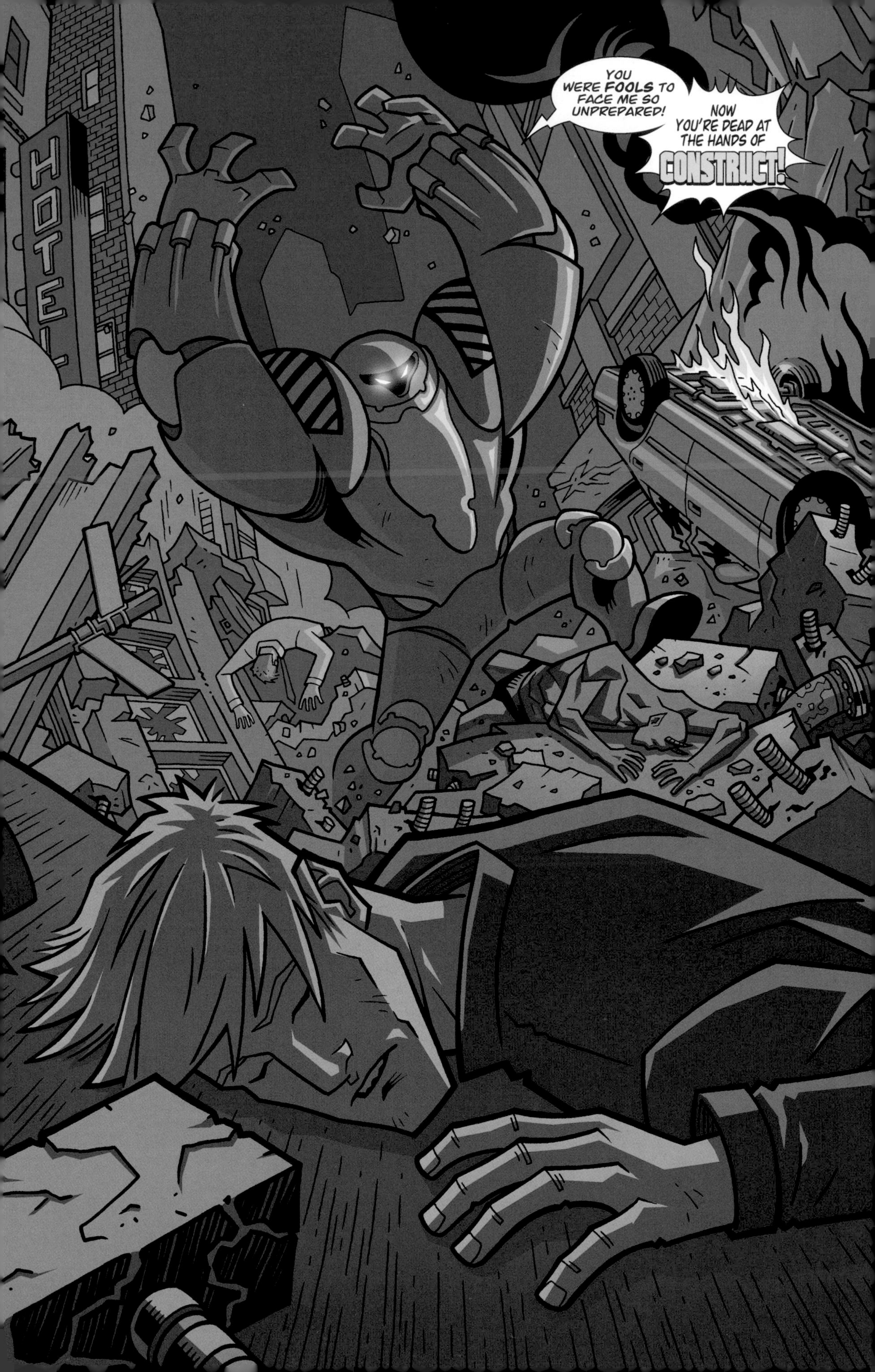
YOU WERE FOOLS TO FACE ME SO UNPREPARED!
NOW YOU'RE DEAD AT THE HANDS OF CONSTRUCT!
HOTEL

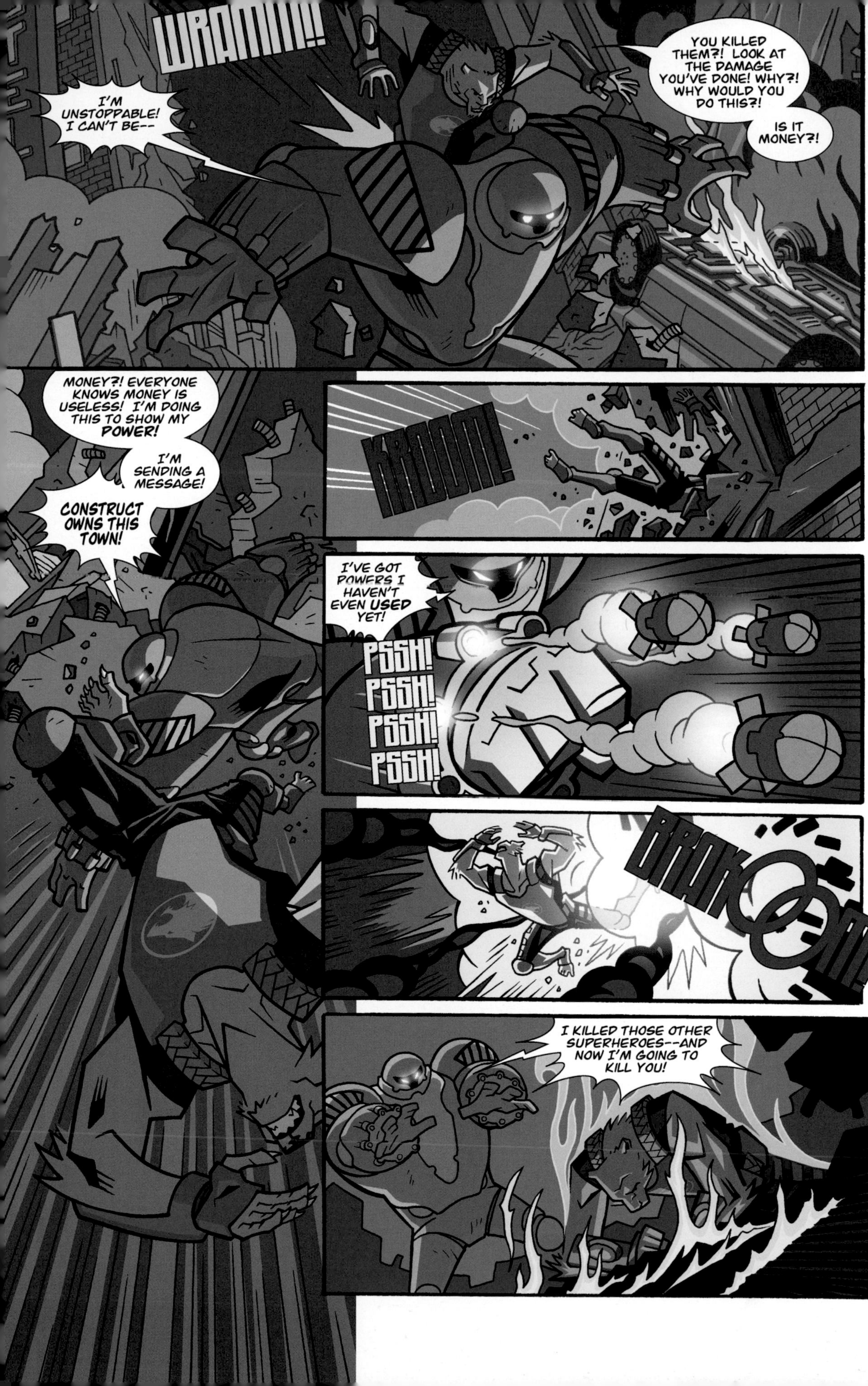
WRAMMM!!
I'M UNSTOPPABLE! I CAN'T BE--
YOU KILLED THEM?! LOOK AT THE DAMAGE YOU'VE DONE! WHY?! WHY WOULD YOU DO THIS?!
IS IT MONEY?!
MONEY?! EVERYONE KNOWS MONEY IS USELESS! I'M DOING THIS TO SHOW MY POWER!
I'M SENDING A MESSAGE!
CONSTRUCT OWNS THIS TOWN!
KROOM!
I'VE GOT POWERS I HAVEN'T EVEN USED YET!
PSSH! PSSH! PSSH! PSSH!
BRAKOOOM!
I KILLED THOSE OTHER SUPERHEROES--AND NOW I'M GOING TO KILL YOU!

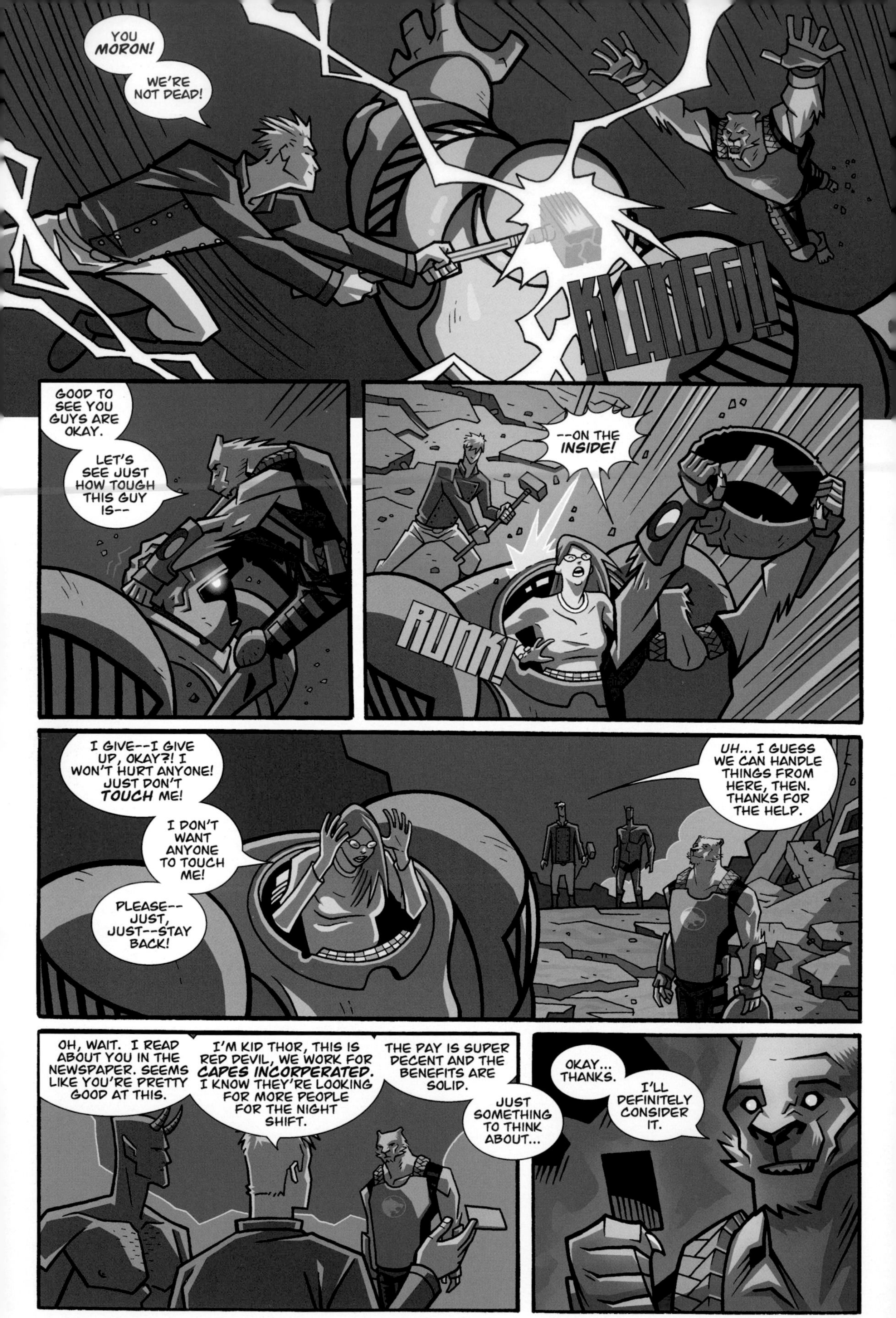
YOU MORON!
WE'RE NOT DEAD!
KLANGG!!
GOOD TO SEE YOU GUYS ARE OKAY.
LET'S SEE JUST HOW TOUGH THIS GUY IS--
--ON THE INSIDE!
RUNK!
I GIVE--I GIVE UP, OKAY?! I WON'T HURT ANYONE! JUST DON'T TOUCH ME!
I DON'T WANT ANYONE TO TOUCH ME!
PLEASE--JUST, JUST--STAY BACK!
UH... I GUESS WE CAN HANDLE THINGS FROM HERE, THEN. THANKS FOR THE HELP.
OH, WAIT. I READ ABOUT YOU IN THE NEWSPAPER. SEEMS LIKE YOU'RE PRETTY GOOD AT THIS.
I'M KID THOR, THIS IS RED DEVIL, WE WORK FOR CAPES INCORPERATED. I KNOW THEY'RE LOOKING FOR MORE PEOPLE FOR THE NIGHT SHIFT.
THE PAY IS SUPER DECENT AND THE BENEFITS ARE SOLID.
JUST SOMETHING TO THINK ABOUT...
OKAY... THANKS.
I'LL DEFINITELY CONSIDER IT.

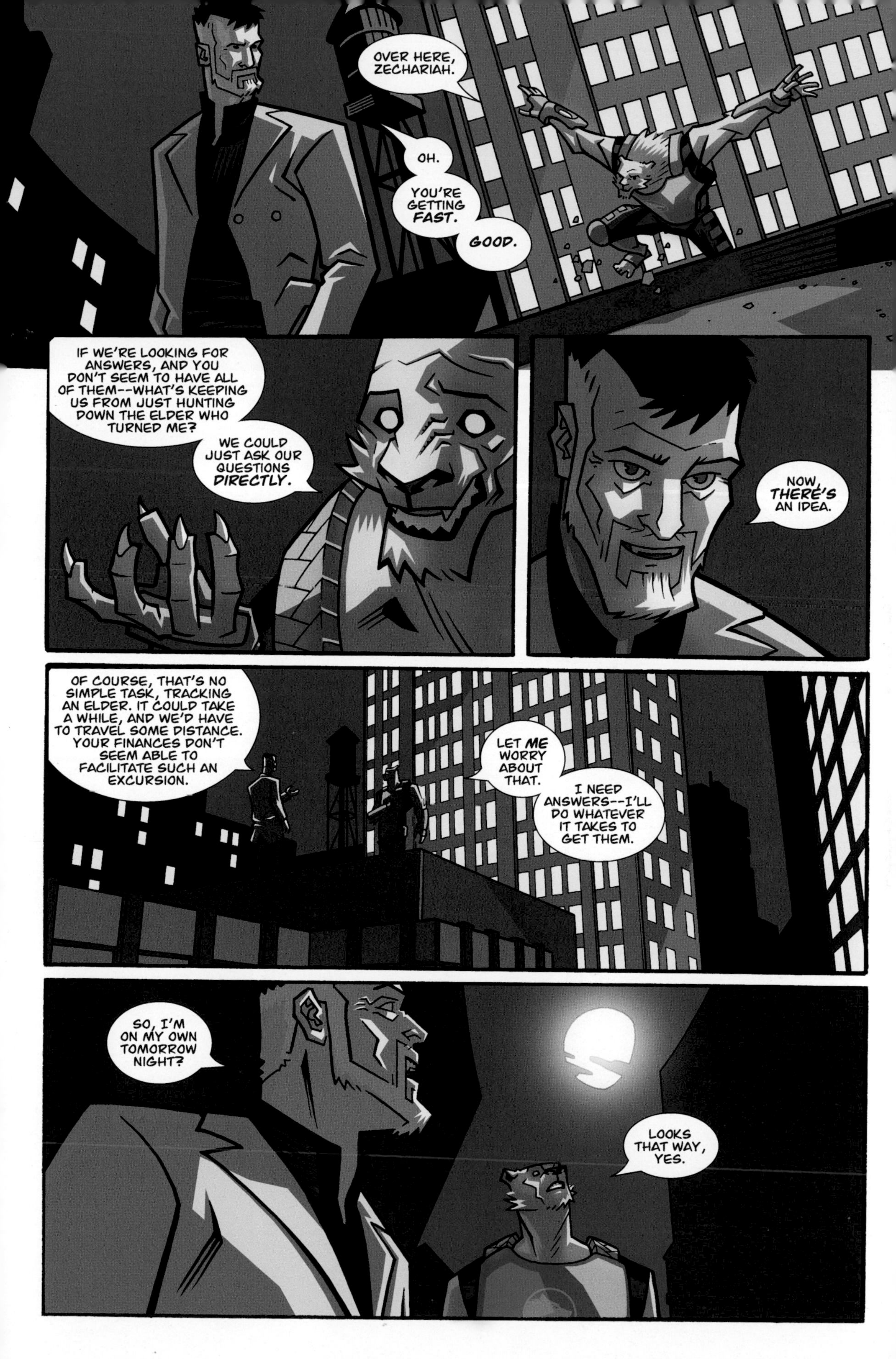
OVER HERE, ZECHARIAH.
OH.
YOU'RE GETTING FAST.
GOOD.
IF WE'RE LOOKING FOR ANSWERS, AND YOU DON'T SEEM TO HAVE ALL OF THEM--WHAT'S KEEPING US FROM JUST HUNTING DOWN THE ELDER WHO TURNED ME?
WE COULD JUST ASK OUR QUESTIONS DIRECTLY.
NOW, THERE'S AN IDEA.
OF COURSE, THAT'S NO SIMPLE TASK, TRACKING AN ELDER. IT COULD TAKE A WHILE, AND WE'D HAVE TO TRAVEL SOME DISTANCE. YOUR FINANCES DON'T SEEM ABLE TO FACILITATE SUCH AN EXCURSION.
LET ME WORRY ABOUT THAT.
I NEED ANSWERS--I'LL DO WHATEVER IT TAKES TO GET THEM.
SO, I'M ON MY OWN TOMORROW NIGHT?
LOOKS THAT WAY, YES.

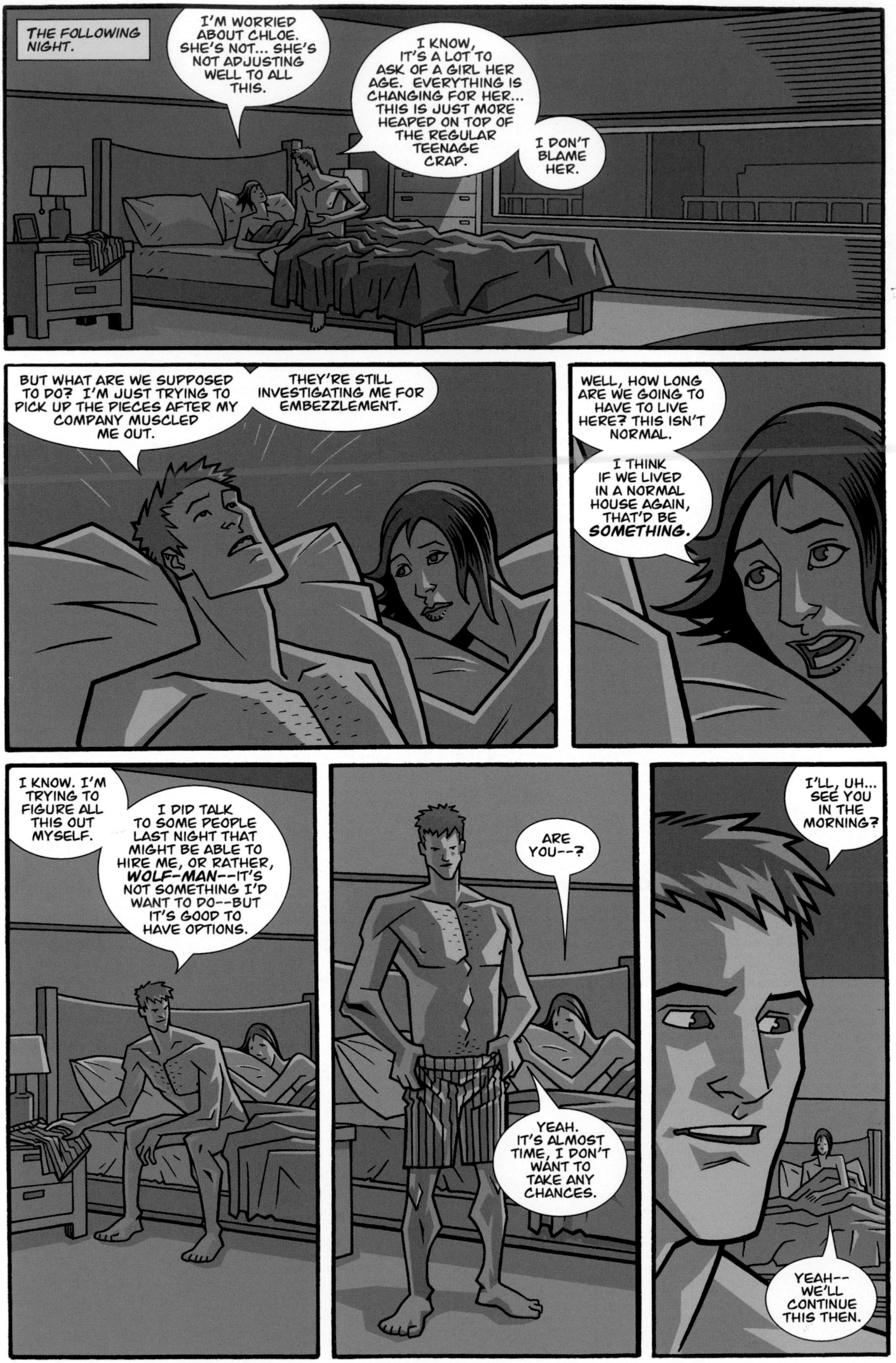
THE FOLLOWING NIGHT.
I'M WORRIED ABOUT CHLOE. SHE'S NOT... SHE'S NOT ADJUSTING WELL TO ALL THIS.
I KNOW, IT'S A LOT TO ASK OF A GIRL HER AGE. EVERYTHING IS CHANGING FOR HER... THIS IS JUST MORE HEAPED ON TOP OF THE REGULAR TEENAGE CRAP.
I DON'T BLAME HER.
BUT WHAT ARE WE SUPPOSED TO DO? I'M JUST TRYING TO PICK UP THE PIECES AFTER MY COMPANY MUSCLED ME OUT.
THEY'RE STILL INVESTIGATING ME FOR EMBEZZLEMENT.
WELL, HOW LONG ARE WE GOING TO HAVE TO LIVE HERE? THIS ISN'T NORMAL.
I THINK IF WE LIVED IN A NORMAL HOUSE AGAIN, THAT'D BE SOMETHING.
I KNOW. I'M TRYING TO FIGURE ALL THIS OUT MYSELF.
I DID TALK TO SOME PEOPLE LAST NIGHT THAT MIGHT BE ABLE TO HIRE ME, OR RATHER, WOLF-MAN--IT'S NOT SOMETHING I'D WANT TO DO--BUT IT'S GOOD TO HAVE OPTIONS.
ARE YOU--?
YEAH. IT'S ALMOST TIME, I DON'T WANT TO TAKE ANY CHANCES.
I'LL, UH... SEE YOU IN THE MORNING?
YEAH--WE'LL CONTINUE THIS THEN.

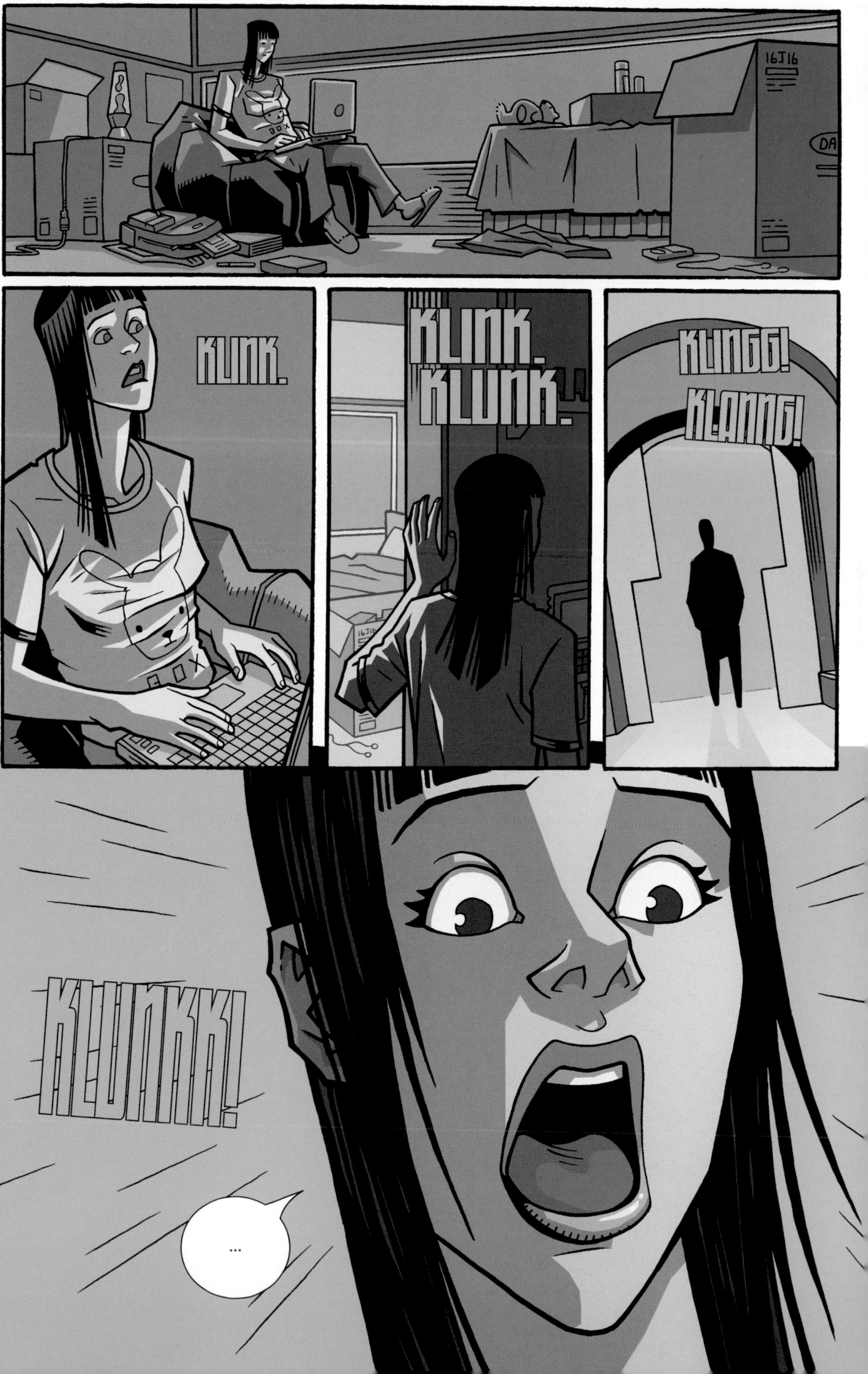

KLINK.
KLINK.
KLUNK.
KLINGG!
KLANNG!
KLUNKK!
...

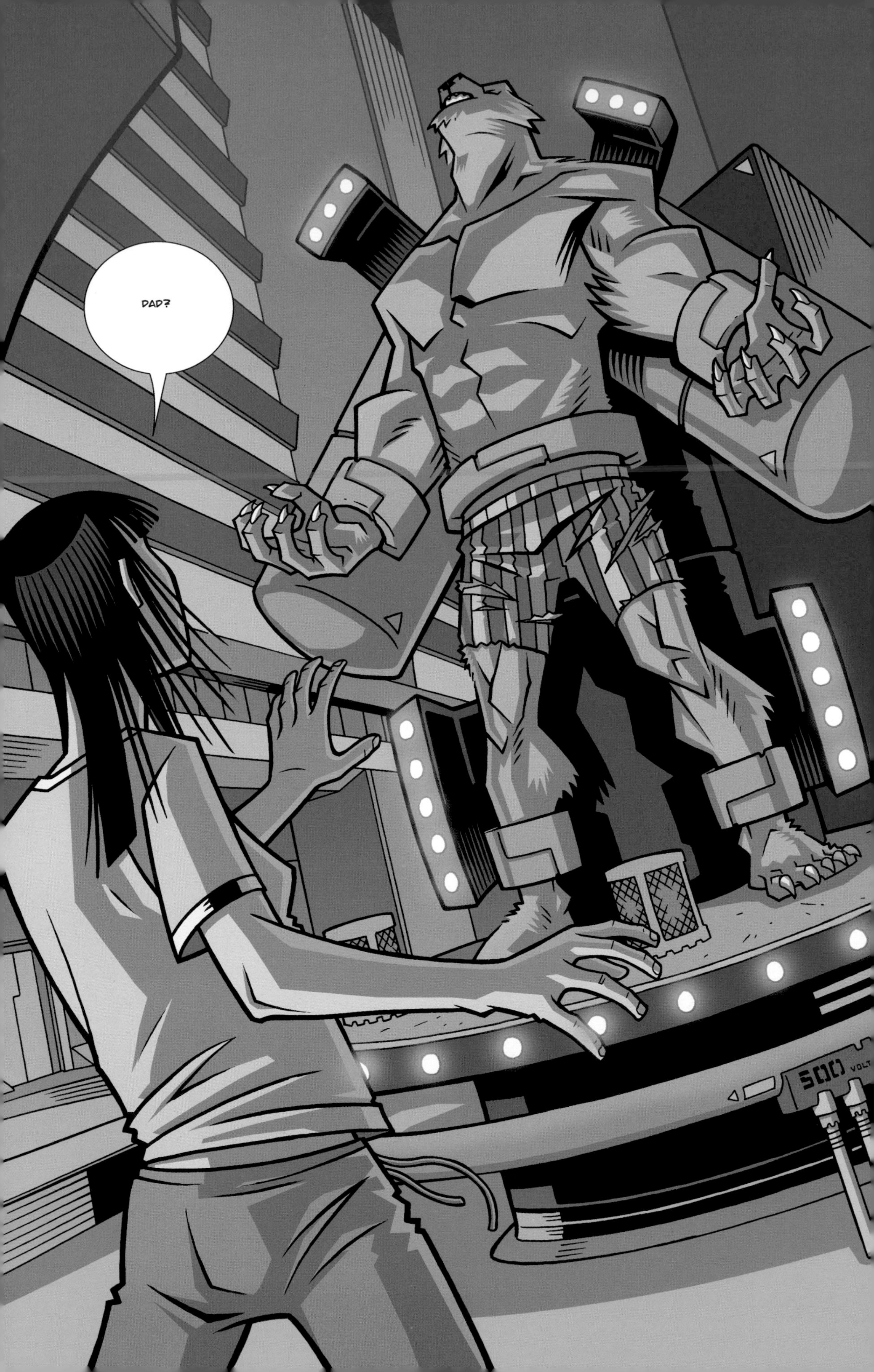
DAD?
500 VOLT

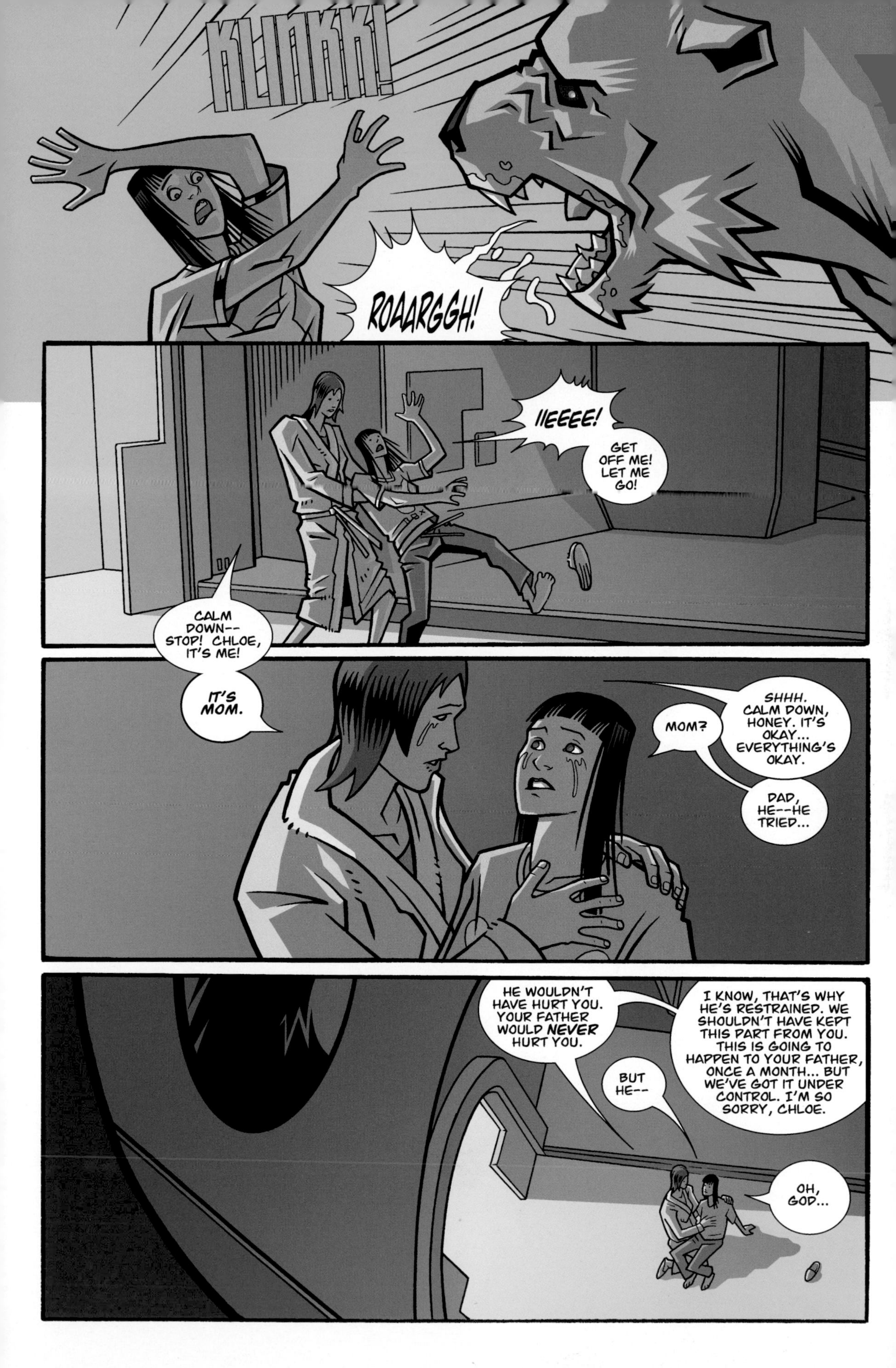
KLINKK!
ROAARGGH!
IIEEEE!
GET OFF ME! LET ME GO!
CALM DOWN-- STOP! CHLOE, IT'S ME!
IT'S MOM.
MOM?
SHHH. CALM DOWN, HONEY. IT'S OKAY... EVERYTHING'S OKAY.
DAD, HE--HE TRIED...
HE WOULDN'T HAVE HURT YOU. YOUR FATHER WOULD NEVER HURT YOU.
BUT HE--
I KNOW, THAT'S WHY HE'S RESTRAINED. WE SHOULDN'T HAVE KEPT THIS PART FROM YOU. THIS IS GOING TO HAPPEN TO YOUR FATHER, ONCE A MONTH... BUT WE'VE GOT IT UNDER CONTROL. I'M SO SORRY, CHLOE.
OH, GOD...

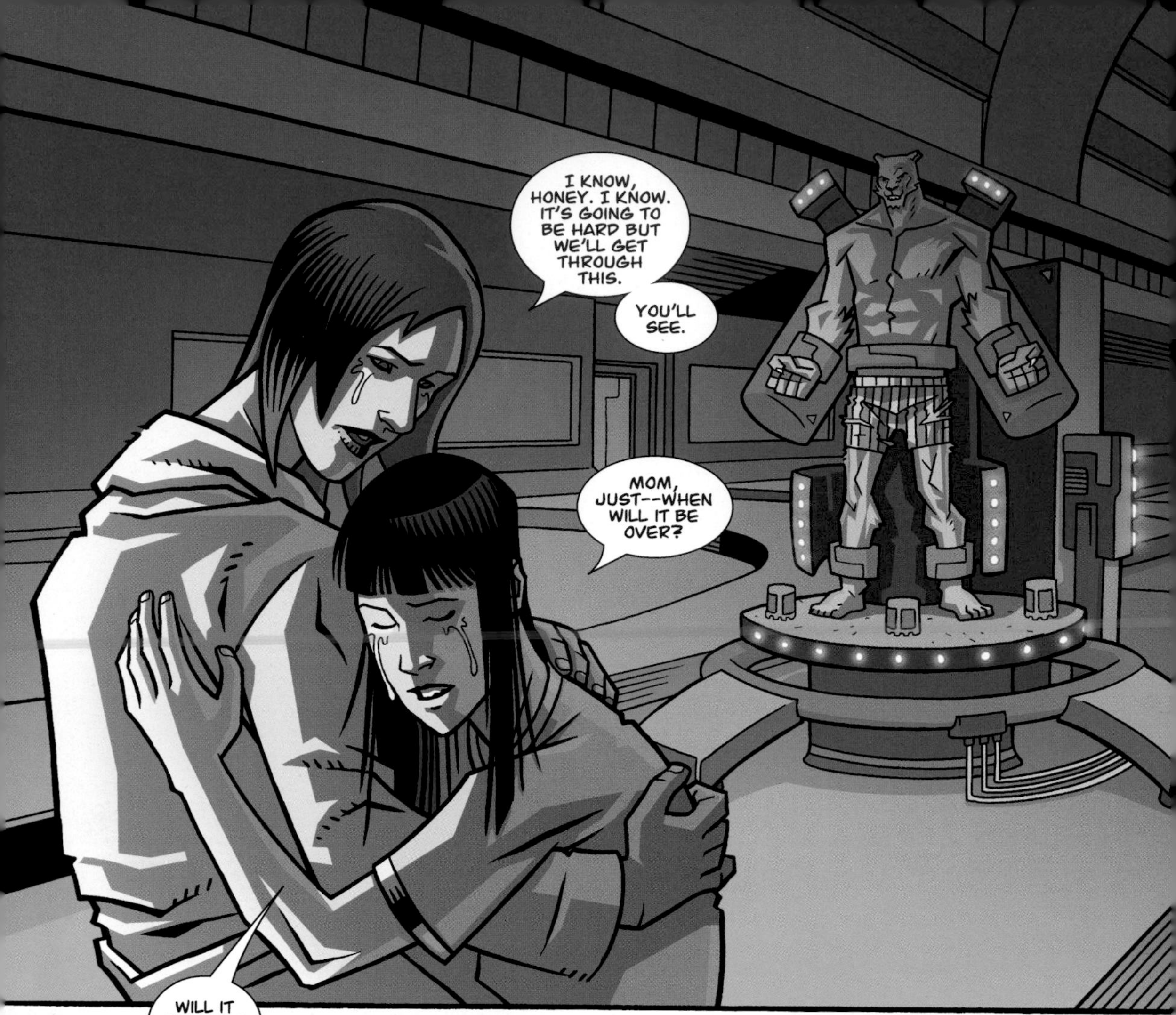
I KNOW, HONEY. I KNOW. IT'S GOING TO BE HARD BUT WE'LL GET THROUGH THIS.
YOU'LL SEE.
MOM, JUST--WHEN WILL IT BE OVER?

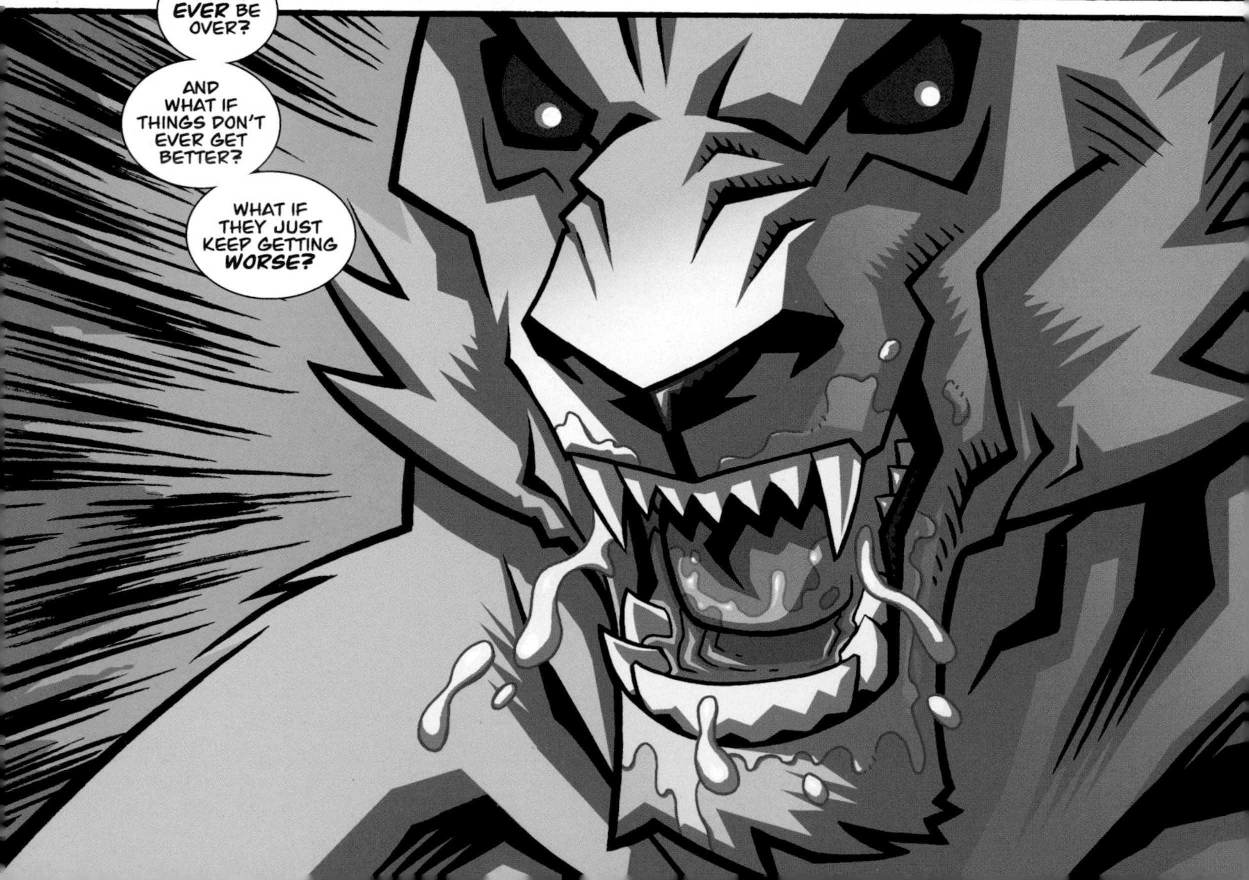
WILL IT EVER BE OVER?
AND WHAT IF THINGS DON'T EVER GET BETTER?
WHAT IF THEY JUST KEEP GETTING WORSE?

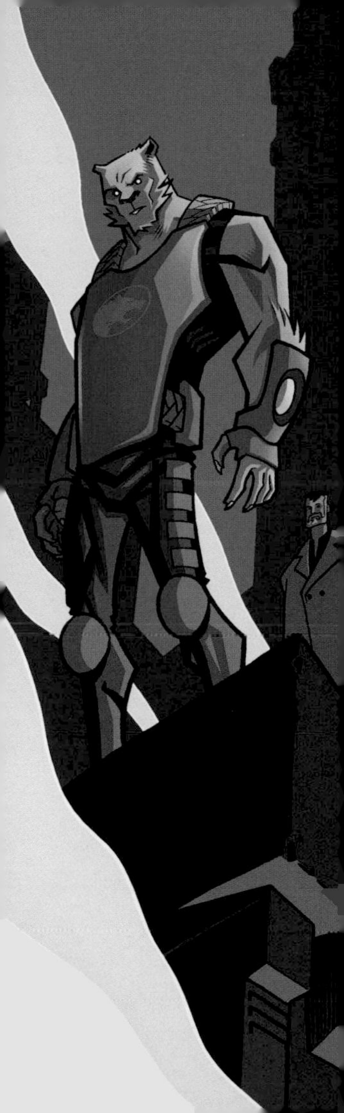

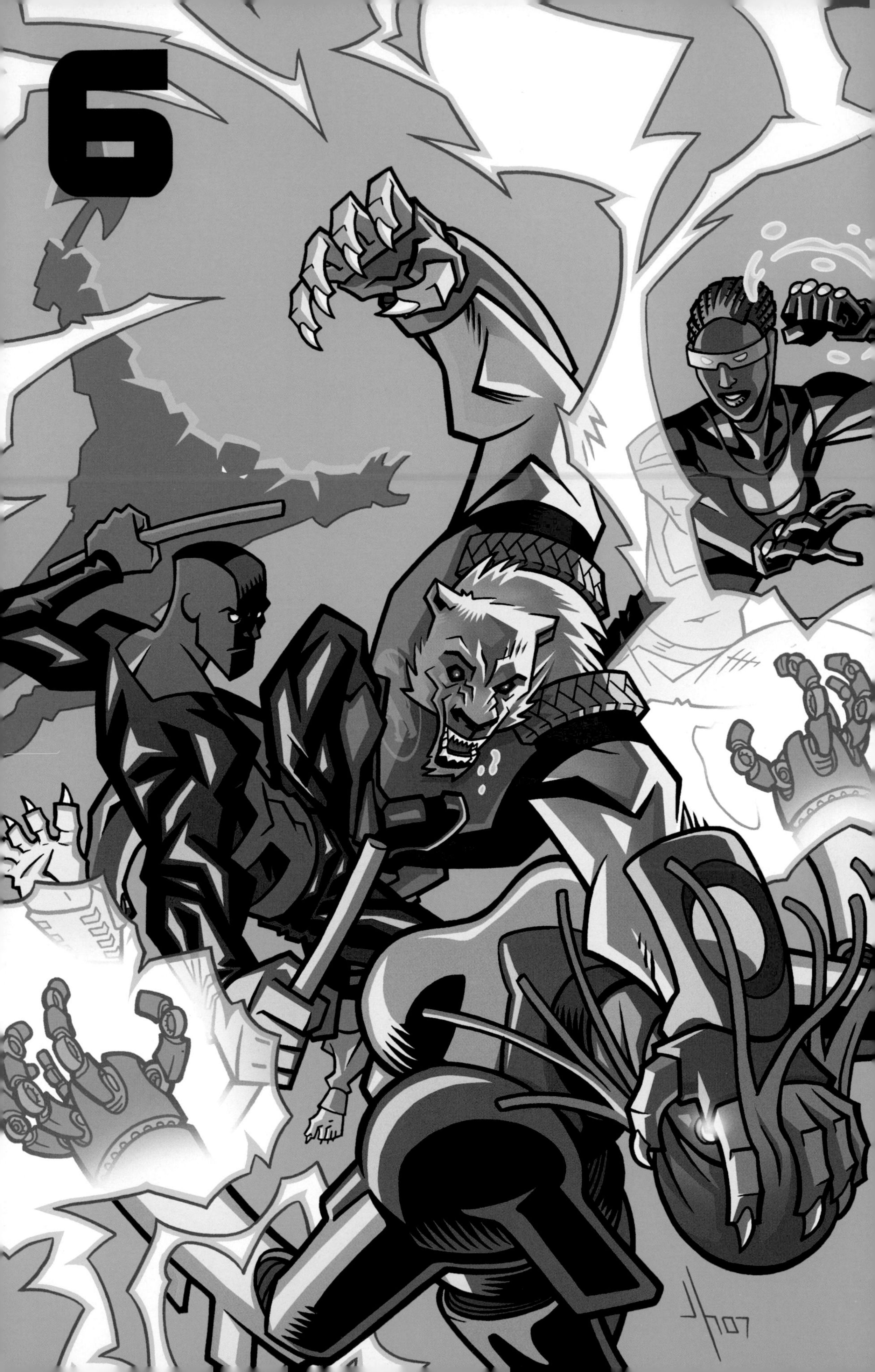
6

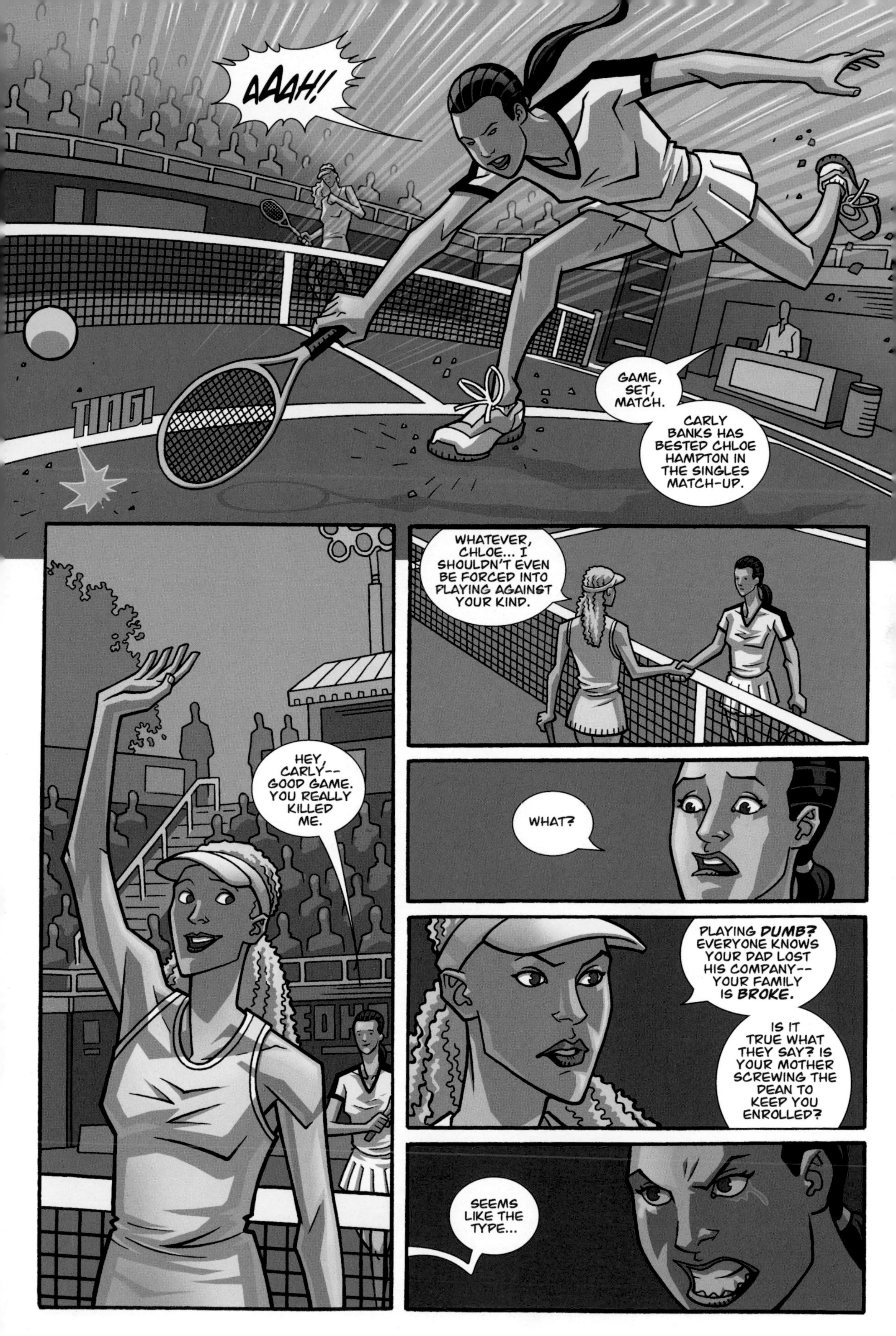
AAAH!
TING!
GAME, SET, MATCH.
CARLY BANKS HAS BESTED CHLOE HAMPTON IN THE SINGLES MATCH-UP.
HEY, CARLY-- GOOD GAME. YOU REALLY KILLED ME.
WHATEVER, CHLOE... I SHOULDN'T EVEN BE FORCED INTO PLAYING AGAINST YOUR KIND.
WHAT?
PLAYING DUMB? EVERYONE KNOWS YOUR DAD LOST HIS COMPANY-- YOUR FAMILY IS BROKE.
IS IT TRUE WHAT THEY SAY? IS YOUR MOTHER SCREWING THE DEAN TO KEEP YOU ENROLLED?
SEEMS LIKE THE TYPE...

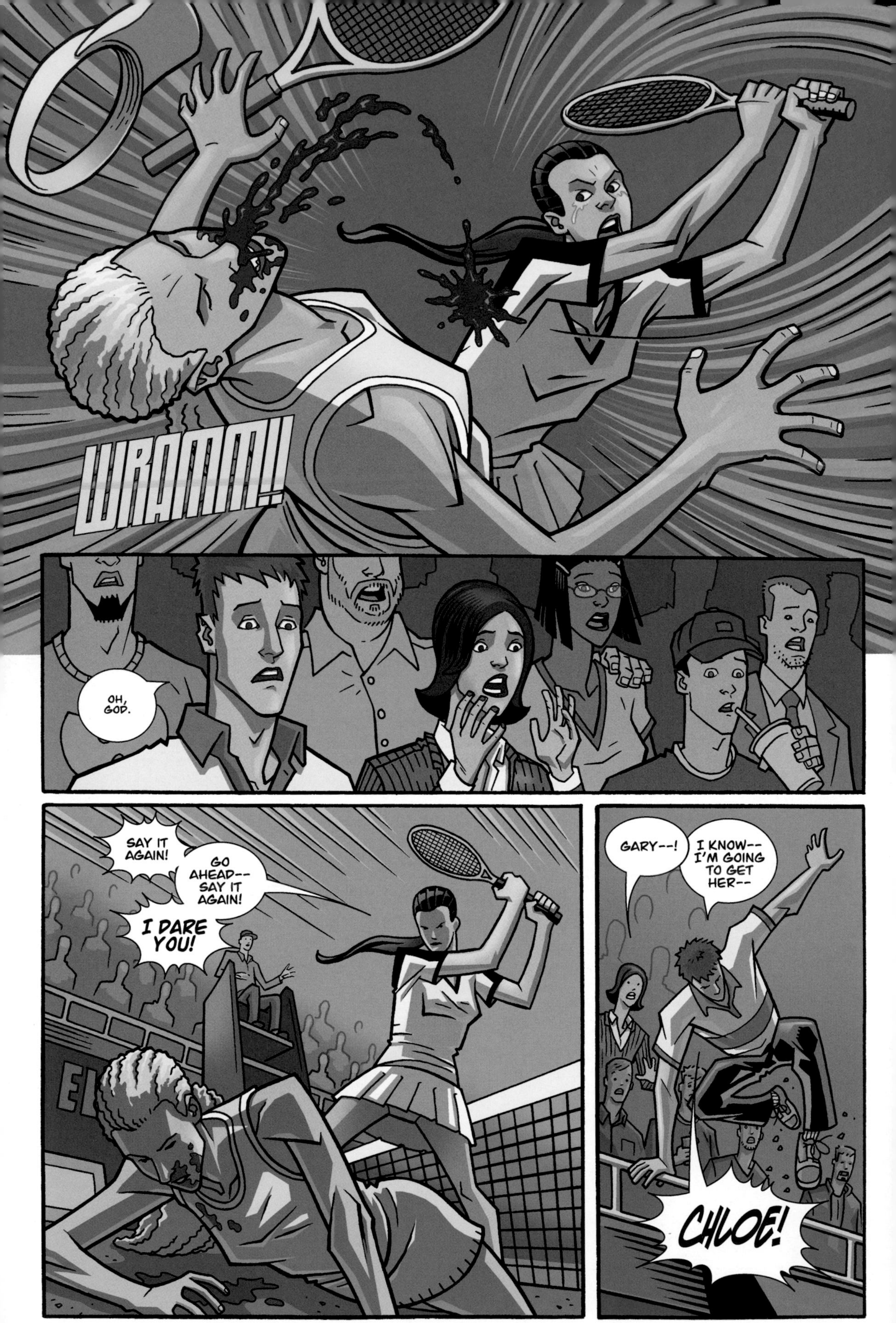
WRAMM!!
OH, GOD.
SAY IT AGAIN!
GO AHEAD-- SAY IT AGAIN!
I DARE YOU!
GARY--!
I KNOW-- I'M GOING TO GET HER--
CHLOE!

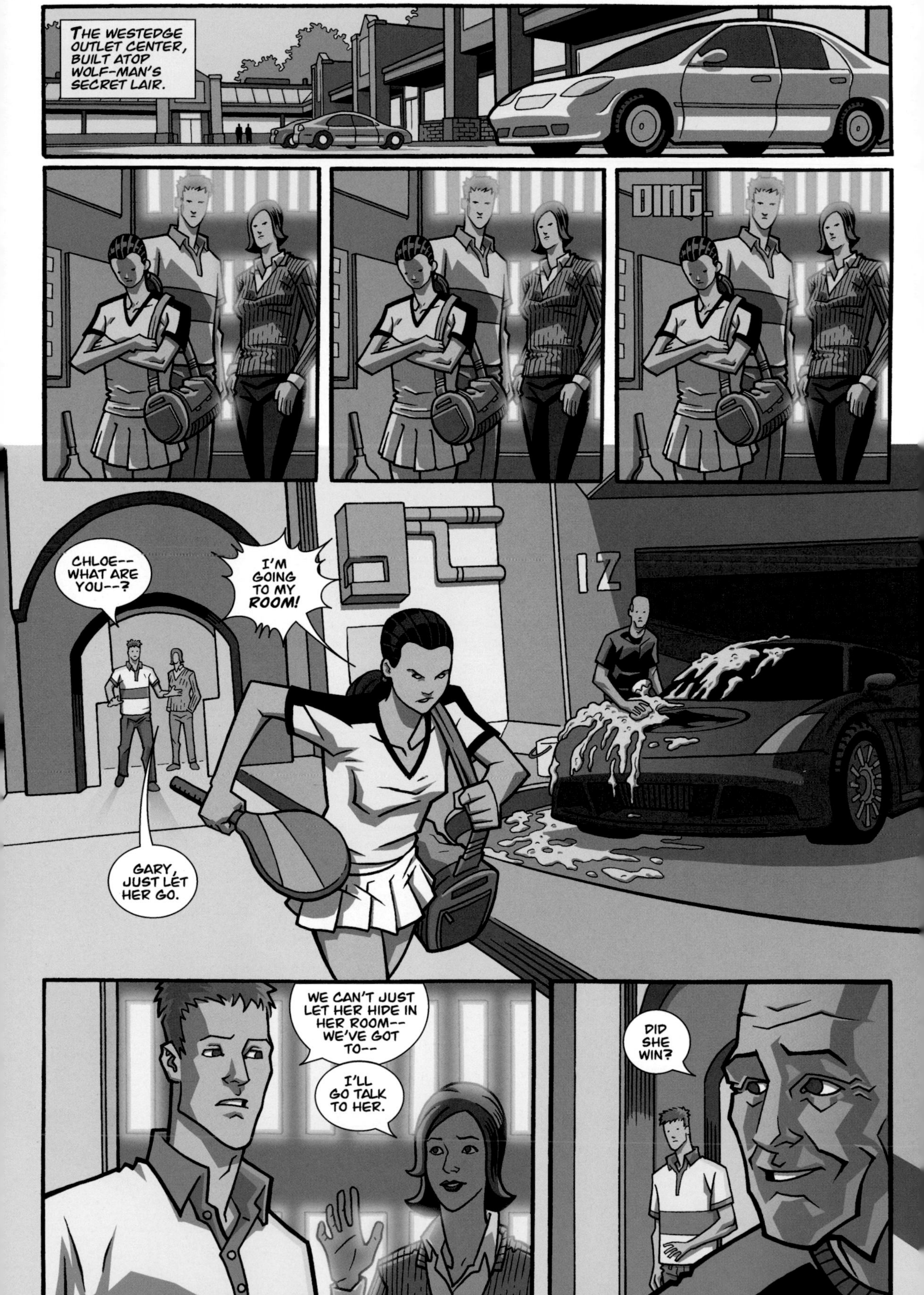
THE WESTEDGE OUTLET CENTER, BUILT ATOP WOLF-MAN'S SECRET LAIR.
DING.
CHLOE-- WHAT ARE YOU--?
I'M GOING TO MY ROOM!
GARY, JUST LET HER GO.
IZ
WE CAN'T JUST LET HER HIDE IN HER ROOM-- WE'VE GOT TO--
I'LL GO TALK TO HER.
DID SHE WIN?

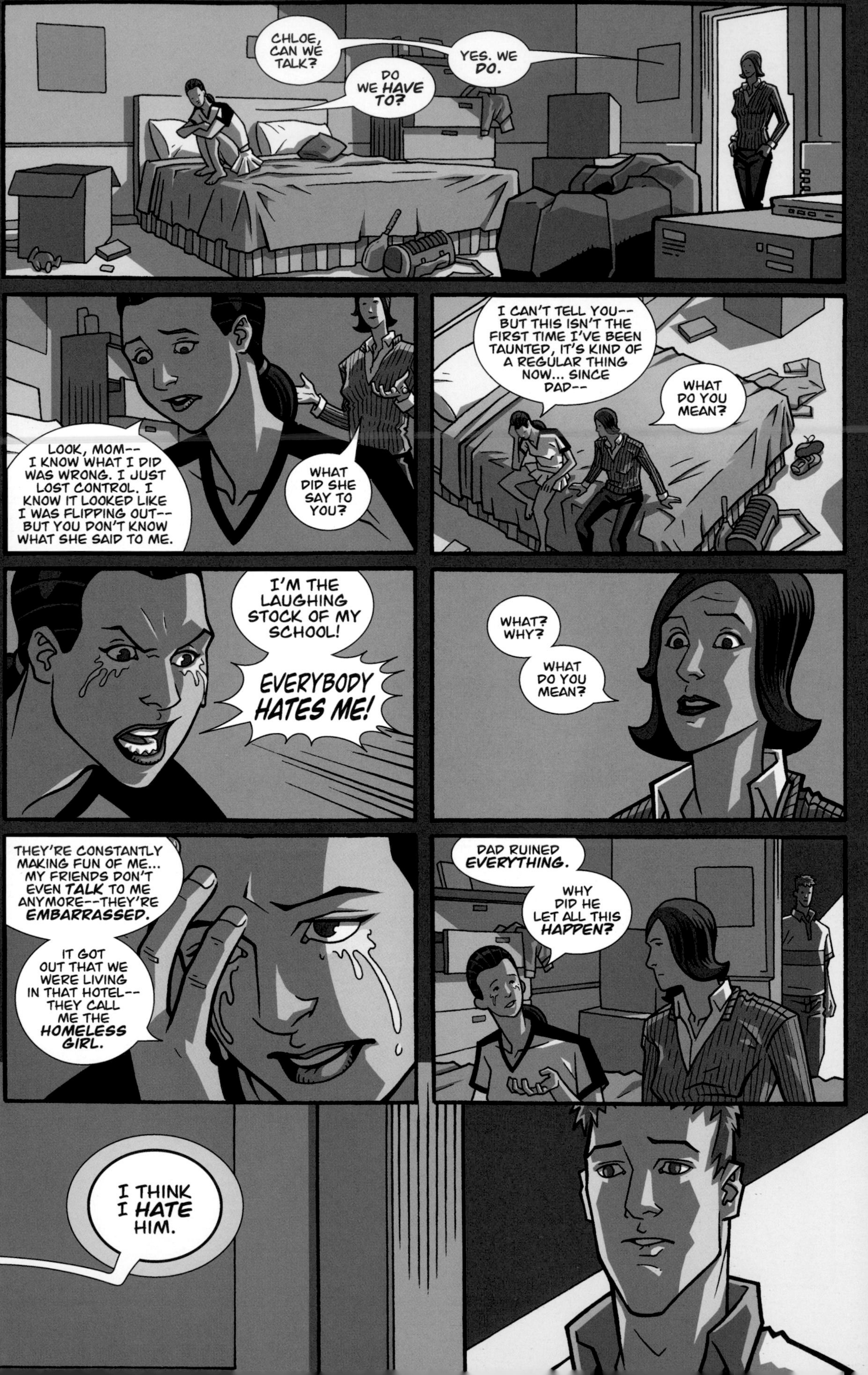
CHLOE, CAN WE TALK?
DO WE HAVE TO?
YES. WE DO.
LOOK, MOM-- I KNOW WHAT I DID WAS WRONG. I JUST LOST CONTROL. I KNOW IT LOOKED LIKE I WAS FLIPPING OUT-- BUT YOU DON'T KNOW WHAT SHE SAID TO ME.
WHAT DID SHE SAY TO YOU?
I CAN'T TELL YOU-- BUT THIS ISN'T THE FIRST TIME I'VE BEEN TAUNTED, IT'S KIND OF A REGULAR THING NOW... SINCE DAD--
WHAT DO YOU MEAN?
I'M THE LAUGHING STOCK OF MY SCHOOL!
EVERYBODY HATES ME!
WHAT? WHY?
WHAT DO YOU MEAN?
THEY'RE CONSTANTLY MAKING FUN OF ME... MY FRIENDS DON'T EVEN TALK TO ME ANYMORE--THEY'RE EMBARRASSED.
IT GOT OUT THAT WE WERE LIVING IN THAT HOTEL-- THEY CALL ME THE HOMELESS GIRL.
DAD RUINED EVERYTHING.
WHY DID HE LET ALL THIS HAPPEN?
I THINK I HATE HIM.

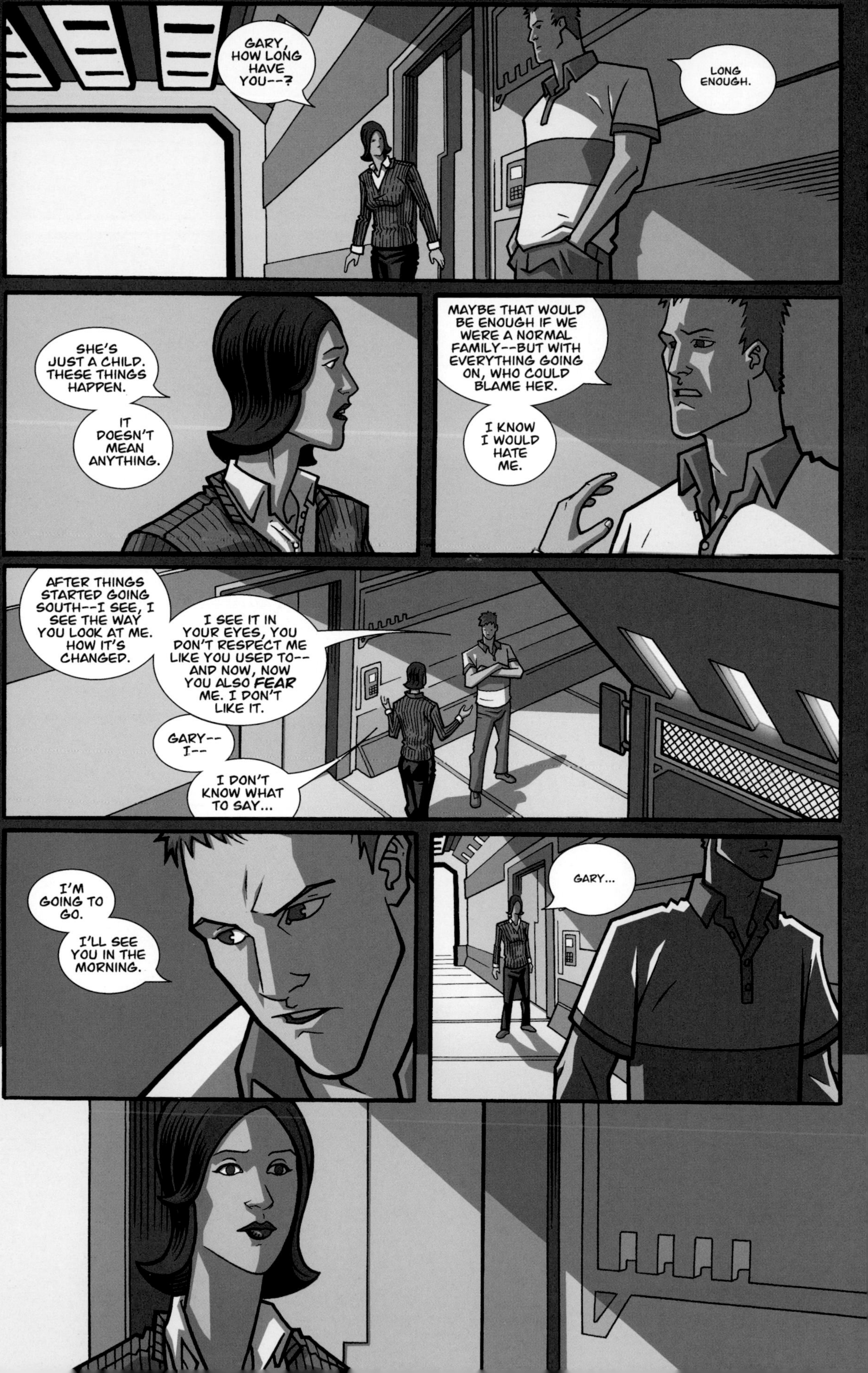
GARY, HOW LONG HAVE YOU--?
LONG ENOUGH.
SHE'S JUST A CHILD. THESE THINGS HAPPEN.
IT DOESN'T MEAN ANYTHING.
MAYBE THAT WOULD BE ENOUGH IF WE WERE A NORMAL FAMILY--BUT WITH EVERYTHING GOING ON, WHO COULD BLAME HER.
I KNOW I WOULD HATE ME.
AFTER THINGS STARTED GOING SOUTH--I SEE, I SEE THE WAY YOU LOOK AT ME. HOW IT'S CHANGED.
I SEE IT IN YOUR EYES, YOU DON'T RESPECT ME LIKE YOU USED TO--AND NOW, NOW YOU ALSO FEAR ME. I DON'T LIKE IT.
GARY-- I--
I DON'T KNOW WHAT TO SAY...
I'M GOING TO GO.
I'LL SEE YOU IN THE MORNING.
GARY...

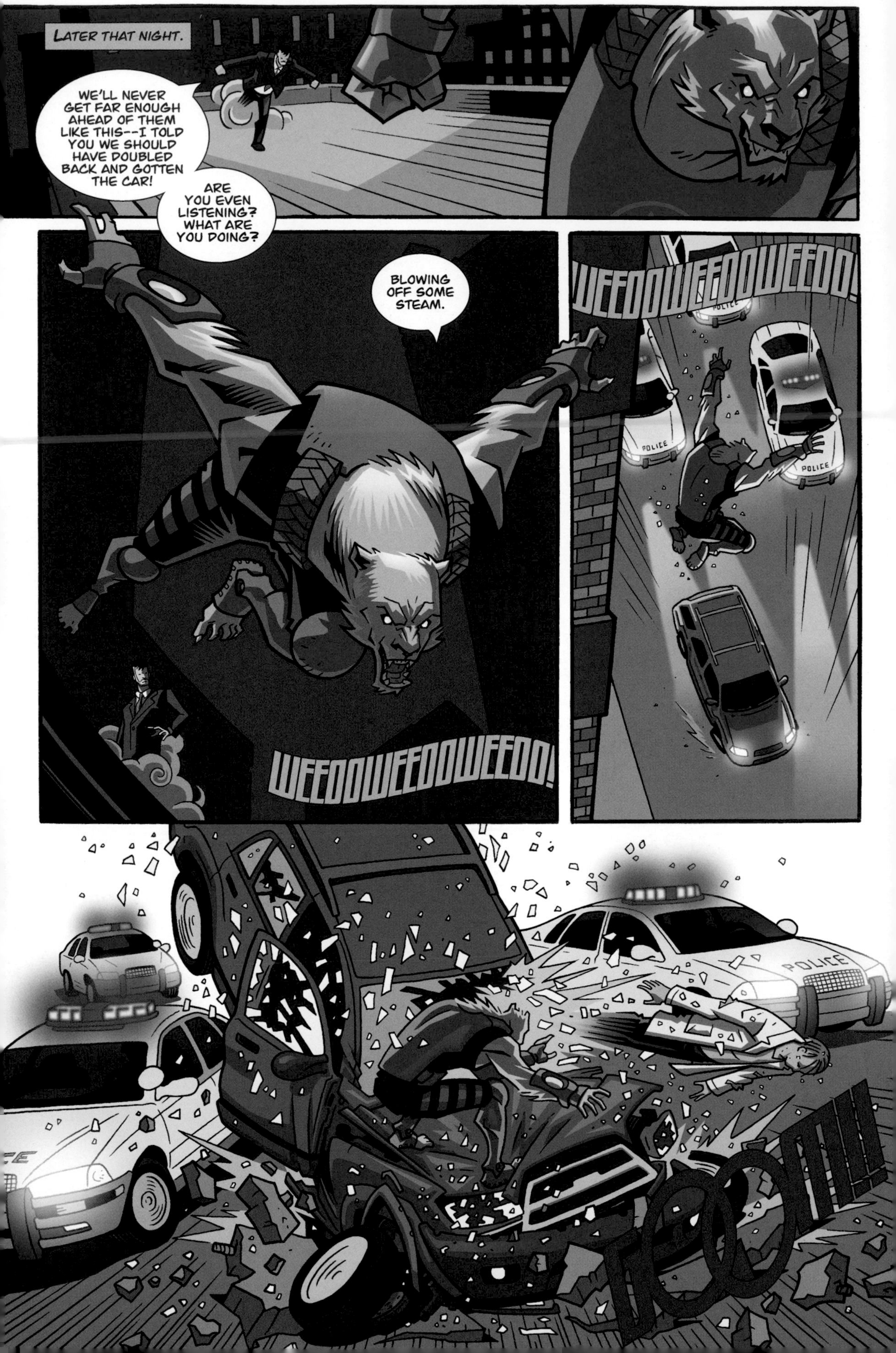
LATER THAT NIGHT.
WE'LL NEVER GET FAR ENOUGH AHEAD OF THEM LIKE THIS--I TOLD YOU WE SHOULD HAVE DOUBLED BACK AND GOTTEN THE CAR!
ARE YOU EVEN LISTENING? WHAT ARE YOU DOING?
BLOWING OFF SOME STEAM.
WEEOOWEEOOWEEOO!
WEEOOWEEOOWEEOO!
POLICE
POLICE
POLICE
POLICE
TCOOM!!

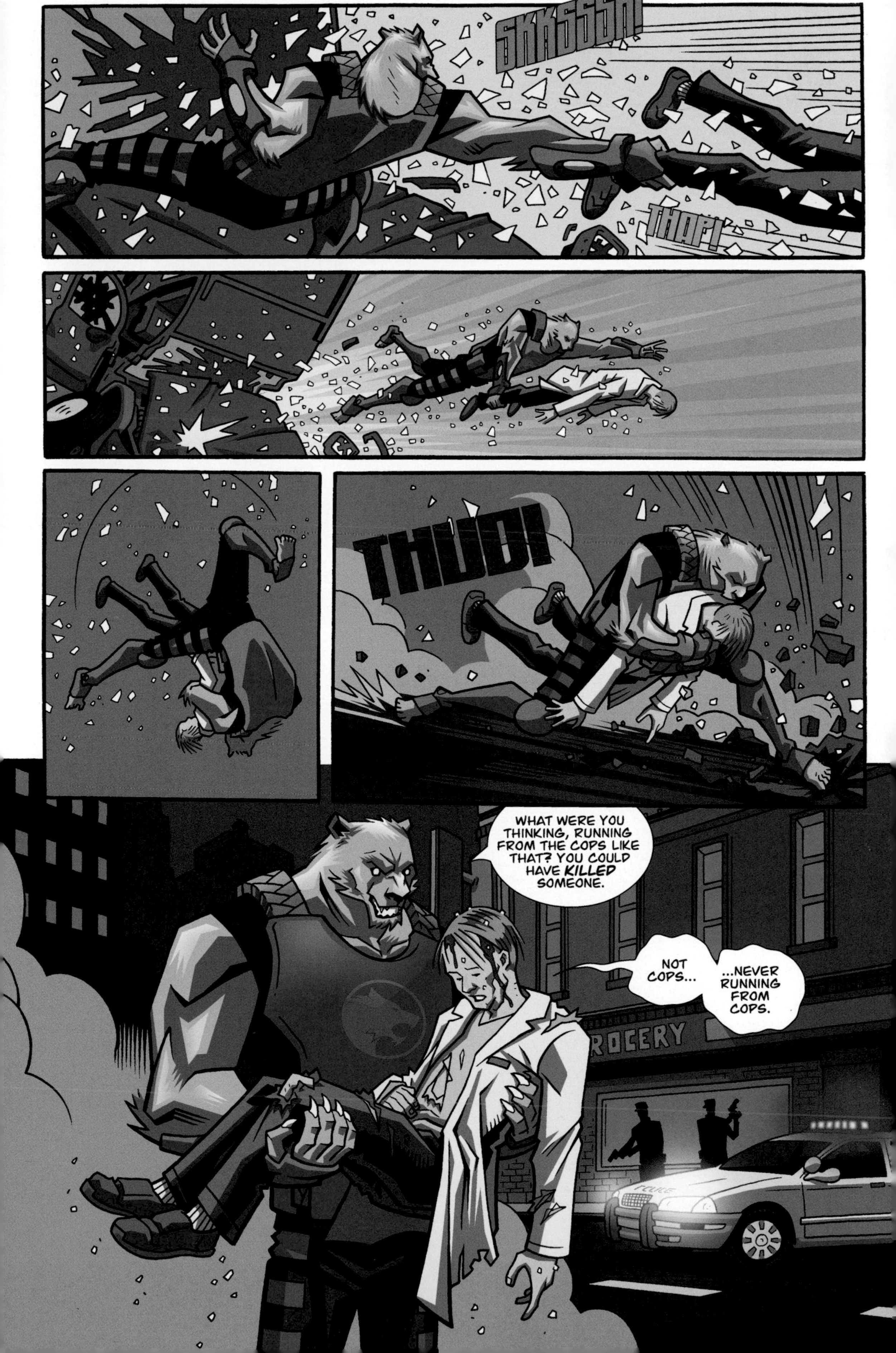
SKKSSSH!
THOP!
THUD!
WHAT WERE YOU THINKING, RUNNING FROM THE COPS LIKE THAT? YOU COULD HAVE KILLED SOMEONE.
NOT COPS...
...NEVER RUNNING FROM COPS.
ROCERY

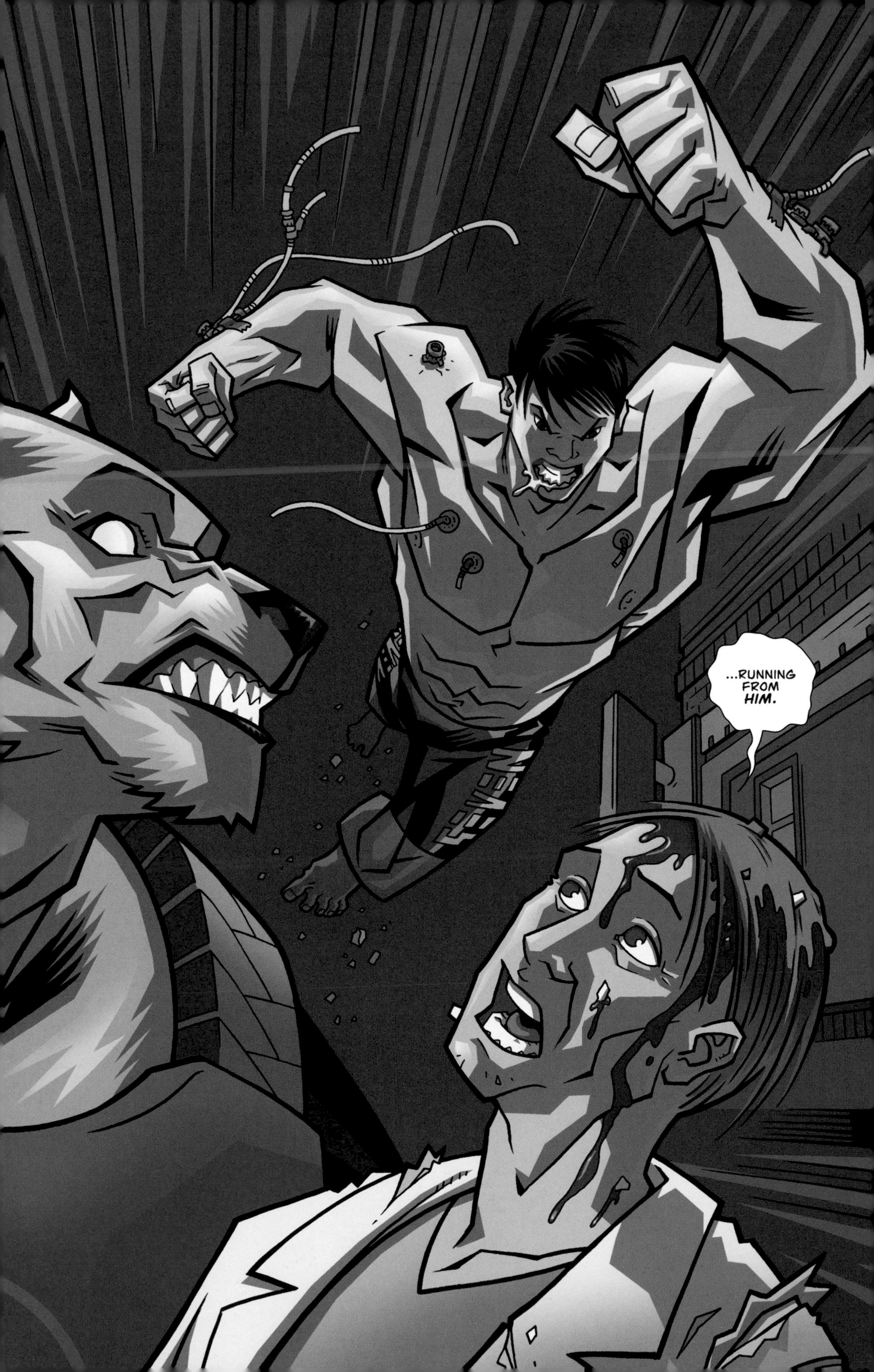
...RUNNING FROM HIM.

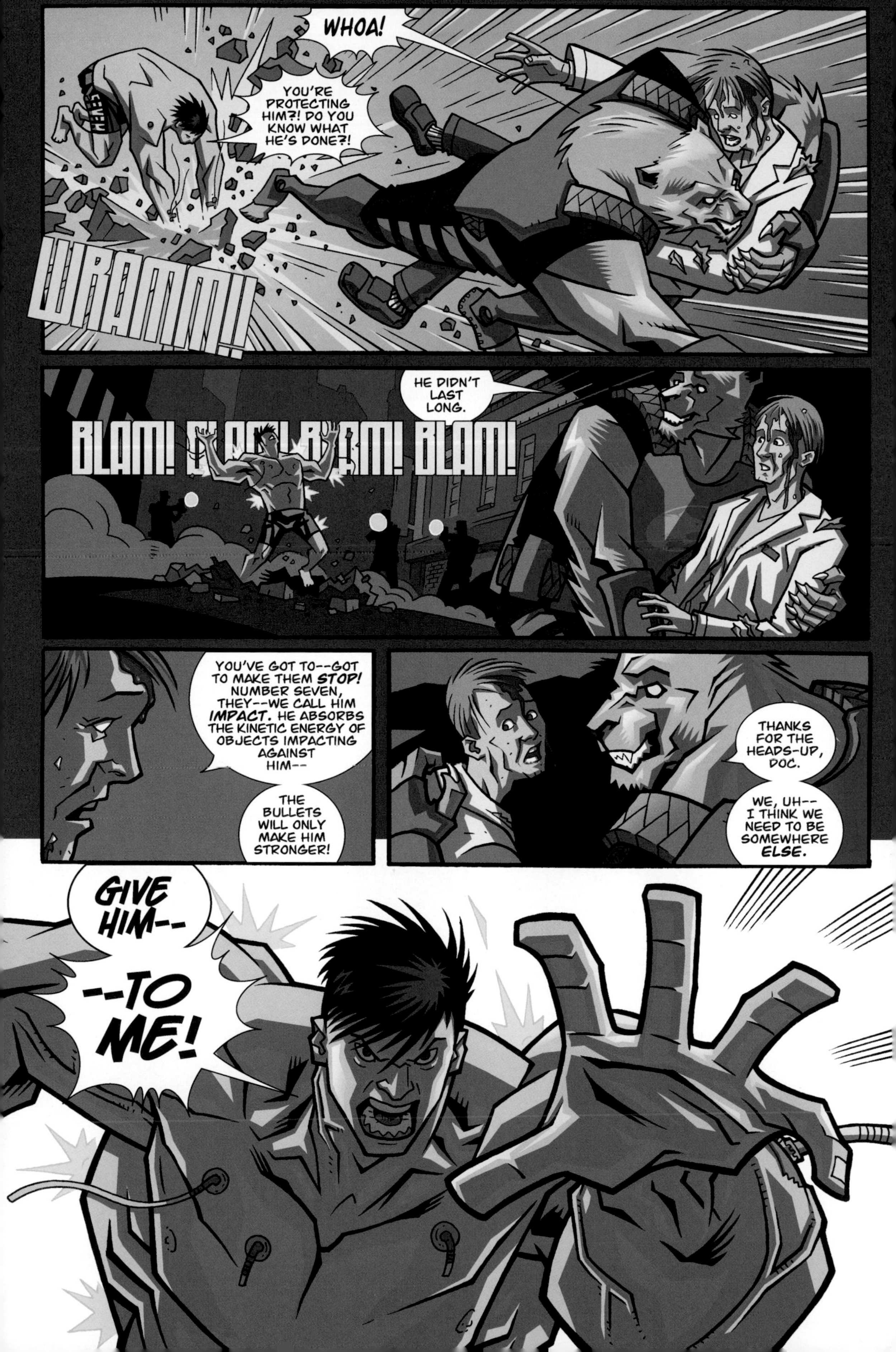
WHOA!
YOU'RE PROTECTING HIM?! DO YOU KNOW WHAT HE'S DONE?!
WRAMMM!!
SEVEN
HE DIDN'T LAST LONG.
BLAM! BLAM! BLAM! BLAM!
YOU'VE GOT TO--GOT TO MAKE THEM STOP! NUMBER SEVEN, THEY--WE CALL HIM IMPACT. HE ABSORBS THE KINETIC ENERGY OF OBJECTS IMPACTING AGAINST HIM--
THE BULLETS WILL ONLY MAKE HIM STRONGER!
THANKS FOR THE HEADS-UP, DOC.
WE, UH-- I THINK WE NEED TO BE SOMEWHERE ELSE.
GIVE HIM--
--TO ME!

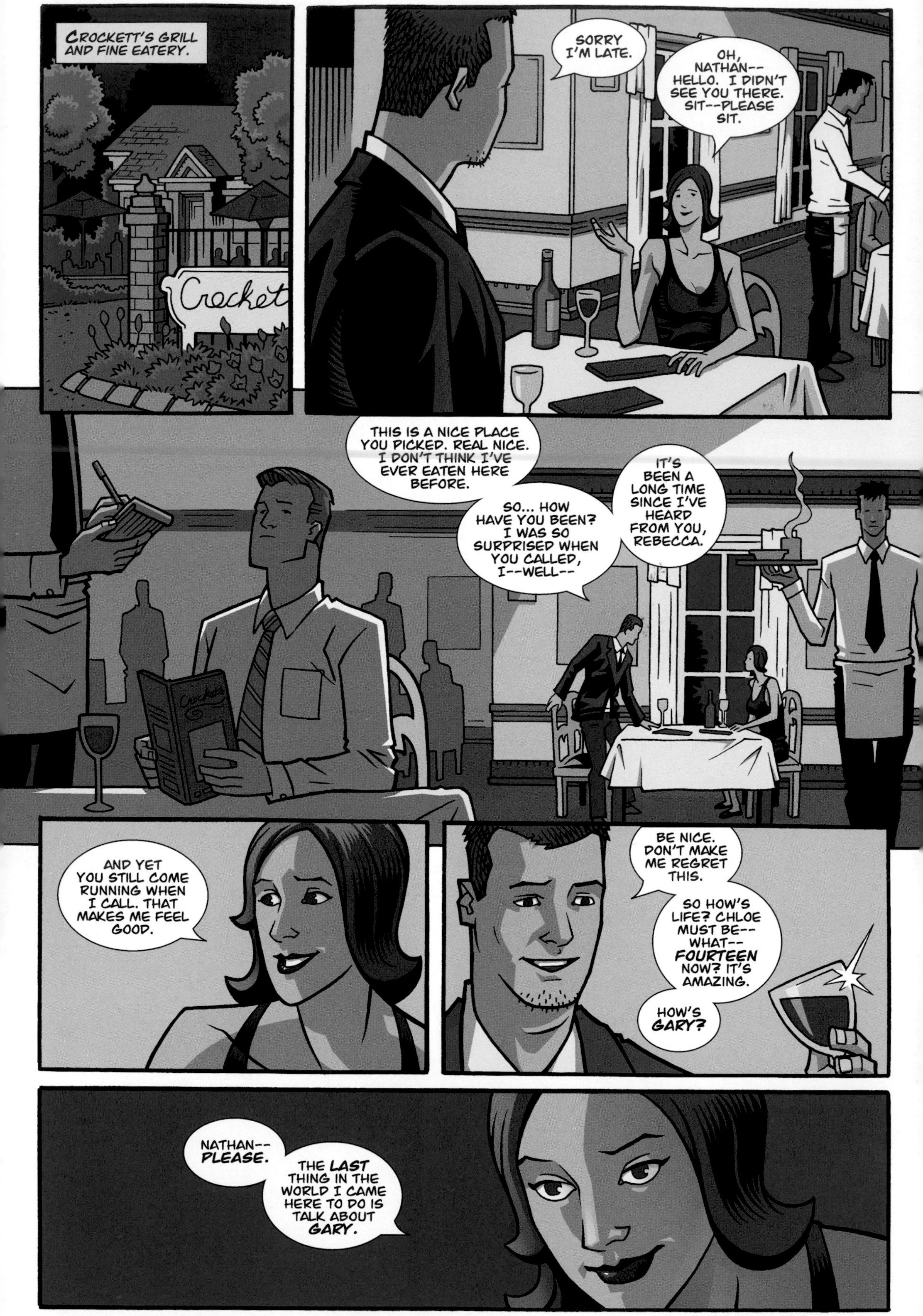
CROCKETT'S GRILL AND FINE EATERY.
Crockett
SORRY I'M LATE.
OH, NATHAN-- HELLO. I DIDN'T SEE YOU THERE. SIT--PLEASE SIT.
THIS IS A NICE PLACE YOU PICKED. REAL NICE. I DON'T THINK I'VE EVER EATEN HERE BEFORE.
SO... HOW HAVE YOU BEEN? I WAS SO SURPRISED WHEN YOU CALLED, I--WELL--
IT'S BEEN A LONG TIME SINCE I'VE HEARD FROM YOU, REBECCA.
AND YET YOU STILL COME RUNNING WHEN I CALL. THAT MAKES ME FEEL GOOD.
BE NICE. DON'T MAKE ME REGRET THIS.
SO HOW'S LIFE? CHLOE MUST BE--WHAT--FOURTEEN NOW? IT'S AMAZING.
HOW'S GARY?
NATHAN--PLEASE.
THE LAST THING IN THE WORLD I CAME HERE TO DO IS TALK ABOUT GARY.

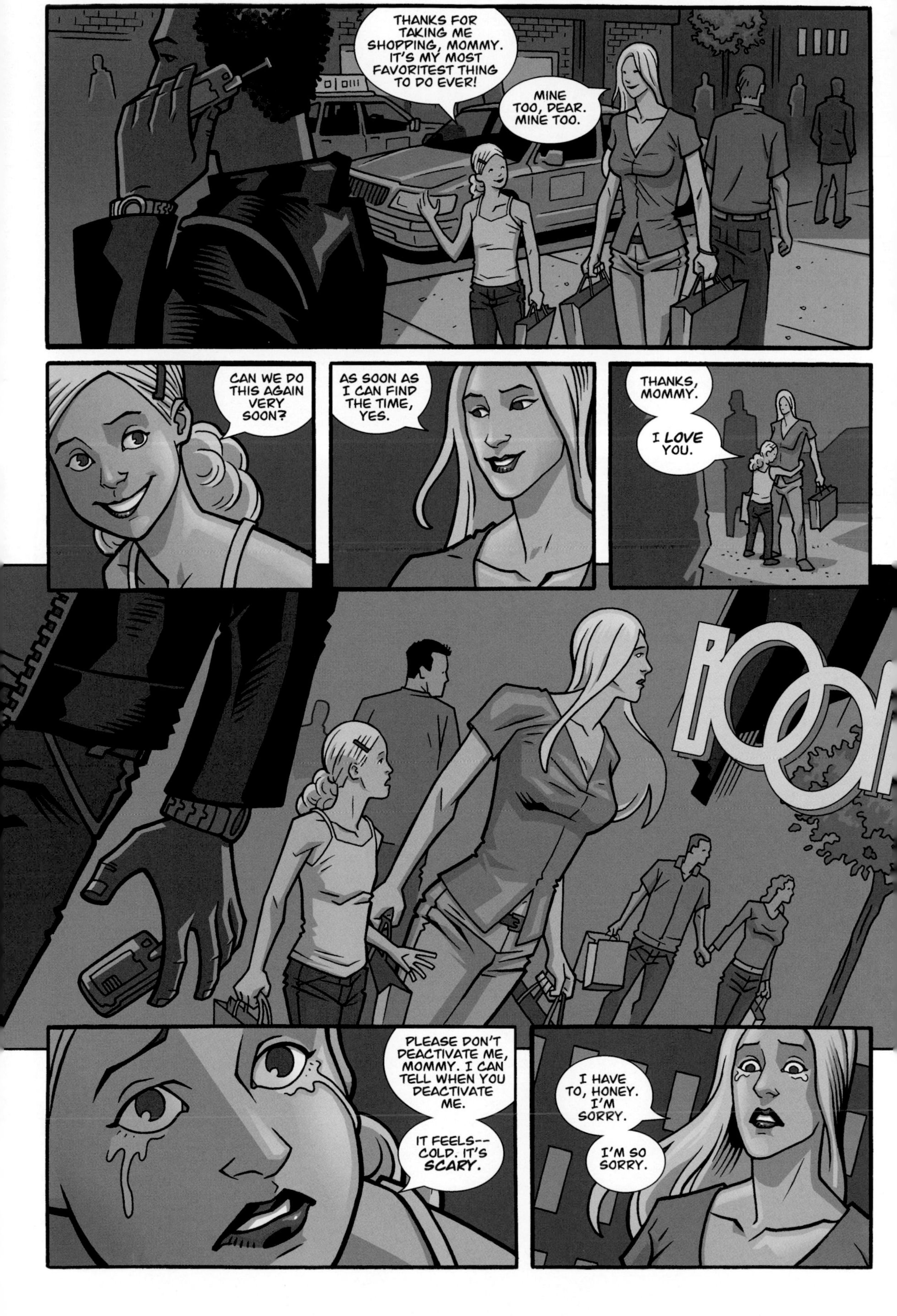
THANKS FOR TAKING ME SHOPPING, MOMMY. IT'S MY MOST FAVORITEST THING TO DO EVER!
MINE TOO, DEAR. MINE TOO.
CAN WE DO THIS AGAIN VERY SOON?
AS SOON AS I CAN FIND THE TIME, YES.
THANKS, MOMMY.
I LOVE YOU.
BOOM
PLEASE DON'T DEACTIVATE ME, MOMMY. I CAN TELL WHEN YOU DEACTIVATE ME.
IT FEELS-- COLD. IT'S SCARY.
I HAVE TO, HONEY. I'M SORRY.
I'M SO SORRY.

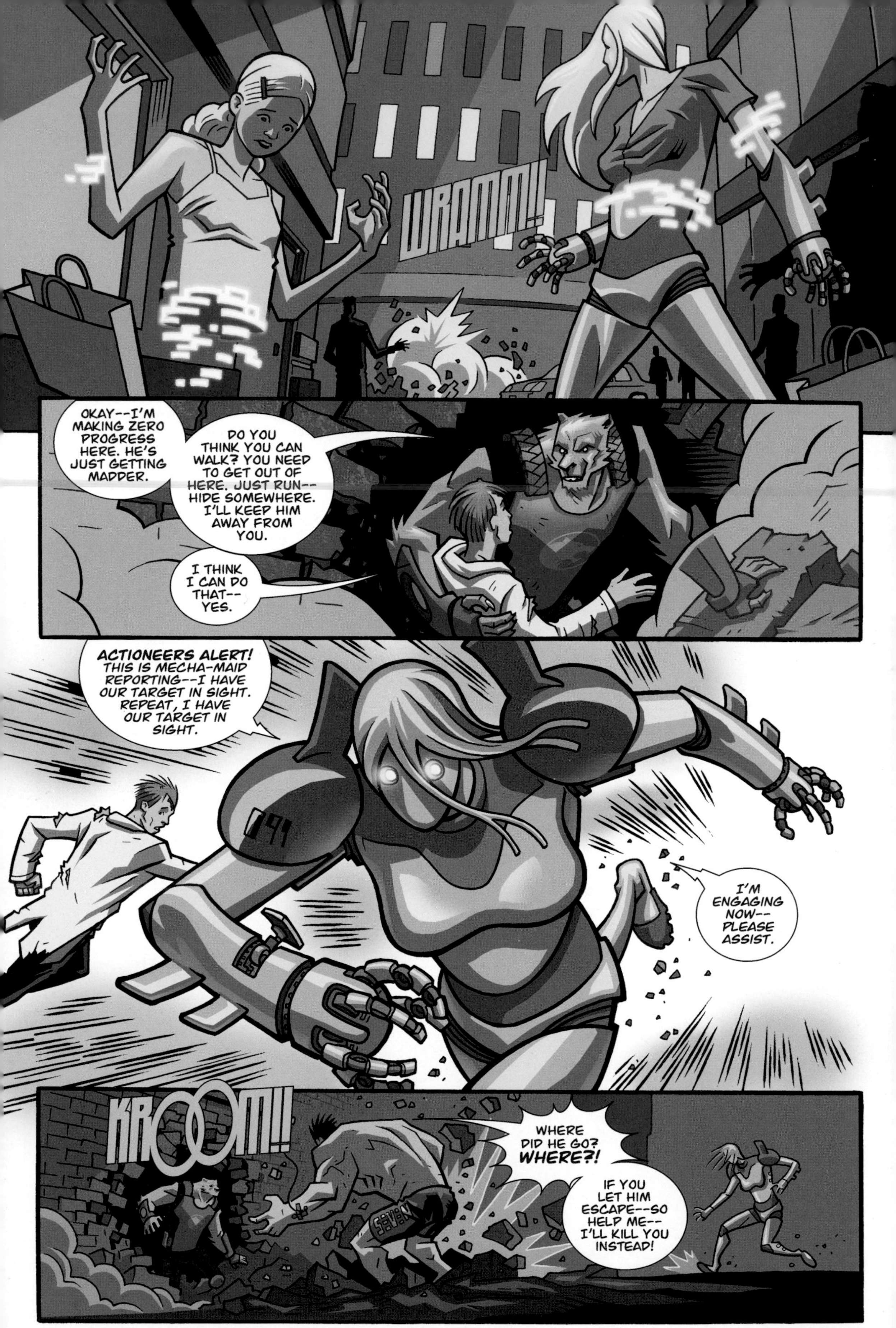
WRAMM!!
OKAY--I'M MAKING ZERO PROGRESS HERE. HE'S JUST GETTING MADDER.
DO YOU THINK YOU CAN WALK? YOU NEED TO GET OUT OF HERE. JUST RUN--HIDE SOMEWHERE. I'LL KEEP HIM AWAY FROM YOU.
I THINK I CAN DO THAT--YES.
ACTIONEERS ALERT! THIS IS MECHA-MAID REPORTING--I HAVE OUR TARGET IN SIGHT. REPEAT, I HAVE OUR TARGET IN SIGHT.
I'M ENGAGING NOW--PLEASE ASSIST.
KROOM!!
WHERE DID HE GO? WHERE?!
IF YOU LET HIM ESCAPE--SO HELP ME--I'LL KILL YOU INSTEAD!

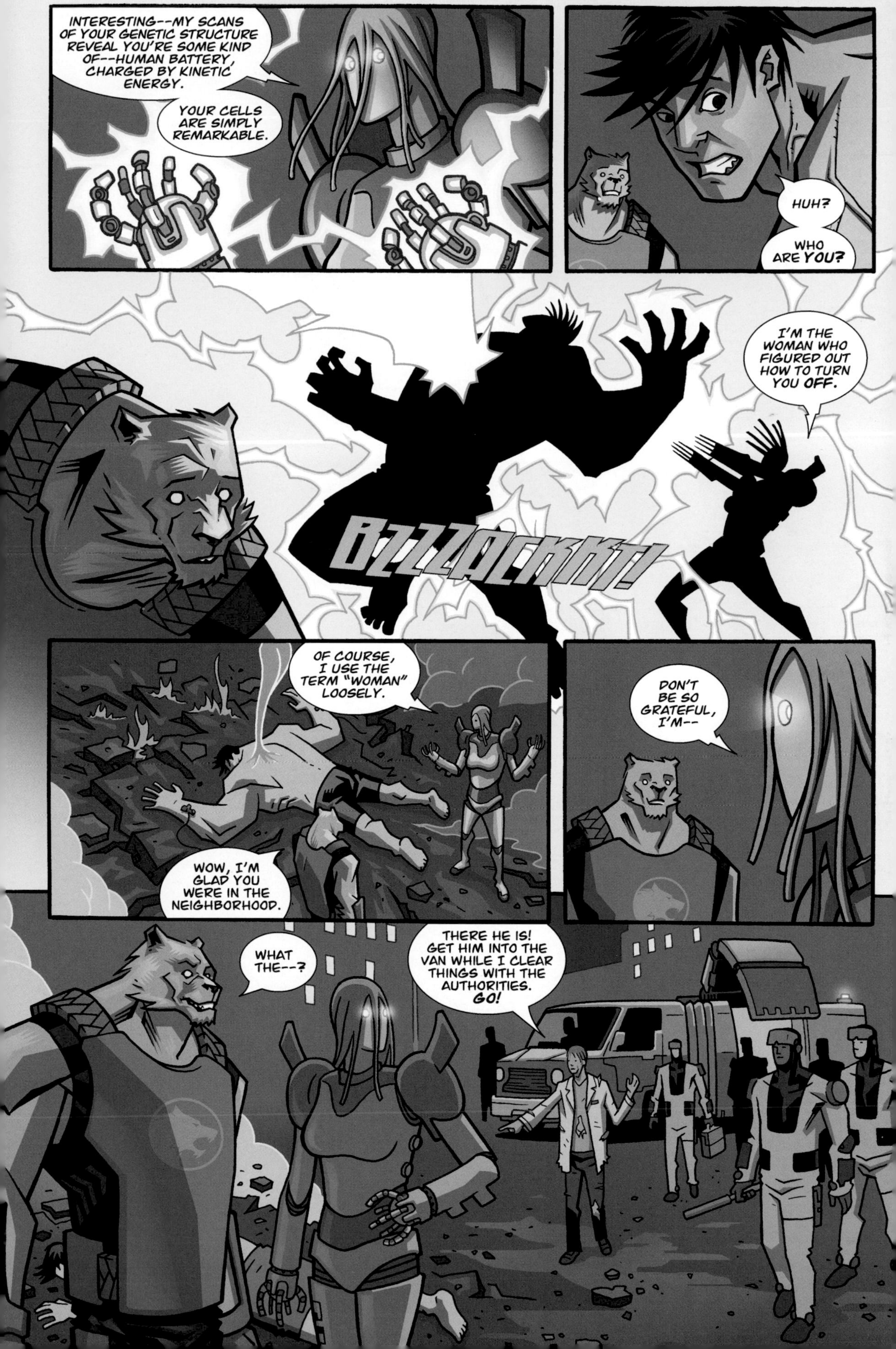
INTERESTING--MY SCANS OF YOUR GENETIC STRUCTURE REVEAL YOU'RE SOME KIND OF--HUMAN BATTERY, CHARGED BY KINETIC ENERGY.
YOUR CELLS ARE SIMPLY REMARKABLE.
HUH?
WHO ARE YOU?
I'M THE WOMAN WHO FIGURED OUT HOW TO TURN YOU OFF.
BZZZACKKKT!
OF COURSE, I USE THE TERM "WOMAN" LOOSELY.
WOW, I'M GLAD YOU WERE IN THE NEIGHBORHOOD.
DON'T BE SO GRATEFUL, I'M--
WHAT THE--?
THERE HE IS! GET HIM INTO THE VAN WHILE I CLEAR THINGS WITH THE AUTHORITIES. GO!

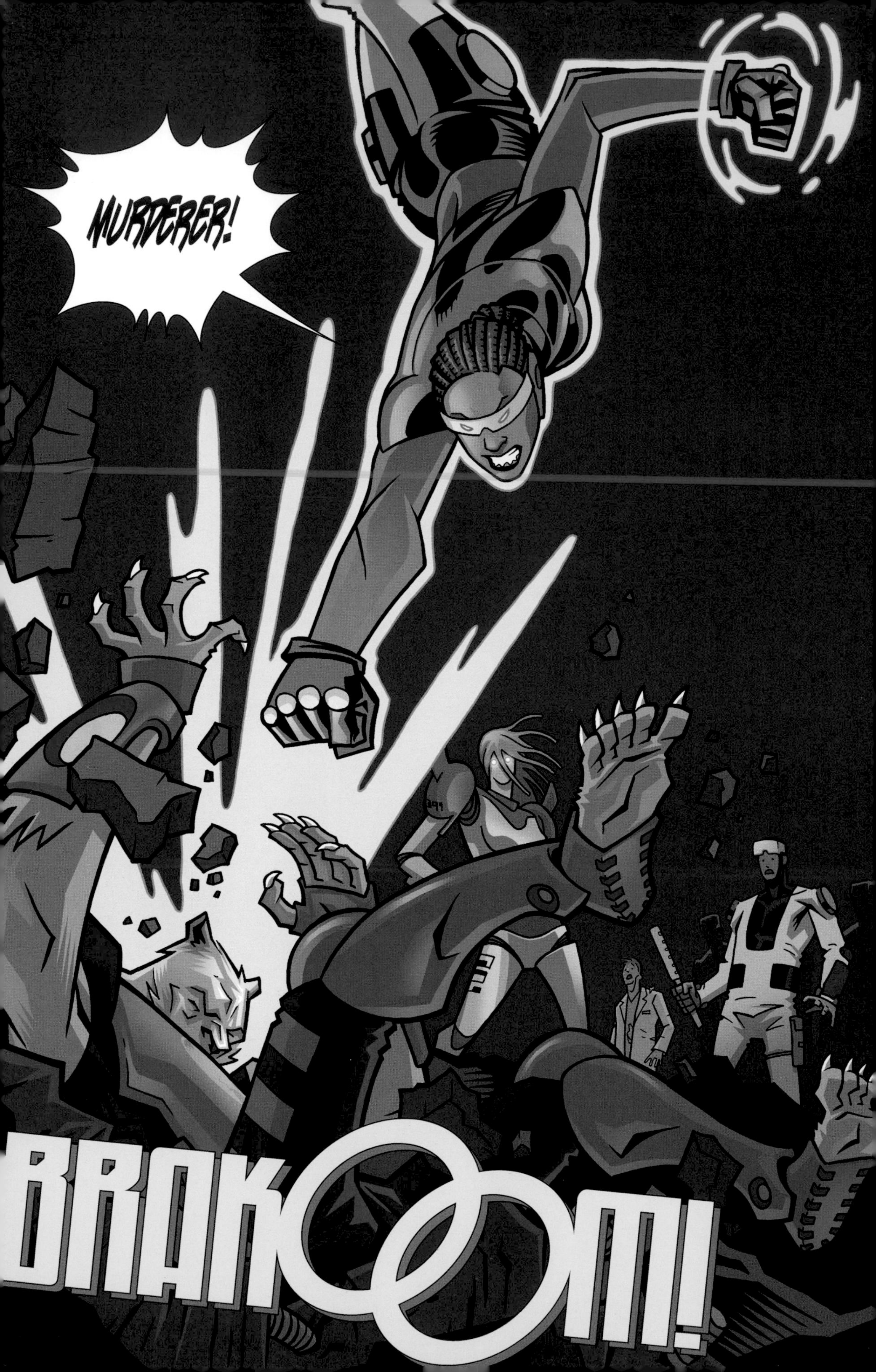
MURDERER!
BRAKOOM!

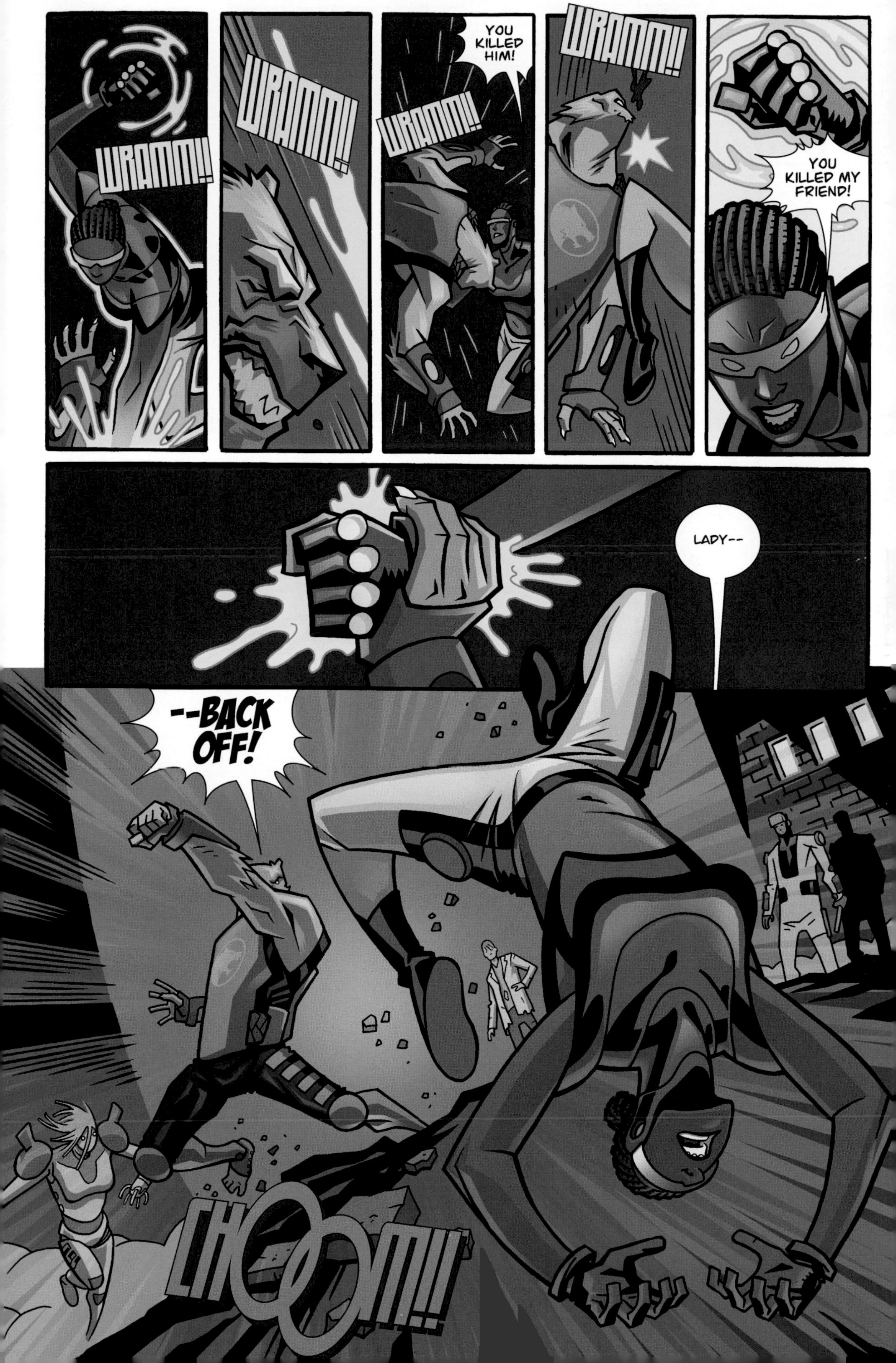
WRAMM!!
WRAMM!!
WRAMM!!
YOU KILLED HIM!
WRAMM!!
YOU KILLED MY FRIEND!
LADY--
--BACK OFF!
CHOOOM!!

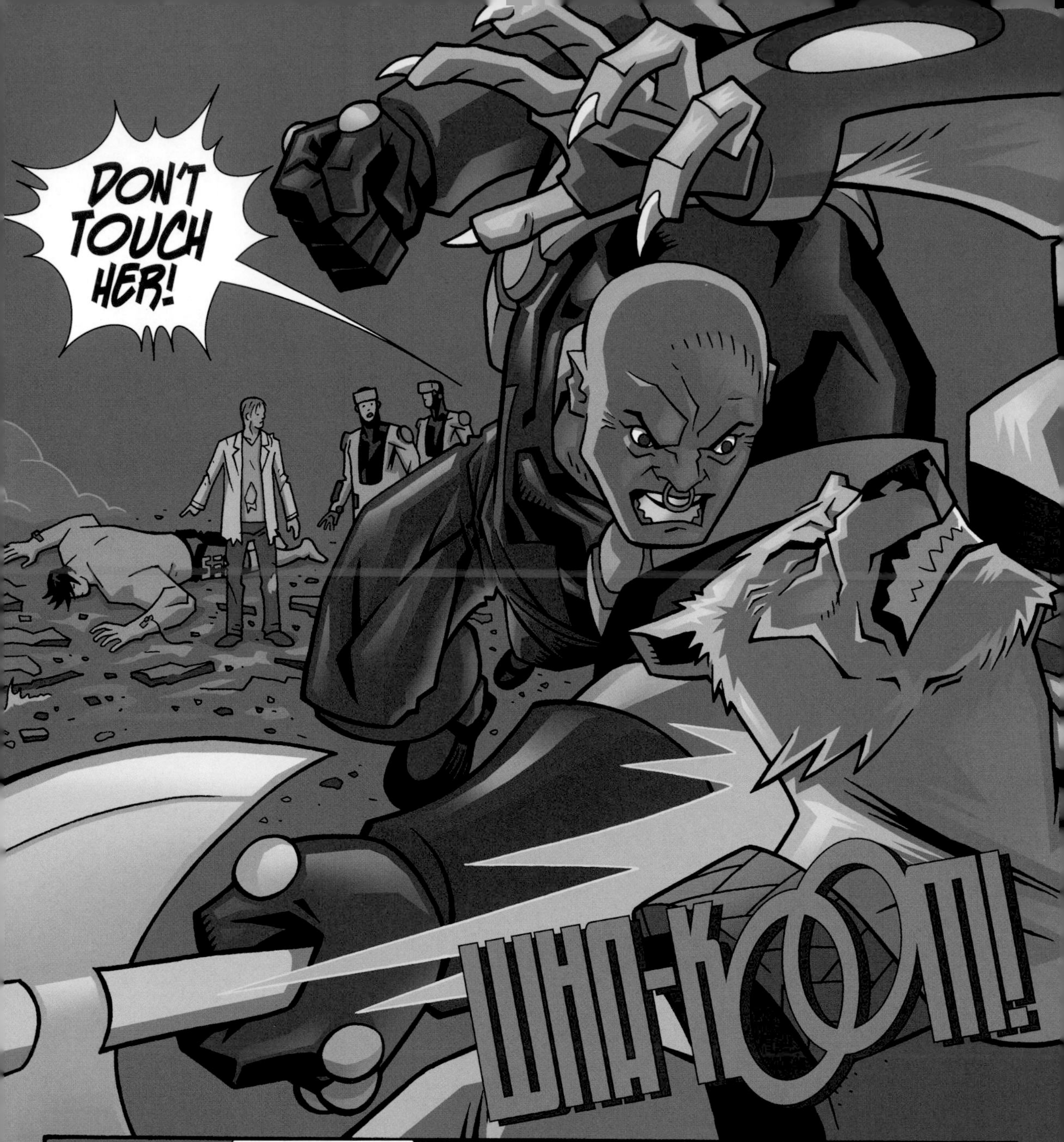
DON'T TOUCH HER!
WHA-KOOM!!

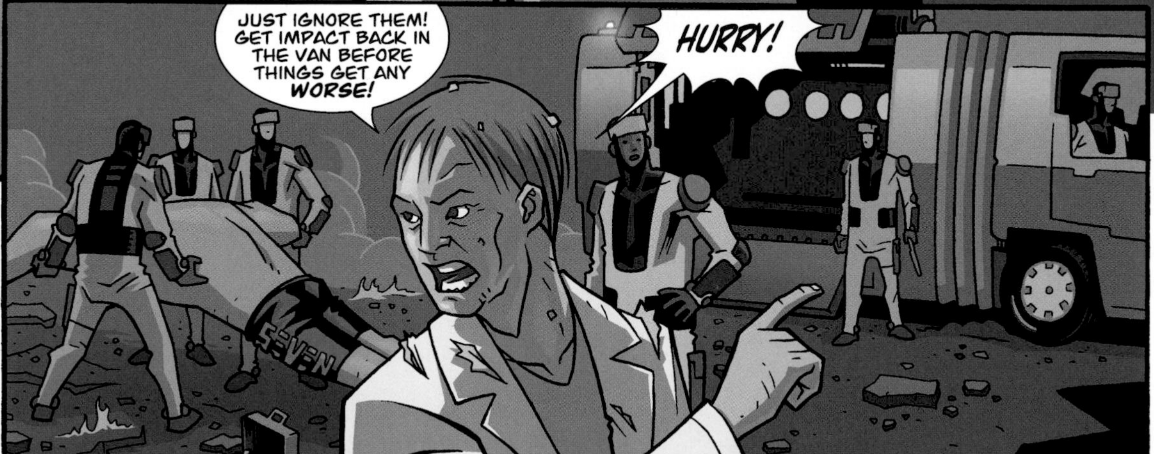
JUST IGNORE THEM! GET IMPACT BACK IN THE VAN BEFORE THINGS GET ANY WORSE!
HURRY!

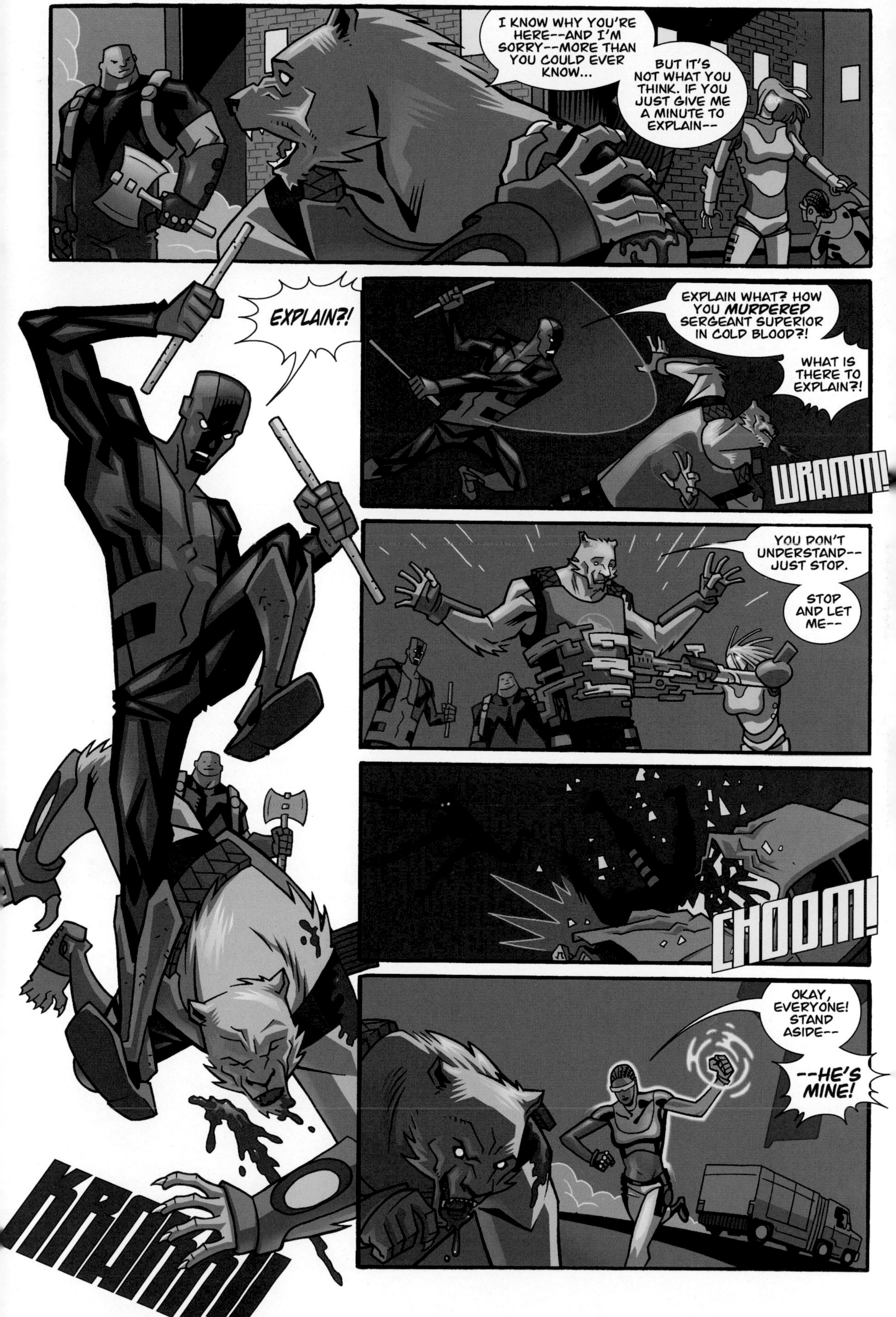

I KNOW WHY YOU'RE HERE--AND I'M SORRY--MORE THAN YOU COULD EVER KNOW...
BUT IT'S NOT WHAT YOU THINK. IF YOU JUST GIVE ME A MINUTE TO EXPLAIN--
EXPLAIN?!
EXPLAIN WHAT? HOW YOU MURDERED SERGEANT SUPERIOR IN COLD BLOOD?!
WHAT IS THERE TO EXPLAIN?!
WRAMM!
YOU DON'T UNDERSTAND--JUST STOP.
STOP AND LET ME--
CHOOM!
OKAY, EVERYONE! STAND ASIDE--
--HE'S MINE!
KRUNN!!

PLEASE! I DON'T WANT TO FIGHT YOU!

I'M NOT GIVING YOU A CHOICE!

CHOOM!

POW!

I WASN'T READY FOR YOU EARLIER—I DIDN'T KNOW HOW FAST YOU WERE. YOU CAUGHT ME OFF GUARD.

I'M GOING TO MAKE YOU PAY FOR WHAT YOU'VE DONE!

NOT THIS TIME—I KNOW WHAT TO EXPECT. YOU'RE GOING DOWN!

WRAMM!

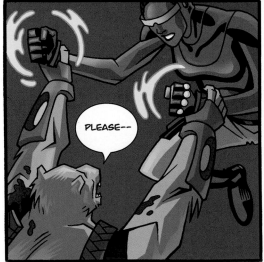

PLEASE—

SHUT UP!

THE LAST THING IN THE WORLD I NEED RIGHT NOW IS TO HEAR YOUR VOICE!

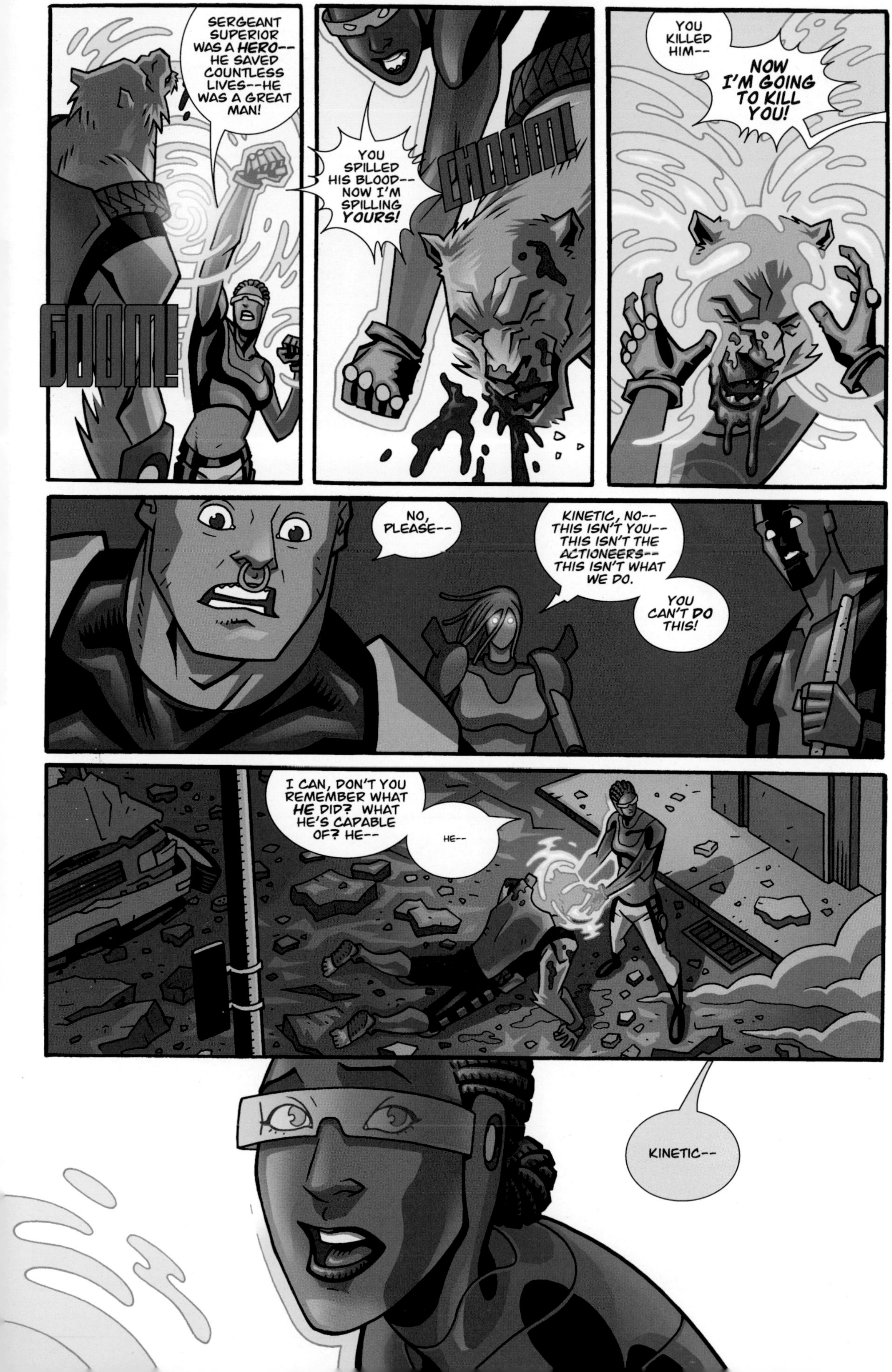
SERGEANT SUPERIOR WAS A HERO--HE SAVED COUNTLESS LIVES--HE WAS A GREAT MAN!
GOOM!
YOU SPILLED HIS BLOOD--NOW I'M SPILLING YOURS!
CHOOM!
YOU KILLED HIM--
NOW I'M GOING TO KILL YOU!
NO, PLEASE--
KINETIC, NO--THIS ISN'T YOU--THIS ISN'T THE ACTIONEERS--THIS ISN'T WHAT WE DO.
YOU CAN'T DO THIS!
I CAN, DON'T YOU REMEMBER WHAT HE DID? WHAT HE'S CAPABLE OF? HE--
HE--
KINETIC--

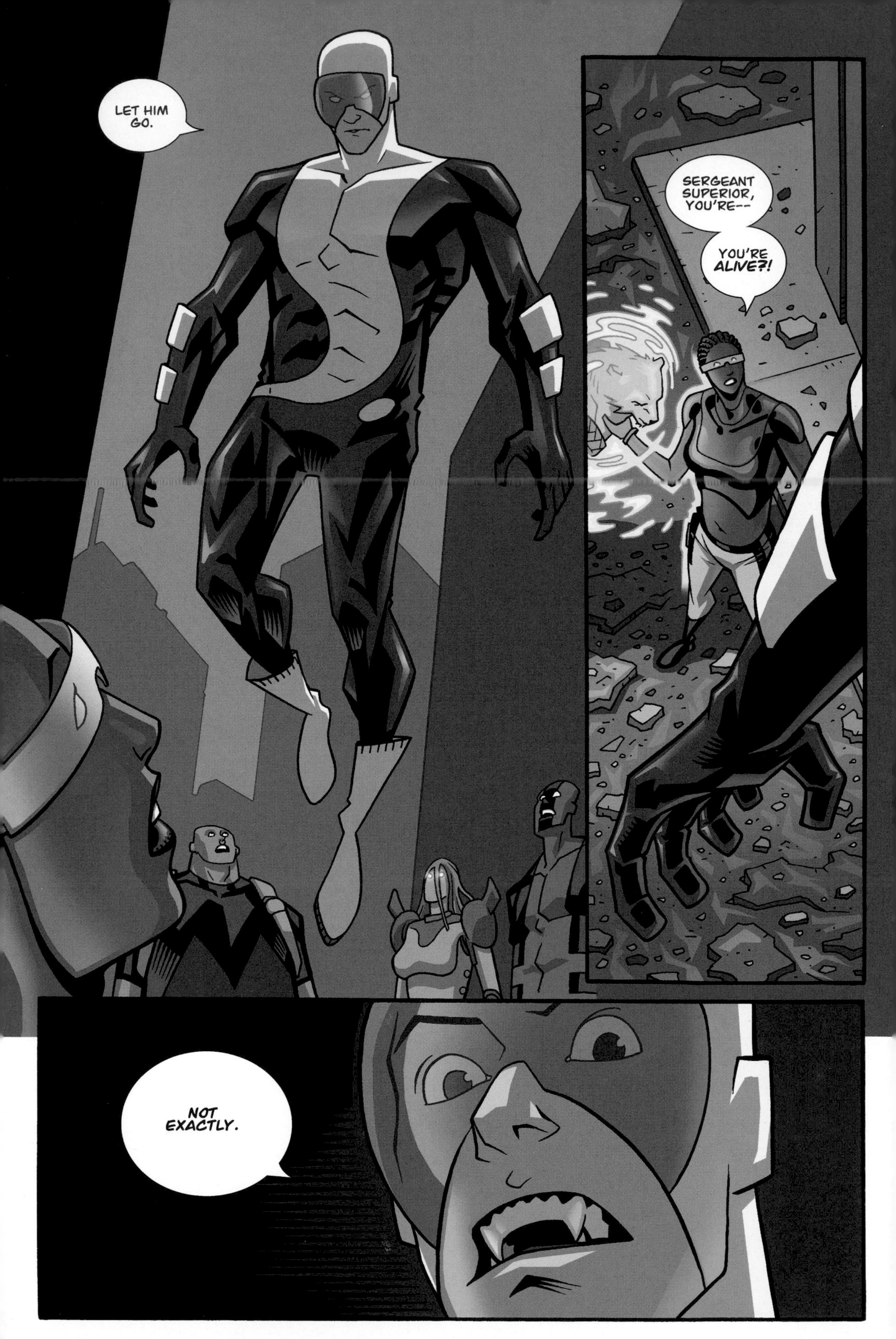
LET HIM GO.
SERGEANT SUPERIOR, YOU'RE--
YOU'RE ALIVE?!
NOT EXACTLY.

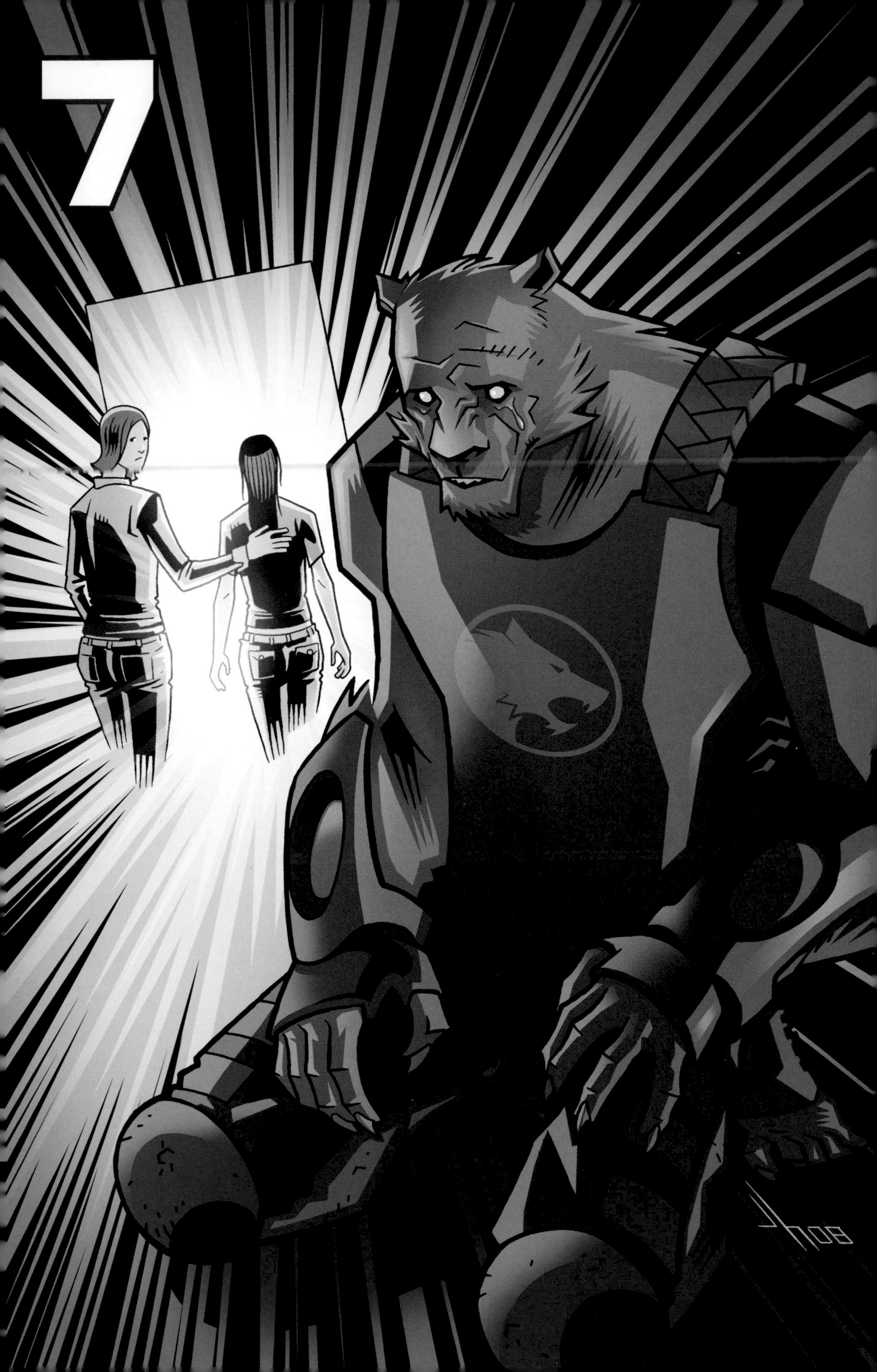
7

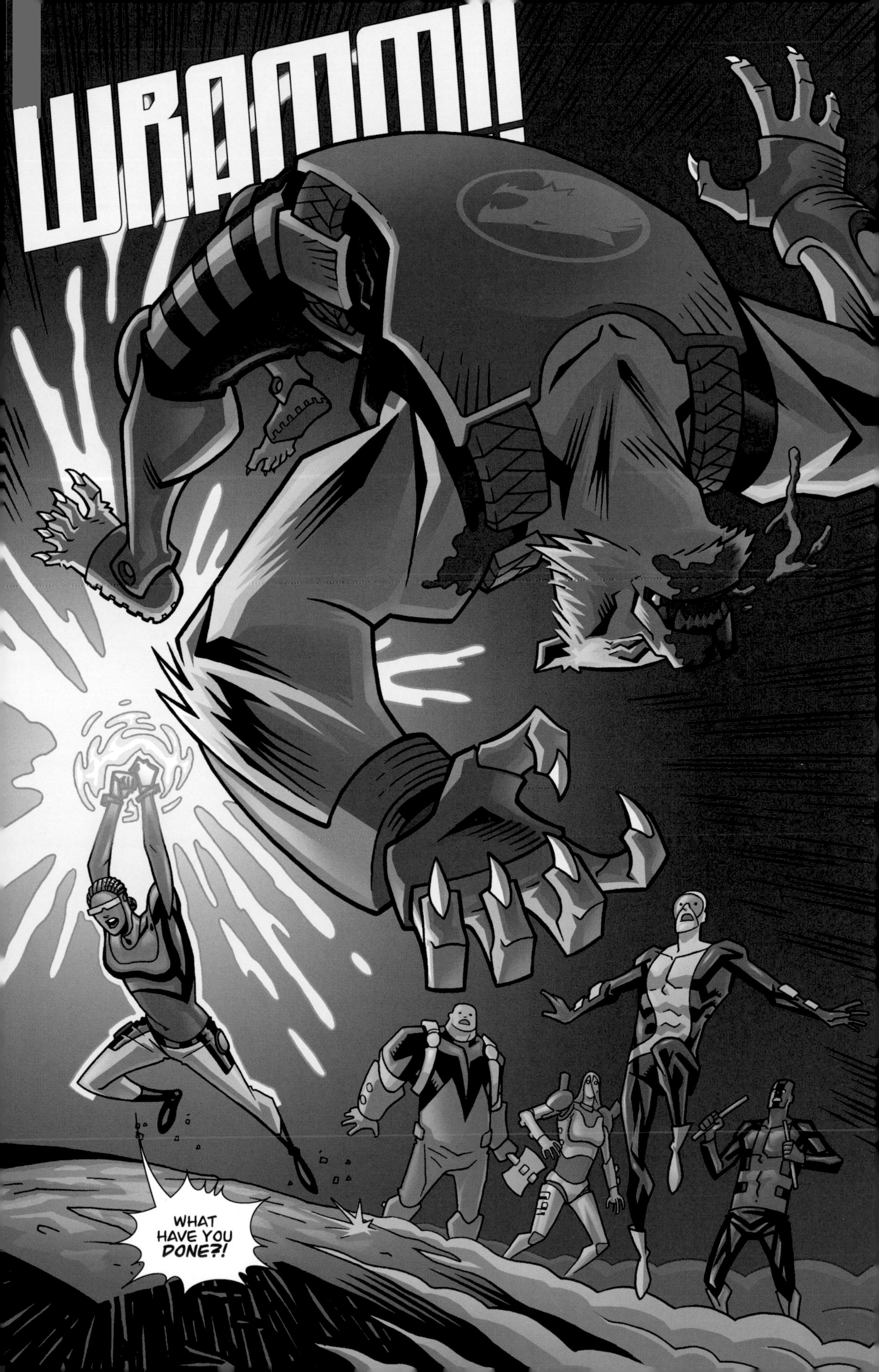
WRAMM!!
WHAT HAVE YOU DONE?!

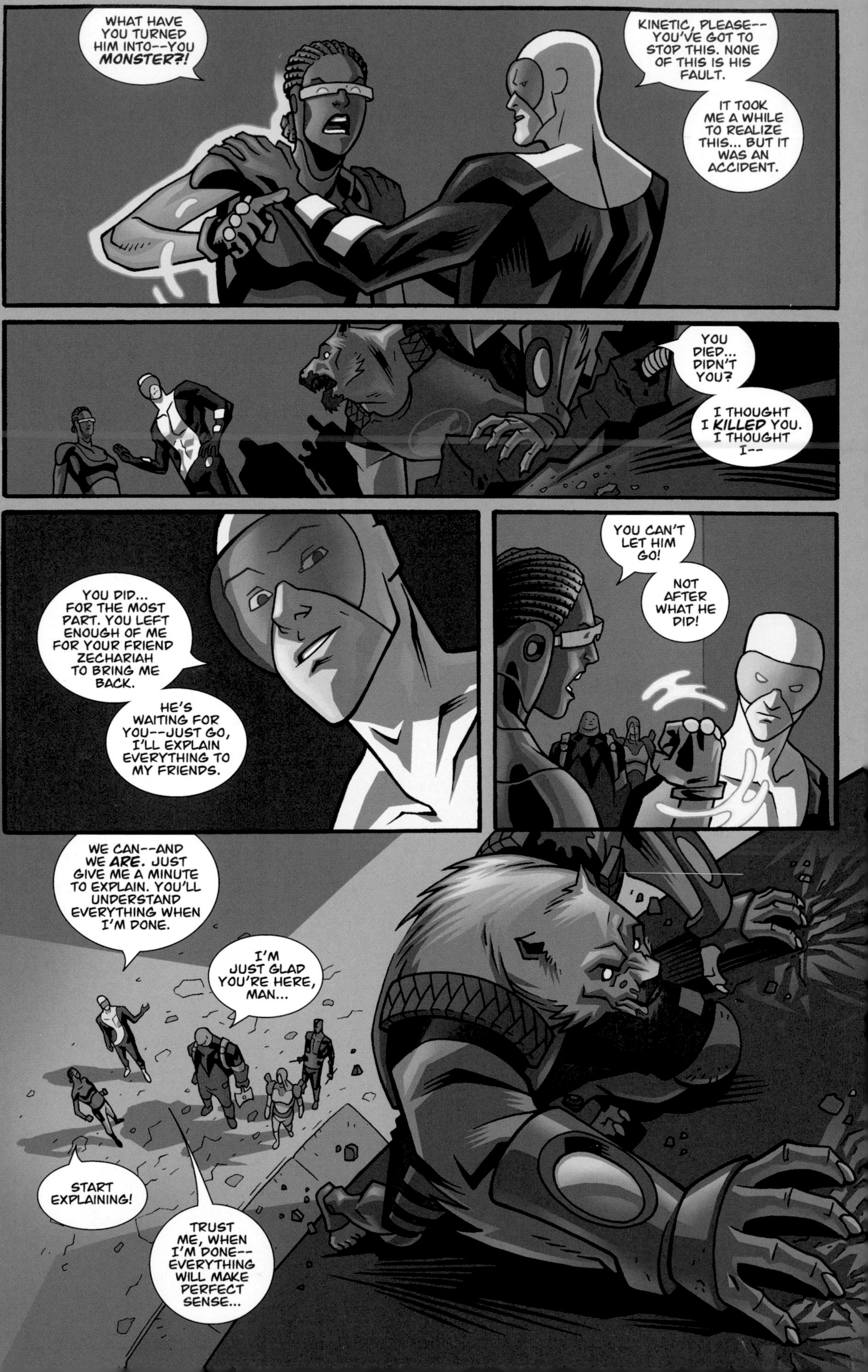
WHAT HAVE YOU TURNED HIM INTO--YOU MONSTER?!
KINETIC, PLEASE-- YOU'VE GOT TO STOP THIS. NONE OF THIS IS HIS FAULT.
IT TOOK ME A WHILE TO REALIZE THIS... BUT IT WAS AN ACCIDENT.
YOU DIED... DIDN'T YOU?
I THOUGHT I KILLED YOU. I THOUGHT I--
YOU DID... FOR THE MOST PART. YOU LEFT ENOUGH OF ME FOR YOUR FRIEND ZECHARIAH TO BRING ME BACK.
HE'S WAITING FOR YOU--JUST GO, I'LL EXPLAIN EVERYTHING TO MY FRIENDS.
YOU CAN'T LET HIM GO!
NOT AFTER WHAT HE DID!
WE CAN--AND WE ARE. JUST GIVE ME A MINUTE TO EXPLAIN. YOU'LL UNDERSTAND EVERYTHING WHEN I'M DONE.
I'M JUST GLAD YOU'RE HERE, MAN...
START EXPLAINING!
TRUST ME, WHEN I'M DONE-- EVERYTHING WILL MAKE PERFECT SENSE...

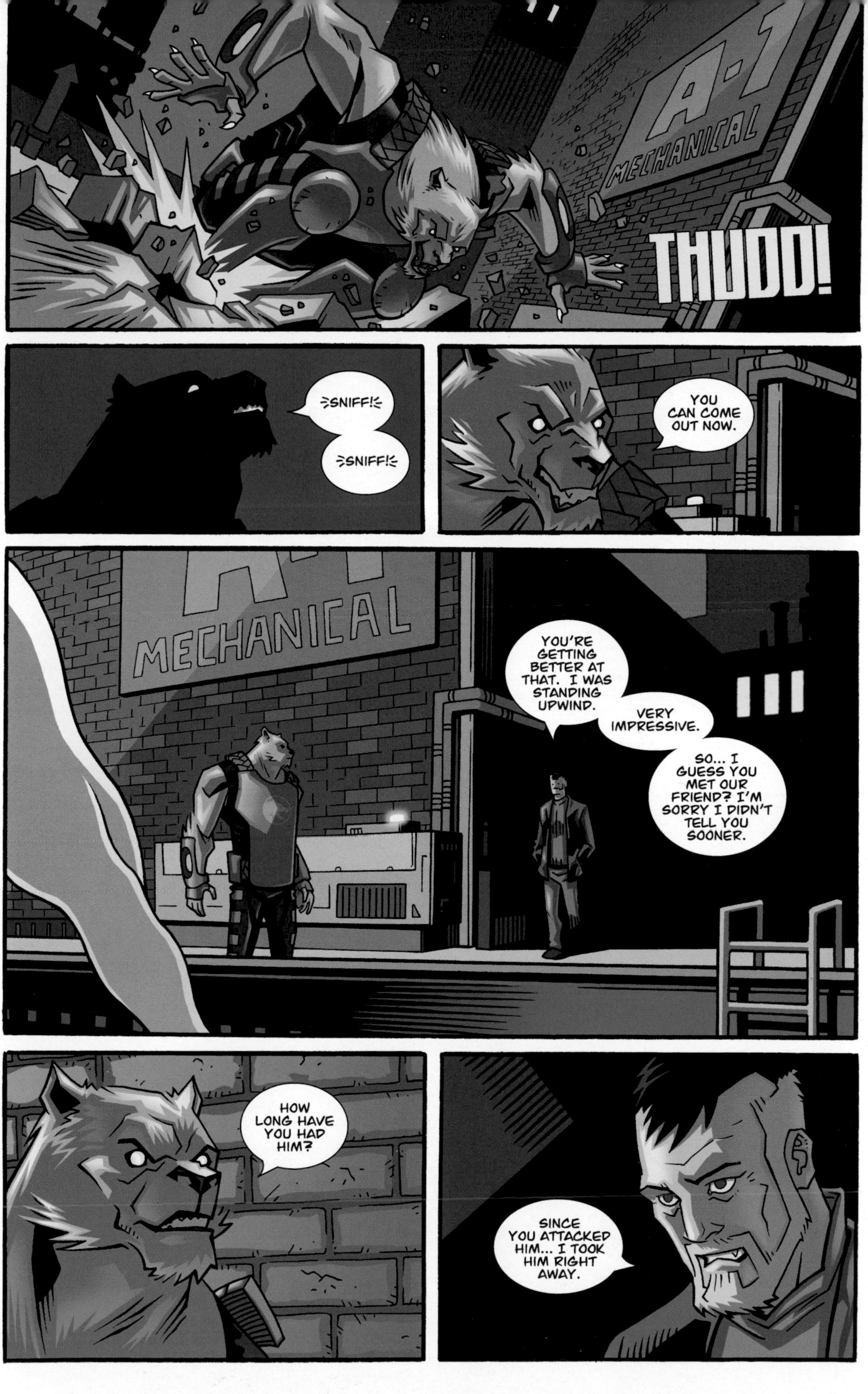
A-1
MECHANICAL
THUDD!
SNIFF!
SNIFF!
YOU CAN COME OUT NOW.
MECHANICAL
YOU'RE GETTING BETTER AT THAT. I WAS STANDING UPWIND.
VERY IMPRESSIVE.
SO... I GUESS YOU MET OUR FRIEND? I'M SORRY I DIDN'T TELL YOU SOONER.
HOW LONG HAVE YOU HAD HIM?
SINCE YOU ATTACKED HIM... I TOOK HIM RIGHT AWAY.

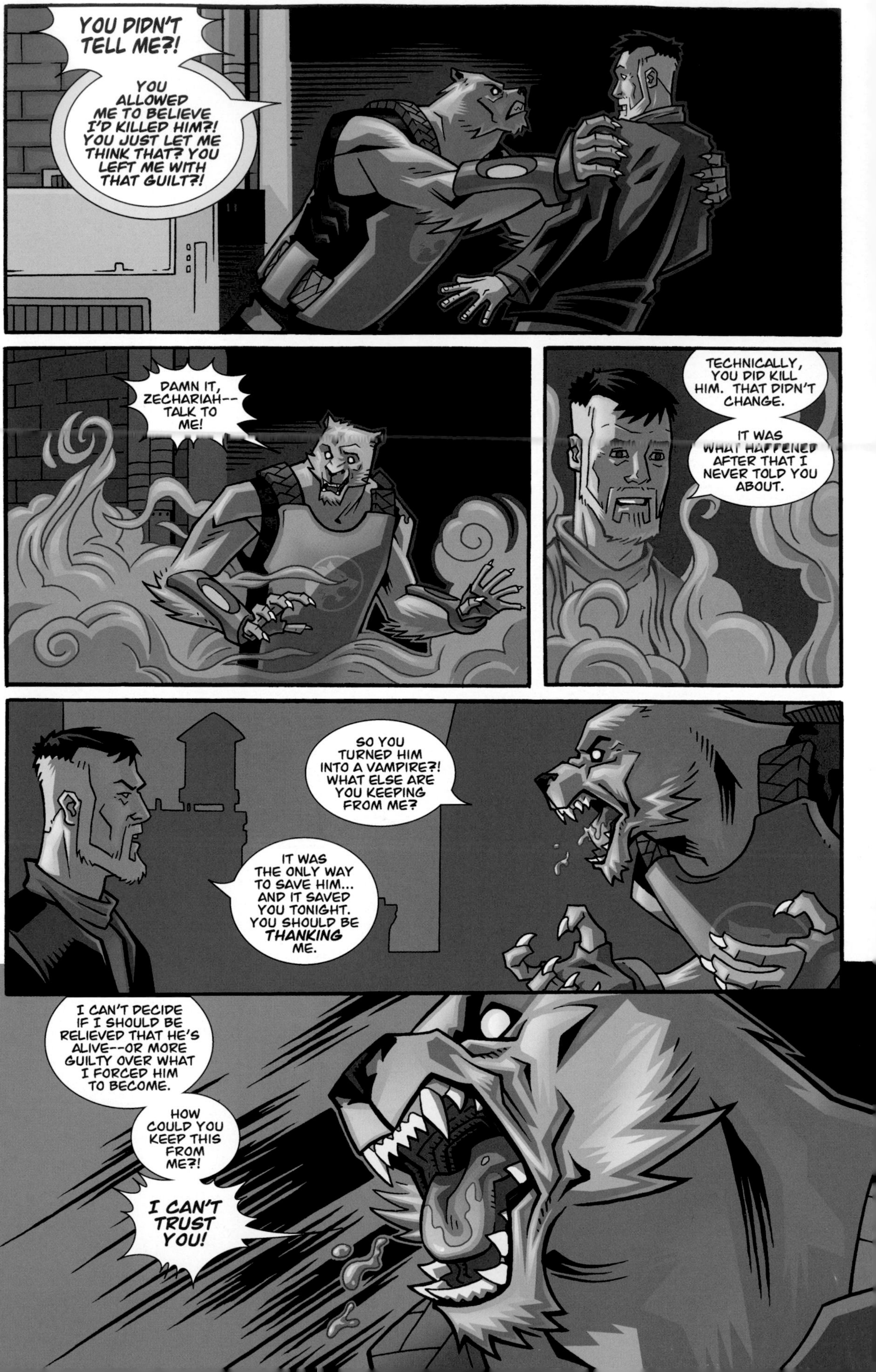
YOU DIDN'T TELL ME?!
YOU ALLOWED ME TO BELIEVE I'D KILLED HIM?! YOU JUST LET ME THINK THAT? YOU LEFT ME WITH THAT GUILT?!
DAMN IT, ZECHARIAH--TALK TO ME!
TECHNICALLY, YOU DID KILL HIM. THAT DIDN'T CHANGE.
IT WAS WHAT HAPPENED AFTER THAT I NEVER TOLD YOU ABOUT.
SO YOU TURNED HIM INTO A VAMPIRE?! WHAT ELSE ARE YOU KEEPING FROM ME?
IT WAS THE ONLY WAY TO SAVE HIM... AND IT SAVED YOU TONIGHT. YOU SHOULD BE THANKING ME.
I CAN'T DECIDE IF I SHOULD BE RELIEVED THAT HE'S ALIVE--OR MORE GUILTY OVER WHAT I FORCED HIM TO BECOME.
HOW COULD YOU KEEP THIS FROM ME?!
I CAN'T TRUST YOU!

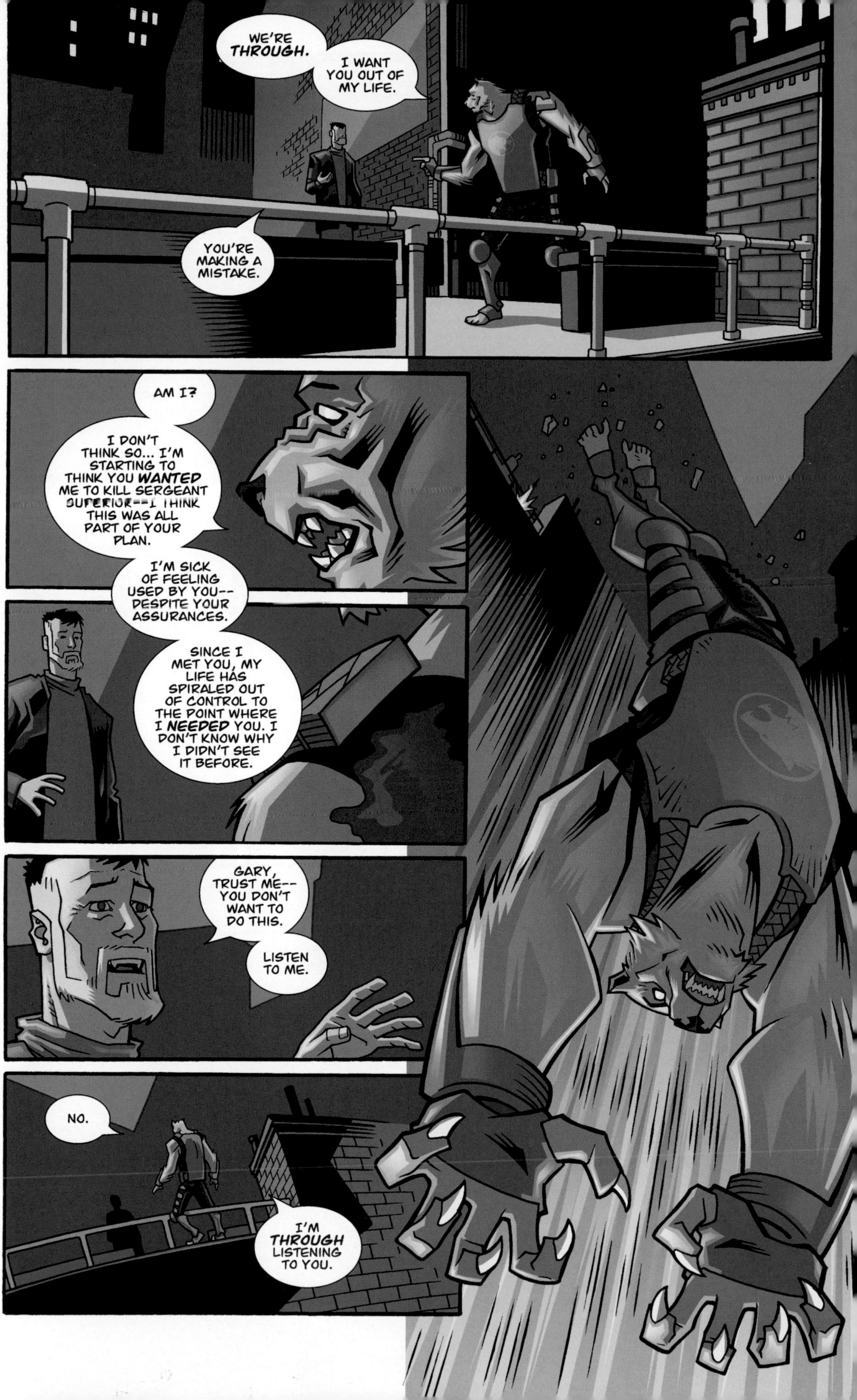
WE'RE THROUGH.
I WANT YOU OUT OF MY LIFE.
YOU'RE MAKING A MISTAKE.
AM I?
I DON'T THINK SO... I'M STARTING TO THINK YOU WANTED ME TO KILL SERGEANT SUPERIOR--I THINK THIS WAS ALL PART OF YOUR PLAN.
I'M SICK OF FEELING USED BY YOU--DESPITE YOUR ASSURANCES.
SINCE I MET YOU, MY LIFE HAS SPIRALED OUT OF CONTROL TO THE POINT WHERE I NEEDED YOU. I DON'T KNOW WHY I DIDN'T SEE IT BEFORE.
GARY, TRUST ME--YOU DON'T WANT TO DO THIS.
LISTEN TO ME.
NO.
I'M THROUGH LISTENING TO YOU.

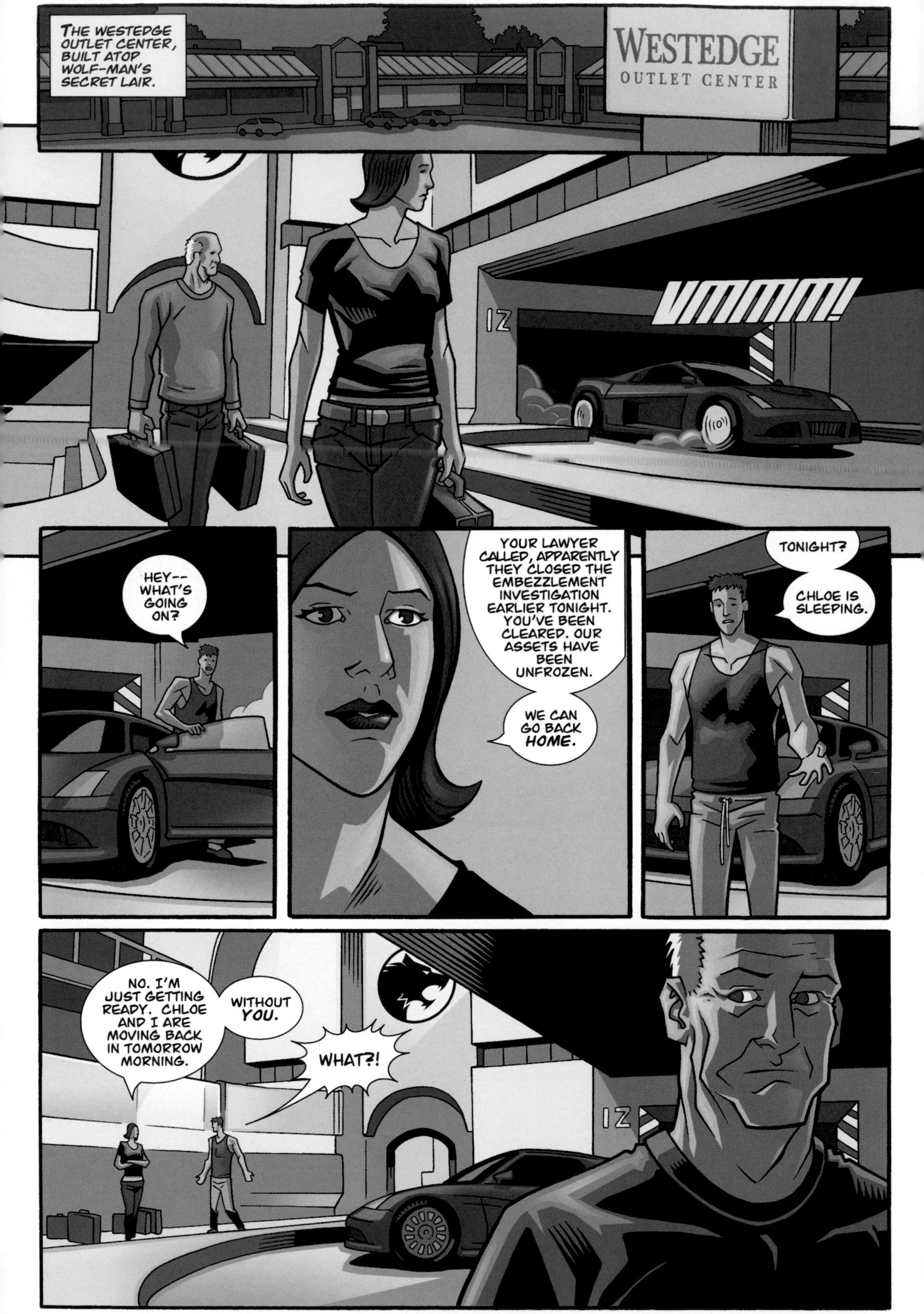

THE WESTEDGE OUTLET CENTER, BUILT ATOP WOLF-MAN'S SECRET LAIR.
WESTEDGE
OUTLET CENTER
VMMMM!
HEY-- WHAT'S GOING ON?
YOUR LAWYER CALLED, APPARENTLY THEY CLOSED THE EMBEZZLEMENT INVESTIGATION EARLIER TONIGHT. YOU'VE BEEN CLEARED. OUR ASSETS HAVE BEEN UNFROZEN.
WE CAN GO BACK HOME.
TONIGHT?
CHLOE IS SLEEPING.
NO. I'M JUST GETTING READY. CHLOE AND I ARE MOVING BACK IN TOMORROW MORNING.
WITHOUT YOU.
WHAT?!

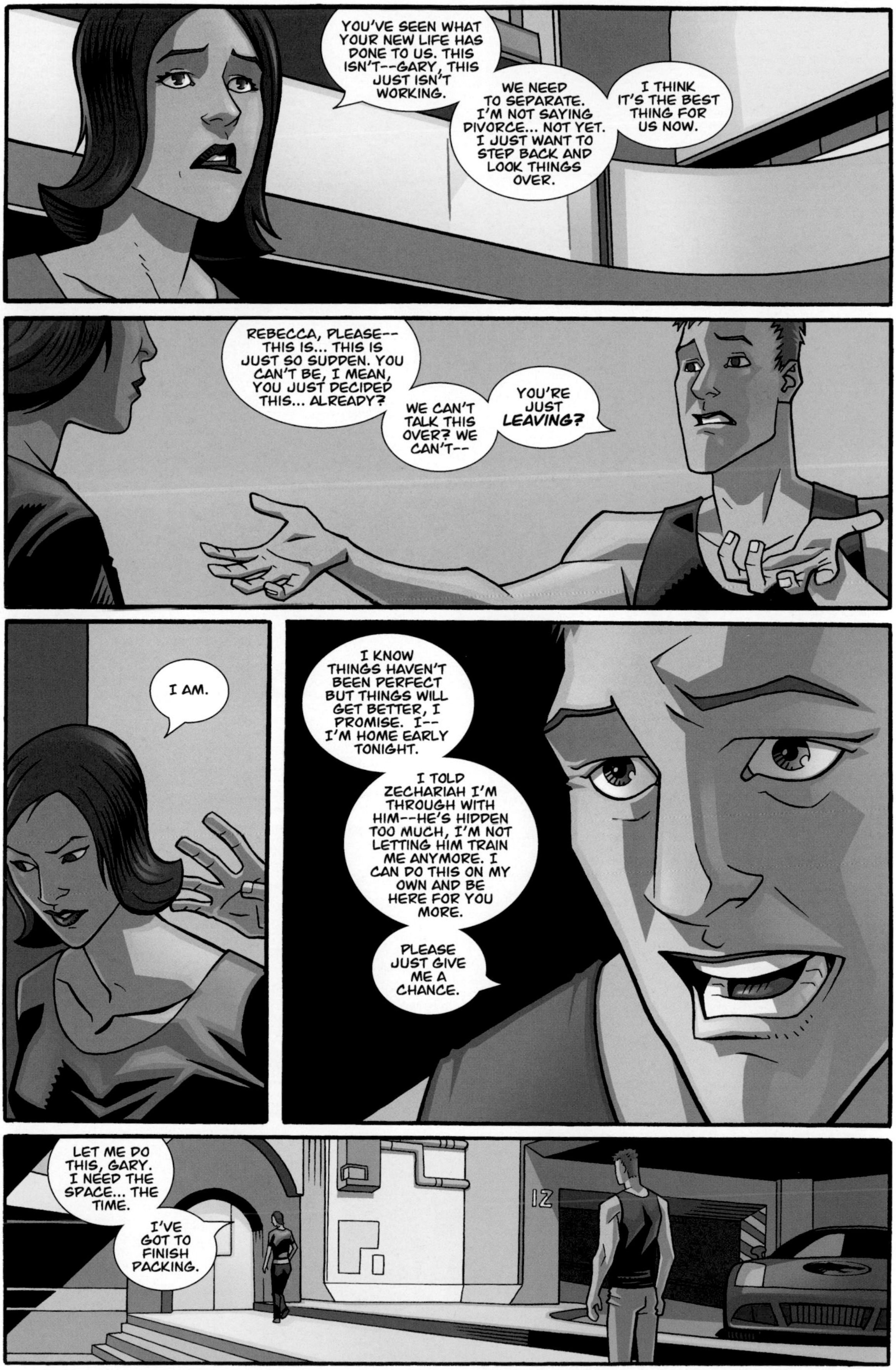
YOU'VE SEEN WHAT YOUR NEW LIFE HAS DONE TO US. THIS ISN'T--GARY, THIS JUST ISN'T WORKING.
WE NEED TO SEPARATE. I'M NOT SAYING DIVORCE... NOT YET. I JUST WANT TO STEP BACK AND LOOK THINGS OVER.
I THINK IT'S THE BEST THING FOR US NOW.
REBECCA, PLEASE-- THIS IS... THIS IS JUST SO SUDDEN. YOU CAN'T BE, I MEAN, YOU JUST DECIDED THIS... ALREADY?
WE CAN'T TALK THIS OVER? WE CAN'T--
YOU'RE JUST LEAVING?
I AM.
I KNOW THINGS HAVEN'T BEEN PERFECT BUT THINGS WILL GET BETTER, I PROMISE. I-- I'M HOME EARLY TONIGHT.
I TOLD ZECHARIAH I'M THROUGH WITH HIM--HE'S HIDDEN TOO MUCH, I'M NOT LETTING HIM TRAIN ME ANYMORE. I CAN DO THIS ON MY OWN AND BE HERE FOR YOU MORE.
PLEASE JUST GIVE ME A CHANCE.
LET ME DO THIS, GARY. I NEED THE SPACE... THE TIME.
I'VE GOT TO FINISH PACKING.
12

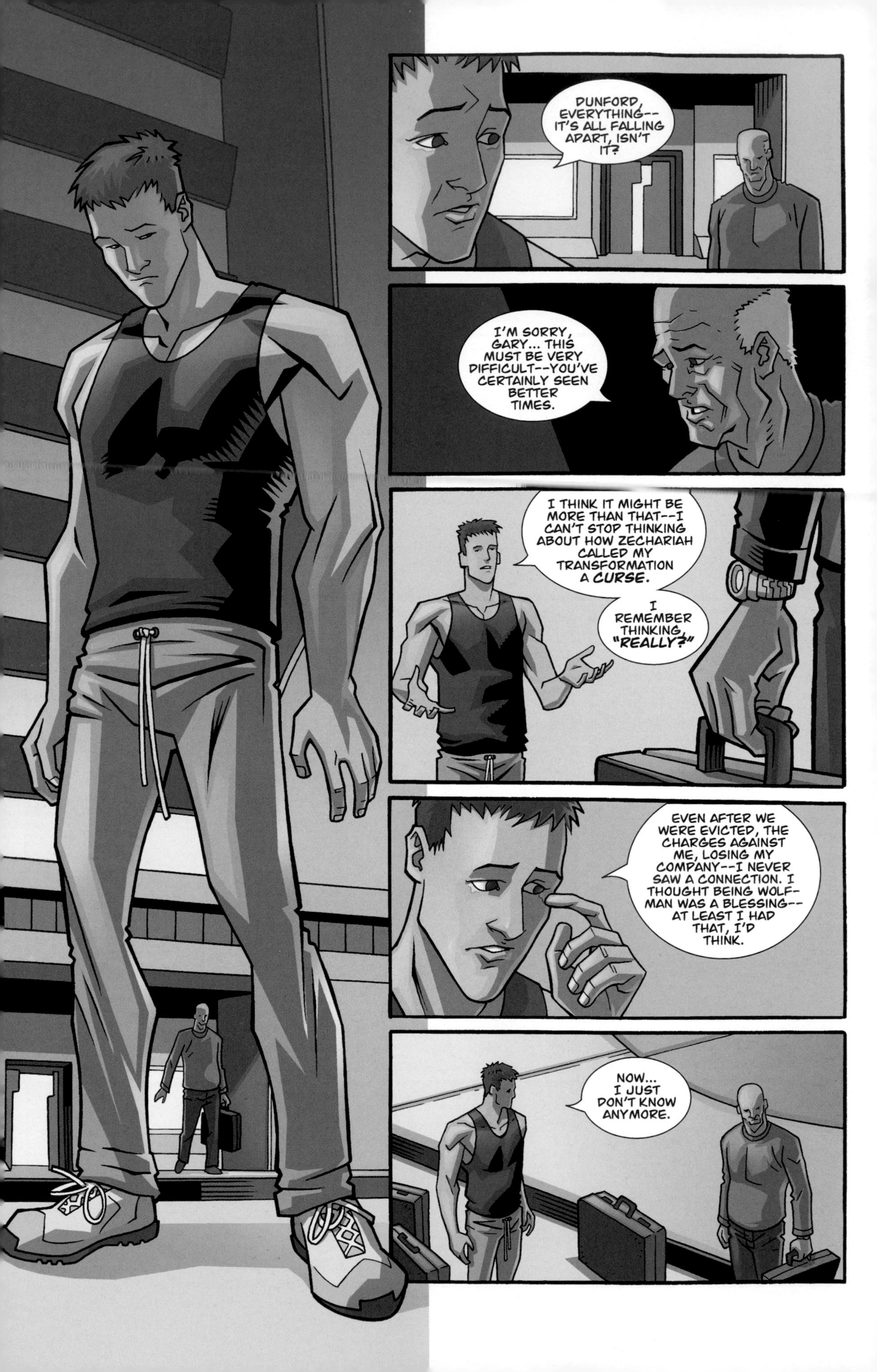
DUNFORD, EVERYTHING-- IT'S ALL FALLING APART, ISN'T IT?
I'M SORRY, GARY... THIS MUST BE VERY DIFFICULT--YOU'VE CERTAINLY SEEN BETTER TIMES.
I THINK IT MIGHT BE MORE THAN THAT--I CAN'T STOP THINKING ABOUT HOW ZECHARIAH CALLED MY TRANSFORMATION A CURSE.
I REMEMBER THINKING, "REALLY?"
EVEN AFTER WE WERE EVICTED, THE CHARGES AGAINST ME, LOSING MY COMPANY--I NEVER SAW A CONNECTION. I THOUGHT BEING WOLF-MAN WAS A BLESSING-- AT LEAST I HAD THAT, I'D THINK.
NOW... I JUST DON'T KNOW ANYMORE.

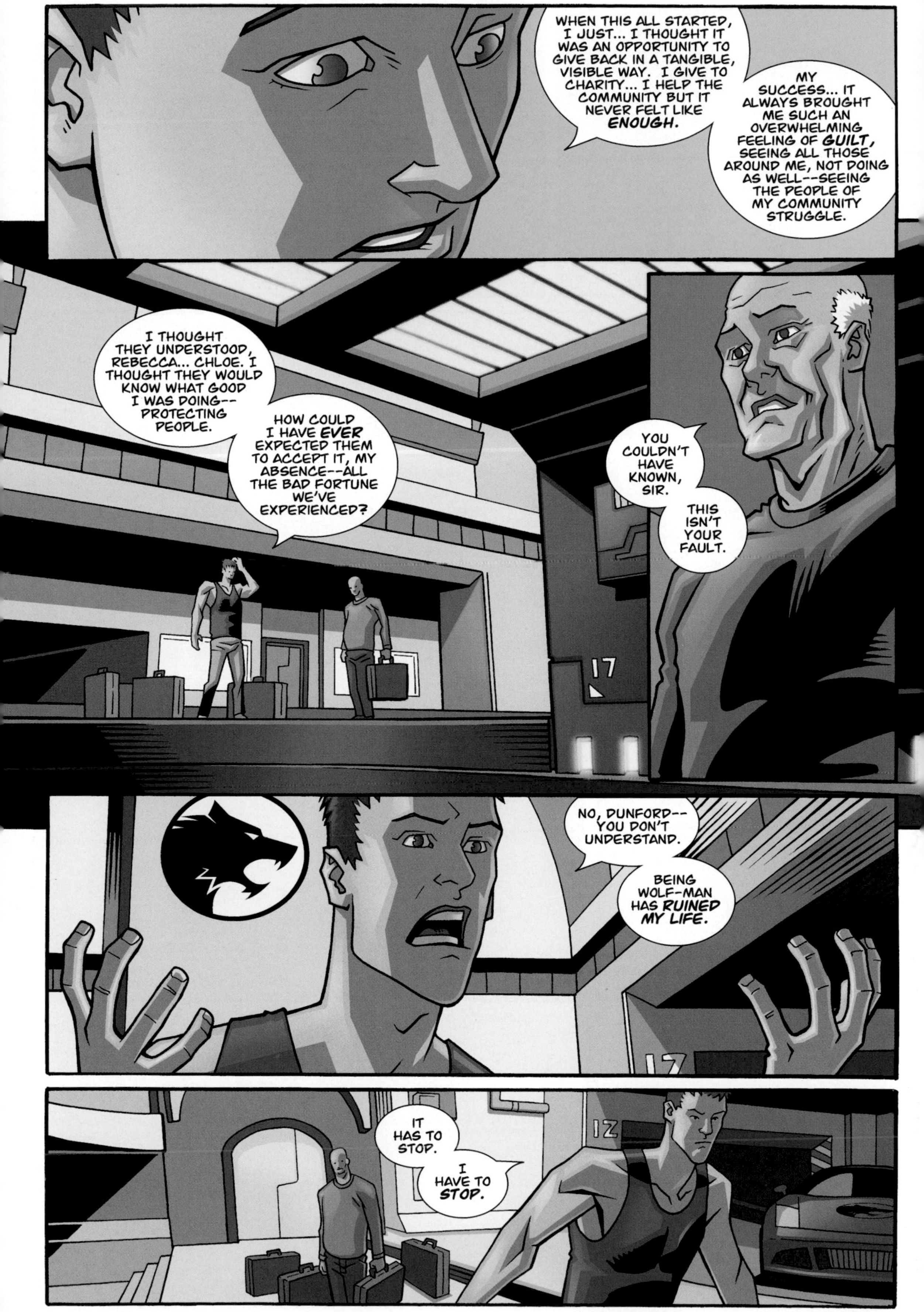
WHEN THIS ALL STARTED, I JUST... I THOUGHT IT WAS AN OPPORTUNITY TO GIVE BACK IN A TANGIBLE, VISIBLE WAY. I GIVE TO CHARITY... I HELP THE COMMUNITY BUT IT NEVER FELT LIKE ENOUGH.
MY SUCCESS... IT ALWAYS BROUGHT ME SUCH AN OVERWHELMING FEELING OF GUILT, SEEING ALL THOSE AROUND ME, NOT DOING AS WELL--SEEING THE PEOPLE OF MY COMMUNITY STRUGGLE.
I THOUGHT THEY UNDERSTOOD, REBECCA... CHLOE. I THOUGHT THEY WOULD KNOW WHAT GOOD I WAS DOING--PROTECTING PEOPLE.
HOW COULD I HAVE EVER EXPECTED THEM TO ACCEPT IT, MY ABSENCE--ALL THE BAD FORTUNE WE'VE EXPERIENCED?
YOU COULDN'T HAVE KNOWN, SIR.
THIS ISN'T YOUR FAULT.
17
NO, DUNFORD--YOU DON'T UNDERSTAND.
BEING WOLF-MAN HAS RUINED MY LIFE.
17
IT HAS TO STOP.
I HAVE TO STOP.
17

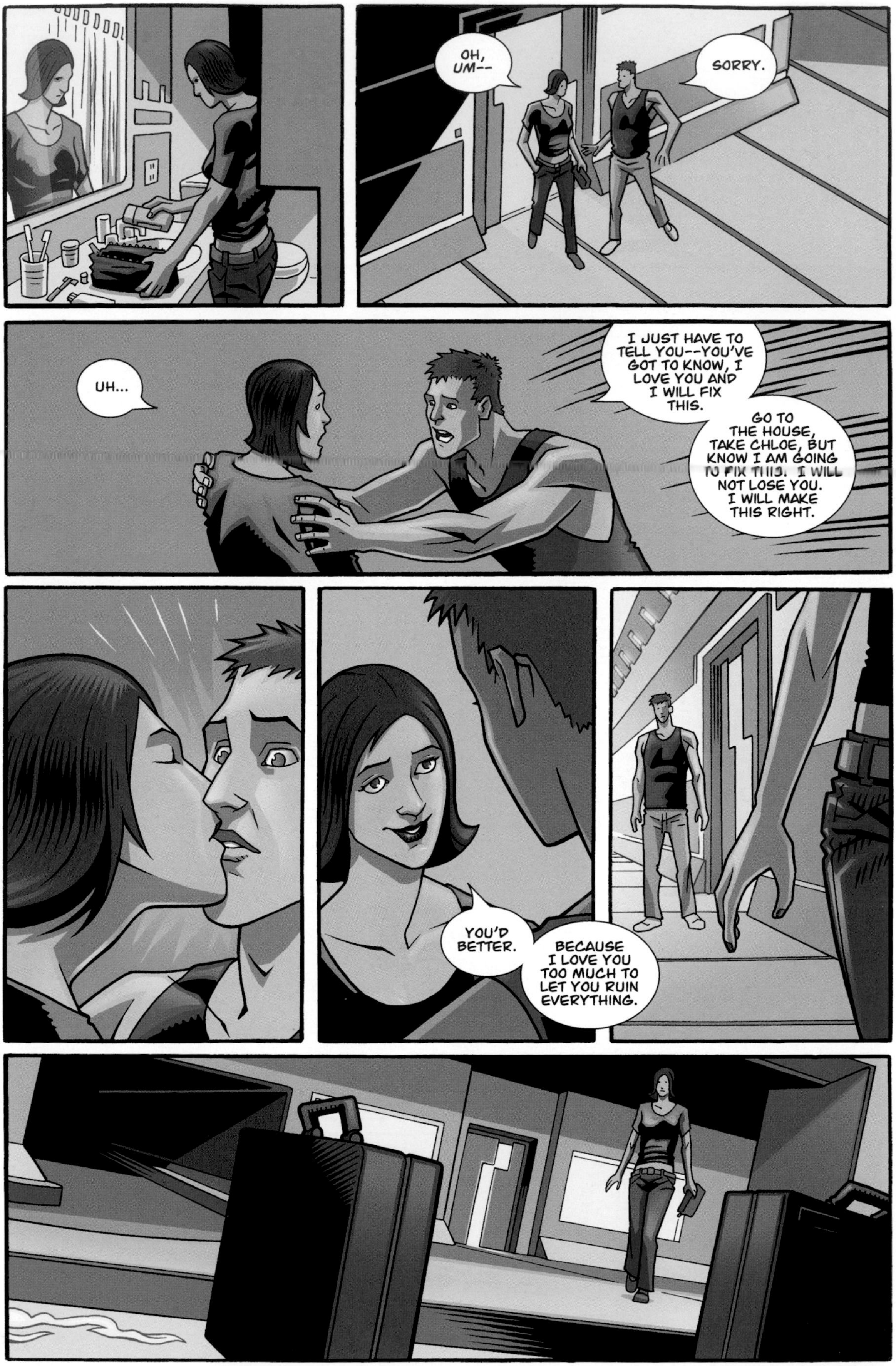
OH, UM--
SORRY.
UH...
I JUST HAVE TO TELL YOU--YOU'VE GOT TO KNOW, I LOVE YOU AND I WILL FIX THIS.
GO TO THE HOUSE, TAKE CHLOE, BUT KNOW I AM GOING TO FIX THIS. I WILL NOT LOSE YOU. I WILL MAKE THIS RIGHT.
YOU'D BETTER.
BECAUSE I LOVE YOU TOO MUCH TO LET YOU RUIN EVERYTHING.

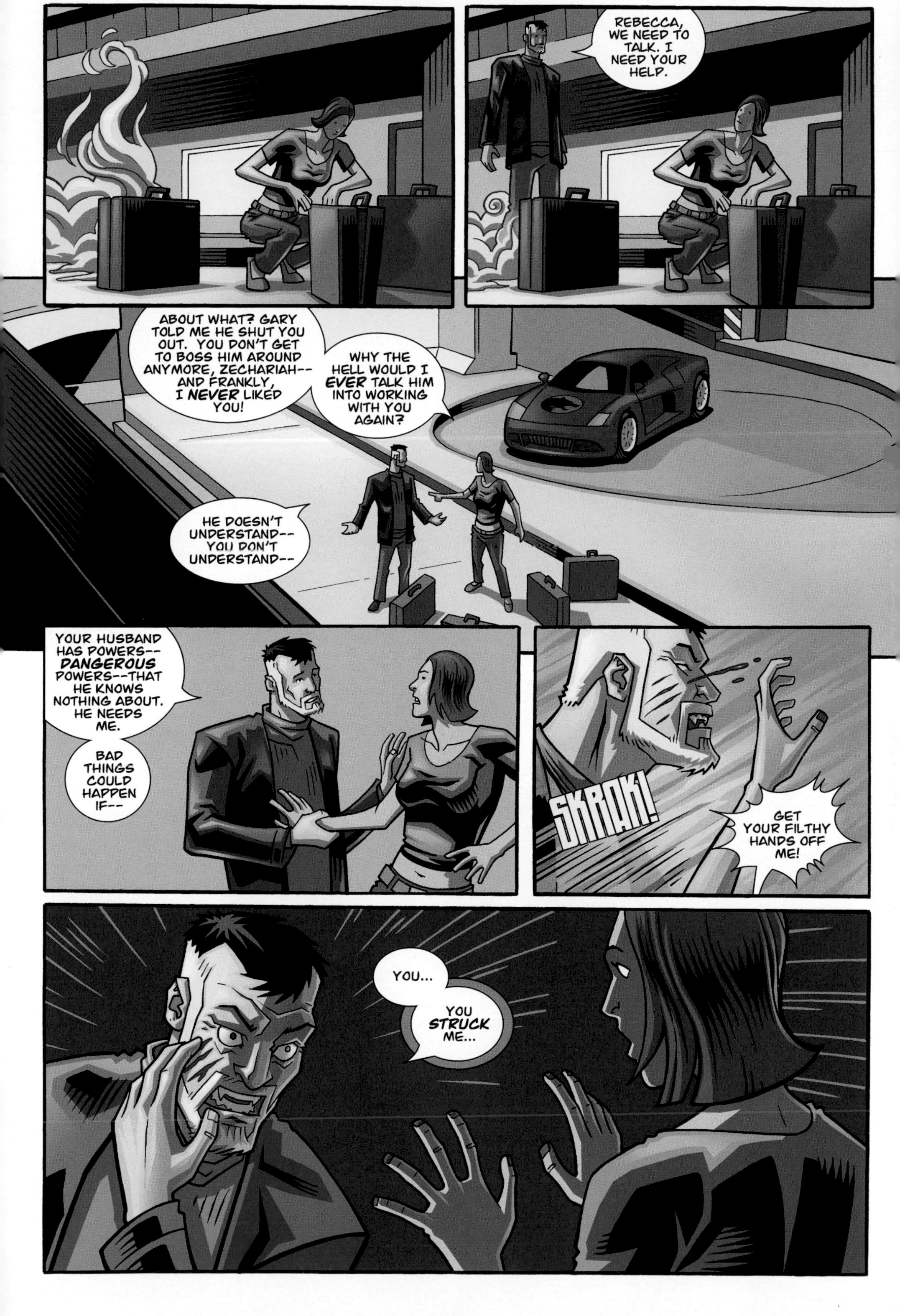
REBECCA, WE NEED TO TALK. I NEED YOUR HELP.
ABOUT WHAT? GARY TOLD ME HE SHUT YOU OUT. YOU DON'T GET TO BOSS HIM AROUND ANYMORE, ZECHARIAH-- AND FRANKLY, I NEVER LIKED YOU!
WHY THE HELL WOULD I EVER TALK HIM INTO WORKING WITH YOU AGAIN?
HE DOESN'T UNDERSTAND-- YOU DON'T UNDERSTAND--
YOUR HUSBAND HAS POWERS-- DANGEROUS POWERS--THAT HE KNOWS NOTHING ABOUT. HE NEEDS ME.
BAD THINGS COULD HAPPEN IF--
SKRAK!
GET YOUR FILTHY HANDS OFF ME!
YOU...
YOU STRUCK ME...

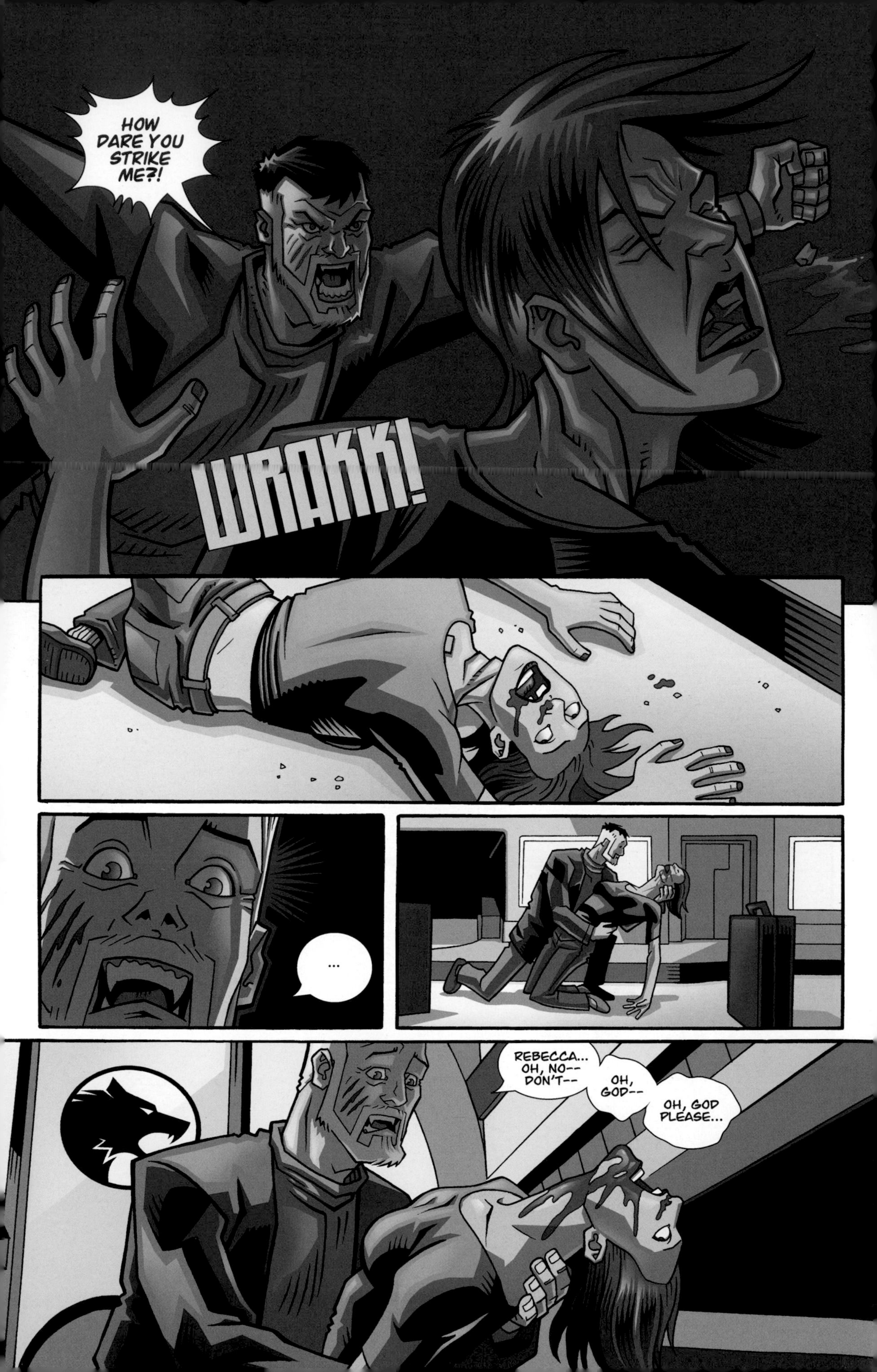
HOW DARE YOU STRIKE ME?!
WRAKK!
...
REBECCA... OH, NO-- DON'T--
OH, GOD--
OH, GOD PLEASE...

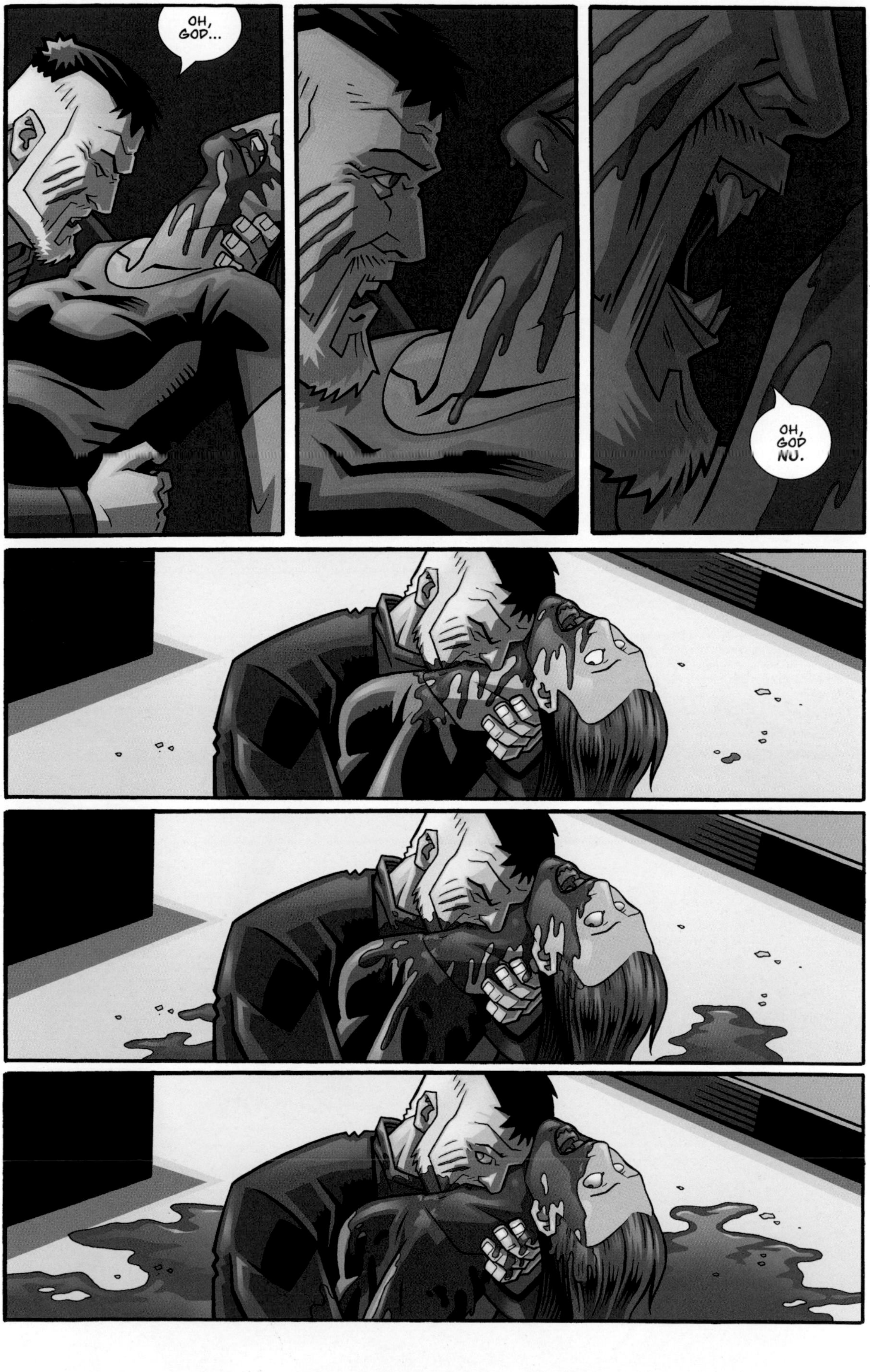
OH, GOD...
OH, GOD NU.

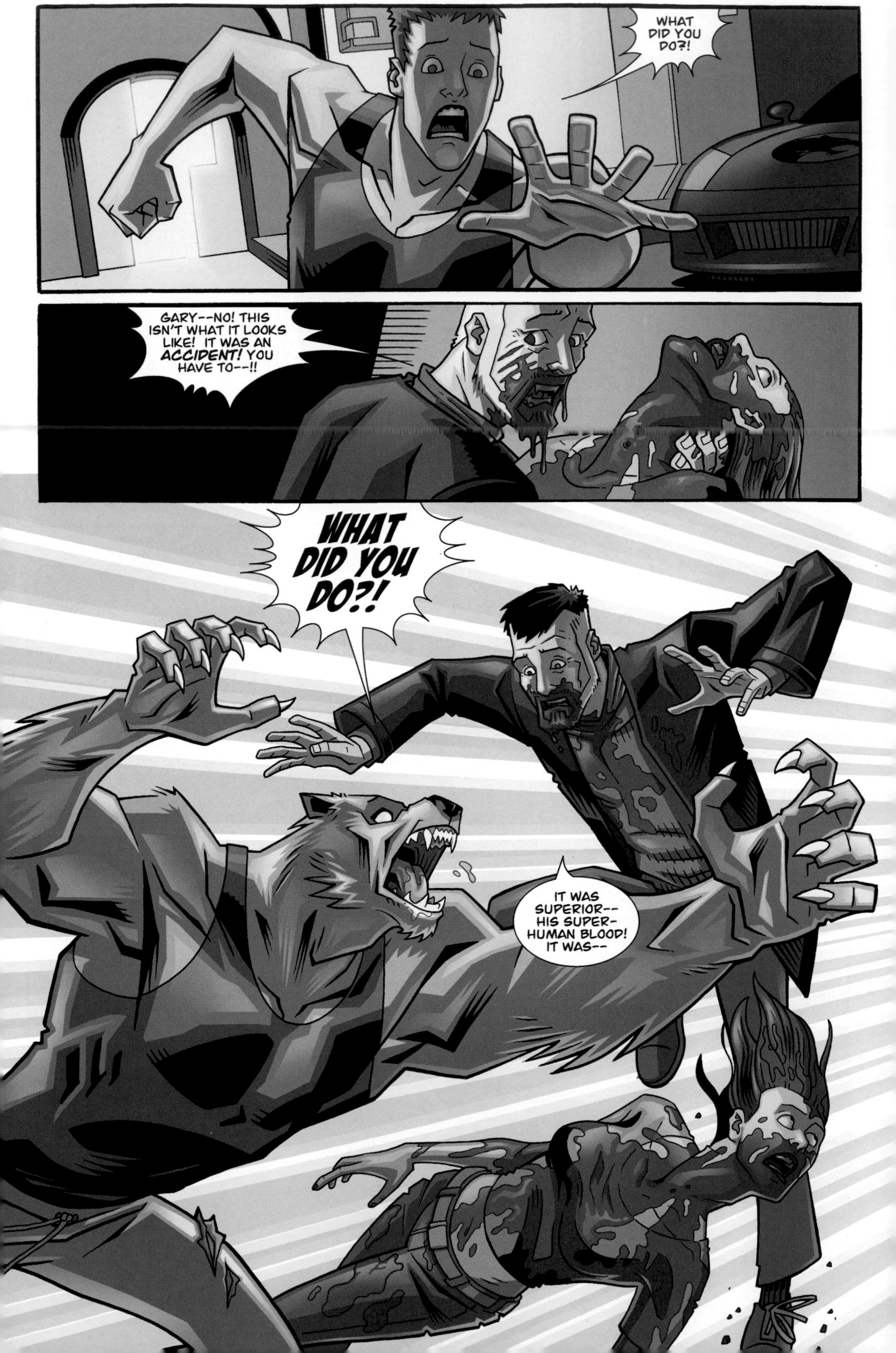
WHAT DID YOU DO?!
GARY--NO! THIS ISN'T WHAT IT LOOKS LIKE! IT WAS AN ACCIDENT! YOU HAVE TO--!!
WHAT DID YOU DO?!
IT WAS SUPERIOR-- HIS SUPER-HUMAN BLOOD! IT WAS--

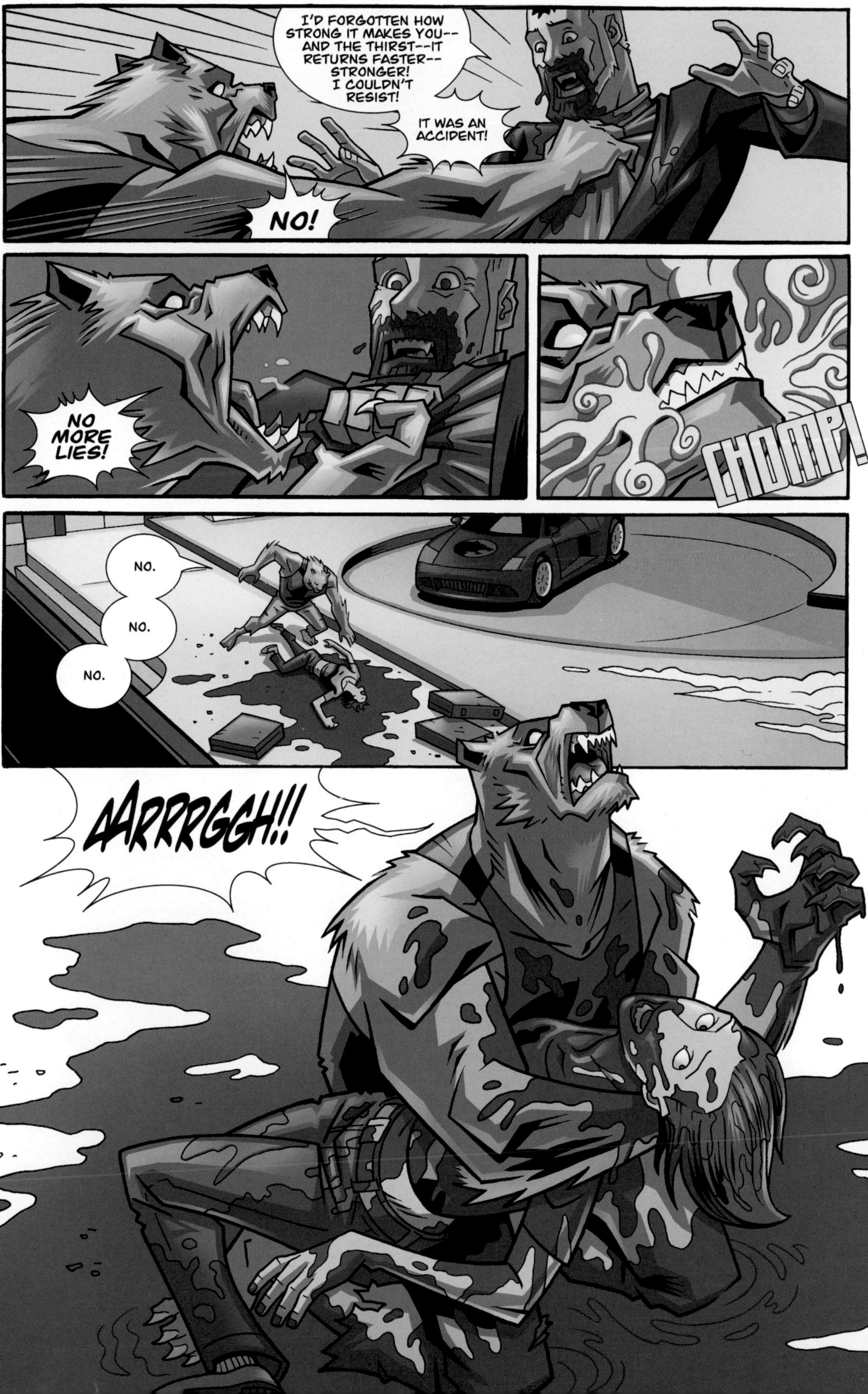
I'D FORGOTTEN HOW STRONG IT MAKES YOU-- AND THE THIRST--IT RETURNS FASTER-- STRONGER! I COULDN'T RESIST!
IT WAS AN ACCIDENT!
NO!
NO MORE LIES!
CHOMP!
NO.
NO.
NO.
AARRRGGH!!

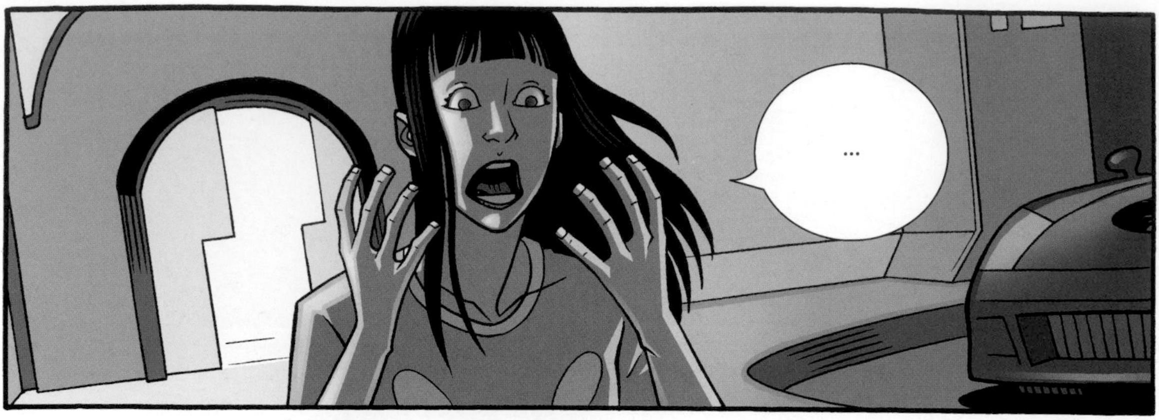
...

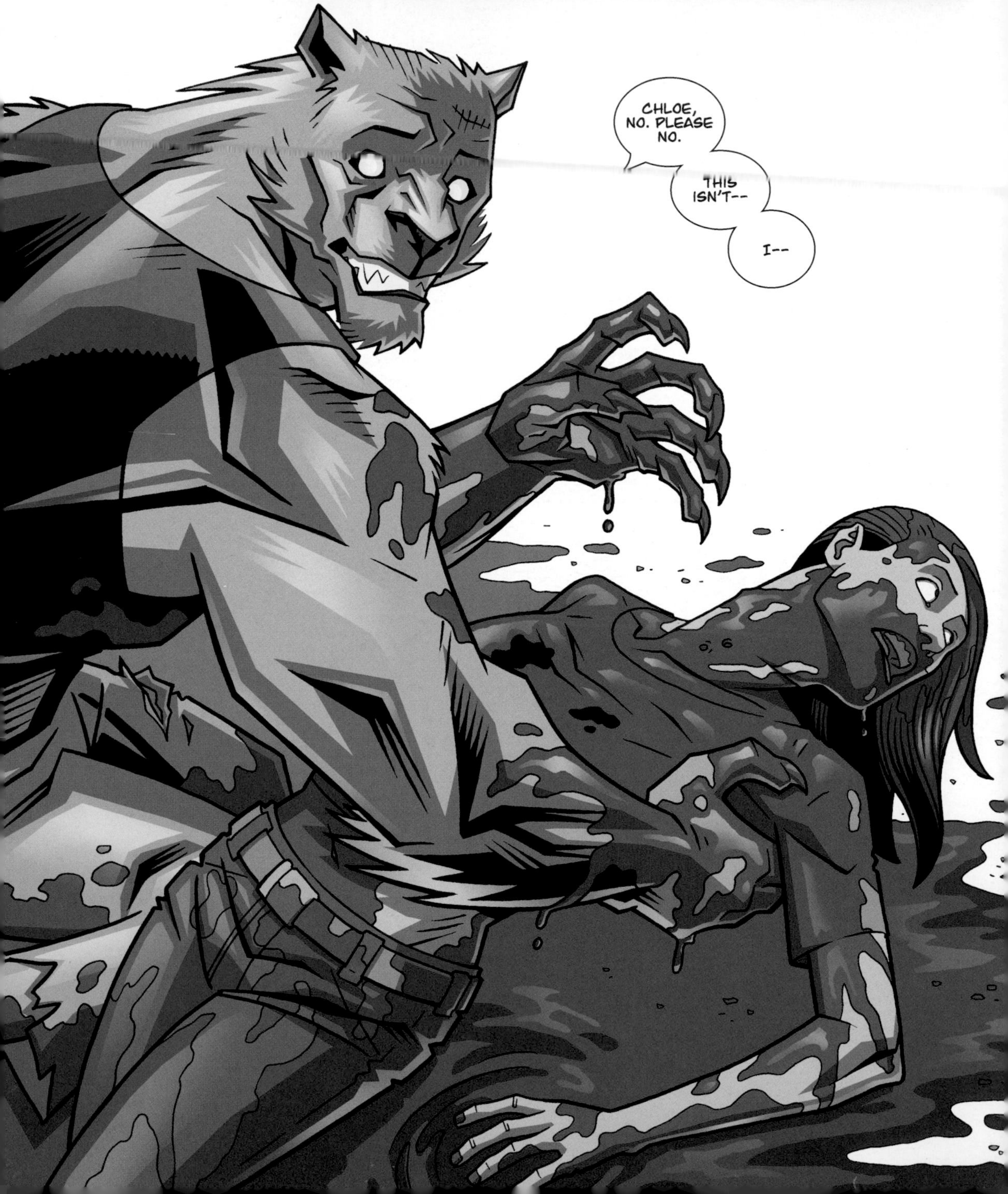
CHLOE, NO. PLEASE NO.
THIS ISN'T--
I--

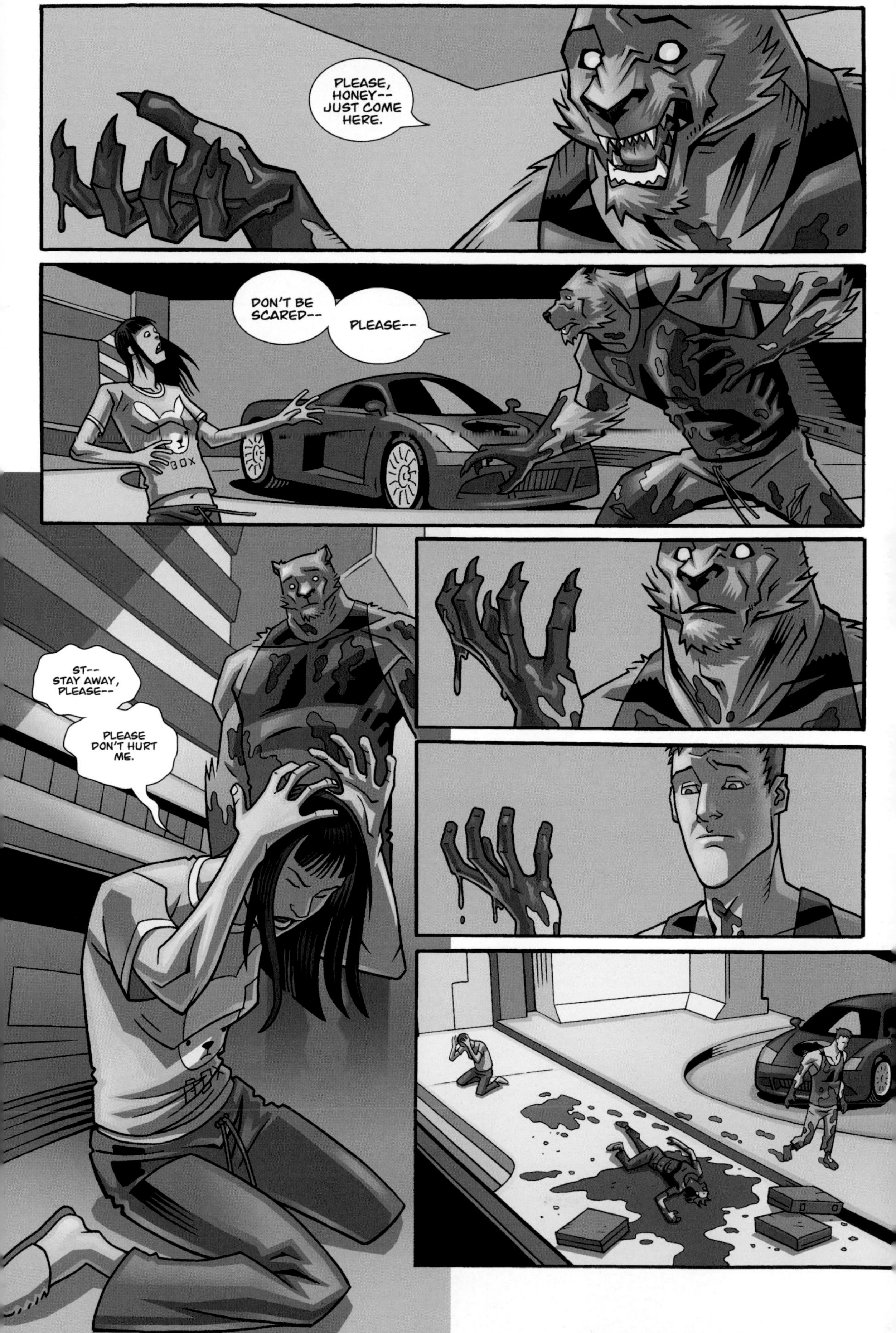
PLEASE, HONEY-- JUST COME HERE.
DON'T BE SCARED--
PLEASE--
ST-- STAY AWAY, PLEASE--
PLEASE DON'T HURT ME.

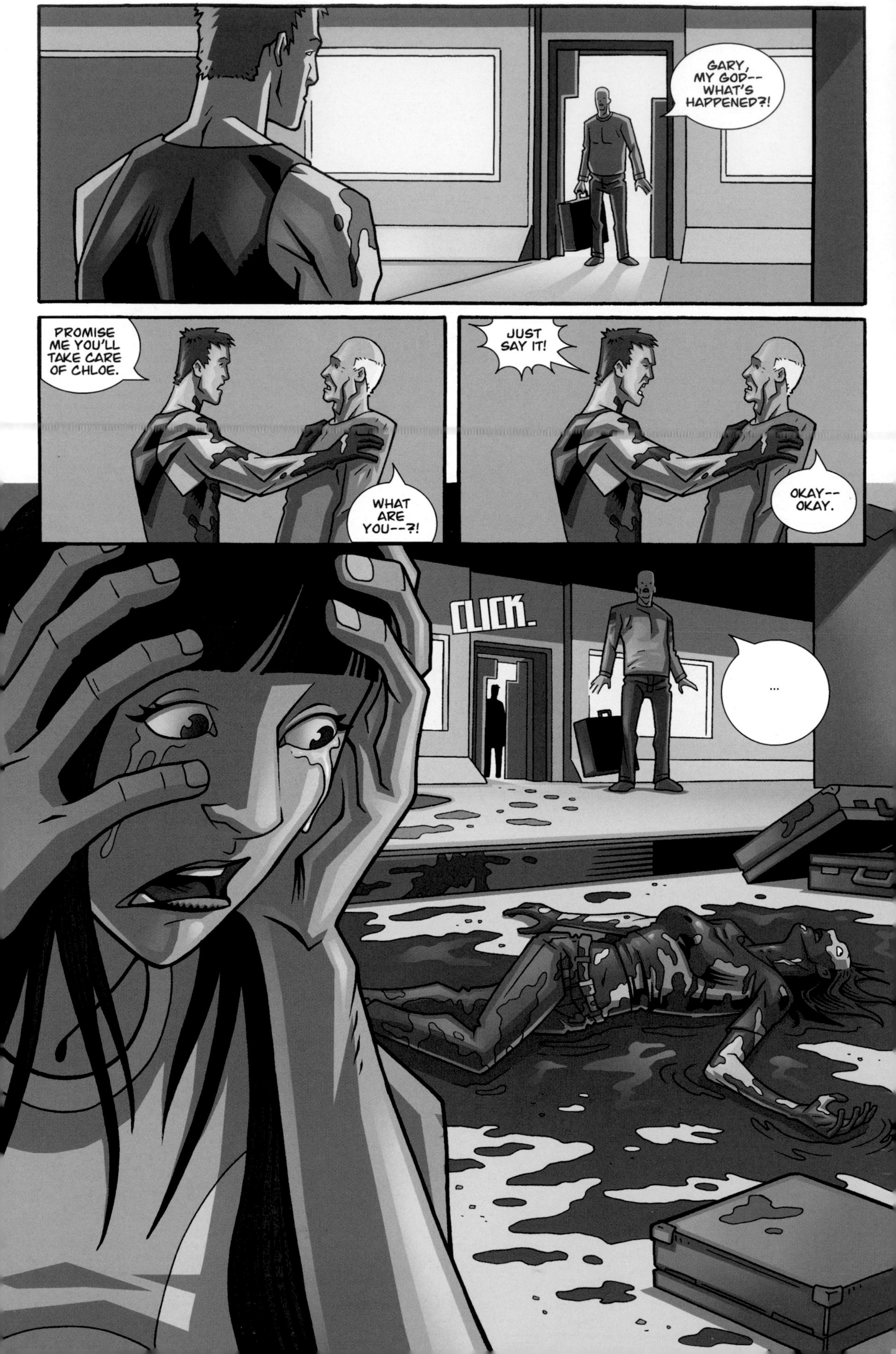
GARY, MY GOD-- WHAT'S HAPPENED?!
PROMISE ME YOU'LL TAKE CARE OF CHLOE.
WHAT ARE YOU--?!
JUST SAY IT!
OKAY-- OKAY.
CLICK.
...

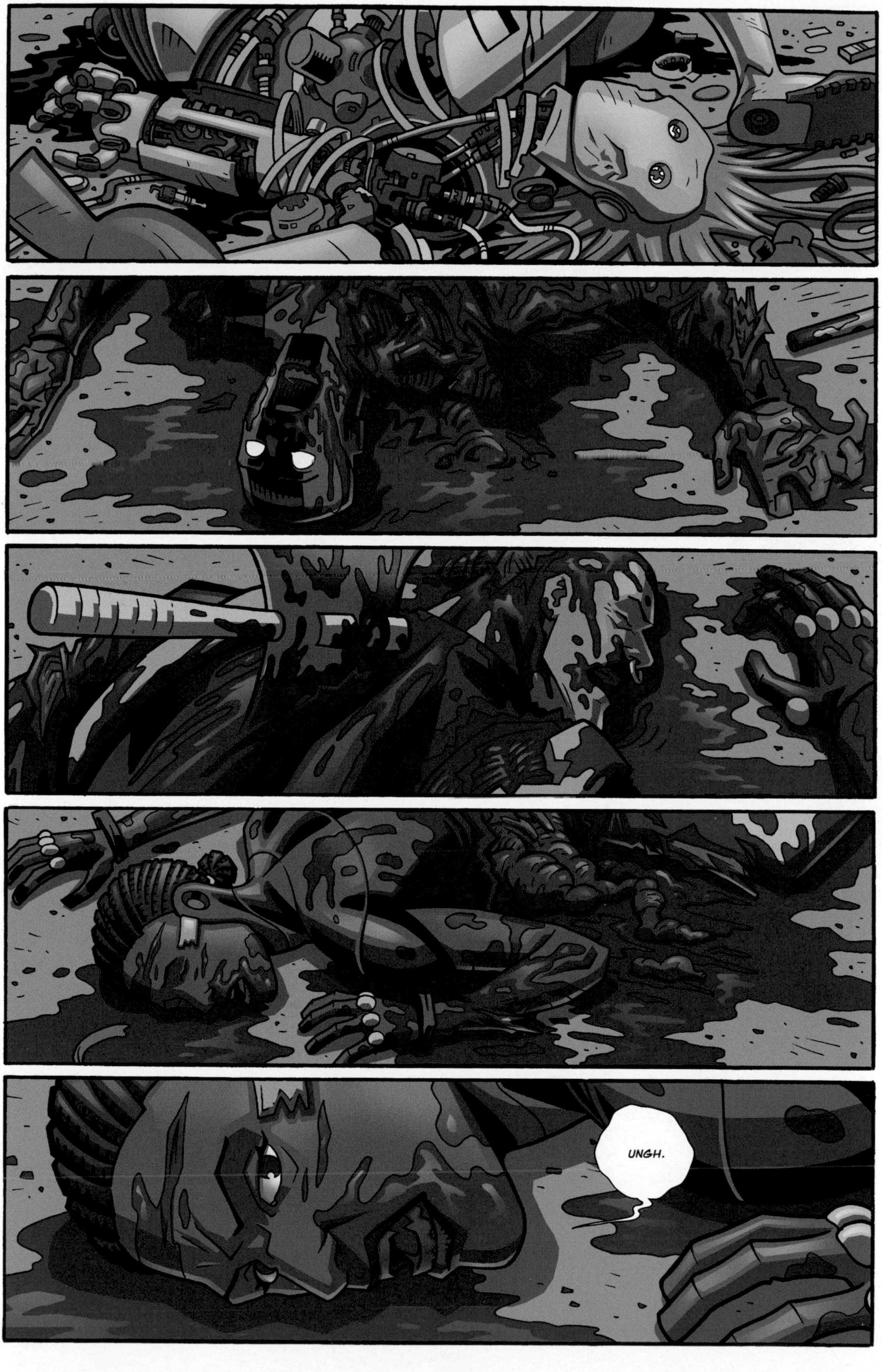
UNGH.

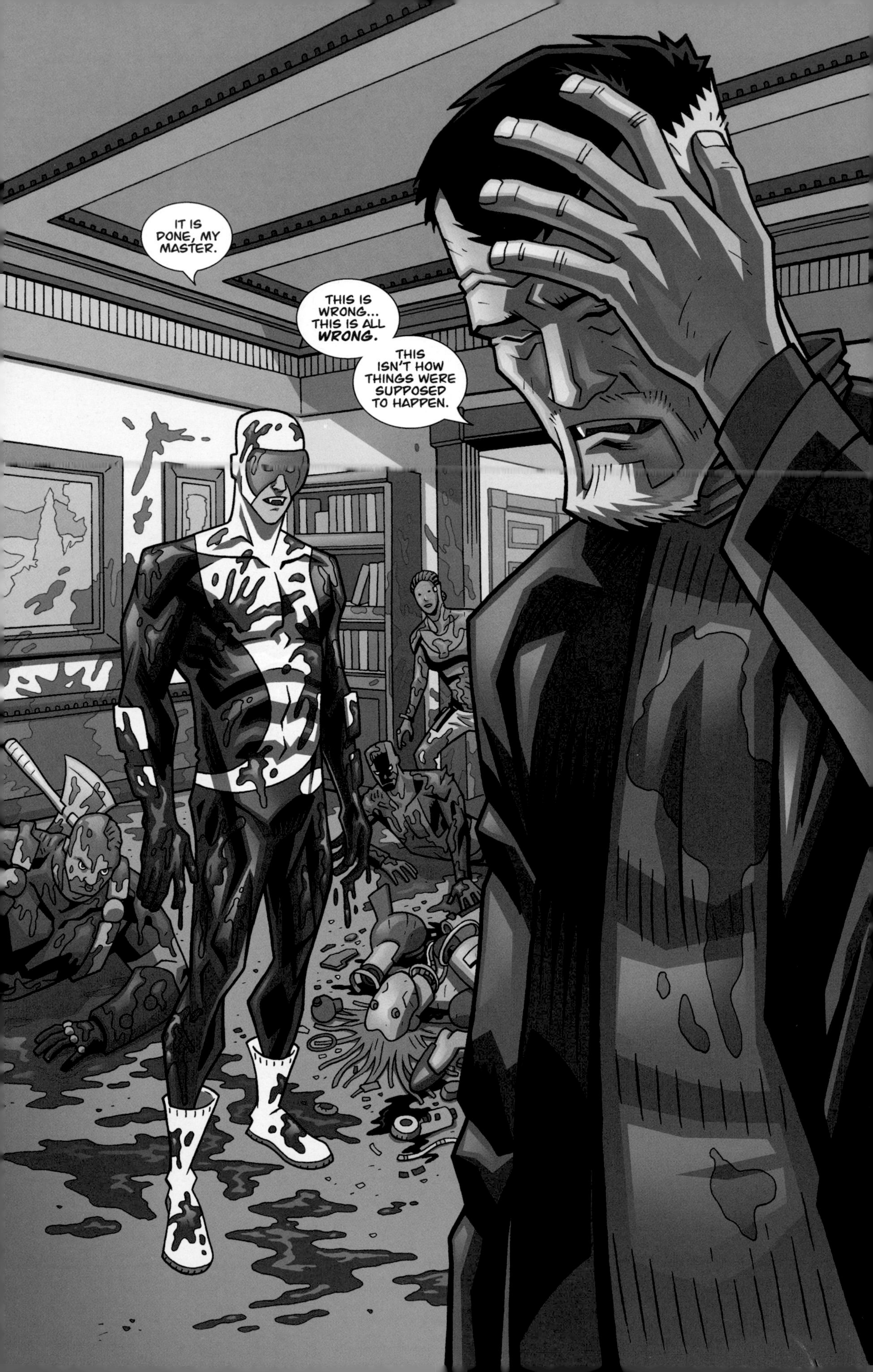
IT IS DONE, MY MASTER.
THIS IS WRONG... THIS IS ALL **WRONG**.
THIS ISN'T HOW THINGS WERE SUPPOSED TO HAPPEN.

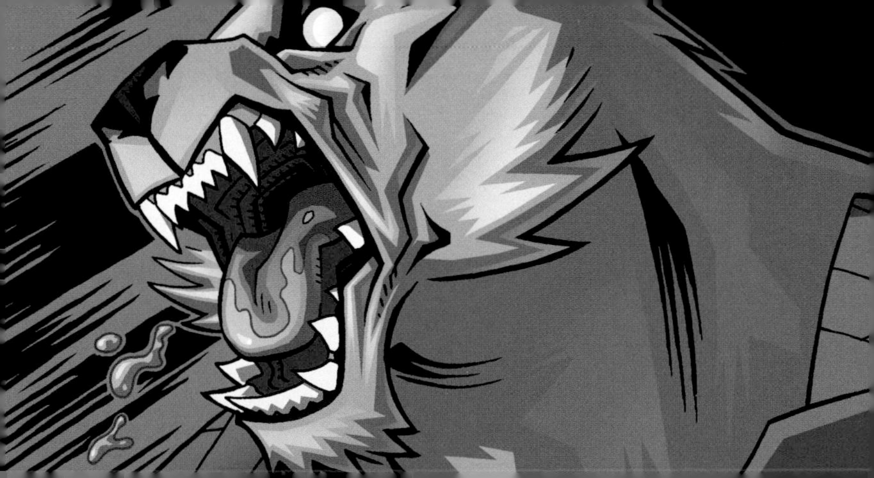

SKETCHBOOK

This is how it all began… a wolf with a man's head pasted on it. Sigh.

I called Jason up when I had the idea of a werewolf superhero called "Wolf-Man." I'd been wanting to work with Jason since we did "The Pact" issue 4 for Jim Valentino and Image and he had just done a Science Dog pin-up for Invincible which let me know he did dudes with fur well. He seemed like the perfect guy for the job. Until I got this.

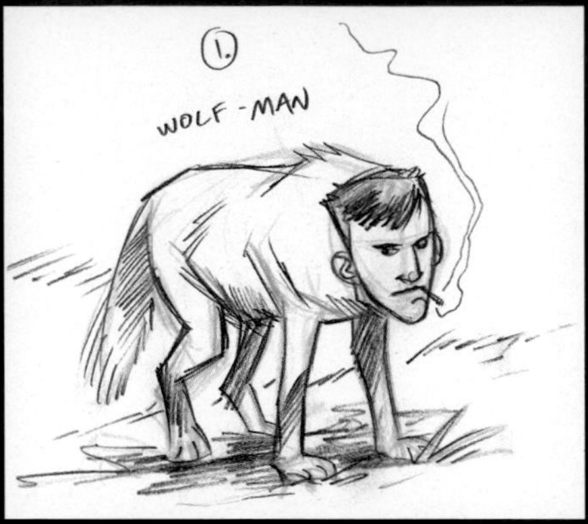
1.
WOLF-MAN

Jason did it as a gag, told me he had the perfect image of the character in mind… and emailed it to me while we were on the phone. He's a funny guy.

Luckily he had more serious designs to send me as well. Things were moving along well.

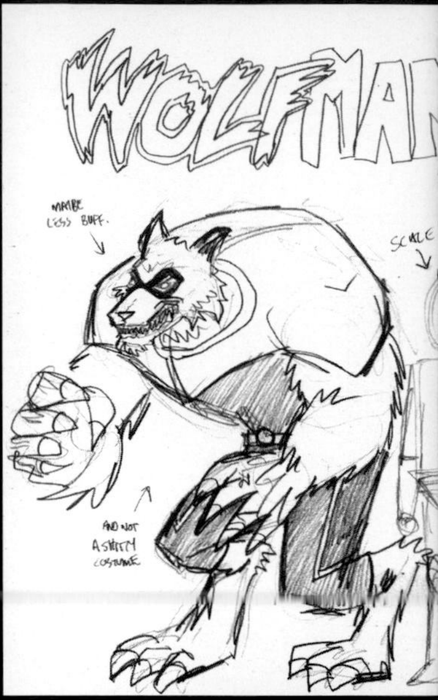
MAYBE LESS BUFF.
SCALE
AND NOT A SHITTY COSTUME

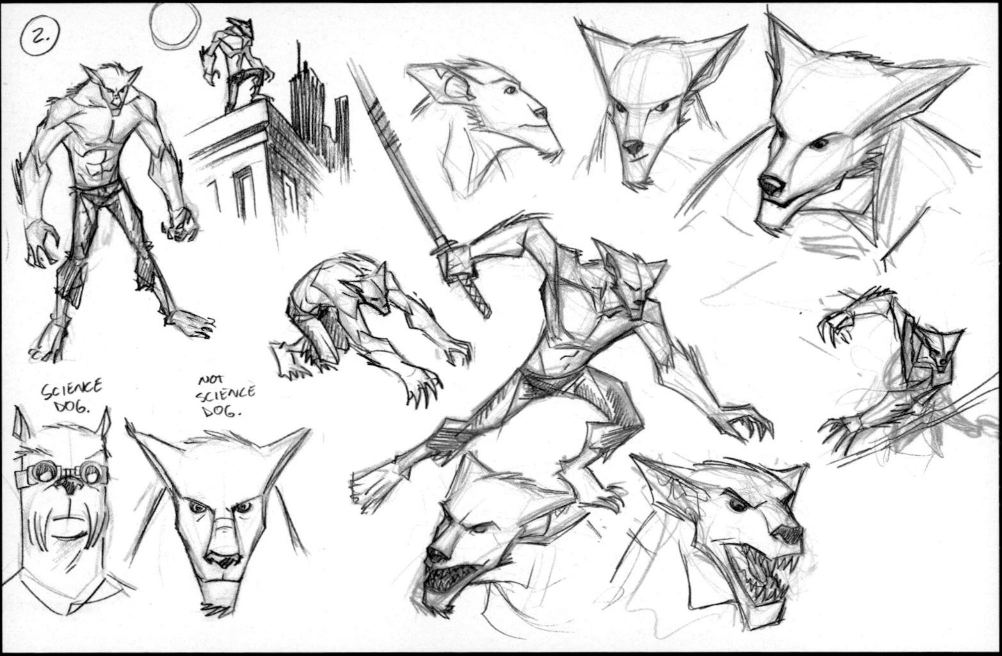
2.
SCIENCE DOG.
NOT SCIENCE DOG.

I had told Jason I wanted to make sure Wolf-Man looked nothing like Science Dog, because that's a book I'd still like to do someday. For whatever reason, Jason's designs, while awesome, started veering too cat-like. So I did my own rendition of how I pictured the character so he could see what I was thinking. I wanted to make it clear just how superheroish I wanted this character to be… VERY.

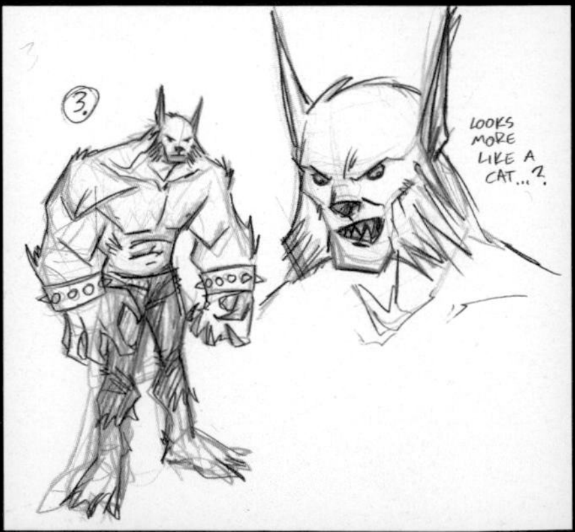
3.
LOOKS MORE LIKE A CAT…?

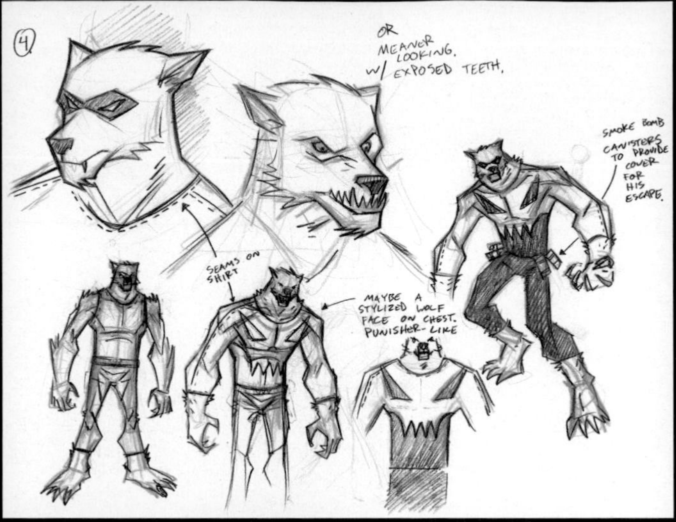
4
OR MEANER LOOKING. W/ EXPOSED TEETH.
SMOKE BOMB CANISTERS TO PROVIDE COVER FOR HIS ESCAPE.
SEAMS ON SHIRT
MAYBE A STYLIZED WOLF FACE ON CHEST. PUNISHER-LIKE

After seeing my horrible sketch, Jason was back on track and things were cooking. He quickly talked me out of the domino mask—which is good, because it was a stupid idea and I'm very ashamed of it. Why would he need to conceal his Wolf-Face any way? Madness.

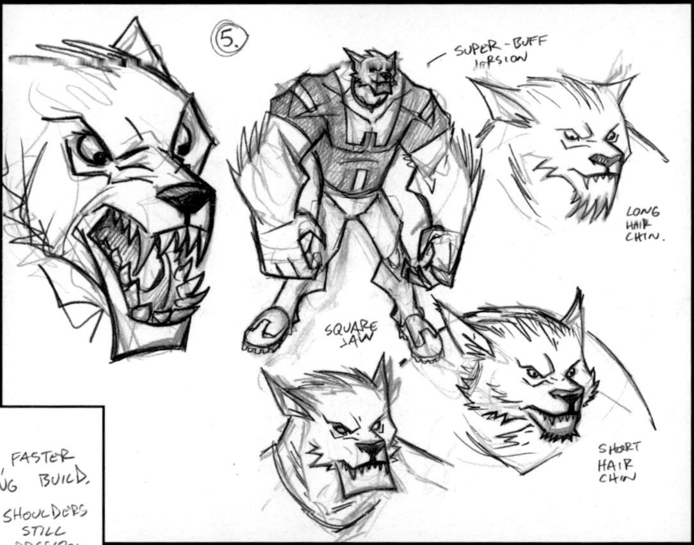
5.
SUPER-BUFF VERSION
LONG HAIR CHIN.
SQUARE JAW
SHORT HAIR CHIN

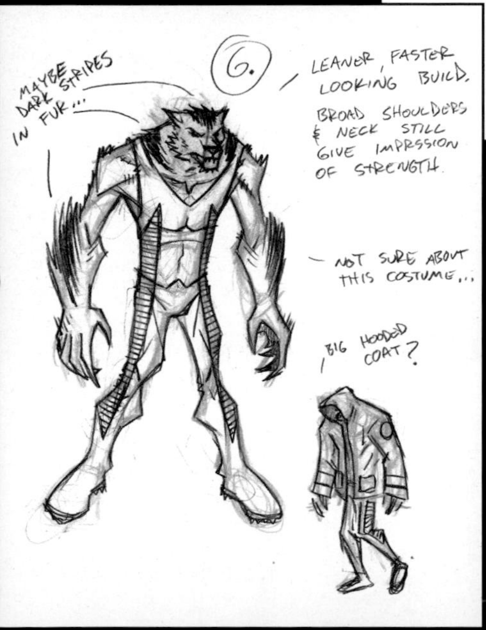
6.
MAYBE DARK STRIPES IN FUR...
LEANER, FASTER LOOKING BUILD.
BROAD SHOULDERS & NECK STILL GIVE IMPRSSION OF STRENGTH.
NOT SURE ABOUT THIS COSTUME...
BIG HOODED COAT?

More designs... starting to get close. I actually really like that hooded coat design... maybe I should think about bringing that into the book at some point. Cool stuff.

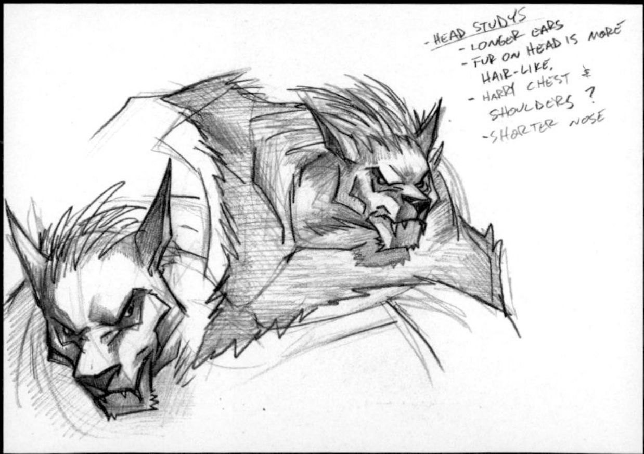
- HEAD STUDYS
- LONGER EARS
- FUR ON HEAD IS MORE HAIR-LIKE.
- HAIRY CHEST & SHOULDERS ?
- SHORTER NOSE

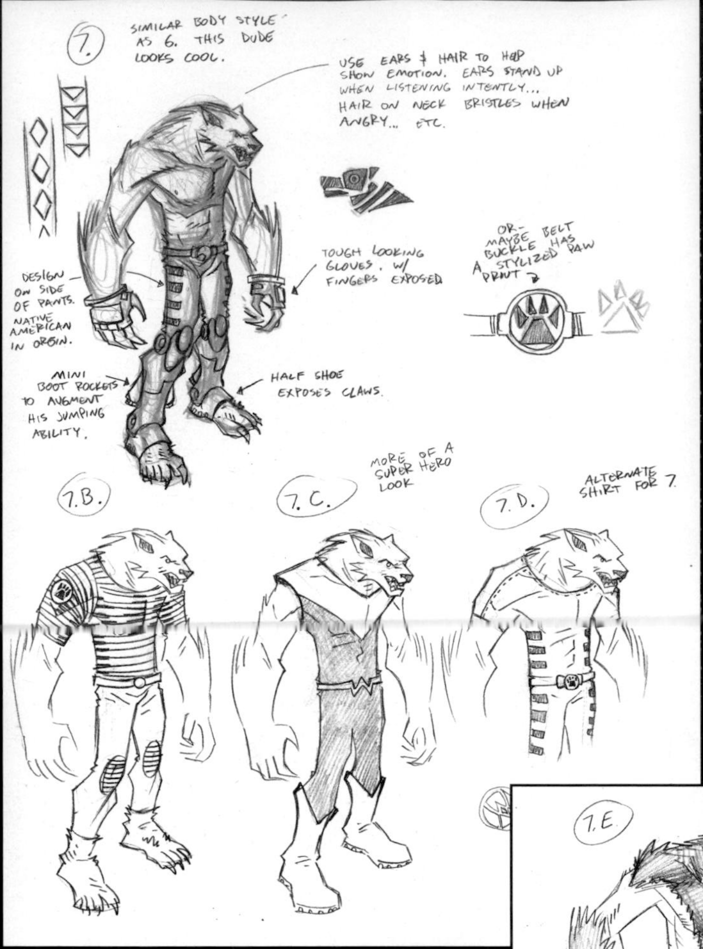

7.
SIMILAR BODY STYLE AS 6. THIS DUDE LOOKS COOL.
USE EARS & HAIR TO HELP SHOW EMOTION. EARS STAND UP WHEN LISTENING INTENTLY... HAIR ON NECK BRISTLES WHEN ANGRY... ETC.
DESIGN ON SIDE OF PANTS. NATIVE AMERICAN IN ORIGIN.
TOUGH LOOKING GLOVES, W/ FINGERS EXPOSED
OR- MAYBE BELT BUCKLE HAS A STYLIZED PAW PRINT
MINI BOOT ROCKETS TO AUGMENT HIS JUMPING ABILITY.
HALF SHOE EXPOSES CLAWS.
7.B.
7.C.
MORE OF A SUPER HERO LOOK
7.D.
ALTERNATE SHIRT FOR 7.

By this point, Jason had pretty much nailed it. I really liked the legs on "7E" and the top on "7F" so I told Jason to combine the two and add gauntlets to match the boot-things and we were done.

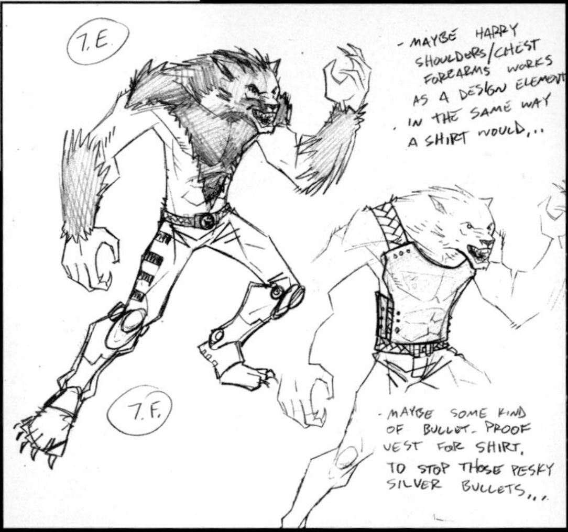

7.E.
- MAYBE HAIRY SHOULDERS/CHEST FOREARMS WORKS AS A DESIGN ELEMENT IN THE SAME WAY A SHIRT WOULD,..
7.F.
- MAYBE SOME KIND OF BULLET-PROOF VEST FOR SHIRT, TO STOP THOSE PESKY SILVER BULLETS...

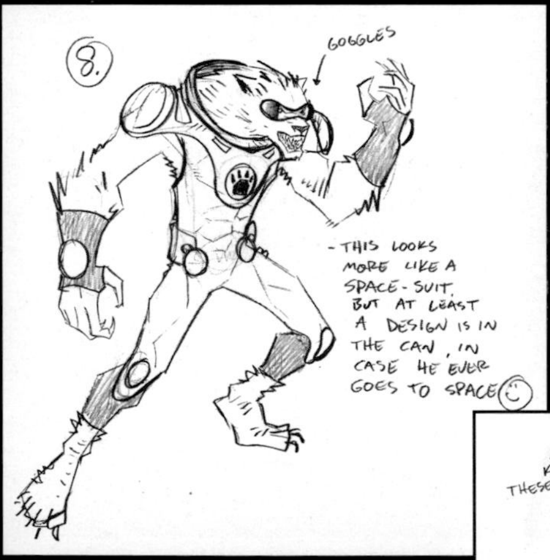

8.
GOGGLES
- THIS LOOKS MORE LIKE A SPACE-SUIT, BUT AT LEAST A DESIGN IS IN THE CAN, IN CASE HE EVER GOES TO SPACE

Jason had already done this keen space-wolf-man design when I had told him to combine the other two designs. He quickly worked up some finished drawings of our boy and we were off to the races.

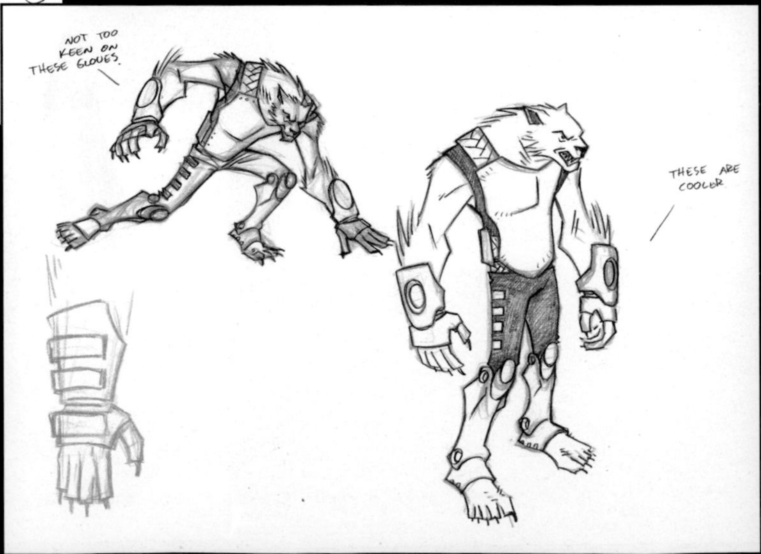

NOT TOO KEEN ON THESE GLOVES.
THESE ARE COOLER

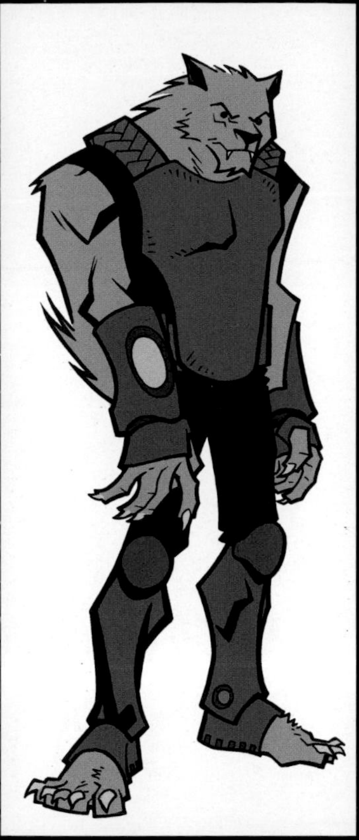

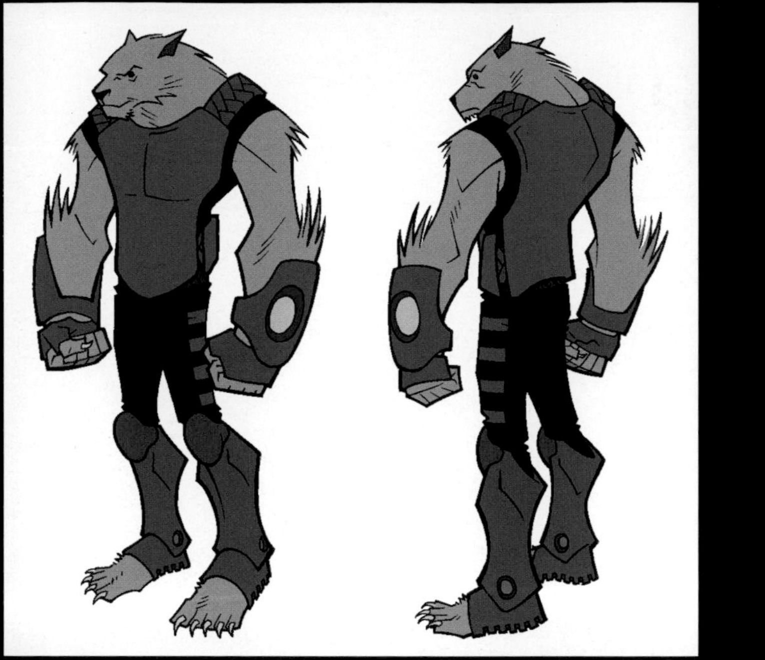

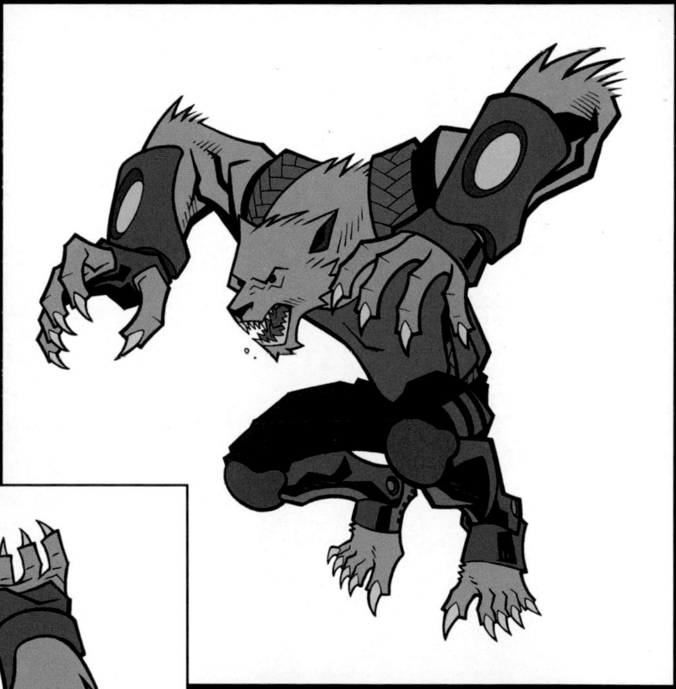

On this page you'll see some finished illustrations of Wolf-Man done by Jason in celebration of nailing down a final design.

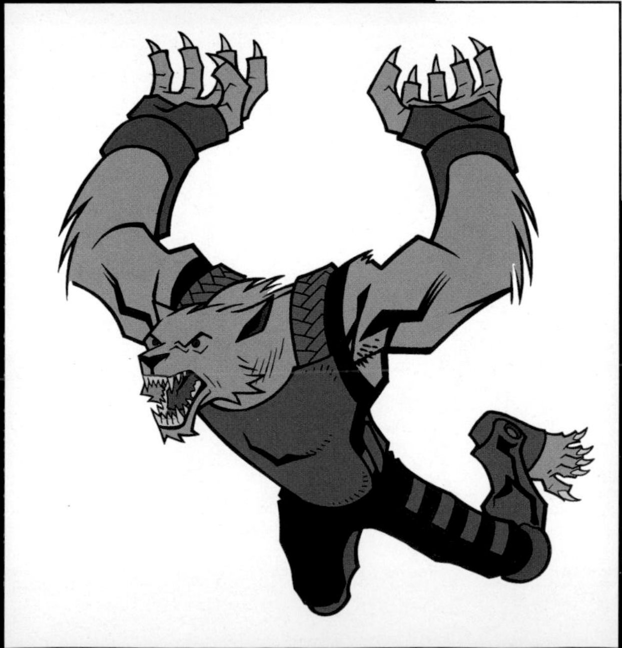

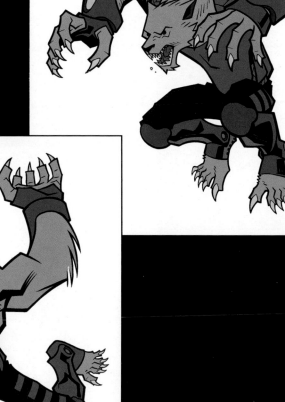

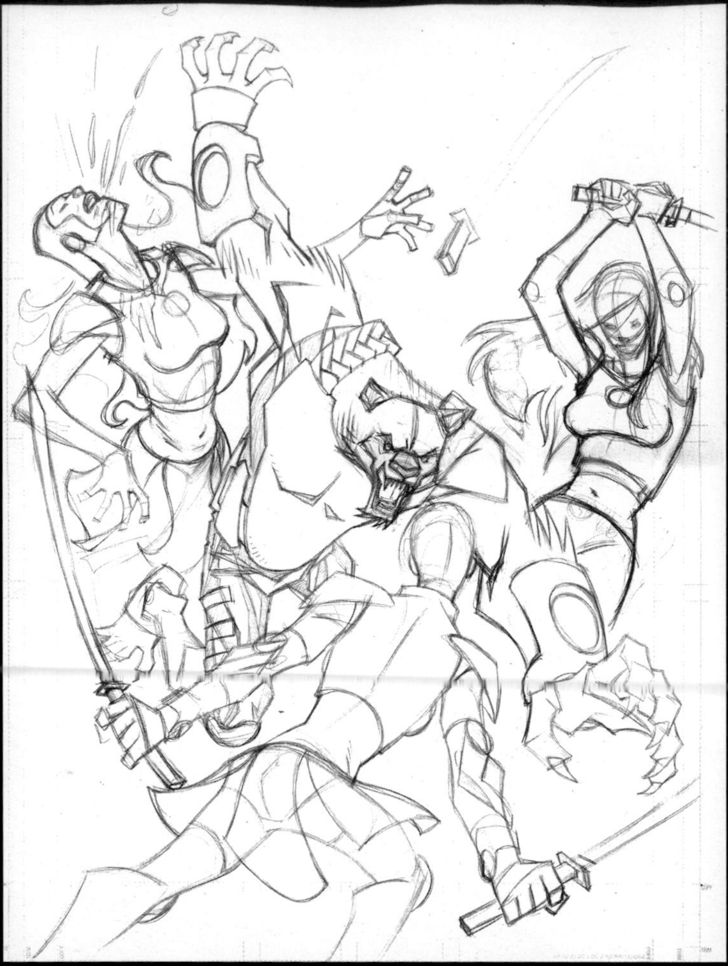

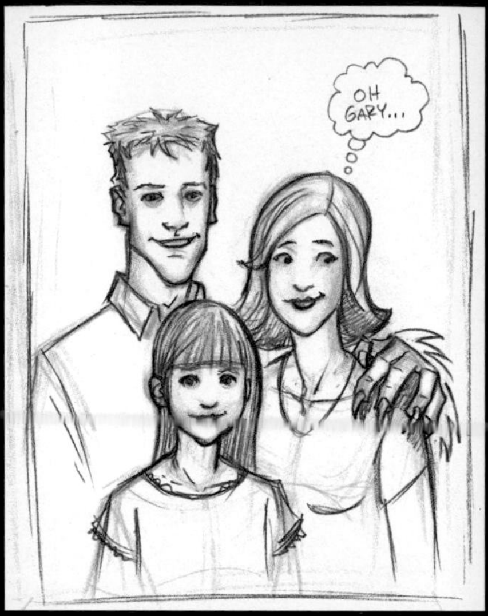
OH GARY...

Some random sketches. If Wolf-Man ever fights some robo-women with swords that could be an upcoming cover… despite being somewhat similar to what Jason did for the cover to issue six.

Jason nailed the Hampton family pretty much right off the bat. What a great looking family… I just couldn't wait to put them through hell after seeing them. This is going to be a fun series.

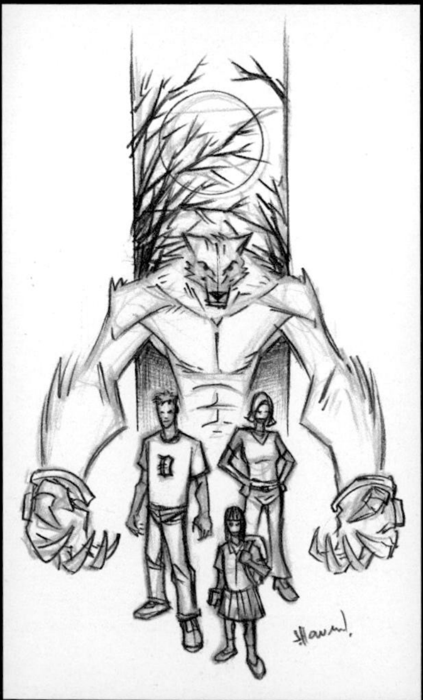

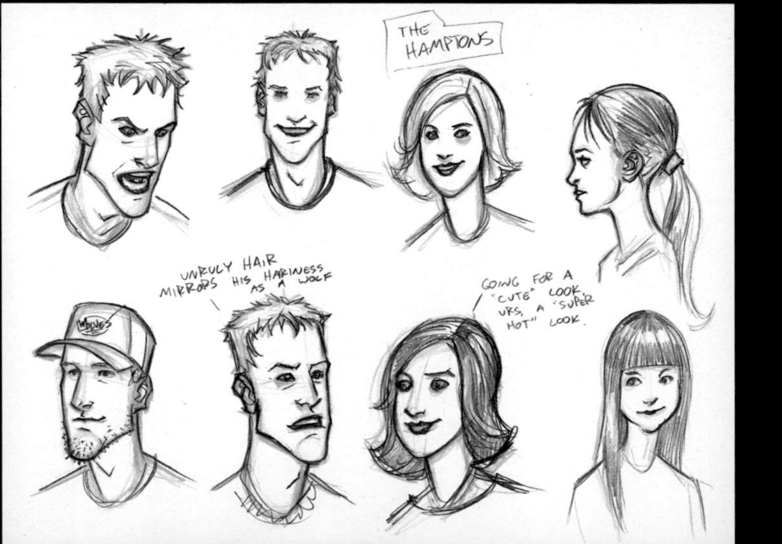
THE HAMPTONS
UNRULY HAIR MIRRORS HIS HAIRINESS AS A WOLF
GOING FOR A "CUTE" LOOK VRS. A "SUPER HOT" LOOK.

Here begins Jason's monumental task of coming up with a look for Zechariah. Jason works pretty fast with the designs, often sending multiple variations at the same time—hence the wealth of choices here.

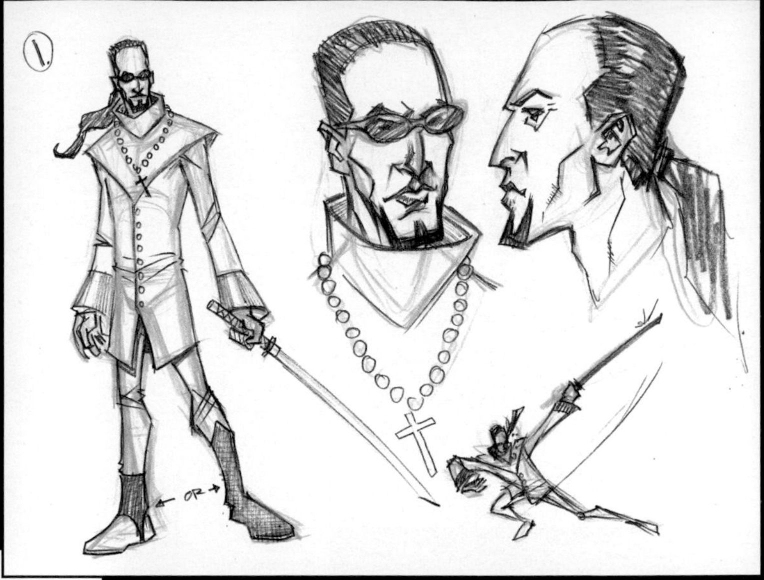
1.
OR

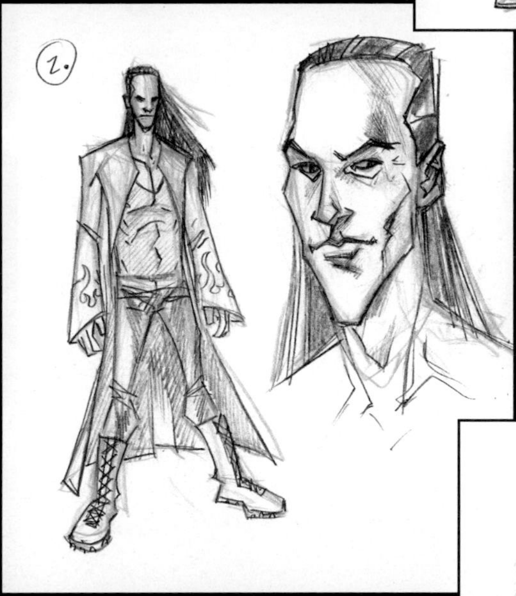
2.

I'm awesome to work with. My only description was "Old Vampire Guy." I wanted something very specific for Zehcariah, but I didn't know what that was. All I knew was that I didn't want these early passes. I eventually told Jason I was picturing a "Skinny Santa Claus." That resulted in the final sketch on the page.

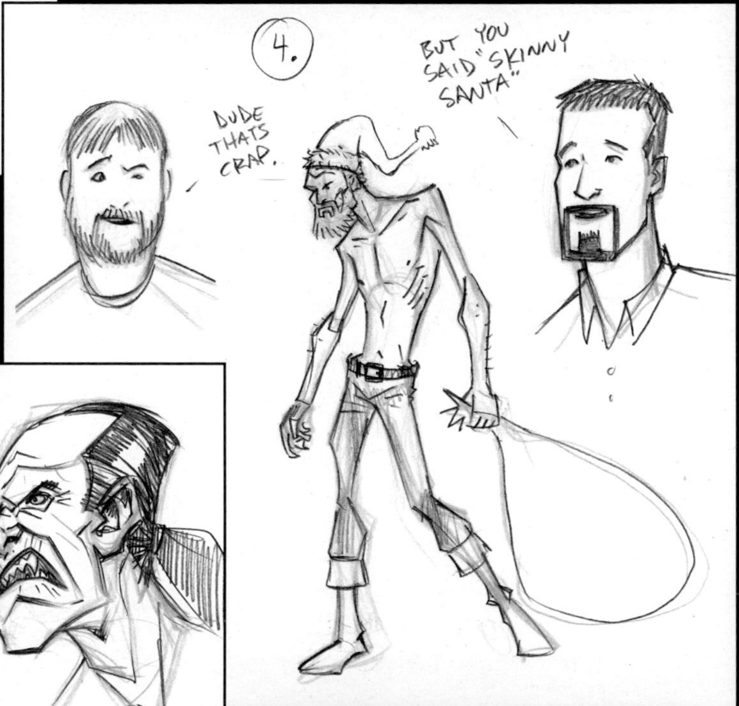
4.
DUDE THATS CRAP.
BUT YOU SAID "SKINNY SANTA"

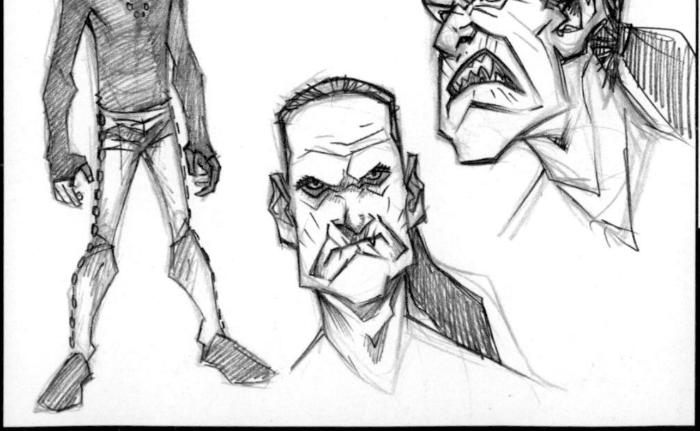
3.

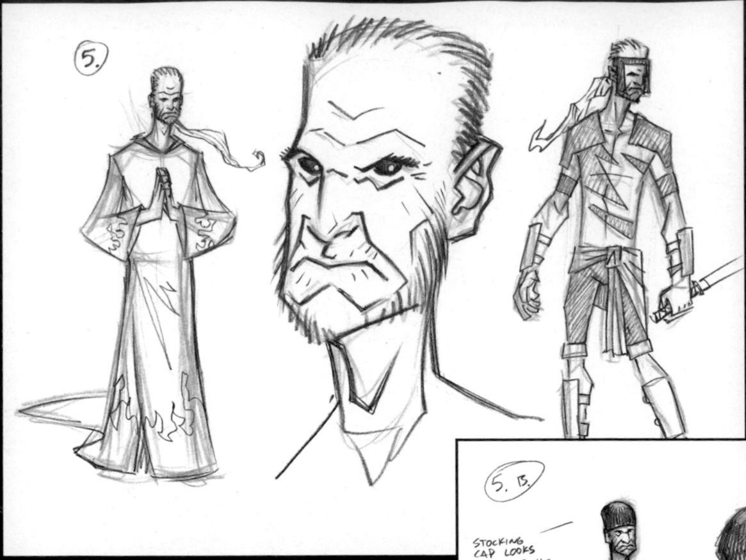
5.

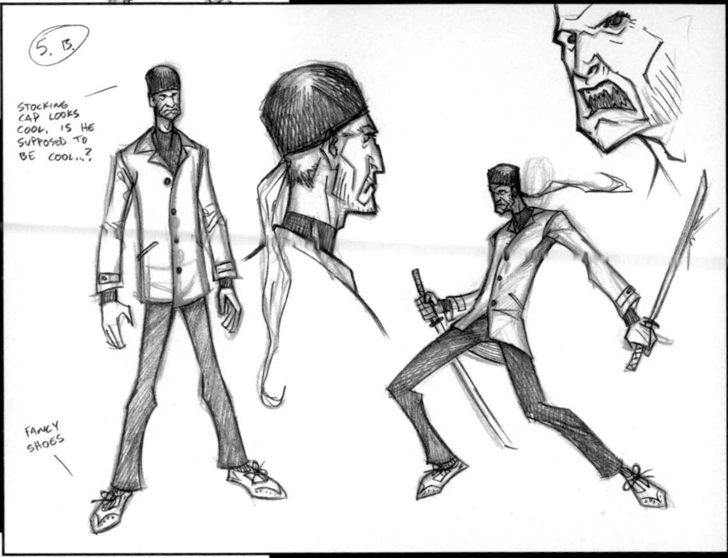
5. B.
STOCKING CAP LOOKS COOL. IS HE SUPPOSED TO BE COOL...?
FANCY SHOES

Here were some very cool designs but they looks too EVIL to me. I eventually came up with the aristocratic take on Zechariah and asked Jason to make sure he could pass for a normal dude at first because I already had the ending scene of issue one planned out. That's when Jason struck gold with the final design on the page here.

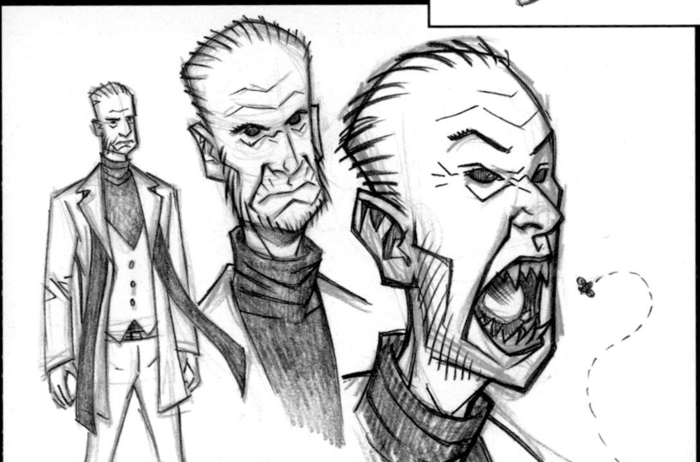

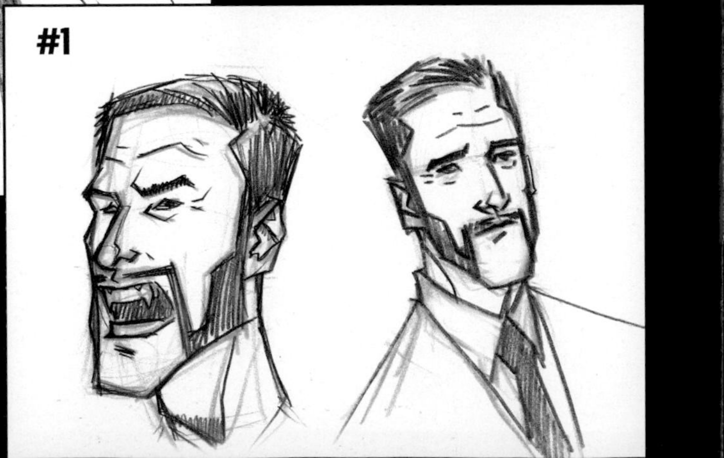
#1

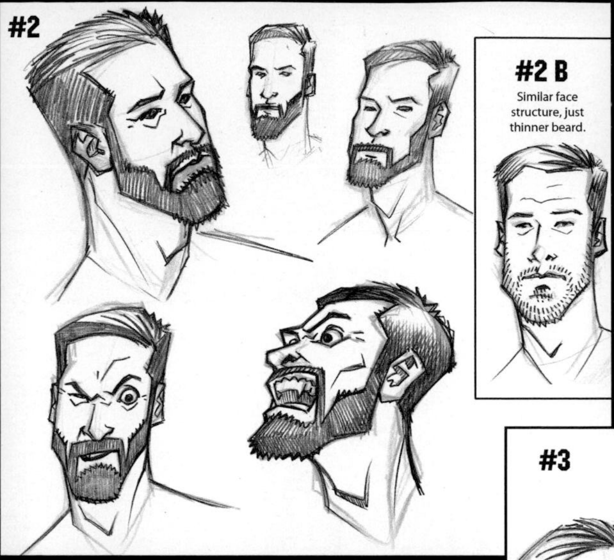
#2
#2 B
Similar face structure, just thinner beard.

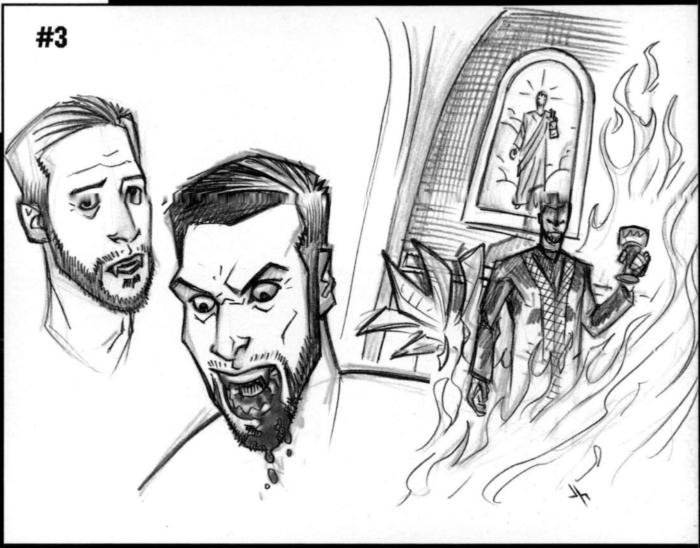
#3

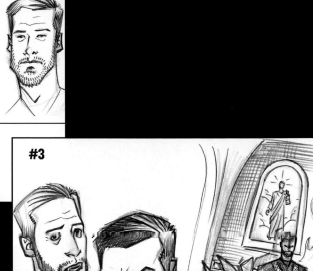

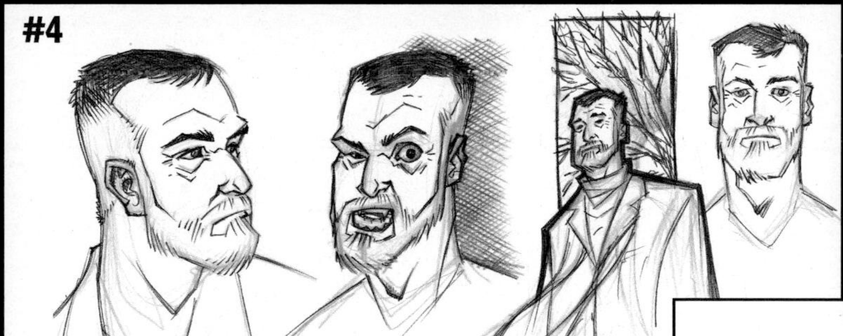
#4

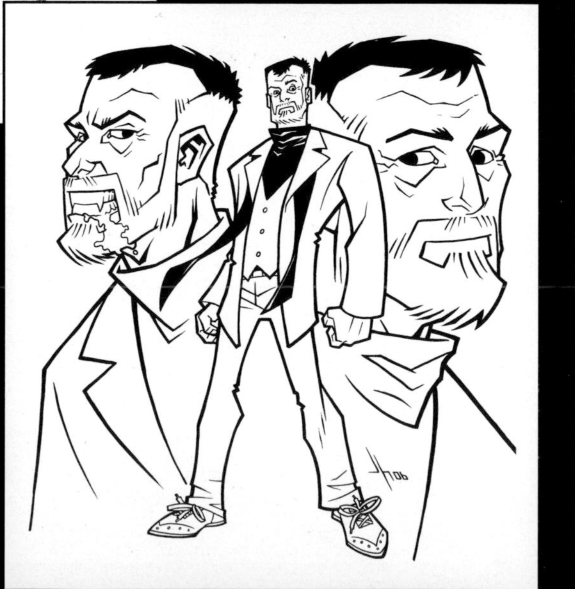

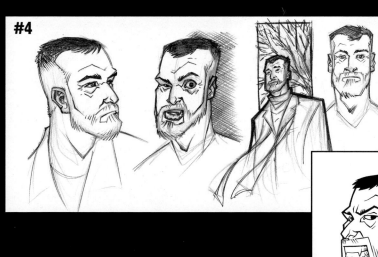

Jason did some variations on this guy until we both decided he should probably look older—so Jason added the gray beard and hair and we had it! Zechariah was born! Jason did that sweet finished drawing seen here to celebrate.

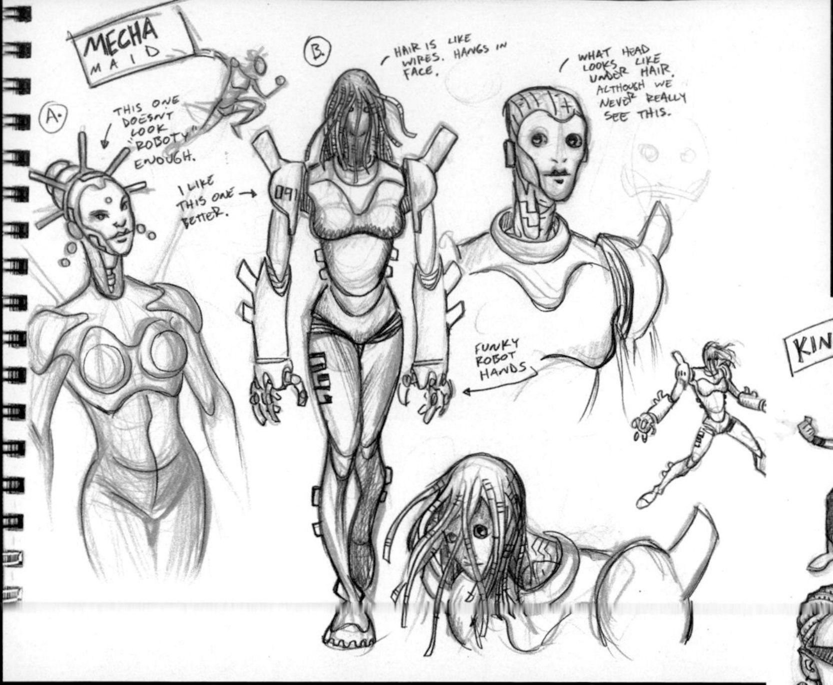
MECHA MAID
A.
B.
THIS ONE DOESN'T LOOK "ROBOTY" ENOUGH.
I LIKE THIS ONE → BETTER.
HAIR IS LIKE WIRES. HANGS IN FACE.
WHAT HEAD LOOKS LIKE UNDER HAIR. ALTHOUGH WE NEVER REALLY SEE THIS.
FUNKY ROBOT HANDS

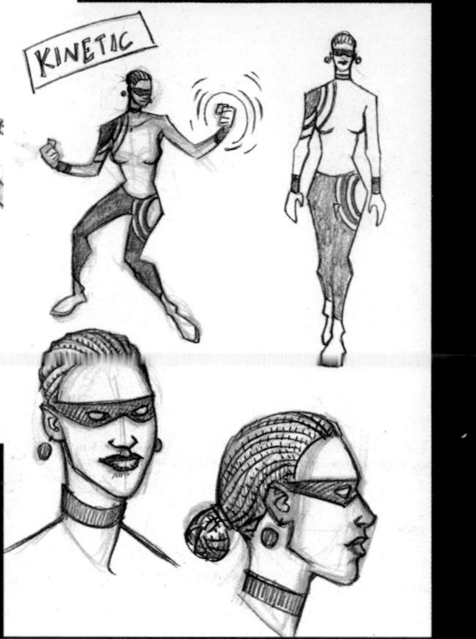
KINETIC

The Actioneers were a lot of fun to create. I think Jason had a list of names to use and I had a list of names and we both picked ones we liked. Sergeant Superior and Mecha Maid were Jason's names and I contributed Kinetic, Minotaur and Code Blue—although Code Blue was just a name I came up with to go with drawings Jason had already done of the character. I know I wanted a black woman to be the team leader—but past that... I think it was pretty much all Jason with these guys—and they really are a cool team. It's almost sad what happened to them in issue 7... but I know what's coming—and it's cool, so don't worry.

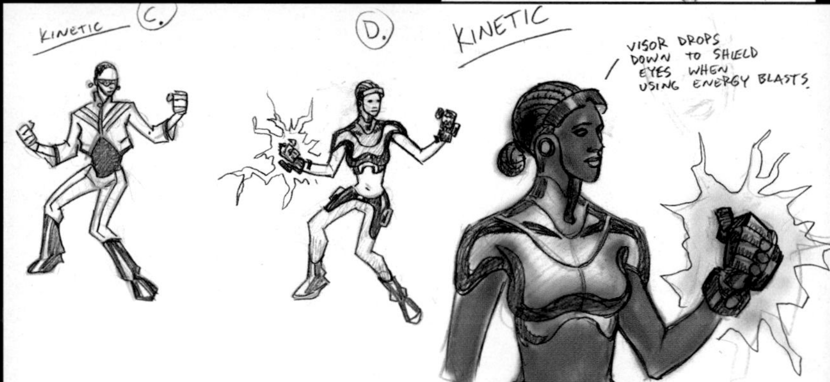
KINETIC
C.
D.
KINETIC
VISOR DROPS DOWN TO SHIELD EYES WHEN USING ENERGY BLASTS.

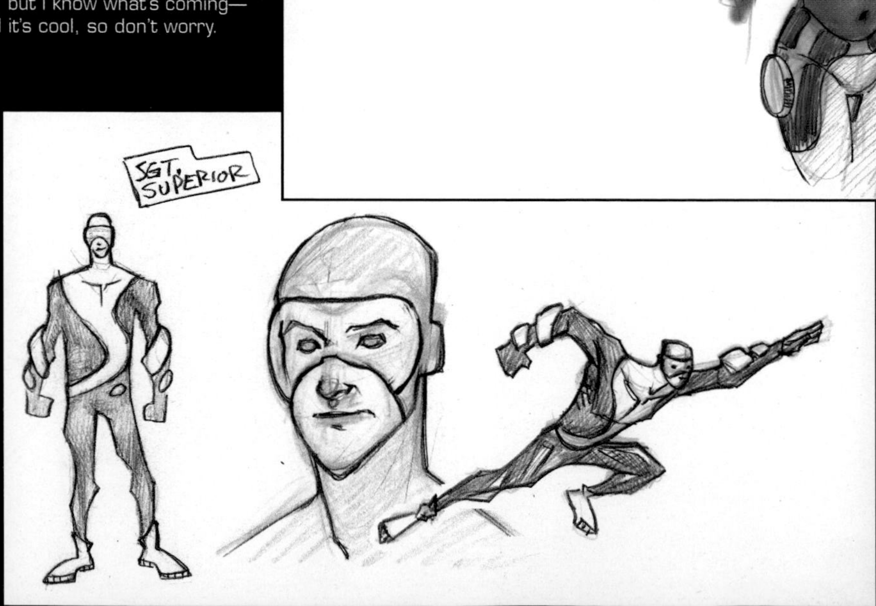
SGT. SUPERIOR

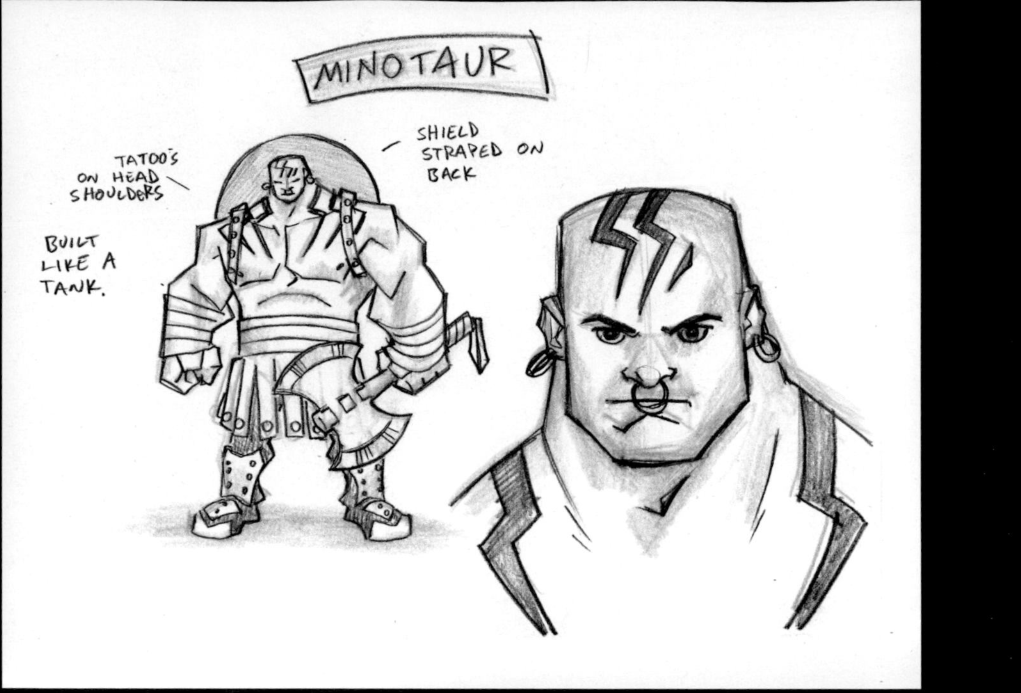
MINOTAUR
SHIELD STRAPED ON BACK
TATOO'S ON HEAD SHOULDERS
BUILT LIKE A TANK.

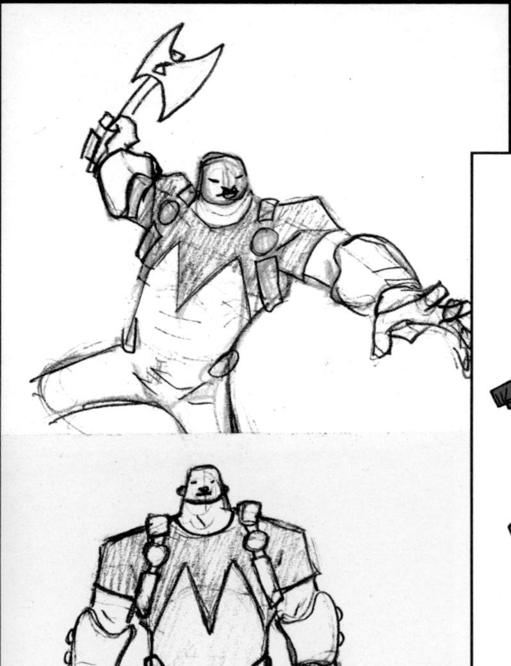

Here's Jason's drawing of Code Blue, done well before the Actioneers were even a thought in my head. Also, the original Minotaur, which I thought was pretty cool—but in the end we decided to do something that was more superheroish so that he'd fit in more with the group.

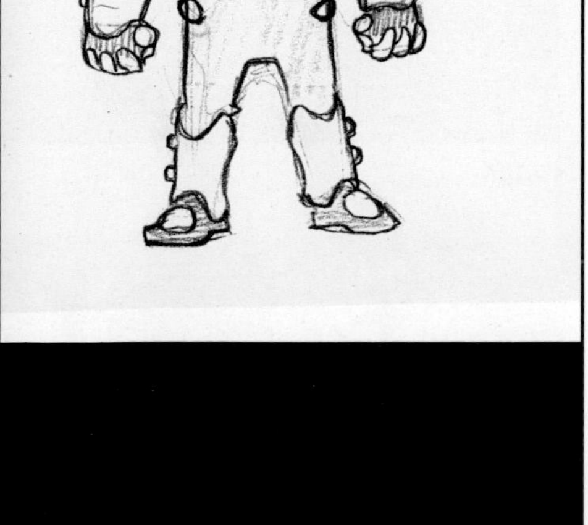

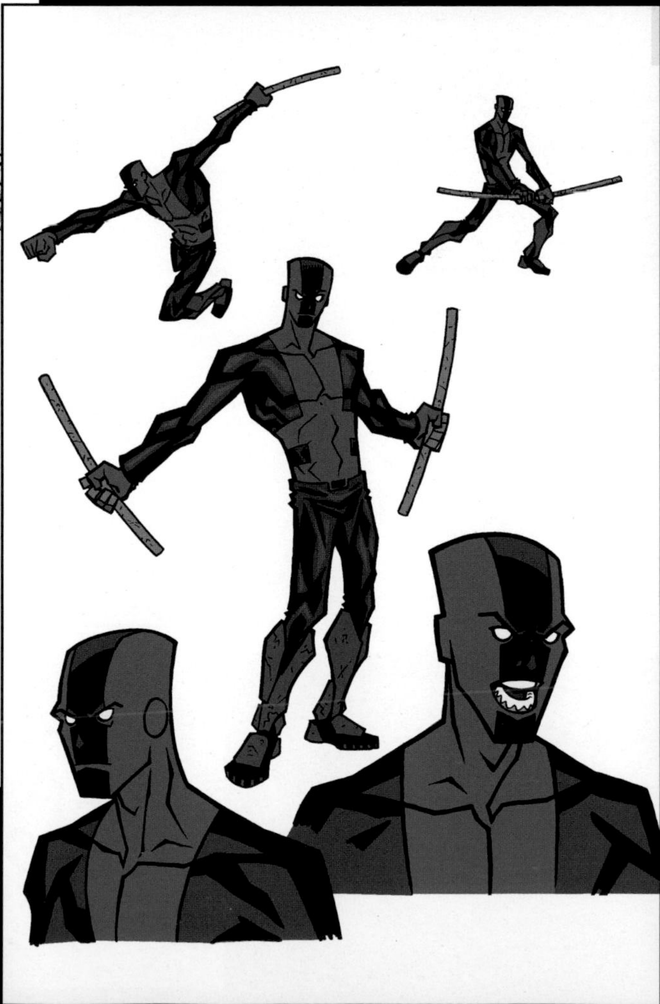

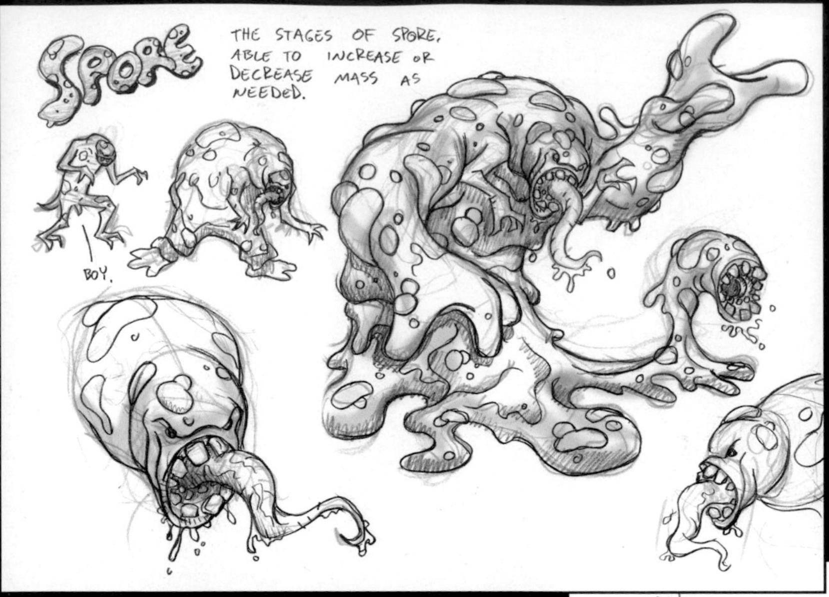
SPORE
THE STAGES OF SPORE, ABLE TO INCREASE OR DECREASE MASS AS NEEDED.
BOY.

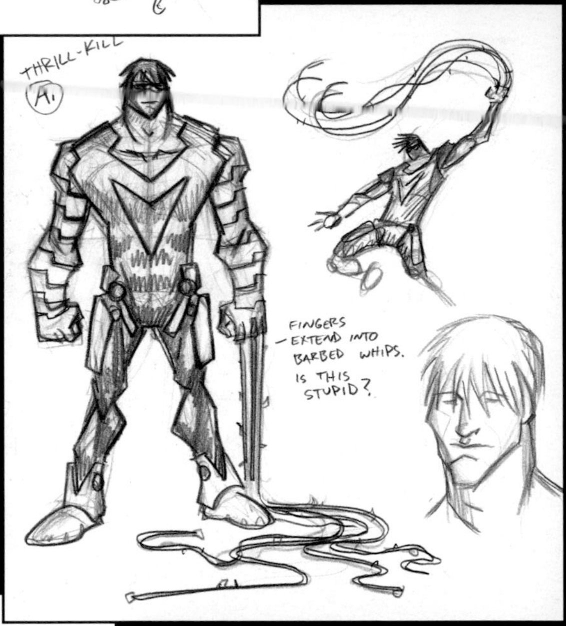
THRILL-KILL
A.
FINGERS
- EXTEND INTO BARBED WHIPS.
IS THIS STUPID?

Villain designs—all of which Jason hit it out of the park on almost the first try. Spore was a home-run from the start—I'm really anxious to get around to showing this guy again, I love Jason's visual for him. Thrill-Kill took a little more time—but I think the end result was worth it.

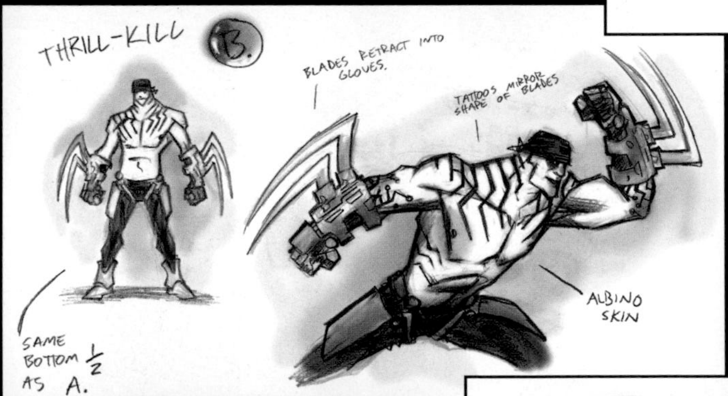
THRILL-KILL
B.
BLADES RETRACT INTO GLOVES.
TATTOOS MIRROR SHAPE OF BLADES
ALBINO SKIN
SAME BOTTOM 1/2 AS A.

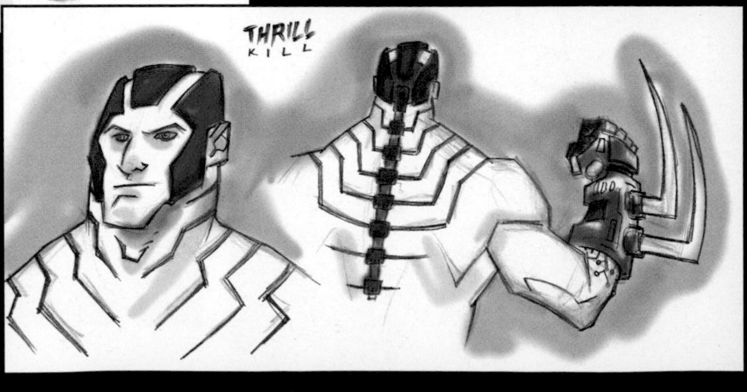
THRILL KILL

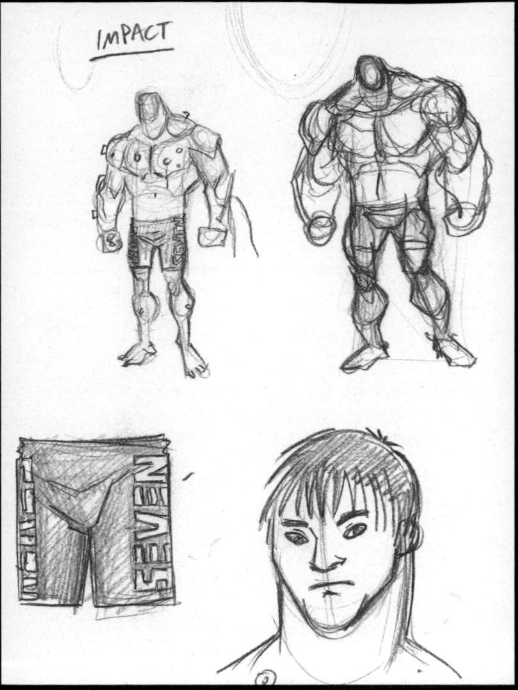
IMPACT
SEVEN

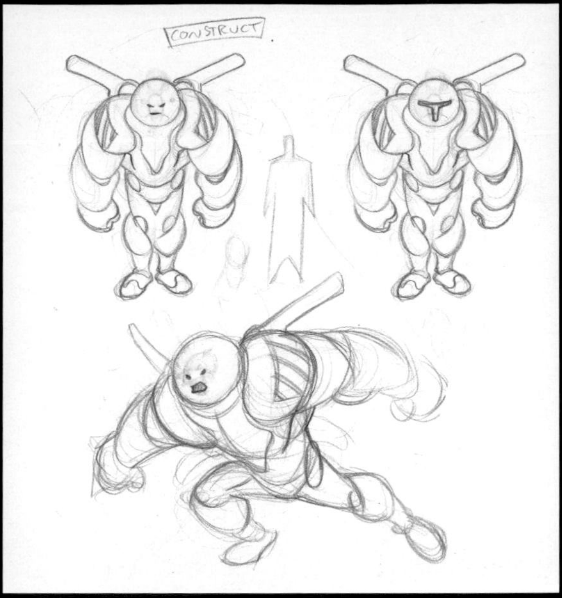
CONSTRUCT

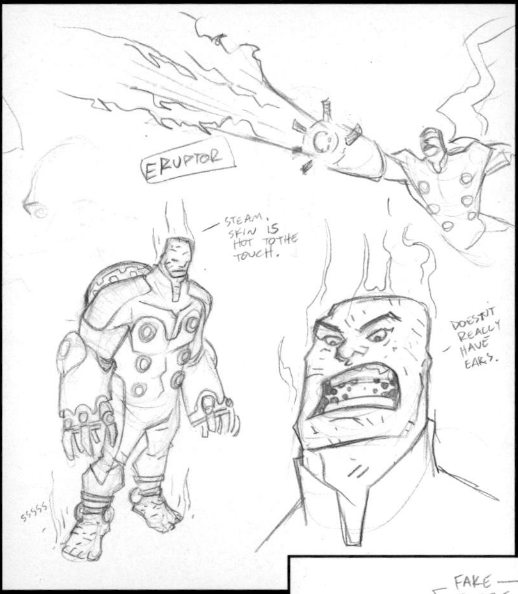
ERUPTOR
STEAM, SKIN IS HOT TO THE TOUCH.
DOESN'T REALLY HAVE EARS.

Construct, Eruptor and Impact... all awesome right off the bat. We'll be seeing more of all these guys eventually. Also on this page, the newspaper staff... who I wanted to make nearly complete opposites of a certain familiar comic-book newspaper staff that will go nameless...

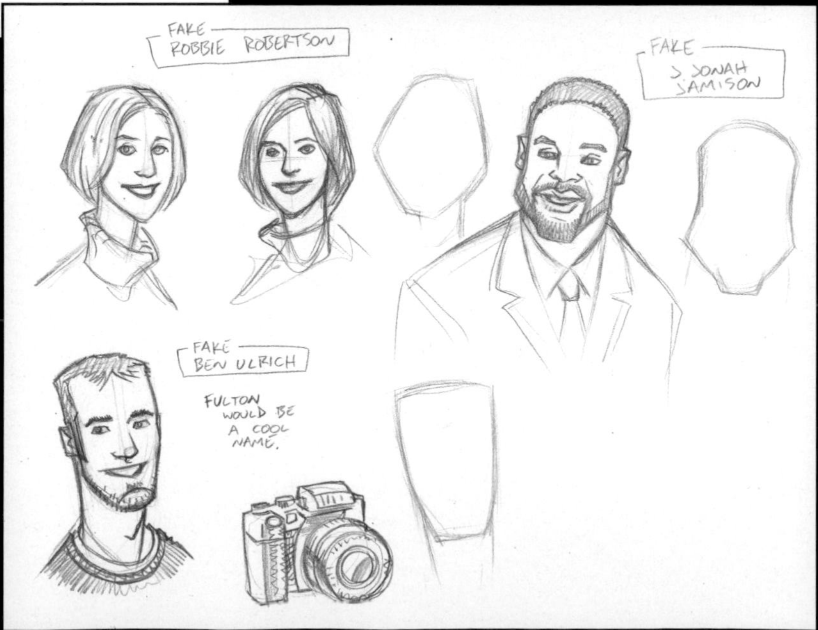
FAKE ROBBIE ROBERTSON
FAKE J. JONAH JAMISON
FAKE BEN ULRICH
FULTON WOULD BE A COOL NAME.

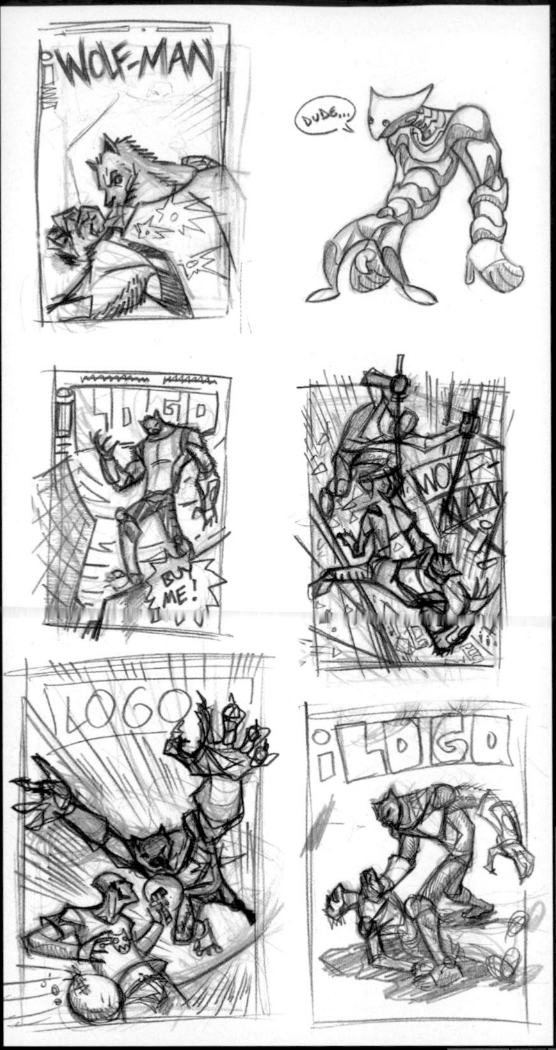
WOLF-MAN
DUDE...
LOGO
WOLF MAN
BUY ME!
LOGO
LOGO

Some cover ideas—and an early promo piece/cover that Jason did early on. It even uses one of the early designs for Zechariah. I don't hate it, but as a general rule I'm not a fan of montage covers. It's an excellent drawing, though. Enjoy!

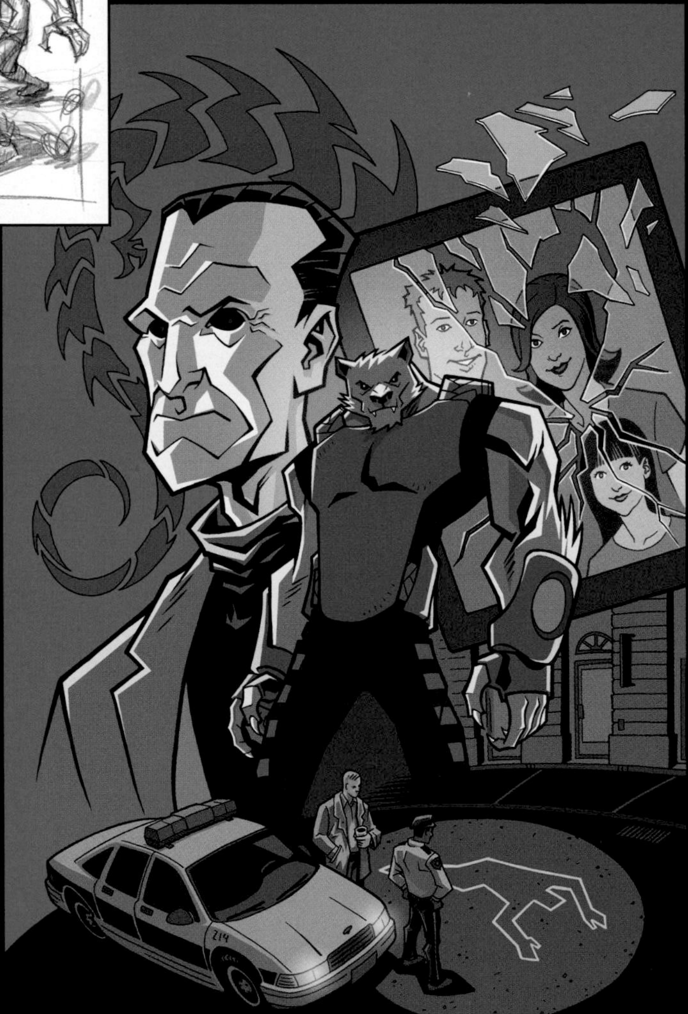

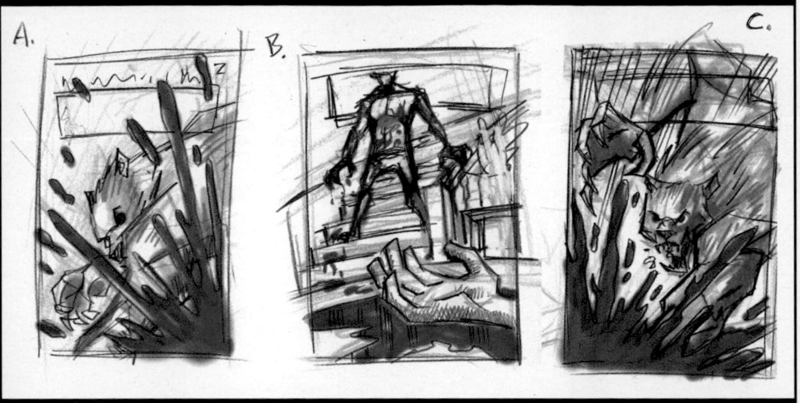
A.
B.
C.

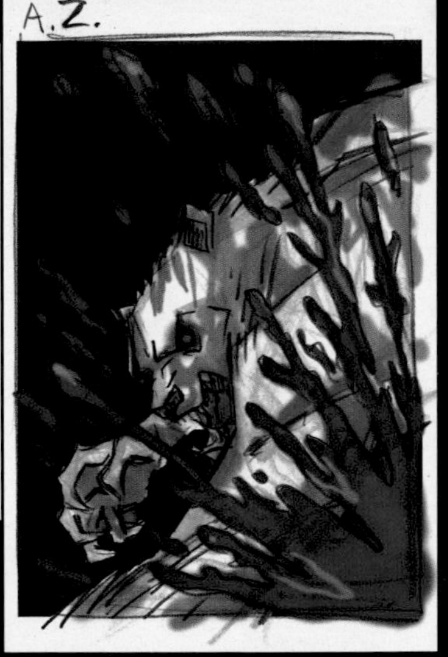
A.Z.

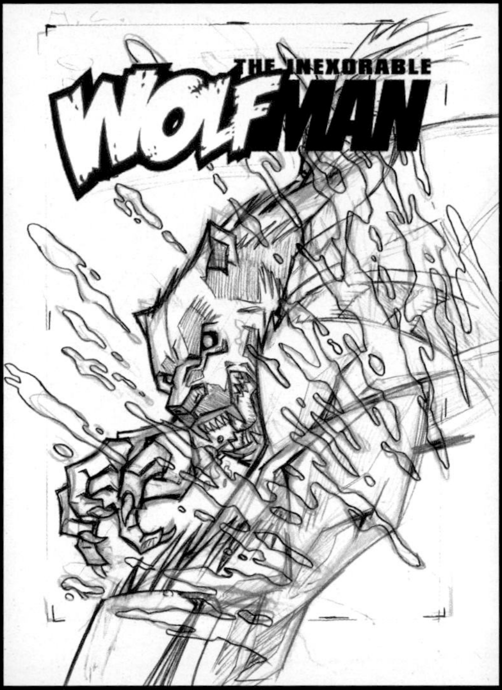
THE INEXORABLE
WOLFMAN

A glimpse into Jason's process for the covers of issues 2 and 3.

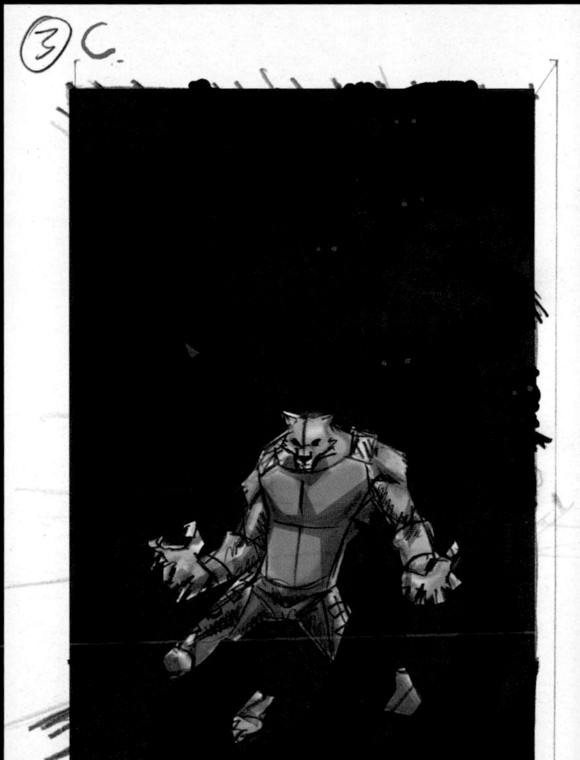
3 C.

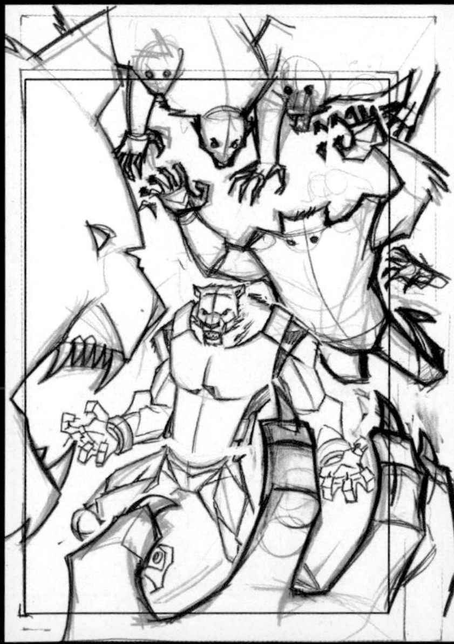

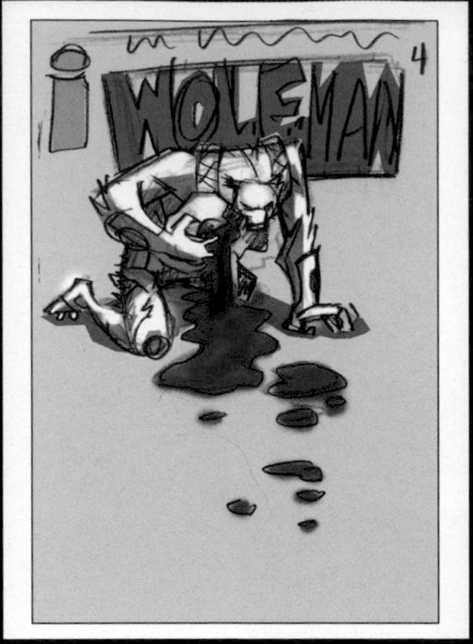
WOLFMAN
4

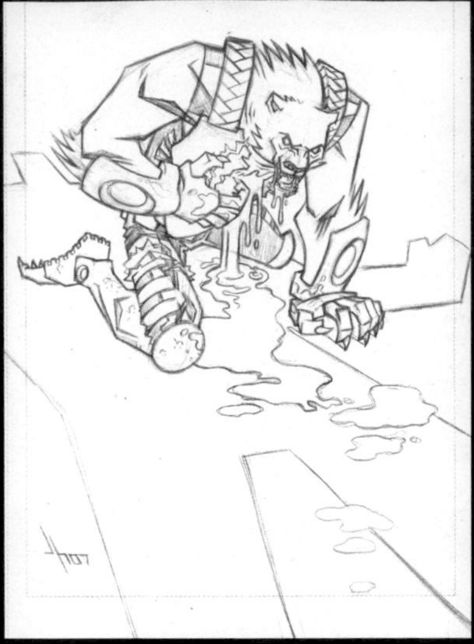

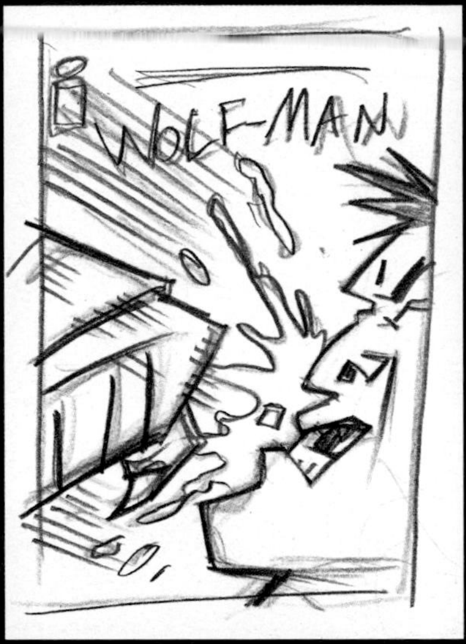
WOLF-MAN

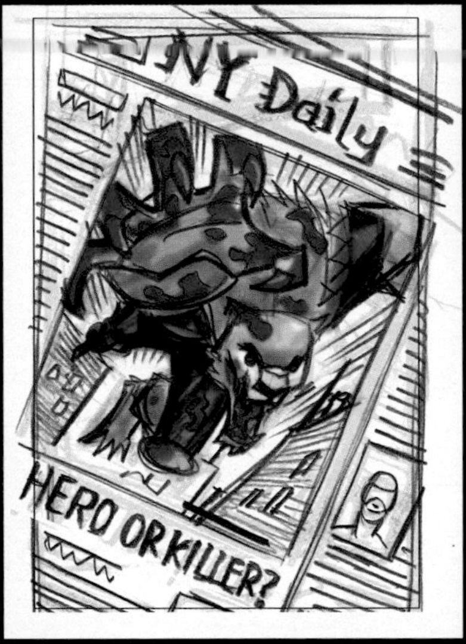
NY Daily
HERO OR KILLER?

Development sketches for covers 4, 5 and 6. Good stuff. The cover to issue 6 is one of my favorites.

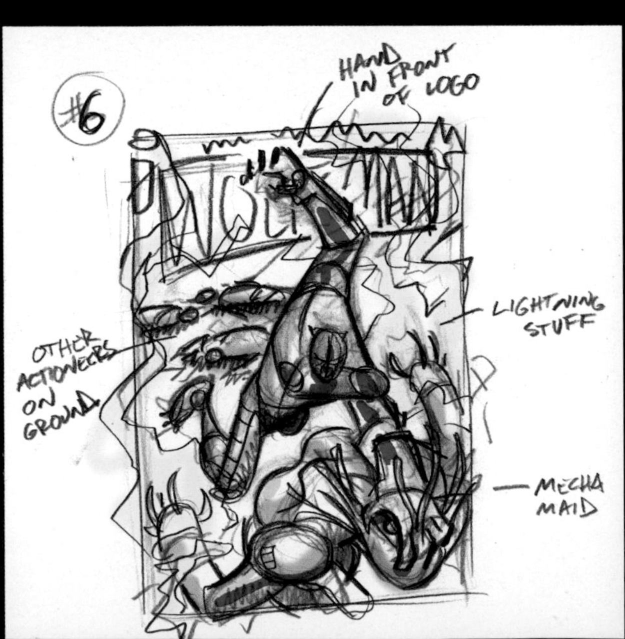
#6
HAND IN FRONT OF LOGO
WOLF-MAN
LIGHTNING STUFF
OTHER ACTIONEERS ON GROUND
MECHA MAID

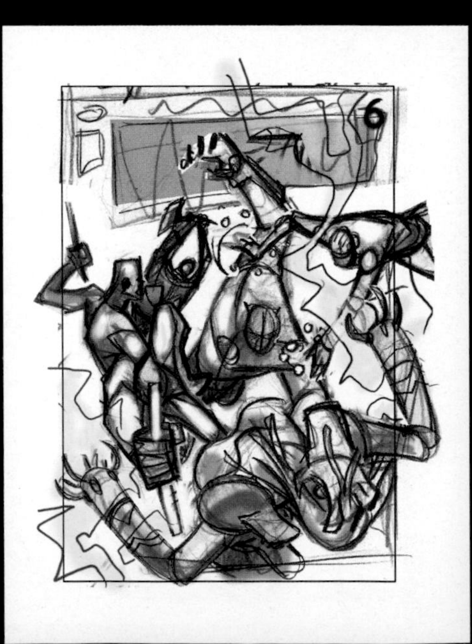
6

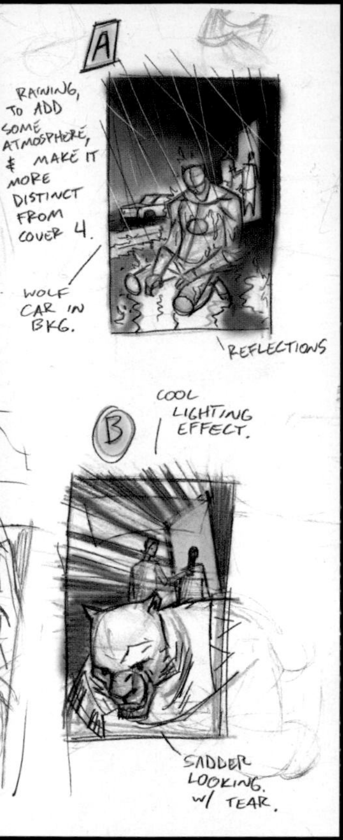
A
RAINING, TO ADD SOME ATMOSPHERE, & MAKE IT MORE DISTINCT FROM COVER 4.
WOLF CAR IN BKG.
REFLECTIONS
COOL LIGHTING EFFECT.
B
SADDER LOOKING. w/ TEAR.

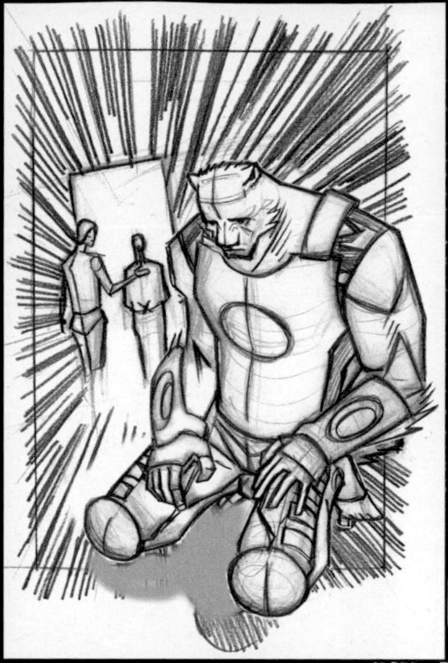

Covers for issue 7 and this volume. The colored version of issue 7 was actually Jason's original version of that cover—but I thought the inking was just too much of a departure from how the book had looked—so I begged him to change it.

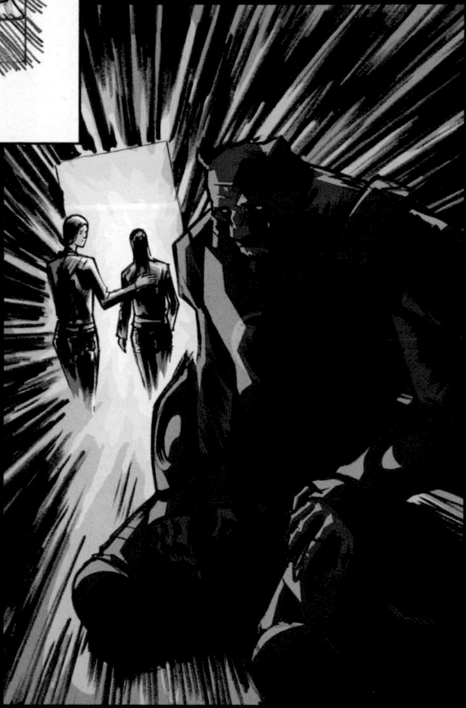

Jason's work on the trade paperback cover is superb. I have no doubt this book looks very classy. I can't wait to see it.

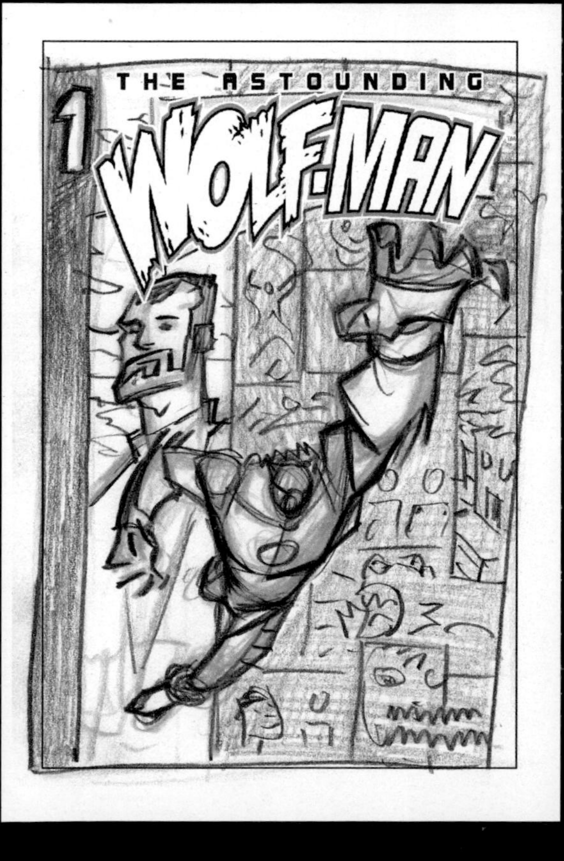
THE ASTOUNDING
1
WOLF-MAN

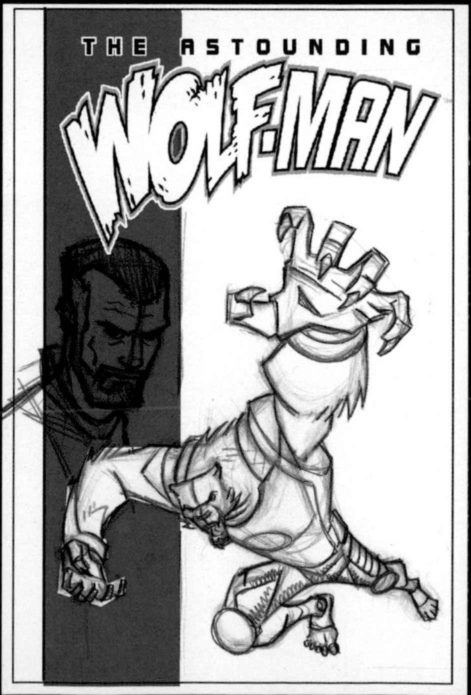
THE ASTOUNDING
WOLF-MAN

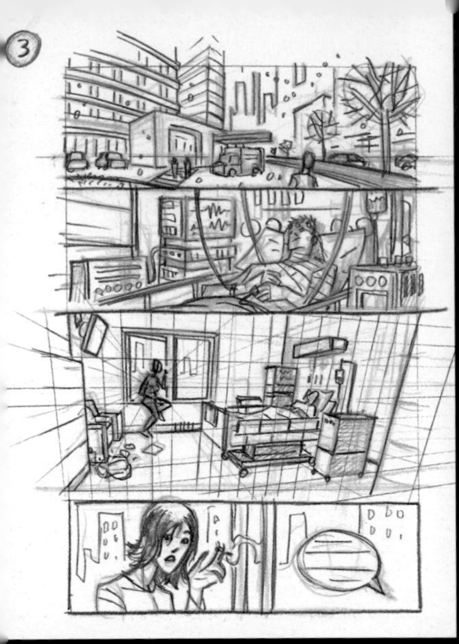
3

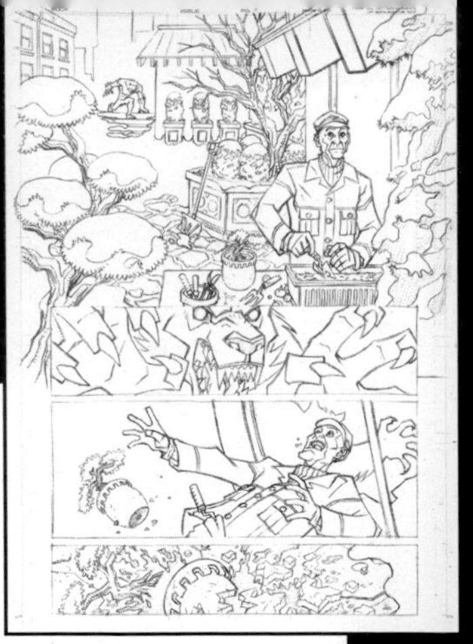

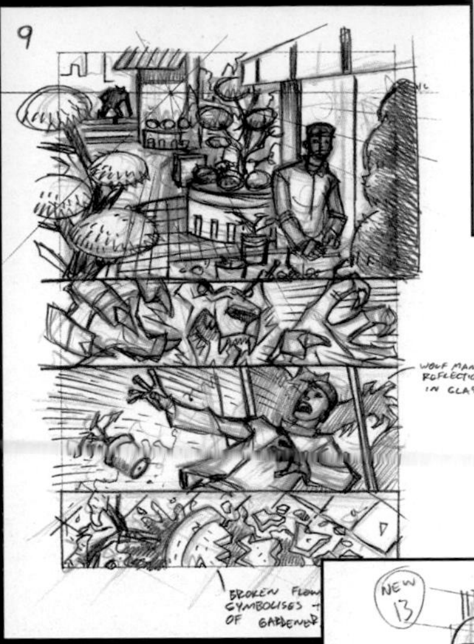
9
WOLF MAN REFLECTION IN GLASS.

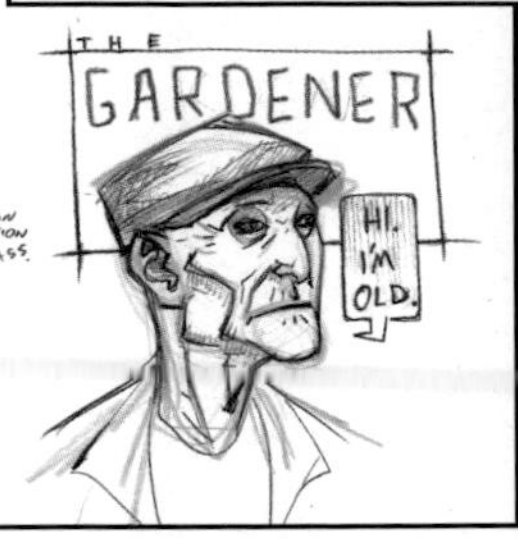
THE GARDENER
HI, I'M OLD.

We'll leave you with a glimpse of Jason's awesome page layouts on the next few pages. You'll see that on a lot of these he also does character designs right next to the layouts. Very cool stuff, enjoy.

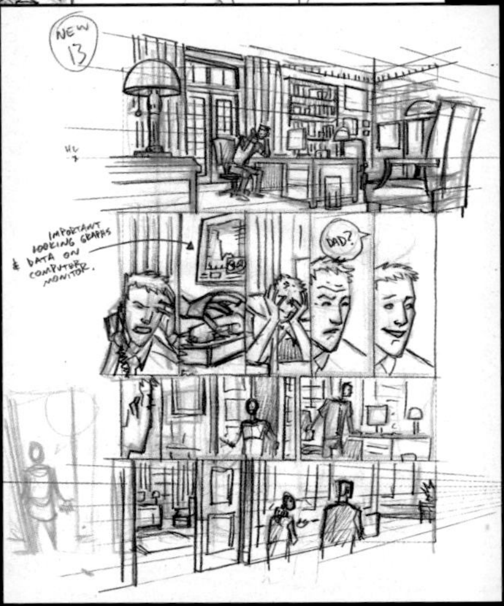
NEW 13
IMPORTANT LOOKING GRAPHS & DATA ON COMPUTER MONITOR.
DAD?

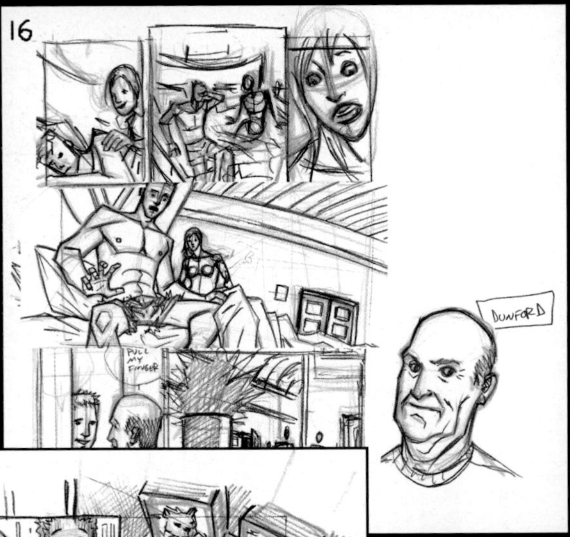
16
PULL MY FINGER
DUNFORD

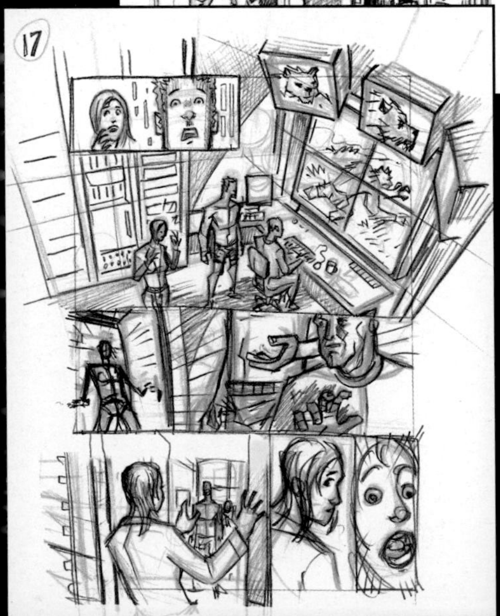
17

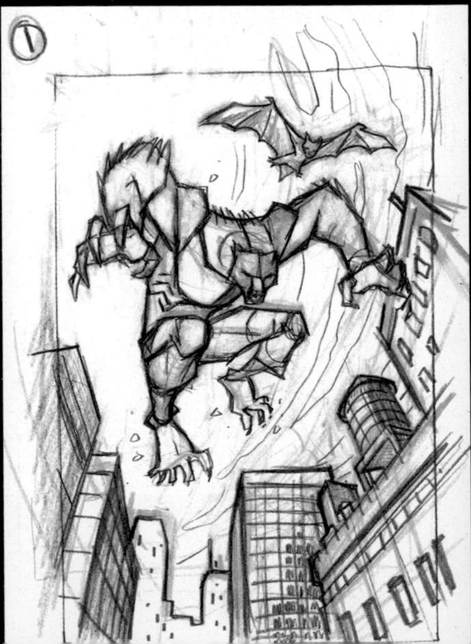
1

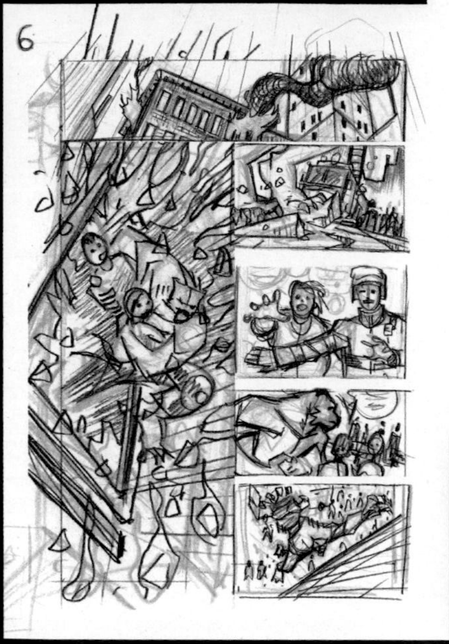

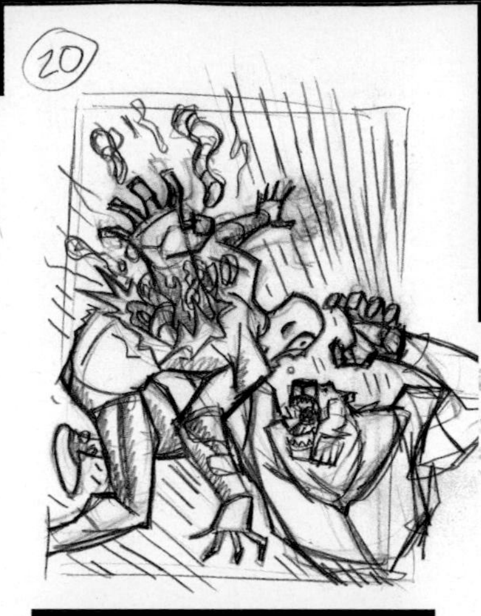

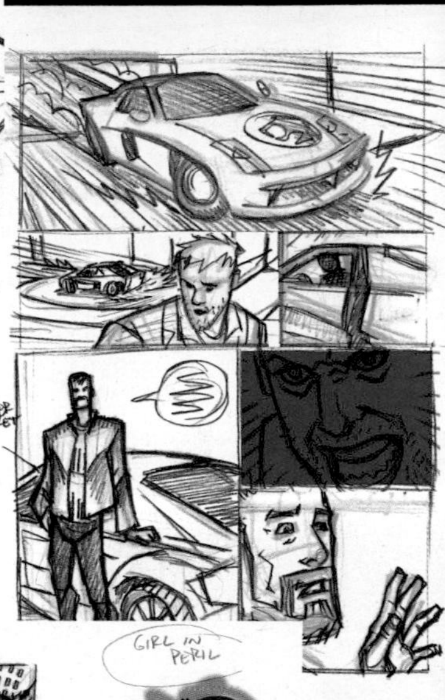
LEATHER JACKET

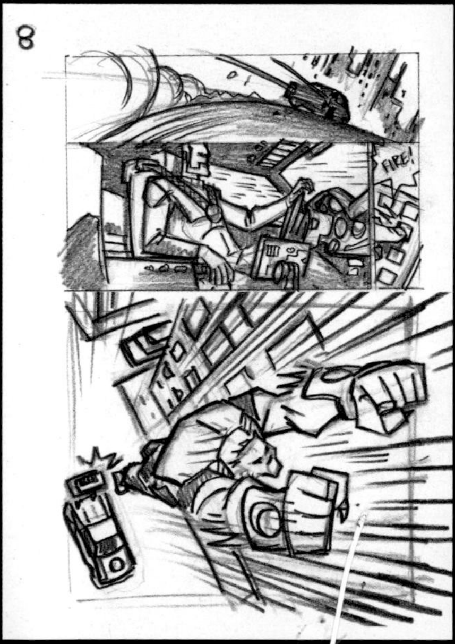
FIRE!

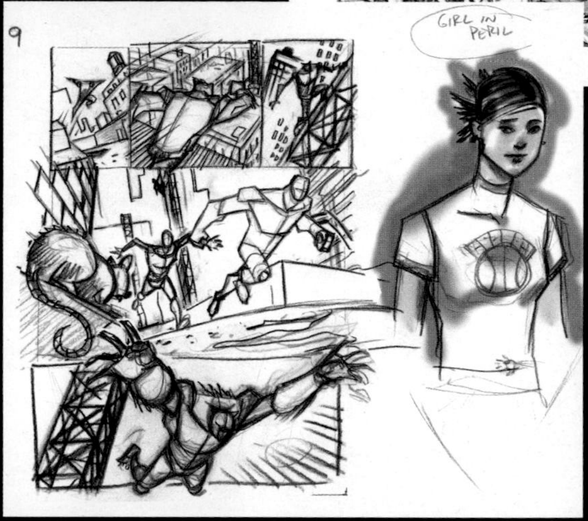
GIRL IN PERIL

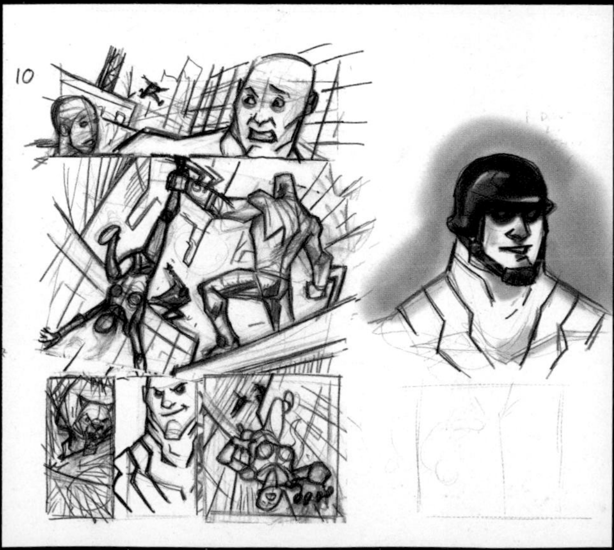

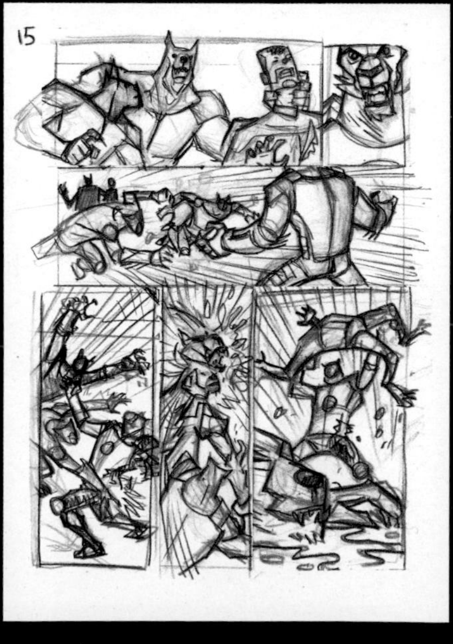

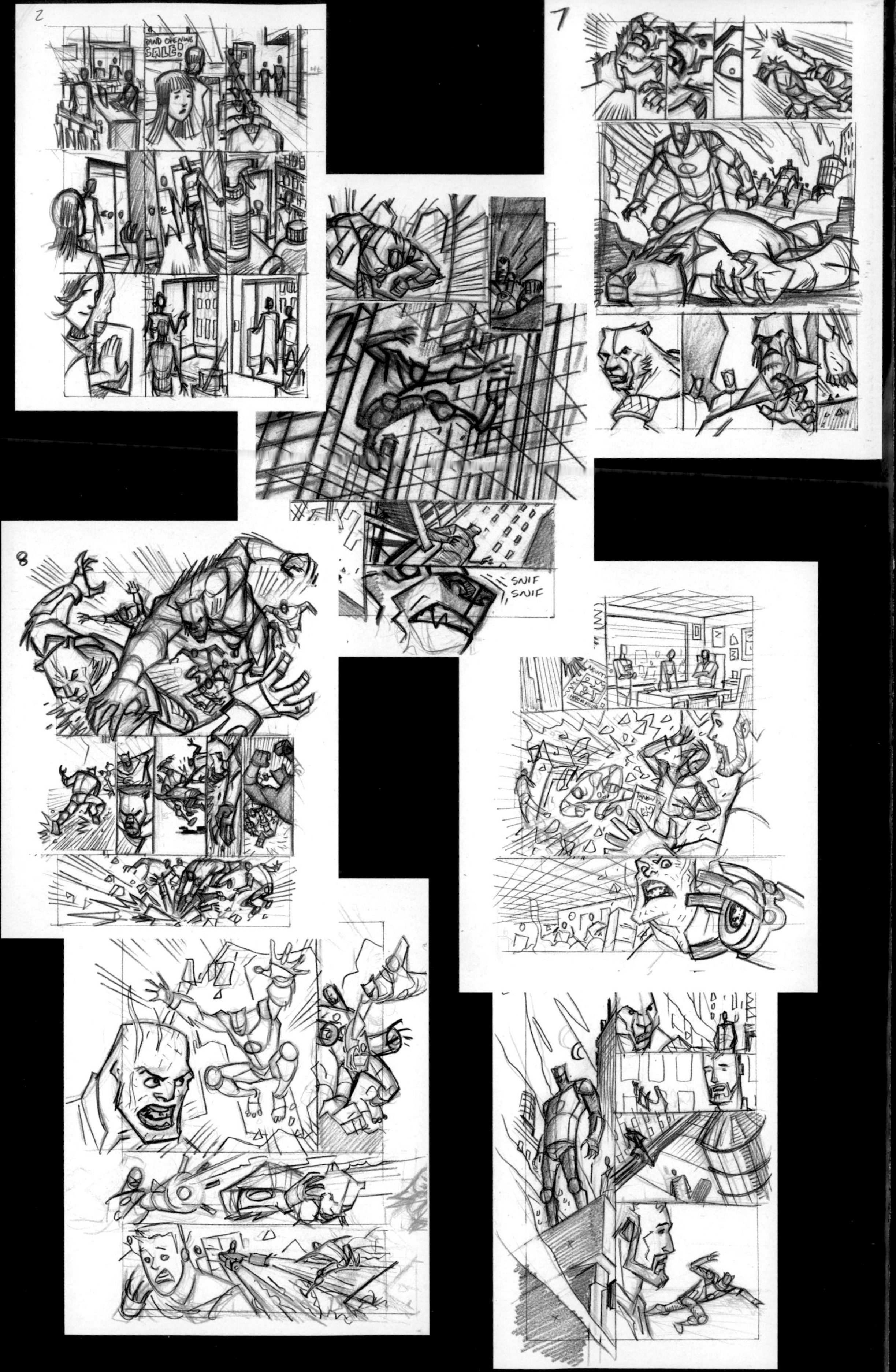
2
RAND OPENING
SALE!
7
8
SNIF
SNIF

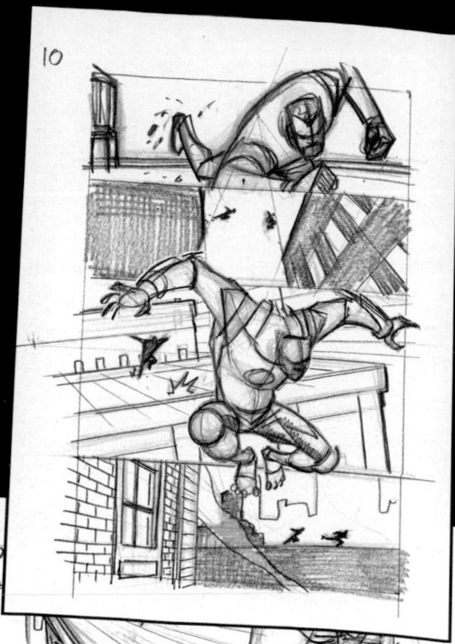

10

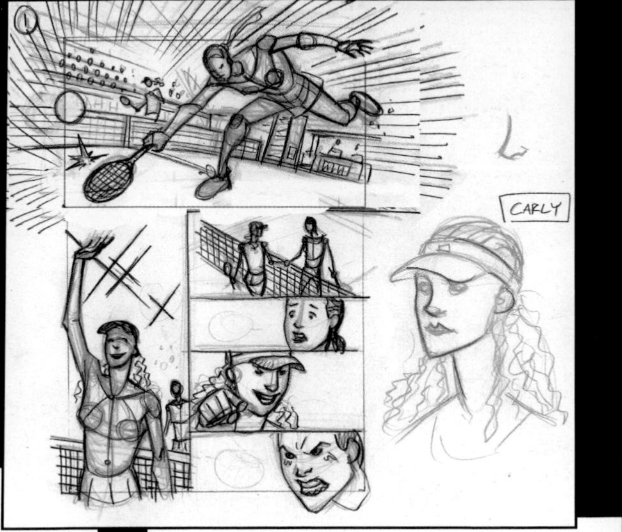

CARLY

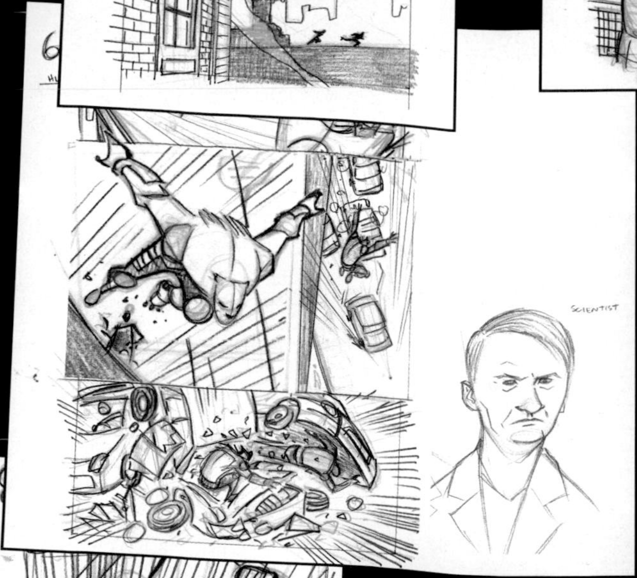

SCIENTIST

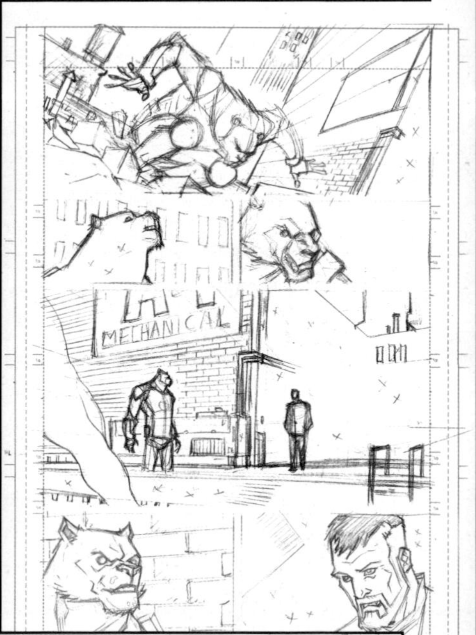

MECHANICAL

Okay, that's all we've got. I hope to see you all back here for volume two.

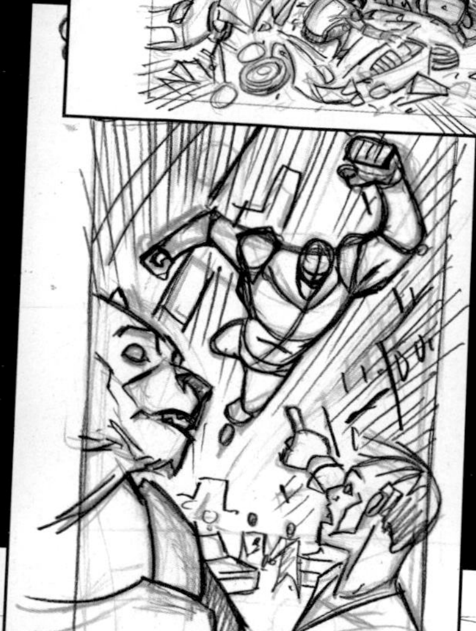

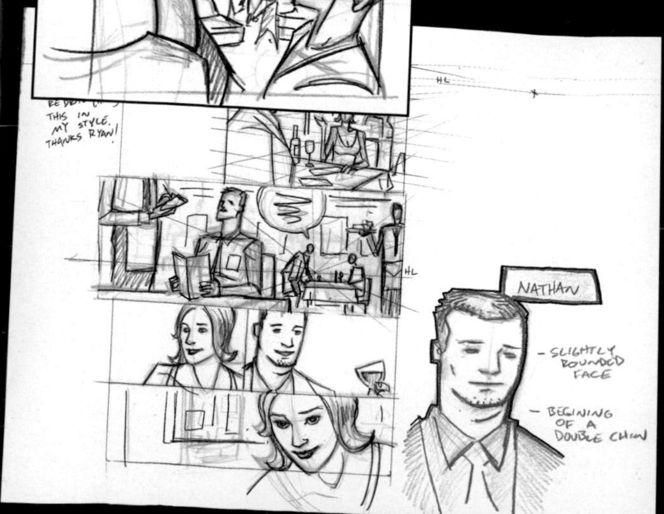

NATHAN
- SLIGHTLY ROUNDED FACE
- BEGINING OF A DOUBLE CHIN

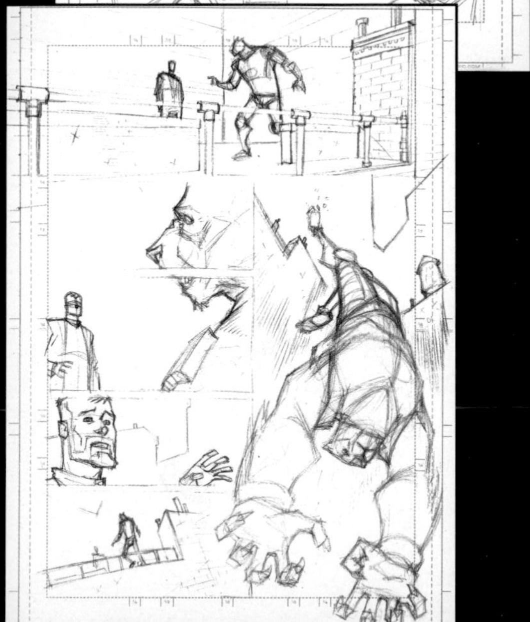

MORE GREAT BOOKS FROM ROBERT KIRKMAN & IMAGE COMICS!

TECH JACKET
THE BOY FROM EARTH
THE WALKING DEAD
BOOK ONE
BRIT
VOLUME THREE: FUBAR
THE WALKING DEAD
REAPER
BRIT
VOLUME ONE

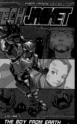

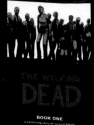

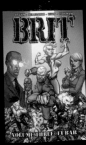

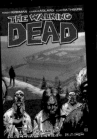

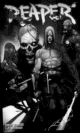

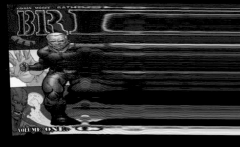

THE ASTOUNDING WOLF-MAN
VOL. 1 TP
ISBN: 978-1-58240-862-0
$14.99
VOL. 2 TP
ISBN: 978-1-60706-007-9
$14.99
VOL. 3 TP
ISBN: 978-1-60706-111-3
$16.99

BATTLE POPE
VOL. 1: GENESIS TP
ISBN: 978-1-58240-572-8
$14.99
VOL. 2: MAYHEM TP
ISBN: 978-1-58240-529-2
$12.99
VOL. 3: PILLOW TALK TP
ISBN: 978-1-58240-677-0
$12.99
VOL. 4: WRATH OF GOD TP
ISBN: 978-1-58240-751-7
$9.99

BRIT
VOL. 1: OLD SOLDIER TP
ISBN: 978-1-58240-678-7
$14.99
VOL. 2: AWOL
ISBN: 978-1-58240-864-4
$14.99
VOL. 3: FUBAR
ISBN: 978-1-60706-061-1
$16.99

CAPES
VOL. 1: PUNCHING THE CLOCK TP
ISBN: 978-1-58240-756-2
$17.99

CLOUDFALL
GRAPHIC NOVEL
$6.95

INVINCIBLE
VOL. 1: FAMILY MATTERS TP
ISBN: 978-1-58240-711-1
$12.99
VOL. 2: EIGHT IS ENOUGH TP
ISBN: 978-1-58240-347-2
$12.99
VOL. 3: PERFECT STRANGERS TP
ISBN: 978-1-58240-793-7
$12.99
VOL. 4: HEAD OF THE CLASS TP
ISBN: 978-1-58240-440-2
$14.95
VOL. 5: THE FACTS OF LIFE TP
ISBN: 978-1-58240-554-4
$14.99
VOL. 6: A DIFFERENT WORLD TP
ISBN: 978-1-58240-579-7
$14.99
VOL. 7: THREE'S COMPANY TP
ISBN: 978-1-58240-656-5
$14.99
VOL. 8: MY FAVORITE MARTIAN TP
ISBN: 978-1-58240-683-1
$14.99
VOL. 9: OUT OF THIS WORLD TP
ISBN: 978-1-58240-827-9
$14.99
VOL. 10: WHO'S THE BOSS TP
ISBN: 978-1-60706-013-0
$16.99
VOL. 11: HAPPY DAYS TP
ISBN: 978-1-60706-062-8
$16.99
ULTIMATE COLLECTION, VOL. 1 HC
ISBN 978-1-58240-500-1
$34.95
ULTIMATE COLLECTION, VOL. 2 HC
ISBN: 978-1-58240-594-0
$34.99
ULTIMATE COLLECTION, VOL. 3 HC
ISBN: 978-1-58240-763-0
$34.99
ULTIMATE COLLECTION, VOL. 4 HC
ISBN: 978-1-58240-989-4
$34.99
ULTIMATE COLLECTION, VOL. 5 HC
ISBN: 978-1-60706-116-8
$34.99
THE OFFICIAL HANDBOOK OF THE INVINCIBLE UNIVERSE TP
ISBN: 978-1-58240-831-6
$12.99
THE COMPLETE INVINCIBLE LIBRARY, VOL. 1 HC
ISBN: 978-1-58240-718-0
$125.00
THE COMPLETE INVINCIBLE LIBRARY, VOL. 2 HC
ISBN: 978-1-60706-112-0
$125.00

THE WALKING DEAD
VOL. 1: DAYS GONE BYE TP
ISBN: 978-1-58240-672-5
$9.99
VOL. 2: MILES BEHIND US TP
ISBN: 978-1-58240-413-4
$14.99
VOL. 3: SAFETY BEHIND BARS TP
ISBN: 978-1-58240-487-5
$14.99
VOL. 4: THE HEART'S DESIRE TP
ISBN: 978-1-58240-530-8
$14.99
VOL. 5: THE BEST DEFENSE TP
ISBN: 978-1-58240-612-1
$14.99
VOL. 6: THIS SORROWFUL LIFE TP
ISBN: 978-1-58240-684-8
$14.99
VOL. 7: THE CALM BEFORE TP
ISBN: 978-1-58240-828-6
$14.99
VOL. 8: MADE TO SUFFER TP
ISBN: 978-1-58240-883-5
$14.99
VOL. 9: HERE [illegible]
ISBN: 978 [illegible]
$14.99
VOL. 10: TH [illegible]
ISBN: 978 [illegible]
$14.99
VOL. 11: FE [illegible]
ISBN: 97 [illegible]
$14.99
BOOK ONE [illegible]
ISBN: 9 [illegible]
$29.99
BOOK TWO [illegible]
ISBN: 9 [illegible]
$29.99
BOOK THR [illegible]
ISBN: 9 [illegible]
$29.99
BOOK FOU [illegible]
ISBN: [illegible]
$29.9 [illegible]
BOOK FIV [illegible]
ISBN: [illegible]
$29.9 [illegible]
THE WAL [illegible]
DELUXE [illegible]
ISBN: [illegible]
$100. [illegible]

REAP [illegible]
GRAPHI [illegible]
$6.9 [illegible]

TECH [illegible]
VOL. 1 [illegible]
ISBN: [illegible]
$14. [illegible]

TALE [illegible]
HARD [illegible]
ISBN [illegible]
$34. [illegible]
TRAD [illegible]
ISBN [illegible]
$14 [illegible]

THE OFFICIAL HANDBOOK OF THE INVINCIBLE UNIVERSE
INVINCIBLE
THREE'S COMPANY
THE ASTOUNDING WOLF-MAN
VOLUME ONE
INVINCIBLE
HAPPY DAYS
THE WALKING DEAD

TO FIND YOUR NEAREST COMIC BOOK STORE, CALL:
1-888-COMIC-BOOK

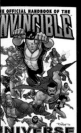

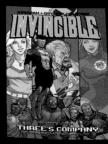

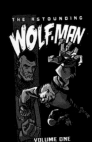

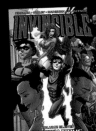

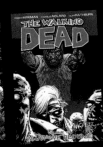

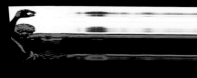

Okay, that's all we've got.
I hope to see you all back
here for volume two.

MORE GREAT BOOKS FROM
ROBERT KIRKMAN & IMAGE COMICS!

TECH JACKET
VOLUME 1
THE BOY FROM EARTH
THE WALKING DEAD
BOOK ONE
BRIT
VOLUME THREE: FUBAR
THE WALKING DEAD
REAPER
BRIT
VOLUME ONE: OLD SOLDIER
PUNCHING THE

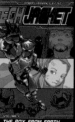

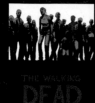

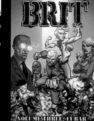

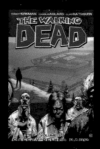

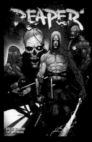

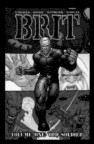

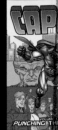

THE ASTOUNDING WOLF-MAN

VOL. 1 TP
ISBN: 978-1-58240-862-0
$14.99
VOL. 2 TP
ISBN: 978-1-60706-007-9
$14.99
VOL. 3 TP
ISBN: 978-1-60706-111-3
$16.99

BATTLE POPE

VOL. 1: GENESIS TP
ISBN: 978-1-58240-572-8
$14.99
VOL. 2: MAYHEM TP
ISBN: 978-1-58240-529-2
$12.99
VOL. 3: PILLOW TALK TP
ISBN: 978-1-58240-677-0
$12.99
VOL. 4: WRATH OF GOD TP
ISBN: 978-1-58240-751-7
$9.99

BRIT

VOL. 1: OLD SOLDIER TP
ISBN: 978-1-58240-678-7
$14.99
VOL. 2: AWOL
ISBN: 978-1-58240-864-4
$14.99
VOL. 3: FUBAR
ISBN: 978-1-60706-061-1
$16.99

CAPES

VOL. 1: PUNCHING THE CLOCK TP
ISBN: 978-1-58240-756-2
$17.99

CLOUDFALL

GRAPHIC NOVEL
$6.95

INVINCIBLE

VOL. 1: FAMILY MATTERS TP
ISBN: 978-1-58240-711-1
$12.99
VOL. 2: EIGHT IS ENOUGH TP
ISBN: 978-1-58240-347-2
$12.99
VOL. 3: PERFECT STRANGERS TP
ISBN: 978-1-58240-793-7
$12.99
VOL. 4: HEAD OF THE CLASS TP
ISBN: 978-1-58240-440-2
$14.95
VOL. 5: THE FACTS OF LIFE TP
ISBN: 978-1-58240-554-4
$14.99
VOL. 6: A DIFFERENT WORLD TP
ISBN: 978-1-58240-579-7
$14.99
VOL. 7: THREE'S COMPANY TP
ISBN: 978-1-58240-656-5
$14.99
VOL. 8: MY FAVORITE MARTIAN TP
ISBN: 978-1-58240-683-1
$14.99
VOL. 9: OUT OF THIS WORLD TP
ISBN: 978-1-58240-827-9
$14.99
VOL. 10: WHO'S THE BOSS TP
ISBN: 978-1-60706-013-0
$16.99
VOL. 11: HAPPY DAYS TP
ISBN: 978-1-60706-062-8
$16.99
ULTIMATE COLLECTION, VOL. 1 HC
ISBN 978-1-58240-500-1
$34.95
ULTIMATE COLLECTION, VOL. 2 HC
ISBN: 978-1-58240-594-0
$34.99
ULTIMATE COLLECTION, VOL. 3 HC
ISBN: 978-1-58240-763-0
$34.99
ULTIMATE COLLECTION, VOL. 4 HC
ISBN: 978-1-58240-989-4
$34.99
ULTIMATE COLLECTION, VOL. 5 HC
ISBN: 978-1-60706-116-8
$34.99
THE OFFICIAL HANDBOOK OF THE INVINCIBLE UNIVERSE TP
ISBN: 978-1-58240-831-6
$12.99
THE COMPLETE INVINCIBLE LIBRARY, VOL. 1 HC
ISBN: 978-1-58240-718-0
$125.00
THE COMPLETE INVINCIBLE LIBRARY, VOL. 2 HC
ISBN: 978-1-60706-112-0
$125.00

THE WALKING DEAD

VOL. 1: DAYS GONE BYE TP
ISBN: 978-1-58240-672-5
$9.99
VOL. 2: MILES BEHIND US TP
ISBN: 978-1-58240-413-4
$14.99
VOL. 3: SAFETY BEHIND BARS TP
ISBN: 978-1-58240-487-5
$14.99
VOL. 4: THE HEART'S DESIRE TP
ISBN: 978-1-58240-530-8
$14.99
VOL. 5: THE BEST DEFENSE TP
ISBN: 978-1-58240-612-1
$14.99
VOL. 6: THIS SORROWFUL LIFE TP
ISBN: 978-1-58240-684-8
$14.99
VOL. 7: THE CALM BEFORE TP
ISBN: 978-1-58240-828-6
$14.99
VOL. 8: MADE TO SUFFER TP
ISBN: 978-1-58240-883-5
$14.99
VOL. 9: HERE WE REMAIN TP
ISBN: 978-1-60706-022-2
$14.99
VOL. 10: THE ROAD AHEAD TP
ISBN: 978-1-60706-075-8
$14.99
VOL. 11: FEAR THE HUNTERS TP
ISBN: 978-1-60706-181-6
$14.99
BOOK ONE HC
ISBN: 978-1-58240-619-0
$29.99
BOOK TWO HC
ISBN: 978-1-58240-698-5
$29.99
BOOK THREE HC
ISBN: 978-1-58240-825-5
$29.99
BOOK FOUR HC
ISBN: 978-1-60706-000-0
$29.99
BOOK FIVE HC
ISBN: 978-1-60706-171-7
$29.99
THE WALKING DEAD DELUXE HARDCOVER, VOL. 2
ISBN: 978-1-60706-029-7
$100.00

REAPER

GRAPHIC NOVEL
$6.95

TECH JACKET

VOL. 1: THE BOY FROM EARTH TP
ISBN: 978-1-58240-771-5
$14.99

TALES OF THE REALM

HARDCOVER
ISBN: 978-1-58240-426-0
$34.95
TRADE PAPERBACK
ISBN: 978-1-58240-394-6
$14.95

THE OFFICIAL HANDBOOK OF THE INVINCIBLE UNIVERSE
INVINCIBLE
THREE'S COMPANY
THE ASTOUNDING WOLF-MAN
VOLUME ONE
INVINCIBLE
HAPPY DAYS
THE WALKING DEAD
THE WALKING DEAD
BOOK THREE
CLOUD

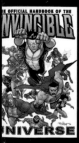

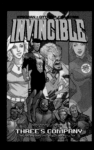

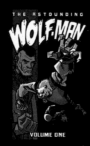

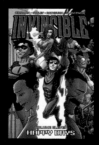

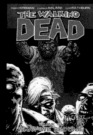

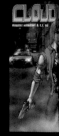

TO FIND YOUR NEAREST COMIC BOOK STORE, CALL:
1-888-COMIC-BOOK

INTRODUCTION by ROBERT KIRKMAN

First of all, let me thank you for purchasing the first volume of my newest creator-owned Image series, The Astounding Wolf-Man. You're getting in on the ground floor of something that I believe will become a worthy addition to the pantheon of creator-owned books I've done at Image... so thanks for taking the plunge and giving it a go. It's very brave of you and I respect that.

There are a lot of things that went into the creation of this series, things that are responsible for its existence, but the thing at the tip top of that list would have to be artist and co-creator, Jason Howard. By and large, you're holding this book in your hands because of him.

Jason and I met in Chicago, although I believe I recall Jason telling me the story more than I remember the actual event. Jason was one of the many nameless faceless convention goers who ask if they can do a pin-up for one of my books, in this case, Invincible. I'd like to think he saw me on the last day of the con, because as the story goes I was very zany and obnoxious, which seems to happen to me by the end of those things... but y'know, it could have just as easily been the first day. I told him I'd print his pin-up, unless it sucked... and then I wouldn't. I'm sure I thought it was funny at the time.

Thankfully, Jason's Invincible pin-up didn't suck.

In fact, it was awesome. Very awesome. Instead of just a good drawing of Invincible, which it also was, it had a story aspect to it—and it was very smart. It was Invincible

swooping down through a drive-thru window at The Burger Mart stealing a soda from a girl in the window. It was eye-catching and unique and everything from the penciling, to the inking, to the coloring was top notch.

I immediately jumped online and googled the hell out of "Jason Howard" until I found a website with his art on it. Lo and behold—it was all as good if not better than that pin-up, he even had sequential pages online that were very good. I was thrilled, this guy was very talented, and was enough of a fan of my work to know what "Burger Mart" was... I thought I could probably get this guy to work with me.

Around that time Jim Valentino had put together a series called THE PACT where Invincible, ShadowHawk, Firebreather and Zephyr from Noble Causes all teamed up and fought stuff. Jim's idea was to have each writer of the four individual series write one issue of this thing. I was excited to do it—but I didn't have an artist. But it was around that time that Jason had done this awesome Invincible pin-up... the job was offered to him and he accepted and we were off to the races.

Kind of.

The Pact came along in a very busy time of my life, my wife was pregnant, I'd taken on a bunch of work at Marvel... and so, I got Jason script in very small bursts and often it was very late. The book even shipped a few months late and it was all my fault. I had a blast doing this issue, and I count it among my favorite

IMAGE COMICS, INC.

Robert Kirkman - Chief Operating Officer
Erik Larsen - Chief Financial Officer
Todd McFarlane - President
Marc Silvestri - Chief Executive Officer
Jim Valentino - Vice-President

ericstephenson - Publisher
Joe Keatinge - PR & Marketing Coordinator
Branwyn Bigglestone - Accounts Manager
Sarah deLaine - Administrative Assistant
Tyler Shainline - Production Manager
Drew Gill - Art Director
Jonathan Chan - Production Artist
Monica Howard - Production Artist
Vincent Kukua - Production Artist

www.imagecomics.com

THE ASTOUNDING WOLF-MAN, VOL. 1
ISBN: 978-1-58240-862-0
Second Printing

PRINTED IN CHINA